KALDOR'S POLITICAL ECONOMY

edited by Tony Lawson, J. Gabriel Palma and John Sender

ACADEMIC PRESS LIMITED
24/28 Oval Road
London NW1 7DX

United States edition published by
ACADEMIC PRESS INC.
San Diego, CA 92101

British Library Cataloguing in Publication Data
Is Available

ISBN 0-12-439640-2

Printed in Great Britain by
Henry Ling Ltd. at the Dorset Press, Dorchester, Dorset

Contents

Preface and acknowledgements

This book is a reprint of the Nicholas Kaldor Memorial Issue of the CJE (Vol 13 No 1), with the addition of a personal appreciation by Luigi Pasinetti. The Cambridge Political Economy Society felt the volume to be sufficiently interesting to deserve the wider audience that a book could reach.

Besides fellow members of the editorial board of the CJE, the editors would like to thank the following people who have been involved in the preparation of this volume: Chris Allsopp, Michael Ball, Alex Cairncross, Betty Clifton, Ricardo Ffrench-Davis, Christopher Gilbert, Martin Hollis, Geoff Hodgson, Charles Kindleberger, David Newbery, Peter Nolan, Luigi Pasinetti, Brian Reddaway, Tibor Scitovsky, Hans Singer, Ron Smith, Bernard Stafford, Ian Steedman, Nick Stern, Frances Stewart, Rosemary Thorp, John Toye and Terry Ward.

The Editors
Cambridge

Nicholas Kaldor
1908–1986

Foreword

I consider myself extraordinarily fortunate to have had Nicholas Kaldor as a most inspiring teacher, and as a close friend and colleague for many years. What I always found so remarkable in him was how openly relevant every bit of his life was to whatever he was currently doing. And he never tried to conceal it; nor, for that matter, did he ever try to conceal *any* feeling. The marks of his past were always clearly visible in his behaviour: his particularly happy childhood, enjoyed in a rather well-off Jewish family; his élitist education in Budapest, one of the major capitals of Central European culture; his bohemian Berlin interlude (1926–27); his disciplined training in economics at the London School of Economics, from which he graduated brilliantly in 1930 (the lectures of Allyn Young continued to exert an impact even on his latest works); his very productive 'orthodox' period as a young lecturer at the LSE, with frequent discussions and intellectual interchange with his teachers (Robbins, Hayek and Hicks) and his contemporaries (Rothbarth, Scitovsky, Maurice Allen); his numerous confrontations with the 'hard facts of power' in his capacity as adviser to several governments all over the world, including of course, Britain; and, finally, and above all, his 'conversion' to the new course of economic theory originating in Keynes's *General Theory*.

This last event was undoubtedly the fundamental turning point in the development of Kaldor's thought. It took place gradually, toward the end of the 1930s, leading up to his two brilliant articles in 1939 (on speculation and stability in the *Review of Economic Studies*) and 1940 (on the trade cycle in the *Economic Journal*), and then, quite naturally and logically, to his moving from London to Cambridge, after the war. By this time, the break with orthodoxy was definitive and complete, making Nicholas Kaldor and Joan Robinson the most active members of that remarkable group of economists (which also included Richard Kahn and Piero Sraffa) who on the trail of Keynes, made post-war Cambridge a major world centre for the development of non-traditional, i.e. *new* economic theory.

It is perhaps too early to assess the significance of the extraordinary contributions to economic theory that have come from this remarkable group of Cambridge post-Keynesian economists. Their lines of thought, by developing in a more or less parallel way, have not always crossed one another, they have sometimes overlapped and reinforced each other, sometimes diverged, sometimes even been in contradiction; in all cases they have cross-fertilised. There can be no doubt that their overall impact has been enormous. I am convinced that it is still potentially much greater than it has been so far.

I had the good fortune to arrive in Cambridge, as a research student, in October 1956, the year of publication of Kaldor's theory income distribution in the *Review of Economic Studies* and of Joan Robinson's *The Accumulation of Capital*. The sense of achievement that one could feel in the on-going debates was indescribable; and the intellectual stimulation for the students was extraordinary. I had the further good fortune, after interludes at Harvard and at Oxford, to become a Fellow of King's College in 1961, the year that followed the publication of Sraffa's book. As the youngest member, I dared to present the results of my work on income distribution to a session of the so called 'Secret Seminar' in King's College (a post-war version of Keynes's more famous 'Circus'). That experience was astonishing. I presented my results as a *criticism* of Kaldor's theory. The audience was stunned and disbelieving, with one exception—Kaldor. He was extraordinarily quick in grasping the gist of the idea and in seeing that the concession of a 'logical slip' led in fact to a generalisation of the post-Keynesian theory of income distribution and of the rate of profits. Kaldor was extremely generous to those who induced him to change his mind.

It must be said that the intellectual atmosphere that Cambridge provided was most congenial to Kaldor—rich as it was in elating interludes, and tense with sudden contrasts. He could move in it at his complete ease, as if he had been there since the beginning; even before Keynes! And in fact, of all the members of the group, Kaldor (though not a pupil of Keynes) was perhaps the one that came nearest to Keynes in his approach to actual economic problems. Theory was never for him a purely intellectual pastime. It may be interesting to recall that he claimed he decided to become an economist at the age of 15, out of curiosity about the mechanism that caused hyper-inflation, as he experienced it directly, 'bargain-hunting for goods at yesterday's prices', while on a family holiday in the Bavarian Alps. His concern with the facts of the real world (crude or 'stylised') was overwhelming; and it was a concern aimed at influencing them. This may well be the basic explanation of his 'conversion' from traditional to Keynesian economics.

The one recurring theme in his criticism of general equilibrium theory (an economic theory which he himself shared, and taught, and to which he made original contributions, in his LSE period) was that it is a purely intellectual exercise with no relevance to the understanding of the real world. He claimed that such theory is founded on highly unrealistic assumptions, the number of which must grow continuously, in order to dodge the increasing objections. A recurring image he used was that of a widening scaffolding with which to sustain a building that could never stand up by itself. And yet many economists were going on to draw out implications *as if* the scaffolding had been removed. Keynesian theory, as he intended it, was doing exactly the opposite.

The affinities of Kaldor and Keynes were manifold. His commuting continually from economic theory to the practical applications of economic policy was only the most obvious one. At a deeper level these affinities concerned their basic vision of the world. Like Keynes, Kaldor was convinced that a revolution is necessary in economic theory, but not in the basic institutional set-up of our societies. He was a great believer in the powerful forces of the market mechanism. But he was at the same time aware of its weaknesses and of the social injustices (in terms both of an unequal distribution of income and wealth, and of too high a level of unemployment) that it is bound to bring about. For this reason, he was a passionate supporter of reforms. He also tended, like Keynes, to overestimate the possibility of cleverness and intelligence overcoming stupidity. He was indeed a great believer in the role of intellectuals, and scornful of the diffused mediocrity of the ruling classes, but he was not—contrary to what has been stated in some superficial evaluations of his behaviour—unconcerned with the lot of the underdog. His social commitment is witnessed by the great pains he took to devise, for Britain and for less developed countries alike, ways and expediencies to make the rich pay taxes, and the poor be relieved of their burden, or get more either for their work or for their goods.

He was disliked precisely for this, by many property-owning people, in those countries whose governments he advised, as he was disliked in recent years in Britain for his very harsh attacks on the monetarist policies of Mrs Thatcher's Government. But he never minded, showing a sort of toughness and nonchalence that irritated his opponents. Yet all those who knew him well could not but feel affection for him.

The death of Nicholas Kaldor sadly deprived his family and his friends of the warmth, wittiness, and brilliancy of his ebullient personality. But his writings remain, for all. His eight volumes of collected essays and the other books and memoranda, in English and in foreign languages, are an immensely rich heritage, full of ideas and stimuli for the generations of economic theorists and political economists yet to come.

Luigi L. Pasinetti
Università Cattolica del Sacro Cuore, Milan

Kaldor's contribution to economics: an introduction

Tony Lawson*, J. Gabriel Palma* and John Sender*

In this memorial issue of the *Cambridge Journal of Economics* we reflect upon the nature, content and influence of Nicholas Kaldor's substantial contribution to political economy. Numerous features of Kaldor's work mark it out as being exceptional: in particular, its breadth of coverage, its originality, its concern for relevance, and the degree to which it was continually developing. These themes are used to structure the comments below.

The wide scope of Kaldor's contribution is indicated by the coverage of the papers which follow. Indeed, although these papers span a wide variety of issues and concerns, so broad were Kaldor's interests and achievements that only a small sample of his thinking can be addressed or represented here. In preparing this collection of papers, various areas were marked out as significant with respect to Kaldor's work, and numerous potential contributors known to have been close to, or influenced by, Kaldor either offered or were invited to contribute—each within a specific broad area. The outcome, inevitably, is a commentary upon Kaldor's work that reflects primarily the concerns and emphases of the contributors, rather than one that attains completeness or a total absence of duplication. This, however, seemed to be a price that was worth paying in order to allow the contributors to commemorate Kaldor in the manner which they perceived to be the most fitting.

The originality of Kaldor's contribution needs little comment here, and is again indicated by the papers included below. It is well known, for example, that Kaldor's work—particularly, perhaps, his writing on growth—initiated numerous research programmes. While the following collection of papers includes commentaries upon those programmes, it also includes substantive contributions which are themselves within the tradition of criticising and refining Kaldor's initial insights.

It is its concern with relevance, however, that distinguishes Kaldor's work from that of many of his contemporaries. In fact, Kaldor spent much of his life working as a policy adviser to various governments—including those of India, Sri Lanka, Chile and Mexico as well as the UK—and a significant proportion of his written work is directed toward specific issues of public policy. However, Kaldor's view of what constitutes relevant economics changed radically in the course of his life—from an economics based upon an approach that proceeds by way of deductive reasoning from rather general macroeconomic axioms, to one involving a more consciously empirical approach. This switch is apparent, for instance, in the contrasting styles of two papers on growth that were both

*University of Cambridge.

published in 1966 (Kaldor, 1966A, 1966B). In connection with the first of these papers, Kaldor was later to observe:

> This paper marked the last of a series of theoretical papers on growth theory which proceeded by way of deductive reasoning from macro-economic axioms of a rather general character. In my subsequent work I followed a different method: I tried to find what kind of regularities can be detected in empirically observed phenomena and then tried to discover what particular testable hypotheses would be capable of explaining the association. I became aware of this more pragmatic approach during the war when it was used by scientists for the purpose of 'operational research'. It is an approach which in one sense is more modest in scope (in not searching for explanations that derive from a comprehensive model of the system) and also more ambitious in that it directly aims at discovering solutions (or remedies) for real problems (Kaldor, 1978A, p. xvii).

This gradual reorientation of his methodological approach is just one example of Kaldor's readiness to subject what he held to be true (or most appropriate in the circumstances) to continual revision in the light of new experience. The same disposition is also reflected in Kaldor's frequently changing theoretical perspective. Arriving at the LSE as an orthodox economist in the late 1920s, Kaldor was initially much influenced by the ideas of Hayek and Robbins. However, by the late 1930s he was far more attracted by the ideas deriving from Keynes' *General Theory,* although he was subsequently horrified by the eventual post-war attempt to synthesise Keynesian macroeconomics with Walrasian (or Marshallian) microeconomics, an endeavour which Kaldor regarded as 'intellectually barren' as well as 'irrelevant' (1978A, p. viii). It was in the attempt to break free from these latter developments—an enterprise which 'entailed finding the crucial changes in assumptions needed to escape from the rigidity of the traditional models and introduce a better insight of how the world really works' (1978A, p. vii)—that the less formal approach of Kaldor's post-war contributions eventually emerged. And since Kaldor's views were continually evolving, he never reached a stage where he considered that his theories were sufficiently final to be put together in a single comprehensive work: 'I have never felt that one's understanding of economic processes has reached a stage where it is no longer liable to radical revision and development in the light of new experience' (1978B, p. xxix).

In the light of such features of Kaldor's work, particularly its wide scope and openness to radical revision and development, it is not surprising that different economists, including the contributors to this volume, choose to emphasise very different aspects or examples of his work. Consequently, the various viewpoints represented here neither provide complete coverage, nor can be regarded as completely mutually consistent. Even so, whatever else they may or may not hold in common, all the contributors seem to be agreed about the value of the heritage left to us in Kaldor's work.

The volume begins with papers primarily concerned with issues of formal theory. These are followed by papers that are more directly concerned with understanding real world economic processes, culminating in papers addressed explicitly to issues of policy. In the opening contribution, John Hicks focuses upon an assumption of economic theory that Kaldor continuously criticised and rejected: the assumption of constant returns to scale. Kaldor was much influenced by the work of Allyn Young (1928), who argued that every reorganisation of production activities creates the opportunity for further changes which would otherwise not have existed. These reorganisations are facilitated when scale increases, leading Young to reason that there exist more or less universal 'increasing returns to scale' in manufacturing. Young was lecturing at the LSE when Kaldor arrived, and had a lasting impact on his views. Hicks too was at the LSE in this period, although he admits to getting less from Young than did Kaldor. In his article here, Hicks provides an historical overview of the alternative assumption of constant returns to scale and questions whether this assumption is quite as irrelevant or inhibiting as Kaldor, following Young, always maintained. Hicks indicates just how much economic theory relies upon the constant returns assumption, concluding, however, that the assumption is not so irrelevant as Kaldor argued.

The next paper, by Jan Graaff, examines Kaldor's contribution to welfare economics and, in particular, Kaldor's (1939) paper on welfare propositions in economics which sets out his still famous compensation test. Kaldor's view is that the test can tell us something about production: that any ability of gainers, following some change, to compensate the losers and yet remain gainers, indicates that physical productivity, aggregate production, total real income, the sum total of wealth, or some such factor, has increased. In the last forty or fifty years that test has been the object of substantial criticism, much of which Kaldor apparently accepted in lectures and in conversation. One specific criticism of the test singled out by Graaff is that in certain situations it can contradict itself. Graaff's paper, then, is concerned with overcoming the limitations of the test, and he argues both for clarity on what is being tested for, and for a tightening of the test itself. Graaff's strategy is to regard Kaldor's compensation test as one of 'economic efficiency', and in order to guard against contradiction, he argues that the possibility of compensation must be calculated in an imaginary 'contracted' economy.

Luigi Pasinetti focuses on the large literature that grew out of Kaldor's 'Keynesian' theory of distribution (Kaldor, 1956). Pasinetti's own earlier work in this area (Pasinetti, 1962) considers the implications for Kaldor's theory arising from a 'long-run Keynesian theory of the rate of profit'. In that earlier paper, Pasinetti contributed to the derivation of what he terms the 'Cambridge Theorem': that, given the constraints of the model, the rate of profit on a long-run equilibrium growth path is determined by the 'natural' rate of growth divided by the propensity to save of capitalists, whatever else may be going on. In the present paper, Pasinetti introduces a hitherto absent analysis of government taxation and expenditure in an attempt to extend and generalise the earlier results. Pasinetti's conclusion is that Kaldor's theory of income distribution and the 'Cambridge' theory of the rate of profit survive the extension both for the case of taxation with balanced budgets and for the case of a government spending deficit, whether financed by public debt or by 'monetary means', so long as certain stated conditions hold.

James Tobin's article also refers to Kaldor's 1956 theory of income distribution. Tobin thus returns, here, to a long debate he had with Kaldor on the question of distribution. He explains that he did not, in that earlier debate, criticise Kaldor's proposition that saving propensities might differ for incomes of different types, as well as for incomes of different magnitudes. What had 'bothered' him was Kaldor's belief that returns to factors have nothing to do with their productivities. If this is so and marginal productivity is dropped as an explanation of income shares to be replaced by the consumption function, then Tobin was unable to understand how aggregate output could be explained. Nevertheless, despite his long-standing differences with Kaldor's approach to distribution, Tobin tries here to develop a model that provides certain insights into Kaldor's ideas in a context where their purpose and relevance may be understood and appreciated by a wider audience. In his model, the distribution of incomes between wages and returns to capital ownership cannot be explained by marginal productivities, because the latter are assumed to be indeterminate. Kaldorian differential saving propensities are shown to be one way to close the model, to determine factor shares, and to equate aggregate saving to technologically required investment. Tobin concludes that the moral of the story is that competitive markets are most likely to exist and to perform well when local incremental decisions are possible. However, societies frequently face all-or-nothing decisions—choices among 'lumpy' alternatives which are often difficult or impossible to reverse. For Tobin, the ordinary tools of neoclassical economics are much less useful for the second class of problems than for the first.

Frank Hahn looks at Kaldor's early post-war attempts to fashion Allyn Young's (1928) views on 'increasing returns to scale' into a formal theory of growth in capitalist economies. Hahn is of the firm opinion that Kaldor advanced numerous important suggestions as to how such a theory might be achieved but that ultimately he failed in this endeavour because of his unwillingness to employ some of the tools of general equilibrium analysis. Allyn Young had pointed to the need for a theory of how 'cumulative causation' was to proceed so that benefits accruing to 'increasing returns' in one sector could be transferred to others. Kaldor's initial 'solution' involved introducing stockholders and merchants of all kinds as essential elements in the analysis, building on his earlier paper (Kaldor, 1939) on speculation and economic stability. However, in Hahn's view, Kaldor's later work on growth is less precise and complete than the 1939 paper, and it is for this reason, according to Hahn, that the ultimate limitations of Kaldor's theories of growth arise. In Hahn's words 'the nuts and bolts of Kaldor's emendation of Allyn Young are missing', and Hahn's own contribution represents 'a rough outline of what he may have had in mind'.

The contributions so far mentioned are concerned mainly with Kaldor's earlier, more formal theorising. Before turning to the papers that address Kaldor's later, more empirical and policy-orientated contributions, Tony Lawson examines explicitly the philosophical underpinnings of this later approach. Throughout the writings in question, Kaldor produced a host of methodological claims and assertions (for example, that equilibrium theory makes the wrong kind of 'abstractions', that analysis should proceed from 'stylized facts', that economics should be concerned with the study of broad 'tendencies', etc.), although he provided little elaboration or substantiation of such claims. Lawson's aim is essentially to provide that elaboration and substantiation. This he attempts to do through demonstrating that Kaldor's assertions, by and large, can be reasonably straightforwardly reconciled with a particular version of philosophical realism. It is also clear from Lawson's arguments that he regards Kaldor's later methodological development as representing an improvement on his earlier more orthodox approach.

In the paper that follows, Geoff Hodgson discusses the work stimulated by Kaldor's later contributions on growth, and particularly those contributions associated with Verdoorn's law and with Kaldor's claim that manufacturing is the 'engine of growth'. Hodgson's strategy is to examine Kaldor's own theories, and various prominent contending theories which have since emerged, in the light of both empirical and theoretical considerations, focusing on recent understanding of how the growth process is affected by inherited institutional structures and social practices. Hodgson singles out the important distinction between codifiable and non-codifiable knowledge; the latter is related to skills and routines, and its development depends upon the transformation and degree of flexibility of social-economic institutions. Drawing on an analysis of the relevance of such factors for the growth process, Hodgson concludes that although weaknesses or faults can be found in parts of Kaldor's theory—so that the latter must properly be qualified—his own alternative 'institutionalist' theory of growth nevertheless supports conclusions similar to many of Kaldor's.

The paper by Ajit Singh stresses the fact that Kaldor was an ardent champion of rapid industrialisation in developing economies and that he was also among the first to call attention to the problem of de-industrialisation in advanced economies. This paper examines the relationship between the growth rates of manufacturing output in newly industrialising countries (NICs) and absolute or relative declines in employment in the manufacturing sectors of advanced economies. It is argued that contracting manufacturing employment/output may indicate 'structural disequilibrium'—by which Singh means that the economy is unable to achieve its long-term growth potential or the full employment of its resources. Singh's analysis is applied to the case of the UK in the period before Mrs Thatcher and before North Sea Oil. The conclusions are that the UK economy was characterised by long-term structural disequilibrium during the 1970s; the reasons for disequilibrium are located not in the trade of services and invisibles, but in the visible and finished manufactures trade flows. Imbalances in manufacturing trade with Japan and other advanced economies, rather than the pattern of UK trade with developing countries, was the chief source of disequilibrium. In fact, UK trade in finished manufactures with the NICs during the 1960s and 1970s resulted in an increase in domestic output and employment. However, Singh also presents evidence to suggest that, in the future, a number of OECD countries are likely to experience trade imbalances with the NICs of a kind similar to the UK's with Japan and other advanced economies, leading to further and widespread structural disequilibria over time.

The subject of Tony Thirlwall's paper is Kaldor's contribution to policy formulation and debate. Here Thirlwall does not confine his analysis to 'official' policy interventions, but assesses Kaldor's remarkably wide-ranging influence over the whole period 1939 to 1980, including episodes when governments or particular departments were often determined to exclude him from the official policy-making process. Several important aspects of Kaldor's work which are dealt with by Thirlwall are also discussed, and often in greater detail, in the papers by Desai (on Kaldor's critique of monetarism); Reddaway (on tax reform in the UK); Toye (on tax reform in developing countries); Spraos (on primary commodities); Griffith-Jones (on international monetary reform); Chakravarty, and Palma and Marcel (on economic problems in India and Chile respectively). However, Thirlwall's paper deals with numerous other policy issues and outlines the essential elements of a complete intellectual and political biography of Kaldor from the late 1930s onwards. Thirlwall's paper contains an analytical discussion of Kaldor's contribution to various aspects of war finance and national income accounting in the early 1940s, as well as of his contribution to post-war reconstruction. Kaldor's role in promoting the political and public acceptance within the UK of the 1944 *Report on Full Employment* is shown to have been crucial, while his work as an applied economist for the Strategic Bombing Survey and the Economic Commission for Europe, and as a policy adviser to the Hungarian and French Governments, made him influential throughout post-war Europe.

The next article, by Brian Reddaway, concerns itself with Kaldor's work on the reform of taxation in the UK, and confines its discussion to an analysis of two books, *An Expenditure Tax* (1955) and Volume VII of Kaldor's *Collected Essays*. Reddaway interprets the former as making a case for an expenditure tax as a replacement for surtax, which involved Kaldor in a thorough review of the problems of income taxes of all kinds. He criticises Kaldor's underestimation of the effects on incentives to tax avoidance and evasion of the 'net' method of expressing the taxation of expenditure. However, Reddaway's praise for

Kaldor's 'outstanding contribution' in devising a completely new form of taxation (the Selective Employment Tax) is less qualified and he concludes by suggesting that the benefits of this tax were substantial.

The paper by Michael Kitson and Solomos Solomou discusses Kaldor's ideas on protectionism as an instrument for economic growth in a flexible regime context. According to these authors, the experience of the UK in the 1930s offers an opportunity for testing Kaldor's hypothesis that the discouragement of imports through tariffs is an effective way of stimulating economic growth. They conclude that evidence relating to the policy shift to protectionism in 1932 supports Kaldor's ideas. By generating a major fall in the manufacturing sector's import propensity, protectionism is claimed to have benefited the British economy via the Harrod foreign trade multiplier; the change towards protectionism was responsible for inducing both the cyclical and relative trend recovery of the economy. In this way, the authors argue, although tariffs by themselves cannot account for all the economic revival of the 1930s, they were a major source of recovery which has been previously underemphasised.

Meghnad Desai's paper concerns itself with Kaldor's writing on monetarism and money. Desai starts out by summarising the many relevant partial statements scattered throughout Kaldor's writings. He connects these with Kaldor's evidence to the Radcliffe Committee, develops Kaldor's view of the endogenous money issue, and brings these matters to bear on a consideration of Kaldor's critique of monetarism. Finally, Desai considers the task of developing a new theory of monetary Keynesianism, building on the insights offered by Kaldor while linking these with developments in the literature on the finance motive.

The next paper, by John Toye, provides a great deal of detail concerning Kaldor's commitment to work on tax reform in developing countries. Three important themes emerge in the course of the discussion. First, it is suggested that the intellectual origins of Kaldor's recommendations for tax reform cannot be found in theoretical work on development economics or growth, nor were they based on detailed study of the history and institutions of the countries concerned. Second, Toye goes a long way towards destroying a number of ideologically-inspired myths concerning the nature and consequences of Kaldor's advice to developing countries. Finally, the implications of the revival in the mid 1980s of applied welfare economics and of the changing emphasis towards the potential of indirect taxation are examined. Toye suggests that those economists currently offering elegant technical solutions to the problems of taxation in poor economies may well experience difficulties which are rather similar to those that were faced by Kaldor in his early missions.

The continuing relevance of Kaldor's work for policy-making is the central theme of John Spraos' paper, in which he discusses Kaldor's preoccupation with the issue of primary commodity prices. Spraos argues that in his early work Kaldor was concerned with providing a theoretical rationale for intervention in primary commodity markets, as well as providing policy proposals which would tackle price instability. The proposals in Kaldor's paper on the International Wheat Agreement (1952) were designed to retain market signals and their desirable allocative effects, while at the same time ensuring that in the long run neither producers nor consumers suffered from adverse distributional consequences. Spraos contrasts and compares these proposals with those of buffer stock schemes, which have been far more prominent in the more recent policy literature. He also demonstrates the similarity between Kaldor's early proposals and compensatory finance schemes, such as STABEX, which have been set up since the 1970s. The second part of

Spraos' paper concentrates on Kaldor's later concerns with macroeconomic issues and, in particular, with policy proposals aimed at achieving growth by minimising the deleterious effects of excessive price fluctuations. Spraos considers that Kaldor's most interesting and powerful arguments focus on the inflationary effects of sharp primary commodity price increases and the excessive social and economic costs of contractionary policy responses to such cost inflation.

In the following article Stephany Griffith-Jones argues that in the field of international monetary reform, Kaldor's work provides both important insights into the malfunctioning of the international monetary and economic system, as well as useful proposals for reform. This author interprets Kaldor as writing very much in the spirit of Keynes, both in the importance he attached to the strengthening of world aggregate demand as a major objective of an efficient international monetary system and in the specific characteristics of his proposals for international commodity control. She also emphasises that Kaldor was one of the first economists working in an advanced capitalist economy to approach these issues taking into account the interests of less developed countries (LDCs), particularly in his emphasis upon the need for a balanced distribution of economic progress in the world. She concludes that the significance of Kaldor's proposals for international monetary reform lies not so much in the detailed schemes themselves, but in the agenda of objectives which he puts forward. This agenda is considered to be particularly relevant in the 1980s.

The impact and influence of Kaldor's work as an economist, rather than as a specialist in the narrower field of taxation, is provided in papers on specific developing countries by Sukhamoy Chakravarty and by Gabriel Palma and Mario Marcel. Chakravarty's discussion of Kaldor's work on Indian economic problems concludes by arguing that Kaldor's general approach remains valid in the late 1980s, especially because of his concern with equity in the design of progressive taxation and because of his appreciation of the positive role of the state in the key sectors of the Indian economy. Palma and Marcel analyse Kaldor's 1956 article on the economic problems of Chile, in which he questions why a country with such enormous potential for economic development (human and natural), had achieved such disappointing rates of economic growth. According to the authors, Kaldor raises some new hypotheses that were to become central to his later work on LDCs. One of them concerned the violation in the LDCs of the traditional post-Keynesian assumption of the saving behaviour of the capitalist class. In particular, Kaldor stressed the contrast between the disproportionately high share of profits in Chile's national income and the strikingly low levels of private savings. According to Kaldor this made it economically (although not necessarily politically) possible to raise domestic savings substantially through taxation, without the need to reduce workers' income, and without requiring large capital inflows from abroad. In this way, Kaldor rejected the case for a worsening income distribution as a necessary condition for growth in LDCs. A second hypothesis postulated by Kaldor concerned the peculiar macroeconomic role of the agricultural sector in some LDCs. He identified agriculture as the main bottleneck that constrained growth and boosted inflation in the Chilean economy, and therefore proceeded to develop a 'structuralist' theory of inflation which was contemporary with the work of Kalecki and the UN Economic Commission for Latin America. Kaldor's ideas are argued to be highly innovative, not least because he explains how the key problems for the Chilean economy did not lie outside the country, but inside it—basically stressing the absence of a really progressive entrepreneurial class.

Although these chapters do not provide complete coverage of Kaldor's work, they are certainly sufficient to indicate that it was extensive and remains highly pertinent. They also indicate its significance in stimulating a number of research programmes—sometimes in areas beyond Kaldor's own. Most of all, however, they reveal its lasting concern with relevance, enlivened by a widely encompassing, if often developing, vision.

Bibliography

Kaldor, N. 1939. Welfare propositions of economics and interpersonal comparisons of utility, *Economic Journal*, vol. 49, September

Kaldor, N. 1952. *A Reconsideration of the Economics of the International Wheat Agreement*, Rome, FAO, Community Studies No. 1

Kaldor, N. 1955. *An Expenditure Tax*, London, George Allen & Unwin

Kaldor, N. 1956. Alternative theories of distribution, *Review of Economic Studies*, vol. 23

Kaldor, N. 1966A. Marginal productivity and the macro-economic theories of distribution, *Review of Economic Studies*, vol. 33, no. 4

Kaldor, N. 1966B. *Causes of the Slow Rate of Economic Growth in the United Kingdom*, Inaugural Lecture, Cambridge, CUP

Kaldor, N. 1978A. *Further Essays in Economic Theory*, London, Duckworth

Kaldor, N. 1978B. *Further Essays in Applied Economics*, London, Duckworth

Pasinetti, L. L. 1962. Rate of profit and income distribution in relation to the rate of economic growth, *Review of Economic Studies*, vol. 29

Young, A. 1928. Increasing returns and economic progress, *Economic Journal*, vol. 38, December

The assumption of constant returns to scale

John Hicks*

I write in this paper about a concept to which Kaldor objected—objected, that is, to its use as a tool of economic analysis. His attitude is perhaps most explicit in the last of his theoretical works—his Okun Memorial Lectures at Yale, *Economics without Equilibrium* (1985); but it is evident, even from what he says in that place, that it goes much further back. For it is expressly associated by him with what he had learned from Allyn Young, whose 'Increasing Returns and Economic Progress' was published in the *Economic Journal* in 1928. During the year when that famous paper was being written, Young was teaching at the London School of Economics; Kaldor, who had just come to LSE, was a member of his seminar. It set a mark on Kaldor, which was never effaced.[1]

I myself got much less from Young. Though I was in a formal sense a member of his department, I am sure he did not think of me as a theorist; nor had I as yet any ambition in that direction. I did not get into touch with Kaldor until I met him at the Robbins postgraduate seminar, nearly a year after Young had died. By then I had just started to work on theory. My first theoretical paper was on elasticity of substitution in relation to distribution, which became known to the Robbins seminar in 1930. It expressly excluded the increasing returns phenomenon, which to Young had been so important. However, by the time it appeared in a well-known chapter of my *Theory of Wages* (1932) I had become aware that my position needed defending; so an attempt at defence, based on what I had found in the first volume of Wicksell's *Lectures*, appears in an Appendix to my book. It is not a good defence; I don't suppose that Kaldor had anything to do with it. But he may well have been one of those who made me feel that something was needed.

The discussion at that time was impeded by the fact that the assumption I was making, in opposition to Young and to Kaldor, had not been named. It may be that I was myself responsible for naming it—as *Constant Returns to Scale* (CRS, as I shall here allow myself to abbreviate it). I am sure that when I first used it I was conscious that I was inventing it;[2] but the name is rather obvious, and there may well be others who have claims. However that may be, the name caught on. Though earlier economists did not have the

*All Souls College, Oxford

[1] Young came to LSE from Harvard, where he had been supervisor of a thesis presented by Edward Chamberlin, to become *The Theory of Monopolistic Competition* in 1933.

[2] In a paper entitled 'Distribution and Economic Progress; a revised version' which appeared in the *Review of Economic Studies* in 1936 and was reprinted in the second edition of *Theory of Wages* (1963). This was itself a reply to a discussion, to which several now notable economists had contributed, that had appeared in an earlier number of that *Review*. I do not find that any of them mentioned CRS explicitly, though they might well have found it convenient to do so.

name, we can see, looking back, that the concept is implied in many of the things they said. It will be useful to look at their story in this light, for it shows, from extensive experience, how hard it is to dispense with CRS. Kaldor wanted to dispense with it, and I sympathise with his desire to dispense with it; but I have not found it easy to do so, certainly not to dispense with it altogether as Kaldor thought he could do.

Beginnings

So let us look at the story, beginning (surely) with Adam Smith. He, one might think, is the last who should be accused of being a CRS victim; for are not increasing returns, division of labour, scale economies, set at the forefront of his teaching, the theme of the very first chapter of the *Wealth of Nations*? But in spite of all he has to say about that in his theory of growth, we still find that in his value theory, his cost of production value theory, he does not get away from CRS. He does not notice this, since he has at the back of his mind what I have myself called his First Model,[1] an agricultural model, taken over from the Physiocrats. This has a natural period, the harvest year, which is self-contained. Production, and distribution, within that period are completely determined by the parameters of that period, the 'labour' supply, the technique of production, the stock that is carried over from the past to that period, divided into the part that is used for further production and the part that is used, as Smith would say, 'unproductively'. There is no reason why these parameters should not be different from one period to the next. There is carry-over of 'corn', but nothing else is carried over.

But as soon as one generalises, as Smith most certainly wanted to do, allowing for half-finished goods to be carried over, both at the start and at the finish of the accounting period, a cost of production theory of value (which is Smith's) will not work unless prices remain the same from period to period. But if output is increasing from period to period, and there are economies of scale which differ as between industries, and/or if the demands for different outputs increase at different rates, some relative prices at least must be changing. That is why I say that in his value theory, Smith does not allow for increasing returns.

I rush on, in this hurried survey, to Ricardo. He has long been supposed to have avoided this trouble in Smith, simply by leaving scale economies out altogether. But though there are no increasing returns in Ricardo, there are diminishing returns, from scarcity of land, and these, as Casarosa (1978) has shown, get him into just the same sort of trouble.[2] He evidently accepts that his productive processes extend outside the current period—beginning before it and continuing after—so he cannot determine his prices (or values) in terms of parameters that are confined to the period he is considering. He needs to have his equilibrium extending further. That would be acceptable, if the same prices continued over time; but in a process of expansion, which is constrained by land scarcity, they cannot do so.

What, however, has this to do with CRS? Ricardo, it has commonly been supposed, did have a sort of CRS production function. It is revealed in his preliminary stage, where there is no land scarcity, so that the employment of all factors, including land, can go on increasing proportionately. Later on, in the world in which he thinks himself to be living, there is land scarcity (and so there is rent), so proportional expansion is no longer possible.

[1] In 'The Social Accounting of Classical Models', a paper which had not been published before it appeared in the third volume of my collected essays, *Classics and Moderns* (see pp. 23–4 of that volume).

[2] Casarosa's view is discussed in my *Causality in Economics* (1979), p. 54.

One can then express the situation in terms of a CRS function, constrained by the fixity of one single factor; alternatively (and this I think would have been more the way of Ricardo's thinking) one can treat the fixity of land as exogenous. The production function must then be expressed in terms of variable factors, and as such it must exhibit diminishing returns. These alternatives are relevant to what happened afterwards. The diminishing returns of Ricardo could be expressed, in later terminology, as diminishing marginal productivity of a bundle of variable factors, applied to the fixed supply of land. But by classifying differently (while following Ricardo in neglecting scale economies) we can have diminishing returns to any factor, employment of the others being regarded as fixed. One can detect this way of thinking in the work of some of Ricardo's successors, Longfield certainly, perhaps von Thunen. It leads on to the *general* marginal productivity doctrine, in which every factor is remunerated according to the value of its marginal product and, then, to the demonstration by Wicksteed (1894) that if the production function is homogeneous of the first degree (which is CRS) and if all factors are remunerated by the values of their marginal products the total product is exhausted. (More generally, the same result is obtained if each firm produces at minimum average cost, as Barone, Walras and Wicksell all knew.) But by the time Wicksted was writing, much else had happened. Marshall's *Principles* had already appeared. And to appreciate the place of Marshall in the story, we must go back to Mill.

The economic theory of Mill (*Principles*, 1848) is based on Ricardo; but he is much more sensitive than Ricardo had been to the difficulties I have been discussing. Though he maintains (or tries to maintain) a cost of production theory of value, he is aware of exceptions; it is true that he does not quite see how big these exceptions are. Increasing returns are one of his exceptions; joint supply is another; but he does not follow them up. What he does follow up is the case of international values. Here he starts from Ricardo's comparative cost theory, which had provided a basis for international specialisation, but had failed to give an explanation of the terms of trade, since (by assumption) 'labour' was not movable between countries. So international values (in Mill) are determined by Reciprocal Demand.

So this is where Demand in a neoclassical sense first comes in—with Mill, long before the time of the so-called 'marginalists', Jevons, Walras, Menger. None of these carried on from Mill (Jevons thought he was reacting against him) but Marshall, in the first of his important theoretical writings, undoubtedly was. His *Pure Theory of Foreign Trade* (1879) descends directly from Mill. He is concerned to indicate exceptions which Mill had not noticed. One of these is inelastic demand; the other arises from increasing returns. So this is the point, one hundred years after Adam Smith, when scale economies win recognition. It is the first time when they win admission to a theory of value.

In Marshall's *Principles* (first edition 1890) of course they are recognised. He has his *increasing cost* (Ricardian) and his *diminishing cost* industries. In the analysis of the behaviour of a single 'industry' he thought that he had found each of them to be manageable; and that for the analysis of international values he had already shown that each was manageable. But he never thought that he had found a place for scale economies in what we should now call a 'macro' model. When he goes 'macro' in the last Part of the *Principles* he relapses into Marginal Productivity. But he is uncomfortable about it; there is less of it in the later editions of his book.

So, though he left much to be done, we may reckon Marshall to have been the founder of the (modern) anti-CRS school. But before following its fortunes further, let us look to see what happened on the other tack.

Walras and the CRS Method

Here we must begin with Walras. Walras is pure CRS. He seems to have been quite uninfluenced by Mill, even by Ricardo. The supply side of his General Equilibrium model is just the cost-of-production theory of Adam Smith, which had filtered down to him through his French predecessors. So he does not have a production function, even a Ricardian production function; he just has a matrix of coefficients, which are stated to be independent of outputs so that they obey the rule of CRS. Though it is only in the first form of his theory (his first edition of 1874) that they are taken to be quite fixed, 'given', as he says, '*a priori*', even in later versions, where substitution in response to changes in factor prices is allowed for, they are still independent of scale. There is not much difference between this later form of Walras's model and the all-round marginal productivity doctrine; it is all CRS.

In one of my own publications, my survey of Linear Theory,[1] I have traced out the pedigree, from Walras to Cassel, from Cassel to Leontief and Wald and von Neumann, from them to DOSSO and much of Samuelson, to Linear Programming and Activity Analysis. I shall not repeat that story here. All I need to do is to emphasise that it is all CRS. It includes a quite major part of what has been done in economic theory in the present century.

Thus there seem to be two traditions, which persist. On the one hand there are those who are so impressed by what has been done by the CRS method that they have come to live with it; on the other, those for whom scale economies are so important that they cannot bring themselves to leave them aside. I do not see that between these views there can be any easy reconciliation. The best that can be done is to keep both in play, being willing to work on the one line or the other depending upon which seems to be more suitable for the problem in hand. It then rather appears that it would be in microeconomics that we should most often find ourselves having to attend to scale economies; while (in spite of Adam Smith and Allyn Young) it would be for macro-problems that we might more often allow ourselves the convenience of leaving them out. But to this rule, as we shall find, there are exceptions.

Competition between firms

A 'micro' field where the CRS approach has most obviously nothing to offer is the study of competition between firms in an 'industry'. The Walrasian, indeed, has never heard of firms! Marshall had raised that issue; but even the most devoted Marshallians were obliged to admit, after the celebrated article by Piero Sraffa, 'The Laws of Returns under competitive conditions' (1926), that Marshall's analysis, at best, was incomplete. He had not shown, at all persuasively, what limited the size of a firm.[2] Sraffa's solution, at the end of his paper, was to suppose that each firm had its own particular market, since its product was a little different from those of its competitors—a solution which was to be formalised, very much formalised, by Joan Robinson (*The Economics of Imperfect Competition*, 1933)

[1] First published in the *Economic Journal* in 1960 and in one of the IBA survey volumes which appeared at that time. It is reprinted in the third volume of my *Collected Essays* (1983A).

[2] There may be more to be said for Marshall on this matter than is commonly thought. I remember being shown by the economic historian T. S. Ashton who had been brought up in Lancashire and had a deep knowledge of its history, that the Marshall model was a very good fit to the cotton industry of Marshall's time. This was the major British industry at the time when Marshall was writing. It was *vertically* highly disintegrated, with firms selling to merchants, who sold to other firms. External economies were of central importance. Forty years later such a structure had become exceptional.

and less so by Chamberlin, whose *Monopolistic Competition* was published in that same year.

Kaldor and I—we were working at that time quite closely together—published in the very next year (1934) articles which in effect were critiques of these now famous works. Kaldor's was essentially an attack on the concept of long-period equilibrium of the firm, and hence of the industry, which had so far been taken over from Marshall. He showed that there would be nothing left, in its internal conditions, to limit the size of the firm in that long-period equilibrium, when that is taken strictly, save one residual indivisibility: that must be a matter of the coordination of its activities; and this is a function which in static conditions, also taken strictly, must tend to disappear. So we seem to be left in that long-period equilibrium with what is essentially a CRS production function; and this he claimed, and I think he was justified in claiming, is inconsistent with the maintenance of competition. (In all this he was carrying on, in a different direction from the others, from the Sraffa paper of 1926.) Economists accordingly are left with two alternatives; either to go CRS, admitting that this leaves them with nothing to say about the structure of industry; or, if they want to attend to the structure of industry and to use an equilibrium method in analysing it, to admit that the equilibrium is less 'long-period', so that the firm can be left with a fixed nucleus of plant and so on. It is easy to see which of these alternatives Kaldor preferred.

My own, more or less contemporary paper, 'The theory of monopoly', was largely expository. Its main critical point was to question the identification, which Joan Robinson in particular had taken for granted, between heterogeneity of firms and heterogeneity of products—the 'single product firm'. A new product does not involve a new firm; it could come from an existing firm. Quite a small quantity of it could then be produced at no excessive cost, since overheads could be shared. But this was a matter which could be better treated by the consumers' surplus apparatus, in the development of which both Kaldor and I were going to take a hand.

CRS and the 'New Welfare Economics'

The 'New Welfare Economics', as it came to be called, is commonly associated with a little note of Kaldor's and a much longer paper of my own which appeared in successive issues of the *Economic Journal* (1939). The part played by Kaldor was, however, much greater than would be suggested by the relative length of our published contributions. It was not just that I had his note in my possession before I began to write my paper, so that he was the inventor of the compensation test by which the Pareto optimum could be shown to be of some significance;[1] it was also that he was the inventor of the geometrical apparatus by which the properties of that optimum could be explained whether the system studied had scale economies or not. It was the first of these contributions which for years attracted almost exclusive attention, the test being criticised from various angles. I need not do more than refer to the Scitovsky paradox (Scitovsky, 1941)—that there could be cases where the test would show, on the one hand that A was 'better' than B, and on the other that B was 'better' than A. That was due to an income effect; but in many 'particular' applications—the introduction of a new product, or of a new firm into an industry—an

[1] The critical passage is on p. 337 of the Italian edition and on p. 354 of the French. I must confess that although I had in 1939 been familiar with Pareto's book for more than ten years (I used to carry the Italian version in my pocket like a prayer-book) the significance of this passage had escaped me.

income effect was unlikely to be important. If the new product could be sold, in competition with varieties previously available, it must offer an advantage, to somebody, but this might be outweighed by the effects of loss of scale economies in production of the goods displaced (Hicks, 1941). Cost–benefit analysis, to which a way was thus opened up, was for long the chief thing which came out of our work.

There was, however, another direction which might have been explored. It is on the side of production that scale economies are important, so there is much to be said about them without bothering about the consumption side. The optimum need do no more than mark a maximum efficiency of production. There should then be a list of products of which, from given resources, as much as possible was to be produced—in the sense that no more could be produced of any one without some sacrifice of output of another, or others. How far could an optimum, in that sense, be reached by the use of a price-system? By the authority, that is, whose wants are to be supplied, setting *suitable* prices, and telling all those in charge of resources to produce as much *value* as they can at those given prices? The complications that are introduced by scale economies into such a problem can be rather precisely defined.[1]

CRS and positive economics

I now turn to consider some instances of CRS propositions intended to be used in more positive economics. In spite of the restrictiveness of the assumptions on which they are based, assumptions which cannot be claimed to be realistic, they can nevertheless to some extent be a help. For the propositions would not have been noticed unless we had begun by making these assumptions. Having reached them, we can proceed to enquire how far they would be affected if scale economies were admitted; so the ladder by which we have got up can be kicked down.

Once again I go back to Sraffa. His *Production of Commodities by Means of Commodities* was published in 1960, but he tells us himself that he began to work on it in the twenties: 'the central propositions took shape in the late 1920s' (Sraffa, 1960, p. vi). So to take it together with his 'Laws of Returns' of 1926 would seem to be fair. Yet the strange thing about the book is that it has nothing to say about Laws of Returns: 'No changes in output', he tells us himself, 'are considered' (*ibid*, p.v.). He is looking away from the questions on which he had been so illuminating.

Though economists may decide to forget about changes in output, is it appropriate for them to allow the actors in their models to do so? The actors must surely be supposed to have some idea of what they were doing yesterday, and of what they are planning to do tomorrow. If their ideas on these matters are to be neglected, that can only be because between the dates in question there is no change. Like Wicksell's and those of other economists who have found themselves similarly baffled, his model lapses into a Stationary State.

The reason why he is content with a model of this static character can only be because it is distribution, not production, which is his concern. So he allows himself to forget about quantities, in order to fix his attention on (relative) prices. Now relative prices can remain constant over time, even though quantities are varying, provided, first, that there is CRS and, second, that the ratios between quantities produced and quantities absorbed in

[1] My 'Optimisation and Specialisation' had never appeared until it was published in the first volume of my *Collected Essays* (*Wealth and Welfare*, 1981). It had waited long enough, but if it had waited a little longer it might have been dedicated to Mr Gorbachev—or to the Russian economists who must be writing textbooks to be used in his universities.

producing them remain constant over time; so the economy is in what had been called a steady state.

Now the point of a steady state model is that it is a representative of an economy in which the capital stock, in all its heterogeneity, is fully adjusted to the production required from it at the moment (like the long-period equilibrium of Marshall). If there is no CRS, any expansion of production must upset this adjustment; the economy has then to adjust itself, in some way or other, to what would have to be regarded, in these Walrasian terms, as a new *technique*. That adjustments of this sort are a very real problem can hardly be questioned. It is what I have called the Problem of Traverse. I have found two ways of approaching this problem,[1] and there may well be others. Differences between them are not important here. What is important, either way, is that the CRS steady state is a *help* in constructing a model in which the issue comes up so sharply that we can at least begin to do something about it.

CRS, factor price equalisation and the elasticity of substitution

I conclude with two examples of a similar procedure which have come up in quite different writings of my own. Neither of them has received much attention, but I would claim that each has some validity. The first concerned the 'Factor Price Equalisation Theorem' of Samuelson, his contention that free movement of goods between countries, without any movement of factors, would tend in the long run to equalise factor prices also between them (see Samuelson, 1948 and 1949). This depended on very CRS assumptions. In a paper I wrote on the subject,[2] I first examined what international trade would look like if the Walrasian assumptions were universally valid. I next introduced variations in natural resources and other geographical differences, which did not change the model save in rather obvious ways. But then in the final page or two, I brought in economies of scale. I found that they led to a transformation:

> There will be a stronger tendency to specialisation, even among equally endowed countries, than there is in the Samuelson model; but they will still be geared together by the possibility of adjusting the kinds of things they produce to the nature of their resources. So, as between 'advanced' or 'industrialised' countries, there should be a tendency to equalisation . . . but as between them and the non-industrialised countries, the case is very different. There is no tendency to equalisation between them and the industrialised countries, nor among the non-industrialised themselves. They may be rich or poor according to their endowment with natural resources. . . Those which are poor in natural resources have no hope save in industrialisation . . . but a small industrialised sector does not develop enough economies to make it competitive, and a large requires so much capital as to be out of reach (Hicks, 1983A, p. 232).

The other example concerns the Elasticity of Substitution, which came in, as has been seen, at the very start of my personal part of the story. Its own story has been tortuous, for it began, at that start, with a mistake. There were two definitions which emerged in the 1932–3 discussions (Hicks, 1932; Robinson, 1933), and it was generally accepted that in conditions to which they both applied (two factors and a CRS production function) they were equivalent. But we can now see, after all that has happened,[3] that this was the wrong way of putting the point. For what is measured, on the Joan Robinson definition, is an

[1] One in Chapter XVI of *Capital and Growth* (1965), the other in *Capital and Time* (1973). They are set out together, in abbreviated versions, in *Methods of Dynamic Economics* (1986).

[2] 'The Factor price equalisation theorem', first published in my *Essays in World Economics* (1959), reprinted in *Collected Essays III* (1983A).

[3] The only complete statement of my later view on this subject is in 'Elasticity of substitution reconsidered', a paper which was not printed until it appeared in the third volume of my *Collected Essays* in 1983.

effect on quantities of a change in factor prices, so it is prices that are independent variables (just as in the conventional demand curve for a final commodity); but on the *Theory of Wages* definition, it is quantities of factors that are independent variables, and it is their effects on prices (or marginal products) which are measured. So it is the reciprocal of 'my' definition which ought to have been taken. If we write c for this elasticity, keeping σ for the Robinson elasticity, the proper statement of the equivalence, in the two-factor case, should have been $\sigma c = 1$. The importance of this change in notation, which is clearly called for on this general ground, is that the extension to the case of many factors then presents no difficulty. We are now to consider the relation between a pair of factors out of many. We have to consider two limiting cases, in one of which the other (background) factors have supplies that are perfectly elastic, while in the other they are fixed. The former case is that to which σ applies; so that the Joan Robinson σ is formally the same as that which presents itself in consumer theory where the prices of other goods in the consumer's budget are taken as fixed (the Slutsky equation). The place of c is in the study of the effects of changes in quantities available, so it is the *quantities* of other factors which are here to be regarded as given. As between that c and that σ, in the 'pair out of many' theory, there is, under CRS, a simple relation

$$A\sigma + Bc = 1$$

where A and B, though not constants, are *necessarily* positive. This is not inconsistent with the $\sigma c = 1$ of the two-factor case; it simply says that in that case both σ and c must be positive. For both σ and c to be positive is however possible, much more generally. But this is not in general the only possibility; either σ or c could be negative, if the other were sufficiently positive.

So we get an intelligible classification. To put it in words, while still calling σ an elasticity of substitution, we should call c an *elasticity of complementarity*. Thus when σ and c are both positive, the two factors would be said to be substitutes one way, complements the other. The relationship between the factors would be 'weak'. As opposed to that, there would be two *strong* cases: (1) strong complements, with c still positive, but σ negative; (2) strong substitutes, with σ still positive but c negative. I suspect that this classification is that to which economists have been feeling their way; it is helpful to have it set out so formally that we can rely upon it. Though we need to have CRS in order to get a formal proof,[1] it is hard to see that the admission of scale economies would make it possible for the relationship between two factors to be such that both σ and c could be negative; and that is what would be needed for the classification to be upset.[2]

My general conclusion is that CRS, if used with proper precaution and in the appropriate contexts, can be a help; but if misused, or if it is applied in the wrong context, it can indeed, as Kaldor thought, be a hindrance.

Bibliography

Casarosa, C. 1978. A new formulation of the Ricardian system, *Oxford Economic Papers*, 30, March

Chamberlin, E. H. 1933. *The Theory of Monopolistic Competition*, Cambridge, Mass. Harvard University Press

Hicks, J. R. 1932. *Theory of Wages*, London, Macmillan (2nd edn, 1963)

[1] The algebra is at last written out, rather clumsily but I think correctly, in the 1983 paper that was cited in the previous note.

[2] It is not excluded that either σ or c might be zero, if the other were positive. It should however be noticed that these, excepting in very special conditions, would be different cases.

Hicks, J. R. 1934. Annual survey of economic theory: the theory of monopoly, *Econometrica,* vol. 3, January, reprinted in Hicks (1983A)
Hicks, J. R. 1936. Distribution and economic progress; a revised version, *Review of Economic Studies,* vol. 4, October
Hicks, J. R. 1941. The rehabilitation of consumers' surplus, *Review of Economic Studies,* vol. 9, February. Reprinted in *Wealth and Welfare, Collected Papers on Economic Theory,* vol. 1, Oxford, Basil Blackwell, 1981
Hicks, J. R. 1959. International trade and the equalisation of factor prices, *Essays in World Economics,* Oxford, Clarendon Press, reprinted in Hicks (1983A)
Hicks, J. R. 1959. *Essays in World Economics,* Oxford, Clarendon Press
Hicks, J. R. 1965. *Capital and Growth,* Oxford, Clarendon Press
Hicks, J. R. 1973. *Capital and Time,* Oxford, Clarendon Press
Hicks, J. R. 1979. *Causality in Economics,* Oxford, Basil Blackwell
Hicks, J. R. 1981. Optimisation and specialisation, in *Collected Essays Vol. 1: Wealth and Welfare,* Oxford, Basil Blackwell
Hicks, J. R. 1983A. *Classics and Moderns (Collected Essays on Economic Theory, Vol. III)* Oxford, Basil Blackwell
Hicks, J. R. 1983B. The social accounting of classical models, in Hicks (1983A)
Hicks, J. R. 1986. *Methods of Dynamic Economics,* Oxford, Clarendon Press
Kaldor, N. 1934. The equilibrium of the firm, Economic Journal, vol. 44, March, reprinted in *Essays in Value and Distribution,* London, Duckworth, 1960
Kaldor, N. 1939. Welfare propositions of economics and interpersonal comparisons of utility, *Economic Journal,* 49, September, reprinted in *Essays in Value and Distribution,* London, Duckworth (1960)
Kaldor, N. 1985. *Economics without equilibrium. The Okun Memorial lectures at Yale University,* Cardiff, University College, Cardiff Press
Marshall, A. 1879. *Pure Theory of Foreign Trade and Domestic Values,* LSE Reprint Series, London, LSE
Marshall, A. 1980. *Principles of Economics,* vol. I, London, Macmillan
Mill, J. S. 1848. *The Principles of Political Economy with some of their applications to Social Philosophy,* in J. M. Robinson (ed.), *Collected works of John Stuart Mill,* vol. II–III, Toronto
Pareto, V. 1925. *Manual of Political Economy* (French edition, 1927; Italian edition, 1919) translated by A. S. Schwier and edited by A. S. Schwier and A. N. Page, London, Macmillan
Robinson, J. 1933. *The Economics of Imperfect Competition,* London, Macmillan (2nd edn, 1969)
Samuelson, P. A. 1948. International trade and the equalisation of factor prices, *Economic Journal,* vol. LVIII, June
Samuelson, P. A. 1949. International factor-price equalisation once again, *Economic Journal,* vol. LIX, June
Scitovsky, T. 1941. A note on welfare propositions in economics, *Review of Economic Studies,* vol. 8, November
Sraffa, P. 1960. *Production of Commodities by Means of Commodities,* Cambridge, CUP
Wicksell, K. 1934. *Lectures on Political Economy,* vol. 1 (translated from the Swedish by Ellassen and edited by L. Robbins), London, Routledge & Kegan Paul
Wicksteed, P. H. 1894. *Essays on the coordination of the Laws of Distribution,* LSE Series of Reprints, London LSE
Young, A. A. 1928. Increasing returns and economic progress, *Economic Journal,* vol. 38, no. 4, December

Kaldor on welfare

J. de V. Graaff*

Kaldor's contribution to the formal body of welfare economics is contained in two brief essays, dating from 1939–40 and to be found in Volume 1 of his *Collected Papers*. They are not of equal importance.

The second, originally published in *Economica* (1940), re-opened the debate on tariffs and the terms of trade. It revived an old argument of Bickerdike's (1906) to the effect that a country enjoying any degree of monopsony power could normally gain at the expense of its trading partners by imposing a small tariff on imports. The conclusion is valid—indeed, if one thinks of a one-man country, it is obvious—but Kaldor employed in his demonstration an apparatus of community indifference curves constructed on compensation criteria that did not for long remain unchallenged (Scitovsky, 1941). It has not stood the test of time.

The first paper, scarcely more than 1,000 words in length, is in a different category. It is reprinted from the 1939 *Economic Journal* under a shortened title: 'Welfare Propositions in Economics'. It states, with characteristic vigour, his compensation test. It is still famous after nearly 50 years.

The compensation test

Kaldor's compensation test asserts that the ability of the gainers from some change to compensate the losers, and still remain gainers, indicates that 'physical productivity', 'aggregate production', 'aggregate real income' or 'the sum total of wealth' has increased. He uses the terms more or less interchangeably, without any attempt at definition, and in much the same sense as Ricardo, writing more than a century earlier, might have spoken of the 'mass' or 'abundance' of commodities. The closest he gets to an explanation is when he refers to Pigou's division of welfare economics into two parts: 'the first relating to production and the second to distribution'. Kaldor's thesis is that the compensation test can be used to tell us something about production, and that what it tells us has 'scientific status'. Statements about distribution, on the other hand, have no such status; and their validity cannot be decided 'on economic grounds'.

These assertions are really no more than shots fired in a contemporary debate on the validity of prescriptive statements in the 'old' welfare economics, which was rooted in utilitarianism. A 'new' version, purged of distributive issues and concentrating on the 'size' of what was to be distributed, was for a time thought to be able to say something

*Cape Town.

useful without having to make interpersonal comparisons of utility. Kaldor's test was offered as a simple way of finding out whether or not the 'size' had in fact increased.

The principle underlying the compensation test was of respectable antiquity when Kaldor wrote. In an essay in *The New Palgrave* (1987), Chipman, giving detailed references, traces it back to Hotelling, Lerner, Pareto, Marshall and Dupuit. Kaldor did not invent it. What he did was to focus attention on it at a time when, if valid, it had a ready-made part to play in a theoretical controversy.

Kaldor's test came under heavy fire, especially in the 1940s and 1950s. This is not the place to catalogue the critics or evaluate the points they made, often extremely well. Chipman's essay does just that, and is readily accessible. It suffices to note that the principal difficulty is that the test can contradict itself. A can be better than B; and, if compensation is not actually carried out, B can at the same time be better than A. This is clearly unsatisfactory.

Kaldor conceded, in lectures and in conversation, that most of the criticism was well founded. His instincts nevertheless told him that the test must mean *something*. They did not, however, enable him to lay his finger on precisely what that something was. Having spread the net so widely in his original paper—which spoke of productivity, production, income and wealth—he was perhaps reluctant to venture a fifth suggestion. Even if he had, the test as formulated could still have led to contradictions. What was needed was reform on two fronts: clarity on what was to be tested for *and* a tightening of the test itself. This paper outlines, with the benefit of hindsight, the sort of answer to which such an approach might have led.

Economic efficiency

In a little noticed passage, Hicks (1939) related Kaldor's contribution to 'the task of examining the efficiency . . . of any given economic organization'. (*Efficiency* is a wider concept than Kaldor's *physical productivity*, because it includes producing the right mix of outputs and allocating them efficiently to consumers who want them.) The suggestion is on the right lines. Consider a move from some inefficient initial position to any Pareto-optimal one—i.e. to any point on the utility–possibility frontier. By definition of the latter, it is in theory always possible to move along the frontier by lump-sum transfers to a point that dominates the initial position. That is to say, the Kaldor test is *always* satisfied for a move from an inefficient to an efficient position. Moreover, as no point on the frontier (i.e. no efficient point) can be dominated by any attainable one, there is no way that the Kaldor test can be satisfied for a move from an efficient point to any other, whether efficient or not. There is thus no possibility of the Kaldor test leading, in these circumstances, to a contradiction.

A test free from the danger of contradicting itself only in respect of movements between efficient and inefficient points, and then capable of saying no more than that the efficient ones are more so than the inefficient, does not get us very far. At the very least we need a modification that would enable us to compare inefficient points with one another. That is what we must seek.

There is a preliminary difficulty. Compensation, or the mere act of transferring wealth, can itself affect efficiency. Two simple examples will make this clear. Consider first a two-person, two-good exchange economy, as might be illustrated by the familiar box diagram. Starting from any inefficient point, there is always a lump-sum transfer that will lead straight to the contract curve. An inefficient point is thus transformed into an efficient one.

Consider next a production economy, distorted by a single monopoly—but by nothing else. Transferring wealth away from the monopolist's customers may (if the income-elasticity of demand is not too low) kill his market and render the distortion irrelevant. The transfer will have turned an inefficient economy into an efficient one. Further examples are not hard to find. Unless great care is taken, using compensation criteria to measure efficiency can be like using elastic to measure length.

The examples just given reflect the economist's traditional dichotomy between efficiency and inefficiency. An engineer measures the efficiency of a machine by relating its output of work to the input of energy, whereas until recently in our profession we have tended to regard the efficiency of an economy as an all-or-nothing affair. It is efficient if you cannot make one person better off without making another worse off. It is inefficient if you can. But how inefficient?

Elsewhere I have proposed a way of answering this question that leans heavily on earlier work of Allais (1943, 1975, 1981) and Debreu (1951). Mention must also be made of a series of papers by Diewert (1981, 1983, 1984, 1985) investigating the measurement of waste in a general equilibrium context—'waste' and 'inefficiency' being virtually identical notions. In what follows I stay with the definitions of Graaff (1976, 1977).

Assume that society's production function is known and define the *degree of efficiency* of the economy as the smallest fraction of potentially available outputs of final goods and services just sufficient to maintain each individual member of the community at his current level of well-being. That is to say, if we could find a mix of final outputs such that 20% of each item in it could be thrown away, we would regard the economy as 80% efficient—or, equivalently, as 20% inefficient. Note that enough labour and other productive services would be being supplied to produce the full 100% of the mix, only 80% of which is required to maintain current levels of well-being. Note too that the degree of efficiency is defined only in relation to the given tastes of a given community with a given production function.

It follows from the definition that an economy that is 80% efficient in relation to its capabilities as described by its genuine production function would be 100% efficient in relation to the capabilities described by a hypothetical production function contracted by 20% in output space—or, more technically, contracted homothetically to its origin in the space of final outputs by that percentage. For brevity we shall refer to an economy facing a contracted constraint of this nature as a *contracted economy*. It turns out that a consideration of such contracted economies helps us understand the application of Kaldor's test to inefficient points in an actual one.

Contracted economies

The utility possibility curve facing a contracted economy is itself contracted—not neatly and homothetically the way the production constraint is assumed to be contracted in the space of final outputs, but in the sense that it must lie everywhere within the utility possibility curve of the original, potentially efficient economy. Moreover, being subject to a tighter constraint, the utility possibility curve relating to an economy contracted by, say, 30% must lie everywhere within that of the same economy contracted by only 20%. There is no way in which utility possibility curves relating to different degrees of contraction of the same economy can intersect. That fact is all we need to compare inefficient points in an actual economy.

Consider a move from B to A, both points being inefficient. Imagine the economy so contracted that A becomes an efficient point, lying on the contracted utility possibility curve. (The percentage contraction of the production function necessary to achieve this tells us how inefficient A is in the actual economy.) If (and only if), within the confines of the contracted utility possibilities, the gainers can compensate the losers and still remain gainers, we can say that *A is more efficient than B*. This is because A lies on the contracted utility possibility curve, while B (given that the compensation test is passed) must lie below it. Lying below it entails that it must lie on the utility possibility curve of an economy that has been still further contracted—which means that B must be more inefficient than A.

The gainers have to be able to compensate the losers 'within the confines of the contracted utility possibilities'. Another way of phrasing this is to say that they have to be able to compensate the losers *without the act of compensation itself increasing the efficiency of the economy*. Elsewhere results have been derived, on certain heroic assumptions, that enable us to take the matter further. They enable us to estimate the percentage change in an economy's degree of efficiency that might be caused by compensation.

The first result (Graaff, 1977) is that, for a small movement that does not affect prices, the percentage change in the degree of efficiency is equal to the percentage change in national income at current prices. In the context of Kaldor's compensation test we would therefore have to say that the gainers would have to be able to compensate the losers *without the act of compensation itself increasing national income, valued at current prices*.

The second result (Graaff, 1979) allows for prices changing from P_1 to P_2 and shows that the proportional change in the degree of efficiency can be approximated by

$$(\sum P_1 \Delta X + \tfrac{1}{2}\sum \Delta P \Delta X)/\sum P_2 X_1$$

where the Xs stand for quantities of final commodities. The Kaldor test would then have to be re-phrased to provide that this expression should not be increased by the hypothetical compensation.

Enthusiasm for these results does not normally survive revelation of the assumptions required for their derivation. They include all those conventionally accepted in calculating a 'true' cost-of-living index. In particular, we have to assume an exchange-efficient economy with fixed hours of work, no international trade, no public goods, no external effects and with consumers who have identical homothetic preferences.

Further work will no doubt permit some weakening of these assumptions. Until it does, compensation tests must be used with caution—even for measuring changes in efficiency.

Concluding remarks

It is probable that Kaldor would have accepted that his compensation test was best regarded as a test of economic efficiency. That was a matter close to his heart. It is, however, less likely that he would have shown much patience with the idea that the possibility of compensation should be calculated in an imaginary contracted economy. His contributions to theory were of a more robust character, driven by a strong social conscience and often devoid of subtleties. That is not criticism, but a measure of him as a man concerned with the affairs of his day whose theoretical work has survived to provoke discussion for half a century.

Bibliography

Allais, M. 1943. *A la recherche d'une discipline économique*, Paris, Ateliers Industria

Allais, M. 1975. The general theory of surplus and Pareto's fundamental contribution, *Convegno Internazionale Vilfredo Pareto*, Rome, Accademia Nazionale dei Lincei
Allais, M. 1981. *La théorie générale des surplus*, Paris, Institut de sciences mathématiques et économiques appliquées (series EM 8, 9)
Bickerdike, C. F. 1906. The theory of incipient taxes, *Economic Journal*, vol. XVI
Chipman J. S. 1987. Compensation Principle, in *The New Palgrave*, London, Macmillan
Debreu, G. 1951. The coefficient of resource utilization, *Econometrica*, July
Diewert, W. E. 1981. The measurement of deadweight loss revisited, *Econometrica*, September
Diewert, W. E. 1983. The measurement of waste within the production sector of an open economy, *Scandinavian Journal of Economics*, vol. 85, no. 2
Diewert, W. E. 1984. The measurement of deadweight loss in an open economy, *Economica*, February
Diewert, W. E. 1985. The measurement of waste and welfare in applied general equilibrium models, in J. Piggot and J. Whalley (eds), *New Developments in Applied General Equilibrium Analysis*, Cambridge, CUP
Graaff, J. de V. 1976. Economic efficiency, in M. L. Truu (ed.), *Public Policy and the South African Economy*, Cape Town, OUP.
Graaff, J. de V. 1977. Equity and efficiency as components of the general welfare, *South African Journal of Economics*, December
Graaff, J. de V. 1979. 'Tastes, values and the foundations of normative economics', paper presented to the Sixth Interlaken Seminar on Analysis and Ideology
Hicks, J. R. 1939. The foundations of welfare economics, *Economic Journal*, December
Kaldor, N. 1939. Welfare propositions of economics and interpersonal comparisons of utility, *Economic Journal*, September (reprinted in Kaldor, 1960)
Kaldor, N. 1940. A note on tariffs and the terms of trade, *Economica*, November (reprinted in Kaldor, 1960)
Kaldor, N. 1946. A comment, *Review of Economic Studies*, vol. XIV, no. 1
Kaldor, N. 1960. *Essays on Value and Distribution*, London, Duckworth, vol. 1 of Kaldor's *Collected Papers*
Scitovsky, T. 1941. A note on welfare propositions in economics, *Review of Economic Studies*, November

Ricardian debt/taxation equivalence in the Kaldor theory of profits and income distribution

Luigi L. Pasinetti*

1. Foreword

Since Nicholas Kaldor published his seminal paper on a 'Keynesian' theory of income distribution between 'capitalists' and 'workers' (Kaldor, 1956), the literature on this topic has grown enormously. I had myself the opportunity of contributing to this development by focussing on the implications for a long-run 'Keynesian' theory of the rate of profits (Pasinetti, 1962); and the major analytical result that was achieved is represented by a remarkable theorem (which for brevity's sake I shall call the 'Cambridge Theorem') stating that, on a long-run equilibrium-growth path, with two categories of savers (the capitalists and the workers), the rate of profits is determined by the natural rate of growth divided by the capitalists' propensity to save, independently of anything else, and, in particular, independently of technology and of the workers' propensity to save.

The considerable amount of literature that was generated by this theorem has gone through two phases. The first phase was characterised by explorations of what happens *outside* the range within which the theorem holds; and here the best-known contributions are those of Meade (1963; 1966) and Samuelson Modigliani (1966), who—in an effort to bring back some relevance for the neoclassical theory of marginal productivity—have analysed the range within which the workers' saving propensity is so high as to make their coexistence with the capitalists impossible on a long-run equilibrium-growth path. They claimed to have provided a completely symmetrical 'Dual Theorem' stating that, on the steady growth path, with only one group of savers left (the workers), the output/capital ratio is determined by the rate of growth divided by the workers' propensity to save, independently of anything else.

In the second phase that followed, many authors proceeded to relax assumptions, trying out new hypotheses and introducing complications of all sorts.[1] This second phase led only to a strengthening of the original Cambridge Theorem (i.e. Kaldor's approach), which has surprisingly proved much more robust to changes of assumptions than the Meade–Samuelson–Modigliani Dual, while the symmetrical aspects, on which Meade, Samuelson and Modigliani relied so much, have receded into the background.

*Catholic University of Milan. I am grateful to Ian Steedman for pointing out an inconsistency in a previous draft. I should like to thank Ian Steedman, Mauro Baranzini, and Geoffrey Harcourt for suggesting, or stimulating, many improvements. All responsibility remains of course mine. Financial support from the Italian Ministry of Education Fund is gratefully acknowledged.

[1] Mauro Baranzini (1988) has recently provided a survey of these developments. An English version of the survey is in Baranzini (1989).

Yet, it is surprising that the various authors, while trying out many extensions, should have paid so little attention to the role of government taxation and expenditure, a topic on which Kaldor worked so much in his life (see Kaldor, 1955 and 1980). A note on this subject, written by Steedman (1972), confirmed the trend mentioned above.[1] A longer article, more recently, by Fleck and Domenghino (1987), came to very pessimistic conclusions. But the Fleck–Domenghino analysis is not correct (see Pasinetti, 1989).

The aim of the present article is to explore the possible extensions of Kaldor's profits and distribution theory when the problems of government taxation and expenditure are explicitly introduced.

2. Introducing government expenditure and taxation

Let me start from my 1962 formulation and simply add government expenditure (G) to consumption (C) and investments (I) in the original over-all equation for national income (Y):

$$Y = C + I + G = W + P_w + P_c, \qquad (2{\cdot}1)$$

where the right hand side represents the income distribution aspect. As usual, W is total wages, P_c is profits accruing to the capitalists and P_w is profits accruing to the workers; all these distributive variables being gross of taxes.

As in all these models, investments are autonomous and in equilibrium. Consumption per unit of income (now, net of taxes) is expressed as the complement to unity of a propensity to save. I shall assume the two usual (marginal and average) propensities to save: s_w for the workers, and s_c for the capitalists, with the (usual) restrictions $0 < s_w < s_c \leqslant 1$.

Now we also have government expenditure, which has to be put into relation with government revenue, i.e. with the proceeds from taxation. We may use a parallel procedure: denoting total taxation by T, we may write

$$G = (1 - s_T)T, \qquad (2{\cdot}2)$$

where s_T represents the proportion of total taxes that is not spent—a sort of 'propensity to save' of the government. Unlike s_w and s_c, s_T may be positive (leading to a government surplus) or negative (leading to a government deficit). Thus $G < T$ or $G > T$ according as $s_T > 0$ or $s_T < 0$, respectively; while $G = T$, the case of a perfectly balanced government budget, when $s_T = 0$.

The equation defining government taxation is more complex, especially if we consider both direct and indirect taxes. We may call t_w the proportional (direct) tax on wages, and t_p the proportional (direct) tax on profits; $0 \leqslant t_w < 1$; $0 \leqslant t_p < 1$. Moreover we may call t_i a proportional (indirect) tax on *all* consumption expenditure of all individuals (workers and capitalists) and of the government itself; $0 \leqslant t_i < 1$. The government total revenue from taxation (T) therefore is:

$$T = t_w W + t_p P_w + t_p P_c + t_i [(1 - s_w)(1 - t_w)W + (1 - s_w)(1 - t_p)P_w + (1 - s_c)(1 - t_p)P_c + G]. \qquad (2{\cdot}3)$$

By substituting (2·2) into (2·3) and rearranging, we may write:

$$T = a\{t_w W + t_p P_w + t_p P_c + t_i[(1 - s_w)(1 - t_w)W + (1 - s_w)(1 - t_p)P_w + (1 - s_c)(1 - t_p)P_c]\}, \qquad (2{\cdot}4)$$

[1] Steedman analysed the case of a perfectly balanced government budget and concluded that 'the existence of taxation and Government expenditure will not affect the nature of a Pasinetti equilibrium [i.e. the Cambridge Theorem],' while, except in special cases, it will '... destroy the possibility of a Meade equilibrium [i.e. the Dual Theorem]' (Steedman, 1972 p. 1394).

where:

$$a = [1 - t_i(1 - s_T)]^{-1}, \tag{2·5}$$

is the correction factor due to the fact that the government also taxes its own expenditure.[1]

Let us now explicitly write the saving functions for the various categories of savers:

$$S_w = s_w(W + P_w - t_w W - t_p P_w), \tag{2·6}$$

$$S_c = s_c(P_c - t_p P_c), \tag{2·7}$$

$$S_G = s_T T, \tag{2·8}$$

where S_w is workers' savings net of both wage and profits taxes, S_c is capitalists' savings net of profits taxes, and S_G is saving by the government. The over-all savings (S) will be the sum of (2·6)–(2·8):

$$S = S_w + S_c + S_G, \tag{2·9}$$

where S_G positively adds something to total savings only if $s_T > 0$. If, on the other hand, $s_T < 0$, government expenditure, by being in excess of taxation revenue, has the over-all effect of destroying part of private savings (public dissavings).

By substituting (2·4) into (2·8) and then (2·6)–(2·8) into (2·9), and rearranging, we obtain:

$$\begin{aligned} S = &\{s_w(1 - t_w) + s_T a[t_w + t_i(1 - s_w)(1 - t_w)]\} W + \\ &\{s_w(1 - t_p) + s_T a[t_p + t_i(1 - s_w)(1 - t_p)]\} P_w + \\ &\{s_c(1 - t_p) + s_T a[t_p + t_i(1 - s_c)(1 - t_p)]\} P_c. \end{aligned} \tag{2·10}$$

This apparently complicated expression is in fact a very interesting one, as will shortly appear. But we must proceed to consider the relevant hypotheses in order.

3. The case of a balanced government budget

The simplest case is that of a balanced government budget, i.e., the case of $s_T = 0$. In this case, government expenditure is exactly covered by explicit taxation. In each of the three braces in (2·10), the second addendum cancels out completely.

The first thing to note is that, with a balanced budget, indirect taxation causes no complications; it simply diverts, from private to public uses, an amount of expenditure that has already been decided.

Direct taxation, on the other hand, makes a difference to individuals' savings. The taxation parameters modify the individuals' propensities to save differently, according to the categories of income. Consequently we end up with three (and no longer two) propensities to save, when these are considered *net* of taxation, namely:

$$s_w(1 - t_w), \tag{3·1}$$

[1] In this paper, as the reader will notice, I am concentrating on the effects of government *expenditure*, with a balanced or an unbalanced budget. I am neglecting other aspects of government activity, such as transfer payments and ownership of public enterprises (with accumulation of public capital).

$$s_w(1-t_p), \tag{3·2}$$

$$s_c(1-t_p), \tag{3·3}$$

except, of course, in the particular case in which $t_w = t_p$. When, as is normally to be expected, $t_w < t_p$, the workers' *net* propensity to save out of wages, $s_w(1-t_w)$, turns out to be higher than the workers' *net* propensity to save out of profits, $s_w(1-t_p)$.

In the economic literature, the case of *different* workers' propensities to save, according as to whether they are out of wages or out of profits, have already been investigated at length (see Chiang, 1973; Maneschi, 1974; Moore, 1974; Mückl, 1978; Fazi–Salvadori, 1981; Pasinetti, 1983). Therefore, if we simply re-define the various propensities to save as being *net* of taxation and call s_{ww} the workers' *net* propensity to save out of wages—in this case (3·1)—and s_{wc} the workers' *net* propensity to save out of profits—in this case (3·2)—respectively, we obtain a model which is reduced to the form already considered in the just-mentioned literature, with the only difference that while in that literature the assumption is normally made that $s_{ww} < s_{wc}$, here, since normally $t_w < t_p$, the opposite will be the case, i.e. $s_w(1-t_w) > s_w(1-t_p)$. Thus, with this reversal of the inequality, we are able to use all the elaborations that have already been developed.

From this point on, the arguments are straightforward. The relevant proportionality relations between savings and capital ownership (for details, see, Pasinetti, 1974, pp. 105–6), namely:

$$(S_w/K_w) = (S_c/K_c) = (S/K) \tag{3·4}$$

(where K_w is capital owned by the workers, K_c is capital owned by the capitalists and $K_w + K_c = K$ is total capital) need only to be supplemented with the other simple relations, namely: (i) the usual $I = S$ (investment equals savings) equilibrium relation, and (ii) the uniformity (which is made here for simplicity) of the rate of profit on all capital, independently of ownership. Then, by substituting from (2·6)–(2·7), S_G being zero, we obtain the usual 'Cambridge Equation':

$$r = \frac{1}{s_c(1-t_p)} g_n, \tag{3·5}$$

which states that the long-run rate of profits (r) is determined by the natural rate of growth (g_n) divided by the capitalists' propensity to save, now 'corrected' by the taxation parameter, independently of anything else. It must also be pointed out that, at this stage already, any symmetry with the Meade–Samuelson–Modigliani case has disappeared. Unless $t_w = t_p$ (i.e. unless the workers' net propensities to save out of wages and out of profits coincide) the Meade–Samuelson–Modigliani Dual Theorem no longer holds, as has been pointed out already by Steedman (1972). The reason is simple. With the introduction of differentiated taxes on wages and on profits, the workers' *net* saving propensities out of wages and out of profits are different. Therefore, the capital/output ratio is no longer determined independently of the rate of profits (and of the distribution of income).

The 'Cambridge Theorem', on the other hand, continues to hold, in the form (3·5). Another way of looking at it is to write it as:

$$r(1-t_p) = (1/s_c) g_n, \tag{3·6}$$

which shows that the 'Cambridge Theorem', in its original form, holds with reference to the rate of profits *net* of profits tax.

The important result that emerges therefore is that the rate of profits and thus the *share* of profits in income, net of taxes, are determined *independently of taxation*. To put it in another way, all taxes are shifted away from profits and on to wages.[1]

This result is, in fact, the clearest expression of the basic idea behind Kaldor's theory of income distribution: on the equilibrium-growth path, profits are sufficiently high as to yield (after deduction of the consumption needs of the capitalists and of the taxation needs of the government) the amount of savings that is necessary to sustain full-employment investments. This is the theory that Kaldor consistently proposed in all his abundant works on taxation. As he openly acknowledged (Kaldor, 1956), the theory is in line with Classical economic analysis, but with a dramatic reversal of the chain of causation. As is well known, Ricardo took wages as exogenously given, and concluded that all taxes on wages are eventually shifted on to profits. For Kaldor the opposite is the case. Profits, by being the source of the savings that are necessary to sustain the exogenously given full-employment investments, have a sort of prior claim on income. Thus, for Kaldor, all taxes on profits are eventually shifted on to wages.

The contribution of the 'Cambridge Theorem' to this discussion has been to show that these results hold independently of workers' savings behaviour.

4. The case of a government budget deficit (or surplus)

Let us now move on to the more complex case of a deficit (or surplus) government budget. When $s_T \neq 0$, the government systematically spends more (or spends less) than it raises from taxation. Note that the adverb 'systematically' is necessary. We are considering here equilibrium-growth paths on which all magnitudes are supposed to grow steadily and indefinitely. Therefore we are considering paths on which s_T, like all other parameters, remains constant through time. The model would not be the appropriate ones to use if we wanted to consider an economic system that sometimes has a government budget surplus and sometimes has a government budget deficit. If we assume $s_T < 0$, the meaning is that the government is, and will always be, in deficit, and similarly if we assume $s_T > 0$, the meaning is that the government is indefinitely in surplus.

These considerations may well lend support to the idea that, after all, the appropriate assumption to make, with these models, is that of a balanced government budget, i.e. the case already considered in the previous section.

However, the case of a permanent government deficit (or surplus) is not inconsistent with the present model, provided that the deficit (or surplus) grows steadily at the same rate as that of all other magnitudes. [The economics literature on steadily growing government deficits has, after all, grown enormously since Domar's well-known article on public debt (Domar, 1944)].

[1] The shares of workers' income (wages plus workers' profits) and of capitalists' income, in total income, are of course more complicated to follow, but the expressions already worked out in the literature (for example in Pasinetti, 1974 and 1983) can easily be used to show that the introduction of taxation on wages and on profits (all other things remaining the same) unambiguously leads to *increases* of P_c/Y and of K_c/K and to *decreases* of $(P_w + W)/Y$ and of K_w/K. Moreover, the same expressions can be used to show that, in the case of a rate of interest that is lower than the rate of profits, the 'Cambridge Equation' (3·6) still continues to hold with respect to the *capitalists*' rate of profits, i.e. it becomes:

$$(P_c/K_c)(1-t_p)=(1/s_c)\,g_n. \qquad (3\cdot 6a)$$

Let us therefore go on to consider the case of a permanent government deficit, i.e. the case of $s_T<0$. For simplicity's sake, we may drop explicit consideration of a systematic government surplus (i.e. the case of $s_T>0$), both because it is hardly justifiable as a long-run policy, and because it is in any case symmetrical (only entailing the reversal of signs) to the case of a government systematic deficit.

Now, if $s_T<0$, and therefore $G>T$, the government is spending more than it receives in taxes. The second addendum in each of the three braces of (2·10) no longer cancels out, as in the previous case of a balanced budget, but becomes negative. From our formulations the effect is straightforward. There is a certain amount of private savings which is destroyed by a corresponding amount of government dissavings. The interesting feature of expression (2·10) is that it divides these government dissavings into three parts, proportional to W, P_w and P_c respectively. The savings propensities separate out nicely for the respective categories of income, without interfering with one another, while taxation parameters and government dissavings make a correction to the categories of private savings to which they refer.

We may therefore define:

$$s'_{ww}=s_w(1-t_w)+s_T\,a[t_w+t_i(1-s_w)\,(1-t_w)], \tag{4·1}$$

$$s'_{wc}=s_w(1-t_p)+s_T\,a[t_p+t_i(1-s_w)\,(1-t_p)], \tag{4·2}$$

$$s'_c=s_c(1-t_p)+s_T\,a[t_p+t_i\,(1-s_c)\,(1-t_p)]. \tag{4·3}$$

Then, after substitution, the over-all saving function (2·10) simply reduces to

$$S=s'_{ww}\,W+s'_{wc}\,P_w+s'_c\,P_c, \tag{4·4}$$

which—with the saving propensities corrected by the effects of government taxation and expenditure—is precisely of the same form as the original saving function in those earlier models where a distinction is made between the workers' savings propensities out of wages and out of profits (see Pasinetti, 1983). The only difference, to be kept in mind here, is that s'_{wc} will normally be less than s'_{ww}, while in the above-mentioned literature the opposite (i.e. $s_{ww}<s_{wc}$) is normally assumed.

We arrive, therefore, at precisely the same formulations that were proposed earlier, though with a re-interpretation of the meaning of the savings propensities.

What needs to be explored now is the extent to which, and the conditions under which, the 'corrected' savings propensities, s'_{ww}, s'_{wc}, s'_c, can legitimately replace the original ones.

5. A further generalisation of Kaldor's profits and distribution theory

Suppose, to begin with, that the conditions (whatever they may be) are satisfied, under which s'_{ww}, s'_{wc}, s'_c may replace the s_{ww}, s_{wc}, s_c of the earlier model. The results, in this case, are really remarkable. After substitution of the 'corrected' propensities to save (4·1)–(4·3) into the savings functions (2·6)–(2·8), the proportionality relations (3·4) again yield the 'Cambridge Equation':

$$r=(1/s'_c)\,g_n. \tag{5·1}$$

Again, the equilibrium rate of profits is determined by the natural rate of growth divided by s'_c, where s'_c is the capitalists' propensity to save, here 'corrected' by the effects *both* of taxation on profits *and* of government deficit spending.[1] This means that, given the rate of taxation and of deficit spending, an equilibrium rate of profits, and consequently an equilibrium share of profits in income, exist, which are sufficiently high as to leave—net of capitalists' consumption, of profits taxes, and of government destruction of savings—that amount of savings that is exactly equal to required equilibrium-growth investments. As in the cases considered earlier in the literature, workers' savings do not have any effect on the determination of this equilibrium rate, and share, of profits.

All this makes wages, as a category of income, rather vulnerable, not only to taxation, but also to government deficit spending. Net profits, on the other hand, emerge as being unaffected by either. Of course, these results must be looked at within a comparative dynamics framework. They allow us to compare different equilibrium-growth paths which have the same workers' and capitalists' saving propensities, but *different* government taxation and deficit spending parameters. Within this comparative dynamics framework, the above results imply that, to any higher government taxation or deficit spending, there corresponds an equilibrium-growth path on which the rate (and the share) of profits are *pro rata* higher by exactly the amount that leaves net profits as they were on the previous equilibrium-growth path, so that—after deduction of capitalists' consumption—they can sustain the same exogenously given equilibrium investments.

Workers can share in this privileged characteristic of profits only to the extent that they themselves save, and thus accumulate capital, and thus receive a share of profits. The possibility is of course open to them of saving even up to the limit of receiving *all* the profits, and thus eliminating the capitalists from the economic system. (This is the case on which Samuelson and Modigliani relied in their elaborations.) But this case—unlikely as it is in any event, see Pasinetti, 1974—becomes even less likely in the present context, as workers' savings would have to be exceptionally high to compensate also for government destruction of savings.[2]

[1] The 'propensity' s'_c is of course a more complicated concept now than in the simple case of the previous section. It may be instructive to consider a special, but revealing, extreme case, namely the case of a 'Classical' propensity to save of the capitalists equal to unity. When $s_c = 1$, expression (4·3) simply reduces to:

$$s'_c = 1 - t_p(1 - s_T a), \qquad (4{\cdot}3a)$$

and the 'Cambridge Equation' (5·1) reduces to:

$$r[1 - t_p(1 - s_T a)] = g_n, \qquad (5{\cdot}1a)$$

which appears not too dissimilar from (3·6). The taxation correction, owing to government deficit spending, appears as accentuated. Note that $s_T < 0$, which makes the factor in round brackets positive and the factor in square brackets lower than it would otherwise be. The rate of growth and the capitalists' propensity to save (here equal to unity) do indeed determine the rate of profits, *net* of taxation and of the effects of government deficit spending. The case of $s_c < 1$, though yielding a more complicated expression, basically has the same meaning.

[2] Note that, with deficit spending (i.e. $s_T < 0$), s_w will have to be not smaller than:

$$(-s_T)\frac{t_w + t_i(1 - t_w)}{(1 - t_w)(1 - t_i)}$$

simply in order to avoid $s'_{ww} < 0$, and not smaller than

$$(-s_T)\frac{t_p + t_i(1 - t_p)}{(1 - t_p)(1 - t_i)}$$

simply in order to avoid $s'_{wc} < 0$ (both expressions being clearly positive, since $s_T < 0$).

These results seem to strengthen Kaldor's intuitive idea of the irrelevance of workers' savings. At the same time they weaken still further the Meade–Samuelson–Modigliani reliance on workers to provide such high savings as to displace the capitalists from the system.

It is interesting to notice that all the asymmetrical effects brought to light by the earlier literature on the Kaldor income distribution theory are here confirmed. To a higher government deficit spending, there corresponds a new equilibrium-growth path on which both capitalists' savings and workers' savings are partly destroyed. But, while in the case of capitalists' savings there is an increase of profits that compensates exactly for the destroyed savings so as to leave net profits as before, in the case of workers' savings, destruction has no compensation. Moreover, wages themselves must be lower, to compensate for the higher gross profits. Workers' savings are thus penalised twice: first through a partial (and uncompensated) destruction, and second through a lower share of income, rendered necessary by the requirements of higher gross profits (in order to leave *net* profits unaffected).

6. Ricardian equivalence

But what are the conditions under which the s'_{ww}, s'_{wc}, s'_c of Section 4 above may replace the s_{ww}, s_{wc}, s_c, of the earlier models?

When the government decides to increase its expenditure beyond explicit taxation and go in for decifit spending (in our case when $s_T < 0$), there are two ways in which it may act: by monetary financing or by debt financing (or by a mixture of both).

Consider, first, monetary financing.

Monetary financing means that the government takes advantage of its privilege as a Monetary Authority and exercises a right of seigniorage by requiring the Central Bank to print paper money, with which to buy more goods than those that tax receipts would entitle it to. To act in this way is equivalent to imposing an implicit extra tax on citizens (what has been called an 'inflation tax') *in addition* to direct and indirect taxation. In real terms, the national income remains what it is, but an increase of the price level transfers some purchasing power from the private to the public sector.

The simplest way to view this transfer of purchasing power, in the present model, is to insist on interpreting the magnitudes that appear in the model as being in *real* terms, and government over-spending ($s_T T$, where $s_T < 0$) as being a diminution (or more specifically a destruction) of private savings. This is precisely what is done by formulation (2·10), where government dissavings are subtracted from the various categories of savings.

This subtraction of public dissavings from private savings is carried out by (2·10), and thus by (4·1)–(4·3), under the least complicating of all assumptions, namely under the assumption of proportionality of the 'implicit' (or inflation) tax to the 'explicit' taxes.

This no doubt crude but very simple assumption is precisely the assumption which, in the case of monetary financing, justifies the replacements of s'_{ww}, s'_{wc}, s'_c for the original s_{ww}, s_{wc}, s_c, leading to the generalisation of the 'Cambridge Equation' expressed by (5·1).

The case of debt financing requires a more sophisticated argument. Public debt may be internal or external. In a closed economy model like the present one, we shall only consider *internal* public debt.

Now, when the government decides to go in for a budget deficit, to be met by a public debt, and issues credit certificates which yield a rate of interest, what in fact happens is that the community, considered as a whole and represented by the government, undertakes a debt obligation towards those individuals who surrender their savings in exchange for credit certificates. The members of the community thus come to play a double role. On the one side, as taxpayers, they become *pro rata* debtors; and on the other side, to the extent that they surrender part of their savings in exchange for public debt certificates, they become creditors towards the government, and hence towards the community as a whole. The second role is played in a voluntary way, while the first role is a necessary consequence of each citizen's liability to taxation. In the model we are considering here, the obvious assumption to make is that, for each group of savers, this liability to taxation is proportional to the explicit taxation to which they are already subject. From an actuarial point of view, this liability to (future) taxation, owing to the existence of a public debt, is equivalent, for each group of savers as taxpayers, to a *negative* stock of capital.

More specifically, we may say that there is a part of each saver's cumulated savings that must be considered as virtually set aside (in a kind of fund) to make up for his/her liability for a quota of the public debt.

This virtual setting aside of savings into a kind of sinking fund precisely is, in the case of a budget deficit financed by a public debt, the interpretation that must be given to the negative addendum in each of the three braces in (4·1)–(4·3). It may be interesting to note, at this point, that this way of conceiving of the meaning and consequences of public debt in fact goes back to Ricardo (see his *Principles*, 1817, 1st ed., chapter 15, and his well-known essay on 'Funding Systems', 1820). These ideas allowed him to argue that the undertaking of a public debt or the imposition of taxes come in the end to have the same effects on the taxpayers—a proposition that has recently become known as the 'Ricardian Equivalence Theorem'.

The Public Finance scholars who have reconsidered Ricardo's arguments (see, for example, De Viti De Marco, 1939; Buchanan, 1987; Abel, 1987) have of course pointed out that the Ricardian Equivalence Theorem requires the satisfaction of certain conditions. Some authors (for example, Barro, 1974) have gone much further, and have introduced further (more restrictive) hypotheses on individuals' behaviour. They have assumed utility maximisation over time so as to transform Ricardo's Equivalence Theorem into a (more stringent) 'Neutrality Theorem', according to which ultra-rational individuals would adapt their savings behaviour over time so as to compensate for *any* type of government tax or debt policy. But this is *not* the kind of behaviour envisaged in Kaldor-like models, where savings assumptions are of a very simple type (constant savings propensities) and where the 'equivalence' is to be understood in the original (less restrictive) Ricardian sense.

It may perhaps be useful to consider briefly, on simple commonsense grounds and without any sophisticated formal model, the basis for this Ricardian Equivalence Theorem within the present context.

Consider first the simplest of all cases. Suppose an ideal economy in which each individual sets aside the correct sinking fund corresponding to his/her quota of public debt (proportional to his/her liability to taxation) and buys public debt certificates for an amount exactly corresponding to it. In this case—if the government imposes a specific tax (proportional to the other taxes) for paying interest—the tax revenue compensates the interest payment not only for the government but also for each single individual (whose two roles—of taxpayer and of lender to the government—exactly cancel each other out). Even the level of the rate of interest in this case (whether high or low, or even null) makes no difference, because tax and interest are always the same for each single individual. The public debt has obviously generated the same effects as direct taxation.

Consider now a more general, and more interesting, case in which the distribution of public debt certificates among savers is not necessarily coincidental with their *pro rata* liability to taxation. In this case, even if they set aside correct sinking funds (not necessarily covered by public debt certificates) and even if a government specific tax (proportional to the other taxes and perceived as such by all savers)[1] exactly covers interest payments, the two roles mentioned above do not necessarily match inside the household of each single saver. Yet, if we add the assumption that the rate of interest on public debt certificates is equal to the rate of interest on private loans, which in turn is equal to the rate of profits in the economic system as a whole (which is the assumption appropriate to the present context) then clearly it does not matter *which* proportion of each saver's assets is made up of public debt certificates, or of private loans, or of real assets. In other words the distribution of the public debt certificates among savers is entirely immaterial. Again we come to the same conclusions as in the previous simpler case. Again the public debt produces the same effects as direct taxation (Ricardian equivalence).[2]

These are basically the conditions that are intended to lie behind the use of (4·1)–(4·3), when a government deficit is met by a public debt. When satisfied, they lead to a complete generalisation of the 'Cambridge Theorem'.

7. Kaldor and Ricardo: a few concluding remarks

The validity of Kaldor's theory of income distribution and of the Cambridge theory of the rate of profits thus seems to go beyond the case of taxation with balanced budgets and extend to the case of a government deficit, whether financed by monetary means or by a public debt, *provided that* Ricardian equivalence holds. New links and similarities emerge between Kaldor and Ricardo.

Is this really surprising? Brief reflection should make one realise that, in fact, this should not be surprising at all.

The relevant step, both in Kaldor's theory and in Ricardo's, is taken at the point where, with government taxation (and a balanced budget), a process is envisaged through which the share of profits, in Kaldor, and of wages, in Ricardo, remains unaffected, as the burden of taxation is fully shifted to the other category of income. When this is granted, then if government expenditure goes beyond the constraints of taxation—but the conditions are satisfied under which taxation and deficit spending (through either monetary or debt financing) come to the same thing—it should be obvious that the original results could not but remain unaffected.

[1] A specific tax, perceived as such, for servicing the public debt, means that the tax is paid by the savers by using the interest received on their ideal funds set aside to cover their *pro rata* liability for the public debt. This means that, for each single saver, interest from the fund and specific tax cancel each other out.

[2] In this case, when substituting s'_{ww}, s'_{wc}, s'_c for the s_{ww}, s_{wc}, s_c of the earlier literature (e.g. in Pasinetti, 1974 and 1983), it should be noticed that the expressions for the shares of capitalists' capital (K_c/K) and of workers' capital (K_w/K), in total capital, are to be interpreted as *net* of the savings set aside in the sinking funds. Therefore the sum $(K_c+K_w)=K$ still represents the total *real* stock of capital. But, in general, K_c and K_w do not correspond to real capital *actually* owned by the capitalists and by the workers (directly or through loans to the capitalists), respectively. If we call K'_c and K'_w, respectively, such amounts of capital *actually* owned, and moreover we call A_c and A_w the amounts of public debt certificates owned by the capitalists and by the workers, respectively, so that (K'_c+A_c) and (K'_w+A_w) are respectively, their total assets, then clearly

$$K'_c+A_c+K'_w+A_w-D=K_c+K_w,$$

where $K'_c \neq K_c$ and $K'_w \neq K_c$, but

$$K'_c+K'_w=K_c+K_w=K$$

and

$$A_c+A_w=D,$$

where D is the total stock of the public debt.

The parts of capitalists' and workers' total assets ideally set aside in the sinking funds will respectively be:

$$A_c-(K_c-K'_c),$$

and

$$A_w-(K_w-K'_w).$$

The question remains of course of tracing out the re-distributive effects of different government policies when the conditions of Ricardian equivalence are not satisfied. For individuals or groups of individuals may behave in a non-rational way, or may be under the effect of financial illusions or of fiscal illusions of one sort or another. This is indeed a wide field of research that remains open and largely unexplored. Many economists—and here I may simply recall, symbolically, Keynes (1936) and Puviani (1903)—have been constantly pointing in this direction. They have also done remarkable pioneering work already. But, so far, we have all been too slow to follow up their leads.

Bibliography

Abel, A. B. 1987. Ricardian Equivalence Theorem, entry in *The New Palgrave Dictionary of Economics*, vol. 4, London, Macmillan.

Baranzini, M. 1988. Un quarto di secolo di dibattito sulla teoria della distribuzione, in F. Targetti, (ed.) *Nicholas Kaldor*, Bari, Laterza pp. 205–228

Baranzini, M. 1989. *A Theory of Capital Accumulation*, Oxford, OUP, forthcoming.

Barro, R. J. 1974. Are Government Bonds Net Wealth? *Journal of Political Economy*, pp. 1095–1117

Buchanan, J. M. 1987. 'Public Debt', entry in *The New Palgrave Dictionary of Economics*, vol. 3, London, Macmillan

Chiang, A. C. 1973. A simple generalization of the Kaldor-Pasinetti theory of profit rate and income distribution, *Economica*, vol. XL, pp. 311–313

De Viti de Marco, A. 1939. *Principî di Economia Finanziaria*, Torino, Einaudi

Domar, E. D. 1944. The 'Burden of the Debt' and the National Income, *American Economic Review*, vol. XXXIV, pp. 798–827

Fazi, E. and Salvadori, N. 1981. The existence of a two-class economy in the Kaldor model of growth and distribution, *Kyklos*, vol. 34, pp. 582–592.

Fleck, F. H. and Domenghino, C. M. 1987. Cambridge (U.K.) versus Cambridge (Mass.): a Keynesian solution of the 'Pasinetti Paradox', *Journal of Post-Keynesian Economics*, vol. X, pp. 22–36.

Kaldor, N. 1955. *An Expenditure Tax*, London, George Allen & Unwin

Kaldor, N. 1956. Alternative theories of distribution, *Review of Economic Studies*, vol. 23, pp. 83–100

Kaldor, N. 1980. *Reports on Taxation*, vols I and II, New York, Holmes and Meier

Keynes, J. M. 1936. *The General Theory of Employment Interest and Money*, London, Macmillan

Maneschi, A. 1974. The existence of a two-class economy in the Kaldor and Pasinetti models of growth and distribution, *Review of Economic Studies*, vol. 41, pp. 149–150

Moore, B. J. 1974. The Pasinetti Paradox revisited, *Review of Economic Studies*, vol. 41, pp. 297–299

Mückl, W. J. 1978. On the existence of a two-class economy in the Cambridge Model of growth and distribution, *Jahrbücher für National ökonomie und Statistik*, Band 193, pp. 508–517

Meade, J. E. 1963. 'The rate of profit in a growing economy', *Economic Journal*, vol. LXXIII, pp. 665–674

Meade, J. E. 1966. The outcome of the Pasinetti Process: a note, *Economic Journal*, vol. LXXVI, pp. 161–165

Pasinetti, L. L. 1962. Rate of profit and income distribution in relation to the rate of economic growth, *Review of Economic Studies*, vol. 29, pp. 103–120 (reprinted in Pasinetti, 1974)

Pasinetti, L. L. 1974. *Growth and Income Distribution—Essays in Economic Theory*, Cambridge, CUP

Pasinetti, L. L. 1983. Conditions of existence of a two-class economy in the Kaldor and more general models of growth and income distribution, *Kyklos*, vol. 36, pp. 91–102

Pasinetti, L. L. 1989. A Reply to Fleck and Domenghino, *Journal of Post-Keynesian Economics*, forthcoming

Puviani, A. 1903. *Teoria dell'illusione finanziaria*, Palermo, Sandron

Ricardo, D. 1817. *On the Principles of Political Economy and Taxation*, in P. Sraffa (ed.), *The Works and Correspondence of David Ricardo*, vol. 1, 1951, Cambridge, CUP

Ricardo, D. 1820. Funding Systems, in P. Sraffa (ed.), *The Works and Correspondence of David Ricardo*, vol. 4, 1951, Cambridge, CUP

Samuelson, P. A. and Modigliani, F. 1966. The Pasinetti Paradox in neo-classical and more general models, and Reply to Pasinetti and Robinson, *Review of Economic Studies*, vol. 33, pp. 269–301 and pp. 321–335

Steedman, I. 1972. The State and the outcome of the Pasinetti process, *Economic Journal*, vol. LXXXII, pp. 1387–1395

Growth and distribution: a neoclassical Kaldor–Robinson exercise

James Tobin*

Retrospect: Kaldorian distribution theory

In 1956 Nicholas Kaldor published his 'Keynesian' theory of the distribution of output between labour and property incomes, and in 1960 I published a short spoof of his article. I was a brash young American. In reprinting that note in a collection of my essays in 1971, I wrote:

> 'Chapter 7 is an irreverent spoof of a distribution theory advanced by Nicholas Kaldor and others . . . [It] is a footnote to the running controversy between neoclassical growth theory and its opponents. Neoclassical theory would have the division of full employment output between investment and consumption depend on the society's propensity to save. If property owners and wage earners differ in their saving behavior, the distribution of income between them would help to determine the share of investment in national output. The income distribution, in turn, depends, in neoclassical theory, on the marginal productivities of capital and labour. Kaldor rejected marginal productivity theory and needed an explanation of factor shares in its place. He regarded the investment share of total output as independently determined by technology and entrepreneurship—something to which the national saving propensity must adapt, rather than vice versa . . . I would like to record here my judgement, which the reading lists of my courses confirm, that Mr Kaldor has made many outstanding contributions to economic theory. He should be excused this aberration (1971, p. 3).

Nicky Kaldor was unperturbed by my note, although he did bother to reply (Kaldor, 1960). Fortunately, we subsequently became good friends and were usually on the same side of macroeconomic controversies. I had the opportunity to express my esteem for him in his presence both at the celebration of the centenary of Keynes's birth at Kings in 1983 and at Yale when Lord Kaldor gave the first set of Okun Memorial Lectures in 1983.[1]

For this symposium in his memory, I return to the subject of our disagreement three decades ago.

I was not criticising the proposition that saving propensities might differ for incomes of different types, as well as for incomes of different magnitudes. After all, one important strand of mainstream saving theory, the life cycle model, also focuses on the difference between human and nonhuman wealth. More important, businesses, especially corporations, may not be acting just as agents of convenience for individual shareowners when they plough back profits. They may be instead institutionalising that compulsion for

*Yale University.

[1] See my 'Comment' on Kaldor's paper 'Keynesian Economics after Fifty Years' at the 1983 conference, in D. Worswick and J. Trevithick, (eds) 1983. See also my Preface to Kaldor, 1985.

accumulation which Marx—and Joan Robinson, Kaldor and other post-Keynesians—have regarded as central to capitalism.

In this institutional spirit, Kaldor himself applied his differential propensities to sources of income, labour or property, rather than to classes of persons, workers and capitalists. For this reason he could not get excited about the long-run implications of recognition that both classes save and accumulate wealth, the discussion triggered by the Pasinetti process.[1] Empirically, it has not been possible to prove that business saving is just a one-for-one substitute for household saving.

Kaldorian saving propensities can easily be built into Swan–Solow type neoclassical growth models where, like other savings functions, they help to determine a stable steady-state capital intensity and corresponding stable values of other variables. Indeed the classical saving function, a popular extreme form of the Kaldorian hypothesis—nothing is saved from wages and nothing is consumed from profits—leads to the 'Golden Rule' optimum, the steady state with maximum consumption per worker. In that equilibrium investment equal profits and, in a Swan–Solow model, the marginal productivity of capital is equal to the growth rate. However, the weight of evidence is against the view that national saving and investment are as large as capital incomes (Abel *et al.*, 1986).

Moreover, if Kaldorian saving propensities are built into a one-good neoclassical growth model, they will help to determine the distribution of income and wealth. The steady-state capital shock is endogenous, dependent on saving behaviour. Therefore the marginal productivities of capital and labour and, except in the special case of the Cobb-Douglas production function, the relative shares of labour and capital incomes are likewise endogenous and dependent on saving behaviour. But differential saving propensities are not, except in the special case of the Leontief production function, *necessary* to determine distributive shares. Almost any saving function, for example the primitive assumption that a constant fraction of income of all kinds is saved, will determine the steady-state capital/labour ratio and thus also marginal productivities and factor shares.

What did bother me thirty years ago? First, I found it hard to believe that factors' returns had nothing to do with their productivities, and my note made fun of some implications of that belief. Second, in relation to macroeconomic theory, my problem was this: If marginal productivity is dropped as an explanation of income shares and the consumption function is drafted to replace it, how is aggregate output to be explained? I was shocked to see a 'Keynesian' model that apparently assumed output to be independent of aggregate demand even in the short run. And given full employment, I thought, the role of the consumption function is to help to determine investment as equal to saving, which it cannot do if it is assigned the burden of determining wages and profits. To me, a model with investment wholly exogenous was both unKeynesian and unpalatable.

Of course, marginal productivities are indeterminate, within limits, when factors are fully employed and technology requires them to be used in constant proportions. Maybe differential savings propensities can help in these circumstances. What determines investment and output remains a problem. Animal spirits? Perhaps, in short-run business cycles. In those circumstances there is no mechanism to insure that capital capacity and

[1] Pasinetti, 1962, pp. 267–79. In the course of the debate provoked by this seminal article, Kaldor wrote . . . 'I have always regarded the high savings propensity out of profits as something which attaches to the nature of business income, and not to the wealth (or other peculiarities) of the individuals who own property. It is the enterprise, not the particular body of individuals owning it at any one time, which finds it necessary . . . to plough back a proportion of the profits earned . . . Hence the high savings propensity attaches to profits as such, not to capitalists as such' (1966).

labour supply stand in the correct proportions to each other. Whether capacity is and is expected to be short relative to labour supply or redundant is surely important in investment decisions. In the long run, capital capacity is adjusted to the requirements of exogenous growth in effective labour supply and of technology.

I take my cue from Joan Robinson:

> The rate of investment . . . can be accounted for in two ways which do not seem to be connected with each other. Investment is determined, in one sense, by profit expectations, the 'animal spirits' of entrepreneurs which incline them to take the risks of investment, and the state of supply of finance, which may be subsumed under the head of the level of interest rates.
>
> In another sense, the rate of investment that can be maintained over the long run depends on the technical conditions and the supply of labour. According to this view, the rate at which the effective supply of labour is growing . . . limits the rate at which capital can accumulate, because there would be no point in bringing capital goods into existence when there is not going to be labour to operate them (Robinson, 1960, p. 146).[1]

Factor shares and saving in a growth model with Leontief technologies

I provide here a simple example of a model in which the distribution of income between wages and returns to capital ownership cannot be explained by marginal productivities, because they are not determinate. The reason is that the technological input/output coefficients are constant *à la* Leontief. Kaldorian differential saving propensities are shown to be one way to close the model, to determine factor shares, and to equate aggregate saving to technologically required investment. Other saving functions, for example the primitive uniform constant propensity to save, cannot do these jobs. One workable neoclassical alternative is to equate the interest rate to a constant rate of time preference, possibly augmented by a constant term for decline in the marginal utility of growing per capita consumption. But the specification that saving is supplied perfectly elastically with respect to the interest rate depends on infinitely long horizons for consumption and saving decisions and other implausible assumptions.

A technology consists of two activities; one produces consumption goods, the other capital goods. The two goods are not the same; the price of capital goods in terms of consumption goods is endogenous. Each activity uses labour and capital services. I shall analyse steady states in which total quantities of labour and capital are fully employed in the two activities. The labour supply is exogenous, growing in effective units at a constant rate, determined by natural increase and/or Harrod-neutral progress. The steady-state capital stock, relative to the labour force, is determined by the technology. The output of capital goods—gross investment—is what is needed to offset depreciation and to equip the increment in labour supply. Capital goods are used in both activities. In production, the capital goods used in the consumption goods activity are the same as those used in the capital goods activity itself. In use, they are different, both in the labour required to operate them and in their speed of depreciation.

Available to the economy are two or more technologies, each defined by the four input/output coefficients describing the consumption and investment activities and by the two depreciation rates. The economy may choose one among whole technologies, but it cannot mix activities. That is, for example, the consumption activity of Technology I cannot co-exist with the investment goods activity of Technology II. The nature of the investment goods produced and used might determine the differential productivities of those goods and of labour in making the two kinds of goods. I believe this assumption is in the

[1] The author says that the paper is 'an amended version of a paper published in French in *Economie Appliqué*, Oct–Nov 1957.'

spirit of some of Joan Robinson's representations of technology.[1] The all-or-nothing choice of technology gives rise to the possibility that different technologies will be chosen at high and low profit rates.

I assume that the economy will be on its factor-price frontier, along which the activities in use break even and it is not possible to increase either wages or capital rentals, both measured in consumption goods, without reducing the other factor's share. The break-even conditions for the two activities determine two prices in terms of consumption goods: the wage and the price of capital goods. They determine these prices, *given the profit rate* (or interest rate), a pure number. The equations do not determine the profit rate. That is the essential indeterminacy, traceable to the fixed-coefficient technology, the vacuum that the Kaldorian saving function may fill. It cannot be filled by a function that says saving is a uniform fraction of all income.

The two factor prices are the wage and the rental of capital, net of depreciation. Both are measured in consumption goods. The dimension of the rental is consumption goods per unit of capital goods per unit of time. These are the prices which, if multiplied by the quantities of the factor inputs, give factor incomes that add up to the value of total output. And it is those factor incomes to which the Kaldorian consumption or saving coefficients apply.

The net rental is, of course, to be distinguished from the profit rate, a pure number per unit time. Within a technology, the net rental is the same in both activities, and so of course is the profit rate. The rental is the price of capital goods times the profit rate. The price varies endogenously with the profit rate, and with the technology. Therefore, the wage/profit frontier, which amounts to the same thing as the wage/rental frontier in a model where the relative price of capital goods is always the same, is not a proper factor-price frontier in the present model. While all capital in contemporaneous use must bear in the same profit rate in a steady state with constant prices, Technology I and II activities are alternatives never in simultaneous use. They imply different price systems. Nothing compels profit rates to be the same in the two technologies, even at switch points of common wages and rentals.

A neoclassical theorist might argue that the consumption/saving decision depends on the profit rate as well as, or even instead of, aggregate profits measured in consumption goods. This dependence would represent the intertemporal substitution effect, Irving Fisher's interest incentive for saving. This is certainly not what Kaldor had in mind. I have not allowed for it in the present model.

For each technology, the steady-state input balance equations determine outputs of consumption goods and investment goods (per effective worker). These are technologically determined, independent of wages, capital goods prices, and interest rates.

[1] See Robinson, 1966, especially Chapter 10, 'The Spectrum of Techniques'. Here she introduces discrete constant-proportion techniques for labour and fixed capital. However, she does not explicitly model technologies with distinct activities for consumption goods and investment goods.

Robinson and Eatwell, 1973, pp. 183–195 sets forth a multi-sector Sraffa type input/output model and derives from it a wage/profit-rate frontier. A uniform mark-up rate is applied to the cost of every intermediate input in the pricing of all intermediate and final outputs. Evidently this corresponds to a uniform one-period lag between inputs and proximate outputs. But no such lag and mark up apply to labour inputs and wages. In any case, this model does not handle fixed capital, or even inventories other than those implicit in the work in progress during the one-period lag.

The general model of alternative 'blueprints', each involving an indivisible technology using different kinds of capital goods that produce together with labour both the capital goods themselves and consumption goods has been discussed in, for example, Pasinetti, 1969, pp. 508–531. The general model is so complex that points of interest depend greatly on simple illustrations, like the one in my text.

'Reverse switching' is quite possible. That is, a lower-consumption technology can be on the factor-price frontier at higher wages and lower profits. Of course, the other direction of switching, which seems more normal, is also possible. However, this model allows no *re*switching, because the relevant factor-price frontier for any technology is linear.

I find this 'switching' implication preferable to the usual examples, which involve curiously rigid alternative sets of time lags between labour inputs and outputs.[1] In the present example, there are no such lags (although they could be added) and the emphasis is on fixed rather than working capital. Another advantage of the present model is that the steady-state output of investment goods is determined quite naturally to meet the requirements of technology and growth.

The formal model

Here is the model: first, the equations for a technology for the outputs of consumption goods C (activity a) and investment goods I (activity b):

$$a_L C + b_L I = 1 \qquad \text{(Labour demand = supply, normalised to 1)}$$

$$a_K C = K_C, \quad b_K I = K_I \qquad \text{(Capital in each industry)}$$

$$a_K(n+d)C + b_K(n+d+s)I = I \qquad \text{(Steady state gross investment)} \qquad (1)$$

$$a_K(n+d)C + [b_K(n+d) - (1 - sb_K)]I = 0 \qquad \text{(Investment goods demand = supply)} \qquad (2)$$

Here n is the growth rate, and d, $d+s$ (≥ 0) are the depreciation rates in the consumption goods and investment goods activities. Equations (1) and (2) may be solved for the steady-state outputs C and I. Let A be the determinant of the input/output coefficients, $a_L b_K - a_K b_L$, and let $v = (1 - sb_K)$. Then:

$$C = [b_K(n+d) - v]/[A(n+d) - va_L], \quad I = -a_K(n+d)/[A(n+d) - va_L] \qquad (3)$$

The factor-price frontier can be found from the 'dual' of the system (1)–(2). The price of consumption goods, the numéraire, is normalised to 1. The wage rate is w. The price of investment goods is p. The profit rate is r. Thus the gross rental cost of capital services is $p(r+d)$ in the consumption goods activity and $p(r+d+s)$ in investment goods production. The break-even equations for the two activities are:

$$a_L w + a_K p(r+d) = 1 \qquad \text{(Consumption goods activity)} \qquad (4)$$

$$b_L w + [b_K(r+d) - (1 - sb_K)]p = 0 \qquad \text{(Investment goods activity)} \qquad (5)$$

These two equations are to be solved for w and p, given r. The solutions are:

$$w = [b_K(r+d) - v]/[A(r+d) - va_L], \quad p = -b_L/[A(r+d) - va_L] \qquad (6)$$

By inspection, comparing (3) and (6) gives the standard 'Golden Rule' result that $w = C$ when $r = n$.

[1] In Chapter 10 of *The Accumulation of Capital*, 'The Spectrum of Techniques', Joan Robinson discusses switching as 'A Curiosum' (Robinson, 1966, pp. 109–113). See Samuelson, 1966 for a review of reswitching possibilities in models with input/output lags.

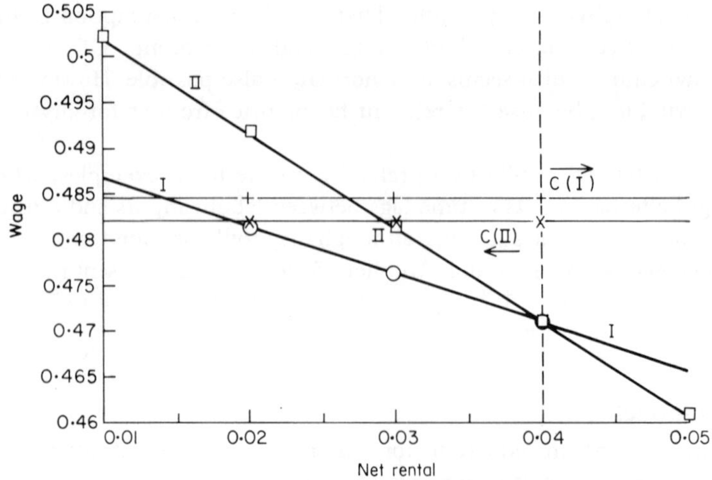

Fig. 1. *Factor prices and consumption: two technologies. Point I is the intersection of the downward sloping factor-price frontier for Technology I (○) with the constant steady-state consumption produced by Technology I. Point II is the similar intersection for Technology II (□). Both points correspond to a profit rate equal to the growth rate, assumed to be 0·03 and independent of technology. The net rental of capital at II is nonetheless higher than at I because the price of capital goods relative to consumption goods, which does depend on the technology, is higher. + = consumption I; × = consumption II.*

Table 1. *Assumed parameter values and key results in illustration (Fig. 1) (labour supply normalised to equal 1)*

	Technology I	Technology II
a_L	2	0·05
a_K	1	2
b_L	0·9	2
b_K	2	0·02
d	0·035	0·47
s	−0·025	0·1
n	0·03	0·03
C	0·485	0·482
I	0·034	0·488
K	0·50	24·64
Price when $r=n$	0·47	0·97
Rental when $r=n$	0·014	0·029
Switch point rental	0·04	0·04
Switch point wage	0·471	0·471

The factor-price frontier relates the wage w to net rental per unit of capital, $R=rp$. It can be derived algebraically from the above equations. It is linear, as follows:

$$w=(b_K d-v)/(Ad-va_L)+va_K R/(Ad-va_L) \tag{7}$$

When $R=np(n)$—where $p(n)$ is calculated from (6) with $r=n$—then $w=C$.

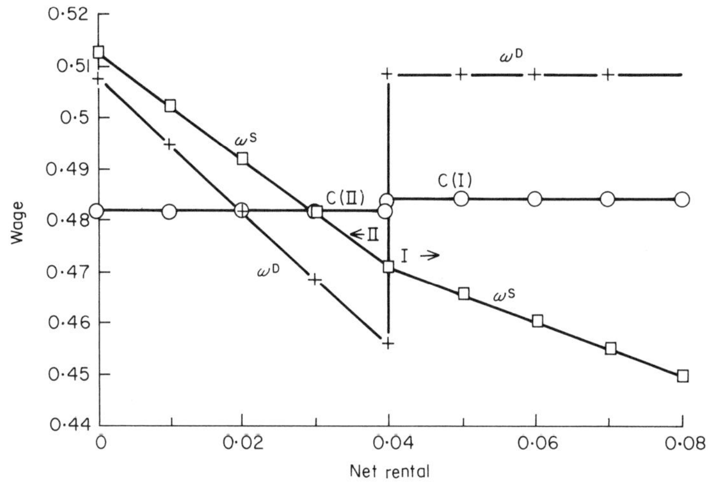

Fig. 2. *Determination of income distribution: equating consumption demand and supply. The switch to Technology I occurs, as in Fig. 1, at a net profit rate just below 0·04. Here the jump in consumption due to the switch is shown, also the kink in the wage-rental frontier ('supply wage', □) due to the switch. 'Demand wage' (+) is, for each value of net rental the wage which, given the two propensities to consume, will make consumption demand equal to the consumption available under the technology in use at that rental. Here the equilibrium is at the switch point.* ○ = *consumption.*

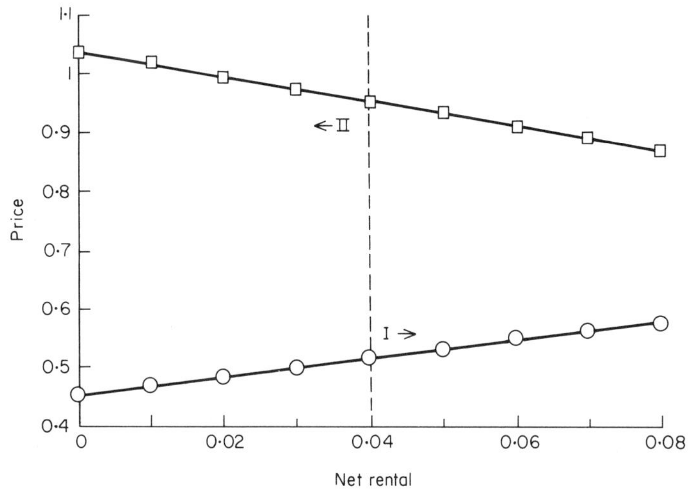

Fig. 3. *Capital goods prices and rentals: two technologies. Technology II (□), the more capital-intensive technology, implies much higher capital goods prices than Technology I (○). Technology II is used to the left of the vertical line, drawn at the switch point rental of 0·04.*

The slope of a wage–rental ($w-R$) frontier like (7) is supposed to be a measure of capital intensity. For example, in the Swan-Solow model—one product, two factors, etc.—the slope is the capital/labour ratio. Here the measure of capital intensity represented by the slope is more complex, but it is there. If d were zero, meaning no depreciation in the consumption goods activity, the slope would be the capital intensity of that activity, a_K/a_L.

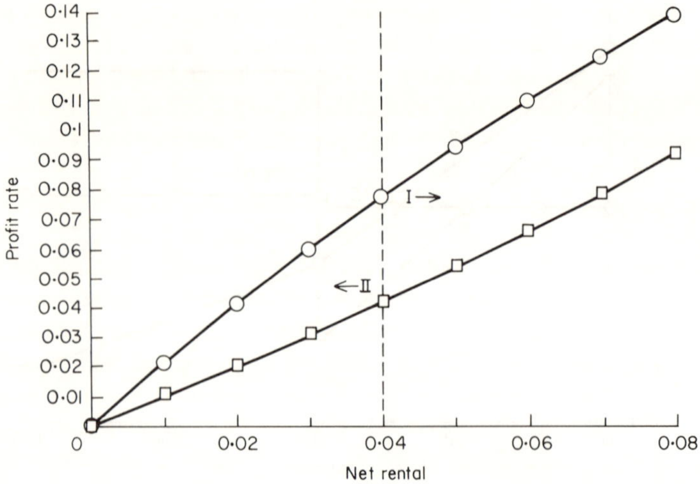

Fig. 4. *Profit rates and net rentals: two technologies. Technology II (□), the more capital intensive technology, implies lower profit rates than Technology I (○). Technology II is in use in the left half of the diagram, at rentals less than 0·04.*

The same calculations can be made for a second technology, indeed for every available technology, each one defined by values of a_L, a_K, b_L, b_K, d, and s. The growth rate n is also exogenous, but it is assumed to be independent of technology. Figure 1 shows illustrative factor-price frontiers for two technologies. Each is linear, with constant and slope dependent on six parameters. With so many degrees of freedom, even when respecting the obvious inequalities, many configurations are possible. The example has been contrived to exhibit reverse switching. Technology II has the lower steady-state consumption, but is used in preference to Technology I at lower net rentals and profit rates. Table 1 tells the numbers assumed in this illustration and reports some of the calculations.

Technology II is highly capital-intensive, in particular in the consumption goods activity, but the capital depreciates rapidly.

All that is needed now is to superimpose a Kaldor consumption function on Figure 1. If nothing is saved from wages and nothing is consumed from capital income, the profit rate is equal to the growth rate, the net rental is $np(n)$ for the technology in use at that profit rate (II in the example), and the wage is equal to the consumption afforded by that technology. In general, consumption demand C^D is equal to $c_L w + c_K RK$, where c_L and c_K are the propensities to consume from labour income and capital income respectively. In equilibrium consumption demand must equal consumption supply C^S, the consumption corresponding to the dominant technology (in the example, Technology I for the high profit rates, II for low).

Figure 2 continues the illustration of Figure 1. C^S is shown, jumping at the profit rate where the two factor-price frontiers cross in Figure 1. The downward-sloping broken line labelled 'supply wage' is the factor-price frontier, taking account of both technologies and the switch from one to the other. The other downward-sloping line, which jumps at the switch-point, is the 'demand wage', i.e. for each rental the wage that, given the propensities to consume, will make consumption demand C^D equal to supply C^S. This is given by:

$$w^D = C^S/c_L - c_K RK/c_L \quad (8)$$

In Figure 2 this is plotted for consumption propensities taken to be 0·95 and 0·05 for labour and capital incomes respectively. In equilibrium the 'demand wage' must equal the 'supply wage'. In the example depicted in Figure 2, this happens to occur only at the switch point. Whichever technology is used, the net rental will be 0·04 and the wage 0·47, on the 'supply wage' locus. Technology I gives the higher aggregate consumption.

Capital goods prices and profit rates vary with rental rates, as illustrated by Figures 3 and 4. Capital goods prices are higher and profit rates lower in Technology II, which is used at rentals less than 0·04, i.e. in the left half of Figures 2, 3, and 4.

In this exercise, I have tried to place certain insights of Nicholas Kaldor and Joan Robinson in a context where their purpose and relevance may be understood and appreciated by a wider audience. Are there morals to the story? Competitive markets are most likely to exist and to perform well when local incremental decisions are possible. However, societies frequently face all-or-nothing decisions, choices among lumpy alternatives, often difficult or impossible to reverse. The ordinary tools of neoclassical economics are much less useful for the second class of problems than for the first.

Bibliography

Abel, A., Mankiw, N., Summers, L. and Zeckhauser, R. 1986. 'Assessing Dynamic Efficiency: Theory and Evidence', National Bureau for Economic Research Working Paper No. 2097

Kaldor, N. 1956. Alternative theories of distribution, *Review of Economic Studies*, vol. XXIII, 83–100

Kaldor, N. 1960. A rejoinder to Mr Atsumi and Professor Tobin, *Review of Economic Studies*, vol. XXVII, 121–3

Kaldor, N. 1966. Marginal productivity and macroeconomic theories of distribution, *Review of Economic Studies*, vol. XXXIII, 309–19

Kaldor, N. 1985. *Economics Without Equilibrium* (The Okun Lectures), Armonk, NY, M.E. Sharpe

Pasinetti, L. L. 1962. Rate of profit and income distribution in relation to the rate of economic growth, *Review of Economic Studies*, vol. XXIX, 267–79

Pasinetti, L. L. 1969. Switches of technique and the 'rate of return' in capital theory, *Economic Journal*, vol. 79, 508–531

Robinson, J. 1960. *Collected Economic Essays*, vol II, Oxford, Blackwell

Robinson, J. 1966. *The Accumulation of Capital*, London, Macmillan

Robinson, J. and Eatwell, J. 1973. *An Introduction to Modern Economics*, London, McGraw-Hill

Samuelson, P. A. 1966. A summing up, *Quarterly Journal of Economics*, vol. 80, 568–583

Tobin, J. 1960. Towards a general Kaldorian theory of distribution: a note, *Review of Economic Studies*, vol. XXVII, 119–20, reprinted as ch. 7 in Tobin (1971)

Tobin, J. 1971. *Essays in Economics: Volume I, Macroeconomics*, Chicago, Markham Publishing Co.

Worswick, D. and Trevithick, J. (eds) 1983. *Keynes and the Modern World*, Cambridge, CUP

Kaldor on growth

F. H. Hahn*

'. . . those individuals who are endowed with a special genius for the subject and have a powerful economic intuition will often be more right in their conclusions and implicit presumptions than in their explanation and explicit statements. That is to say, their intuitions will be in advance of their analysis and their terminology. Great respect, therefore, is due to their general scheme of thought, and it is a poor thing to pester their memories with criticism which is really verbal.' [J. M. Keynes (1924) quoted in Kaldor (1972, p. 1249, n. 1)]

What follows is in no way to be taken as an instance of 'Kaldor scholarship'. I knew Kaldor for forty years and before he became disenchanted with my unsound views we saw a great deal of each other and had very many economics arguments. This period coincided with Kaldor's 'growth phase'. Some of the views which I ascribe to him are taken from our discussions. They may or may not have been published and what I report may indeed not always be consistent with what he did publish. One of Kaldor's virtues was the ease with which he allowed new ideas to drive out old. A learned referee of this piece took me to task for not referring to the quite large literature on Kaldorian themes. I do not know that literature. So the reader of this essay is warned: it is a personal reflection on my debates with an economist of a remarkable mental agility and originality.

Kaldor had a vision of the process of capitalist growth. At first he made great efforts to express it in precise models (1957, 1961). But ultimately he found this too constricting and settled for a more literary and narrative style (1972). He always had interesting things to say and often very illuminating things. But he was in advance of both theoretical tools and empirical research and there must be some delay before his contribution can be properly judged. However, even now one must to conclude that he was more interesting and adventurous than the rest of us who stuck to the straight and narrow of neoclassical theory. When and if precise theory and more evidence catch up with him, it may well be that he will be found to have been largely right. Of course, he was sometimes plainly wrong but that is to be expected when striking out in new directions.

I

What Joan Robinson called the 'book of blueprints' most of us call the production set. Robinson and current theory take this set to have a rather straightforward and unambiguous definition. It simply gives a list of activities available for choice by a producer (an activity is a vector whose components are outputs and inputs). A production function (or more generally a transformation function) characterises the set of efficient activities

*University of Cambridge.

contained in the production set. Robinson was interested in the shape of this function (was it smooth, etc.) and in the problem of expressing it in terms of aggregates such as 'capital', 'output', 'labour', etc. As far as I can tell Kaldor was never interested in these problems.

The reason for this, amongst others, is that he did not think that there was anything defined as a production function or for that matter a production set. Alternative activities (techniques) were not to be taken as given but as discovered. No firm had knowledge of the book of blueprints as it could be assembled by pooling all the knowledge and experience there was in the world. In any case, the size of the book was forever changing and indeed its pages grew larger. That is, new goods, especially new producer goods, were continually appearing. Firms and employees 'learned by doing' (Arrow, 1962) which formally is equivalent to discovering new activities. So the pages in the book as known to the firm were not independent of the firm's choices. As a consequence, no outside observer could, on observing, say, an activity with higher output, judge whether the firm had simply turned to a pre-existing page or found one it had not known before. At one time Kaldor made this into a slogan: 'movements along a production function cannot be distinguished from shifts in this function'. Later we shall see that he did not stick rigorously to this view. However, when he did, he believed the notion of a production function to be non-operational—it could, he claimed, not be estimated. It is obvious from the econometric literature that many did not agree.

So Kaldor invented the 'Technical Progress Function' (1957). In its first incarnation he wrote it as follows:

$$\dot{y} = a + \beta\dot{k}$$

where $y = \log$ (output/man), $k = \log$ (capital/man). The idea was to avoid by this dynamic formulation the distinction between movements along and shifts in the production function. However it was soon pointed out to him that this equation could be integrated into

$$Y = Ae^{at}K^{\beta}$$

(Y = output/man, K = capital/man, A is a constant of integration). This Cobb–Douglas implication was most unwelcome and Kaldor later insisted that the correct formulation required the Technical Progress Function to be non-linear. The justification for this was not at all detailed.

It was left to Arrow (1962) to give this line of reasoning a more concrete formulation. His paper is justly famous and requires no summary here. However, while the Arrowian formulation did lead to the conclusion that socially too little would be invested and produced (learning at any date depended on the integral of output to that date), it did not lead to a drastic break with neoclassical theory. In particular, if learning was regarded as a kind of externality the neoclassical marginal productivity equations continued to play their usual role. In an important sense, then, Arrow did not capture what Kaldor was looking for or what he said he was looking for.

Yet there is substance in the Kaldorian argument. Atkinson and Stiglitz (1969) have pointed out that a change from one technique to another, even to one which is already known to the firm or to other firms, involves learning. Neoclassical theory takes the production set as an objective entity and that is almost certainly the wrong way in which to take it. General Equilibrium Theory is very silent on new knowledge, new goods and on innovation generally. When attempts to take note of these are successful we may find significant changes in that theory.

Kaldor in his later thinking was much influenced by Allyn Young (1928) who also had a vision and, it must be confessed, also found it hard to give it a precise formulation. He believed that 'every reorganisation of production activities creates the opportunity for further change *which would not have existed otherwise*' (Kaldor, 1972). These reorganisations are facilitated when scale increases and Young held the view that this gave rise to more or less universal 'increasing returns to scale' in manufacturing. However, these are not increasing returns in the sense that a firm is faced with a given non-convex production set. Kaldor calls them dynamic increasing returns and it is these that he wished to capture by means of the technical progress function. In any case, once this picture of an ever expanding production set is accepted, 'the whole view of the economic process as a medium for the "allocation of scarce means between alternative uses" falls apart' (Kaldor, 1972). Indeed, 'except in a purely short-term sense, total output can never be *confined* by resources' (Kaldor, 1972). It is not surprising that these assertions have not found wide acceptance. Such a radical departure from traditional views requires a very great deal of argument and evidence. Kaldor produced neither, which, however, does not mean that his vision was false in its essentials.

The Young–Kaldor view of increasing returns to scale, Kaldor attempted to fashion into a theory of growth. In my view he did not succeed in this, although as usual he made a number of suggestions which strike one as deserving further analysis. Young had worried about the means by which the benefits of increasing returns in his sense could be gathered in one sector and transmitted to another so as to cause expansion there and so lead to a process of 'cumulative causation'—that is endogenous growth. He produced an elasticity condition on an offer curve which modern theory cannot, and Kaldor did not, take seriously. (Apart from other objections, the formulation is obscure.) Kaldor put Young's failure down to the circumstance that he was writing before Keynes. Kaldor's failure, in turn, I put down to his unwillingness to use some of the simplest tools of General Equilibrium analysis. He may be right that General Equilibrium Theory abstracts so much from certain essential phenomena (like increasing returns) as to make it unsuitable as a theory of growth. But he himself distinguishes in this criticism between the short and the long run. Young's puzzle concerns a process and a process is indeed a series of short runs.

This process Kaldor often called 'cumulative causation'. But there is also another interpretation of cumulative causation: it may cause an initial advantage of a firm or of a region over competitors to increase through time until competitors are driven out. Kaldor, I think, believed that this consideration told against the UK joining the Common Market: the advantage, say, of German manufacturing industry would lead to the concentration of production there. (Compare this with a neoclassical story of diminishing returns.) Dasgupta and Stiglitz (1987) have recently provided an interesting analysis of this. I shall be mostly concerned with the first of these two concepts of cumulative causation.

Kaldor's solution to the propagation or 'cumulative causation' problem was to introduce stockholders and merchants of all kinds as essential elements. When Sector A expanded and reaped the benefits of dynamic increasing returns, Sector A's prices might fall a great deal since the income of demanders had not expanded. Merchants, etc. who held expectations of a normal price would buy for stock (really for speculative purposes) and in that way allow Sector A's income to increase. This in turn would lead them to demand more from other sectors whose turn it would now be to reap the benefits of increasing returns. In this way growth based on increasing returns would cumulate. He added that all of this required an adaptive monetary policy. Since there seem to have been periods of rapid growth in the past without such a permissive policy one is rather left wondering about the realism of this proposal. Kaldor elaborates the story somewhat by drawing a distinction between those sectors of the economy which he claimed were subject to increasing returns (manufacturing industry) and those which were not (services).

In this theory Kaldor was building on a splendid early paper of his: 'Speculation and Economic Stability' (1939) which was, however, a careful piece of analysis and which was not concerned with growth. One of its contributions was to provide an explanation for Robertson's (1940, ch. 1) contention that increased investment demand could lead to higher output, that is, could take place without an equivalent increase in savings, if idle balances were dishoarded and goods were dishoarded. Kaldor put such dishoarding down to price (and interest rate) stabilising actions of speculators and others whose price expectations were highly inelastic. A similar argument seems to underlie the growth theory, but here i's are not dotted nor t's crossed.

What is missing in the first instance is the accounting equation of agents which we call budget constraints—one of the tools of the discarded neoclassical analysis. In particular the budget constraints of stockholders are not given or discussed. But they are plainly of considerable importance since to perform the task assigned to stockholders by Kaldor they must either have a rotating stock of idle balances or have access to a more or less perfectly elastic supply of credit. Perhaps that is why Kaldor required a permissive monetary policy. However, it is not clear that, given the dynamic increasing returns assumptions, such a policy would not of its own suffice for 'cumulative causation'. For instance, should the expansion in Sector A be accompanied by a rise in money wages there, then an increasing money stock may transmit demand to other sectors and get the process under way.

But the nuts and bolts of Kaldor's emendation of Allyn–Young are missing. What follows now is a rough outline of what he may have had in mind (see also Thirlwall, 1987).

II

Suppose that there are two sectors in the economy labelled one and two. Households receive at date t the profits and wages from the production of the previous period. All prices are expressed in terms of an (ideal) price index (which is homogeneous of degree one in all prices). Let x_i be household demand for good i, y_i be output of good i, p_i the price, in terms of the index, of good i and m_i^h the stock of money held by households; again measured in terms of the index. Let the operator Δ be defined by $\Delta\, z(t)=z(t)-z(t-1)$ for any variable $z(t)$. Then the household budget constraint is given by

$$\Sigma p_i(t)x_i(t)+\Delta m_i^h(t)=\Sigma\, p_i(t-1)y_i(t-1). \tag{1}$$

Suppose now that there are merchants who do not consume, who are capable of issuing money on their own account and who hold stocks $s_i(t)$ of good i. Then

$$\Sigma\, p_i(t)\Delta s_i(t)+\Delta m^s(t)=0, \tag{2}$$

where $\Delta m^s(t)>0$ is absorption and $\Delta m^s(t)<0$ is new supply of money by merchants. Now make the extreme Kaldorian assumptions that (a) merchants are intent on stabilising prices completely and (b) that this is done by choosing

$$\Delta s_i(t)=y_i(t)-x_i(t). \tag{3}$$

From now on, set $p_i(t)=p_i$ all t. Using (2) and (3) in (1) we obtain

$$\Sigma p_i \Delta y_i(t) + \Delta m^s(t) + \Delta m^h(t) = 0. \tag{4}$$

In all of this the amalgamation of merchants and banks into a single entity, and the neglect of borrowing at interest, cannot matter for the general aim of interpreting Kaldor.

Suppose we start in a situation where $\Delta s_i = 0$, $i = 1, 2$. At date $t = 1$ sector one (perhaps through Schumpeterian animal spirits) decides to expand output by $\Delta y(1)$ while sector two stays at its old output. Since at $t = 1$ households have experienced no change in income and merchants stabilise prices, we obtain

$$\Delta s_i(1) = \Delta y_i(1) + [y_i(0) - x_i(0)] = \Delta y_i(1) \tag{5}$$

and a corresponding increase in the real money stock.

At $t = 2$ receipts of households have increased by $\Delta y_i(1) p_i$. This is assumed to increase their demand for both goods. Hence (a) the amount of good one which merchants have to put to stock at $t = 2$ is less than it was at $t - 1$ and (b) they will have to decumulate some stocks of good two if sector two has not increased its output. At $t = 3$ output of sector two rises, thereby adding to demand for the output of sector one at $t = 3$. Each time output goes up in either sector there are benefits of increasing returns to be reaped. These are made implicit in this account by not putting any physical constraints on output.

The above is not much more satisfactory than is Kaldor's own account. One wants the agents involved to be at least partly governed by rational considerations, and one wants the 'lack of physical constraint on output' spelled out in detail and one surely wants to check that it all leads to a virtuous cumulative process. There is of course also the problem that merchants may either run out of stocks or be continuously accumulating them. Let us try for a little more detail.

Kaldor certainly did not wish us to postulate perfect competition. Let us write the demand for the representative firm in sector i as

$$\log x_i(t) = \varepsilon_{ii} \log p_i + \varepsilon_{ij} \log p_j + \log g_i[y(t-1)] \tag{6}$$

where (a) I continue to suppose $p_i(t) = p_i$ for all t, (b) $y = \Sigma p_i y_i$, (c) $\varepsilon_{ii} < -1$, for $i = 1, 2$. The firm has a cost function $c_i(y_i)$ with $c_i'(y_i) > 0$, $c_i'(y_i) < 0$. In deciding on its output the firm takes the price of the other sector and *total income* as given. If it is profit maximising then for $i = 1, 2$,

$$c_i'(y_i) = p_i \frac{1 + \varepsilon_{ii}}{\varepsilon_{ii}}$$

and also (7)

$$c_i''(y_i) > \frac{p_i}{\mathrm{x_i}} \frac{1 + \varepsilon_{ii}}{(\varepsilon_{ii})^2}.$$

Let us start the story with an equilibrium denoted by asterisk superscripts. Choose units such that $p_1^* = p_2^* = 1$. Then

$$y_i^* = g_i(y^*) = x_i^*, \; i = 1, 2. \tag{8}$$

We do not here worry about the existence of an equilibrium but it should be understood as a stationary state.

Now suppose—say by mistake—that firms in Sector 1 decide that they will produce more at $t = 0$ for sale at $t = 1$. (Recall that households only receive income from period 0 production from the proceeds of sales in period one.) We calculate

$$\frac{\partial x_i(1)}{\partial y_1(0)} = \varepsilon_{iy} \frac{x_i}{y^\star} \qquad i = 1, 2 \tag{9}$$

where ε_{iy} is the income elasticity of demand for the output of Sector i. If merchants are to meet any shortfall of demand at the equilibrium prices then

$$\left.\begin{aligned} \Delta s_1(1) &= \left[1 - \varepsilon_{iy} \frac{x_1^\star}{y^\star}\right] \Delta y_1(0) \\ \Delta s_2(1) &= \varepsilon_{2y} \frac{x_2^\star}{y^\star} \Delta y_1(0). \end{aligned}\right\} \tag{10}$$

Suppose that the desired level of money holdings of households per unit income is a constant k. Then from (1)

$$\Sigma \varepsilon_{iy} \frac{x_i^\star}{y^\star} = 1 - k. \tag{11}$$

Hence if neither good is inferior:

$$\Delta s_i(1) > 0, i = 1, 2. \tag{12}$$

From (4) we then find that merchants augment the money stock as required:

$$-\Delta m_t^s = k \Delta y_i(0). \tag{13}$$

But now at $t = 1$ both kinds of firms perceive that their demand curves have shifted to the right. However, we are at once faced with a problem. If firms realise that speculators will always take up stock to stabilise prices then, as far as they are concerned, they are facing a perfectly elastic demand with dire consequences in view of the postulate of continuing increasing returns. Kaldor is not very explicit although one could read him as arguing that there are limits to the increase in output in any time interval. That is, we are allowed to suppose that in the 'short run' cost curves are U-shaped. But that is not much help since it is then obvious that firms will expand output in every period and one does not have to appeal to 'cumulative causation'.

There are several ways out and I do not know which Kaldor would have favoured. One is that firms never learn the postulated behaviour of merchants so that they always believe themselves to be facing negatively sloped demand curves. Another is that merchants are rational and that they base their actions on expectations of prices and on the level of stocks which they hold. In that case a possible assumption is that firms accurately take account of the actions of merchants. Neither of these routes is simple to follow nor is either particularly attractive. Kaldor left these crucial details out of his account. Certainly it is not obvious that $\Delta y_1(0) > 0$ will start the desired cumulative process.

I find it more reasonable to assume that firms anticipate the actions of merchants. Accordingly I now re-tell the story under this assumption which we know entails that prices are completely stabilised by merchants.

Let aggregate demand for firm i be written as X_i so

$$X_i = x_i + \Delta s_i.$$

Note that Δs_i is not restricted in sign—a supply by merchants leaves firm i with a smaller residual demand to satisfy. Let $h_t = \{p_{t-1}, p_{t-2} \ldots\}$ be the history of prices up to date t, where $p=(p_1, p_2)$. Then using (6) we write

$$x_i(t)=\xi_i[p(t), h_t, y(t-1)] \tag{14}$$

Define $\sigma_i=\partial\log\ \Delta s_i(t)/\partial\log\ p_i(t)$. Kaldor calls σ_i the elasticity of speculation. We are supposing that it is not infinite. Then η_i, the elasticity of aggregate demand is given by

$$\eta_i=\frac{x_i}{X_i}\varepsilon_{ii}+\frac{\Delta s_i}{X_i}\sigma_i. \tag{15}$$

It is important to note that η_i will in general depend on all the variables in the economy.

Firms choose to produce a profit maximising output on the aggregate demand curve. So for equilibrium we have

$$y_i(t)=\xi_i[p(t), h_t, y(t-1)], \qquad i=1,2 \tag{16}$$

$$c_i'[y_i(t)]=p_i(t)\frac{1+\eta_i(t)}{\eta_i(t)}, \qquad i=1,2 \tag{17}$$

and second order conditions. Since we also have

$$y(t-1)=\sum_i p_i(t-1)y_i(t-1)$$

we should now be able to trace the time paths of outputs from given initial conditions. Notice now that since the elasticity of speculation is finite, prices need not be constant along this path and merchants will not be, say, augmenting the nominal stock in proportion with their purchases. Hence we shall need a further dynamic equation to give us the change in the price index (price level) required to keep the demand for real balances in equality with their supply. Recall however that p_i is expressed in terms of the 'index good' so that relative prices as solved for by (16) and (17) will not be affected. (If demand for goods depended on the real money stock as well as on income this would not be true. The 'money clearing equation' and the appropriate (16) and (17) would need to be solved together.)

It will be seen that it will not be easy to obtain an analytical solution even when we have given all the relevant functions some suitable parametric form. But I shall not try to do this and simply note the obvious point that it will not be true that this economy *must* be characterised by continuous expansion of output. This will 'depend'. To this must be added the caution that the model is highly simplified. For instance, if the government does not properly augment the money stock, the falling price level may have unfortunate consequences for investment and for merchants' willingness to stock.

I have gone through this exercise in order to illustrate a general feature of Kaldor's later work on growth. He painted with a broad brush and often revealed features of an economy which had been unduly neglected—in this case dynamic increasing returns and the role of merchants in transmitting expansion in one sector to another. But he was then inclined to take these neglected matters—and he was right in holding that the neglect was unjustified—as being the whole story. He was impatient of detail and so was in danger of being himself neglected. That is a pity since, possibly by simulation, it may be feasible to analyse a theory of growth which incorporates his main ideas. My guess is that one will find that some economies characterised at some time by certain expectations and dynamic increasing returns will, at least for a stretch, behave as he predicted. Others will not. But it seems unlikely that one will ever be justified in following Kaldor in his belief that there are 'no resource constraints in the long run'. Human ingenuity after all is a resource constraint itself and one can think of others. Kaldor was inclined to claim too much too soon and so his important insights often went unnoticed.

III

Kaldor's more detailed work on growth (1962) is much easier to discuss. I can be brief since that contribution is intimately connected to the distribution theory which he sponsored and that theory is discussed elsewhere in this issue.

Harrod had left no room for any mechanism which could bring equality between the natural and warranted rate of growth. I believe that writers on Harrods' model are mistaken in their claim that he posited fixed coefficients of production. Rather I believe that he had in mind a minimum real interest rate below which accumulation would cease and so a lower bound on the marginal return on investment. (But it must be admitted that Harrod like Kaldor employed a broad brush.) Kaldor, as we have seen, was not prepared to think in terms of a choice of coefficients of production at all. His mechanism for bringing the natural and warranted growth rate into equality was an adaptive change in the distribution of income between profit and wage income which, owing to the difference in the savings propensities of the two groups, would do the trick. I had also hit on this mechanism in my PhD thesis (1951; see Hahn, 1972) but did not argue from this that the steady state real wage of labour was divorced from its marginal product.

Kaldor was adamant in his opposition to marginal productivity playing any role because he was adamant in his objection to the notion of a production function or production set. I could never, and cannot now, understand why his very important insight into dynamic economies of scale should preclude a firm from comparing the cost and advantage of hiring another hour of work. After all, at any moment of time machines, etc. are in place and it makes sense to ask the usual marginal product question. It is true that if labour cannot be hired by the hour, or even the week, benefits can only be calculated on the basis of expectations. But *something* must be compared when labour is hired or fired and Kaldor always lacked one equation. It is paradoxical for a Keynesian that in his growth work Kaldor always *postulated* full employment and never asked what was needed to ensure this.

So Kaldor growth models (unlike Robinson growth models) were always full-employment steady states. Kaldor, no doubt influenced by Kalecki, thought of the equation: warranted equals natural growth, as determining the economy's 'average degree of monopoly', i.e. the Kaleckian distribution of shares. The latter, however, was motivated by a traditional marginal cost equals marginal revenue account which, as far as I can judge, Kaldor did not accept.

In his early formal model Kaldor used the technical progress function which I have already given. In his far more ambitious work with Mirrlees (1962), Kaldor adopted a vintage approach and stipulated

$$\dot{y}_t/y_t = F(\dot{I}_t/I_t)$$

where y_t is output per man on vintage t machines and I_t is gross investment at t. Gross investment was governed by two conditions. Firstly, given the correctly anticipated 'Golden Age' rate of growth in real wages and given the prevailing net rate of profit, the investment must at least earn that rate. Secondly, under the same expectational assumption the undiscounted sum of quasi-rents on the investment of date t must at least cover the cost of the investment at date t in a fixed interval of time.

It is not clear from the paper whether Kaldor realised where Mirrlees's mathematics was leading him. For in the grand finale of the 'Golden Age' both conditions are taken to hold with equality. So the prevailing Golden Age rate of profit has adapted to the payoff period and so in the Golden Age equilibrium will measure what Keynes called the marginal efficiency of investment. Of course, the latter is not straightforward to calculate since it will depend on the endogenous obsolescence date of investment of a given vintage and so really on all the variables. But by adopting the pay-off period approach Kaldor surely hoped to have an alternative means of characterising profits and the rate of profit which did not seem to involve any 'marginal what nots'. But whether Kaldor approved of the step of making both the conditionals on investment binding must, as I have already noted, remain doubtful. Yet without it he would have been one equation short to determine the net rate of profit. So the 'New Model' had a soft neoclassical underbelly.

It is shown that steady state must entail

$$\dot{y}_t/y_t = \dot{I}_t/I_t$$

since otherwise real wages will experience accelerating growth or decline. So the rate of growth of output per man is determined endogenously and not as, say, in Harrod or most neoclassical models, exogenously. Here Kaldor and Arrow reach similar results although Arrow used a different and, as Kaldor conceded, more plausible technical progress function.

The remainder of the model, besides the usual vintage equations for obsolescence and total output, etc., employs the Cambridge saving hypothesis to close the model. The wage at any date t must equal the quasi-rent per worker of the machine scrapped at t and since we know the Golden Age growth rate, wages at all t are determined. However we are not told how to determine the number of workers which will be employed with each vintage. I assume that it is supposed that there is no choice. Had there been choice then indeed both boundary conditions which investment must satisfy would hold with equality, with the consequence which I have already discussed.

In his comments on Arrow's (1962) 'Learning by Doing', Kaldor distinguishes his model from the 'neoclassical Arrow' by supposing that there is an increase in the production of machines. He claims that for Arrow that will entail a rise in the share of wages but for him it will entail a fall. This is 'the broad brush' again. It is not clear from what position the rise in the production of machines is to be taken. What I believe he has in mind is not a 'rise' but a comparison of two economies in steady state, one of which is investing a larger fraction of income than is the other. Given his savings assumption Kaldor properly concludes that the share of profit will be higher in the economy with a larger investment–income ratio. But there is nothing anti-neoclassical in this savings assumption. The model has eleven simultaneous equations (when the rate of profit is determinate) and if two economies differ in their steady state investment–income ratio then they will differ in other respects as well. Kaldor is here committing a sin which Joan Robinson was always condemning: he confused comparison of equilibria with changes in an equilibrium. In any event, it is of course by now well-known that stark neoclassicism (e.g. a Cobb–Douglas production function) combined with a Cambridge savings function yields a perfectly satisfactory growth model—provided one does not ask causality questions of a system of simultaneous equations.

Kaldor's models, as well as all other models of growth, are now out of favour and there is little work on these kinds of problems to be found in the current journals. One of the reasons no doubt is the concentration on steady state equilibria which resulted from the difficulties of studying more general equilibrium paths except in rather simple cases. A more important reason is actually Kaldorian: the formal models do not seem to capture the history of capitalist development as we know it. That is why Kaldor turned to the more speculative and less formal mode of his later work. But while we may have exhausted what we can, or want to, say concerning steady state growth, the theories of the fifties and sixties did teach us some quite important economics and Kaldor's models were no exception.

IV

I have not discussed Kaldor's more empirical work on growth nor his incorporation of growth theory in a theory of development. The reason why I omit this is that I am not really qualified to assess it. For instance, I do not know whether 'Verdoorn's Law' is now regarded as a law (see Kaldor, 1966).

But Kaldor took his own theories seriously when it came to practical economics and for a time he was in a position to induce governments to take the actions which he advocated. The Selective Employment Tax was an example of this. Basically it was justified on the Marshallian-Pigouvian grounds of subsidising increasing returns sectors at the expense of those with decreasing returns. It was not clear why this was best accomplished by the subsiding and taxing of employment. For a thorough analysis the interested reader is referred to Reddaway *et al.* (1973).

For the UK, Kaldor was an advocate of export-led growth (1966, 1971). But I do not know of any formal model of his which studies growth for an open economy. His less formal arguments certainly were not unpersuasive and incorporated his idea of rising productivity in expanding industrial sectors. There is one important criticism which one can make of some of his policy proposals which involved other countries in an essential way. He ignored what for short one can call the 'reaction functions' of other countries. Nowadays, game theory is being applied to these problems of interaction. Kaldor cannot be blamed for not doing so himself. But he is open to criticism for ignoring these matters altogether.

V

It is inevitable that an economist of the originality, verve and devotion to his subject as Kaldor was should invite criticism of some kind. But that should not detract from the judgement that he possessed rare qualities of insight and imagination. It will not be at all surprising if at some future time he will be hailed as an important precursor in the understanding of the processes of growth. At present the scale of his intellectual picture blurred its details and much of this was in any case only loosely sketched. It is too early to make up this deficiency. But when it is done it may turn out to be a very fine and indeed a very reasonable picture.

Bibiography

Arrow, K. J. 1962. The economic implication of learning by doing, *Review of Economic Studies*, XXIX, pp. 155–73

Atkinson, A. B. and Stiglitz, J. E. 1969. A new view of technological change, *Economic Journal*, vol. LXXIV, pp. 573–578

Dasgupta, P. and Stiglitz, J. 1987. 'Learning-by-Doing, Market Structure and Industrial and Trade Policies', mimeo.

Hahn, F. 1972. *The Share of Wages in The National Income*, London, Weidenfeld and Nicholson

Kaldor, N. 1939. Speculation and economic stability, *Review of Economic Studies*, vol. VII

Kaldor, N. 1957. A model of economic growth, *Economic Journal*, vol. LXVII, December
Kaldor, N. 1961. Capital accumulation and economic growth, in Lutz, F. A. and Hague, D. C. (eds) *The Theory of Capital*, London, Macmillan
Kaldor, N. 1966. *Causes of the Slow Rate of Economic Growth in the United Kingdom*, Inaugural Lecture at Cambridge, CUP
Kaldor, N. 1971. Conflict in national economic objectives, *Economic Journal*, vol. LXXXI
Kaldor, N. 1972. The irrelevance of equilibrium economics, *Economic Journal*, no. 328, pp. 1237–1255
Kaldor, N. and Mirrlees, J. 1962. A new model of economic growth, *Review of Economic Studies*, XXIX, pp. 174–92
Reddaway, B. *et al.* 1973. *Effects of the Selective Employment Tax—Final Report*, Department of Applied Economics Occasional Papers 32, Cambridge, CUP
Robertson, D. H. 1940. *Essays in Monetary Theory*, London and New York, Staples Press
Thirlwall, A. P. 1987. *Nicholas Kaldor*, Brighton, Wheatsheaf Books
Young, A. 1928. Increasing returns and economic progress, *Economic Journal*, vol. XXXVIII, December

Abstraction, tendencies and stylised facts: a realist approach to economic analysis

Tony Lawson*

1. Introduction

In numerous methodological asides and assertions that feature in his more empirically oriented, post-war contributions, Kaldor makes frequent reference to notions of *abstraction, tendencies* and *stylised facts*. The following statement is fairly typical:

Any theory must necessarily be based on abstractions; but the type of abstraction chosen cannot be decided in a vacuum: it must be appropriate to the characteristic features of the economic process as recorded by experience. Hence the theorist, in choosing a particular theoretical approach, ought to start off with a summary of the facts which he regards as relevant to his problem. Since facts, as recorded by statisticians, are always subject to numerous snags and qualifications, and for that reason are incapable of being accurately summarized, the theorist, in my view, should be free to start off with a 'stylised' view of the facts—i.e. concentrate on broad tendencies, ignoring individual detail, and proceed on the 'as if' method, i.e. construct a hypothesis that could account for these 'stylised facts' without necessarily committing himself to the historical accuracy, or sufficiency, of the facts or tendencies thus summarized (Kaldor, 1961, 1978A, p. 2).[1]

Features of analysis such as abstraction, etc., do, of course, figure in much applied economic analysis in general (albeit apparently understood or interpreted differently in different contributions), and typically are employed in consequential ways. At the same time such features seem rarely, if ever, to be explicitly questioned, justified or explicated. And this observation is as true of Kaldor's contributions as of anyone else's.

However, Kaldor, perhaps unlike most other contributors, does at least indicate that, for him, such terms can be used in appropriate (and inappropriate) ways. Even so, what makes a particular usage satisfactory or otherwise is not really made clear. For example, what exactly is meant by the claim that an abstraction 'must be appropriate to the characteristic feature of the economic process as recorded by experience'? Kaldor does not elaborate. Certainly, though, the idea of an appropriate abstraction is significant in Kaldor's writings for, amongst other things, it is said to underpin his well known opposition to formal 'Economic Theory' in general and General Equilibrium analysis in particular:

My basic objection to the theory of general equilibrium is not that it is abstract—all theory is abstract and must necessarily be so since there can be no analysis without abstraction—but that it starts from the wrong kind of abstraction, and therefore gives a misleading 'paradigm' . . . of the world as it is: it gives a misleading impression of the nature and manner of operation of economic forces (Kaldor, 1975, 1978A, p. 202).

*University of Cambridge. For helpful comments on an earlier draft of this paper I am very grateful to Lilli Basile, Geoff Hodgson and John Lovering.

[1]Where a paper has been reprinted in Kaldor's *Collected Economic Essays* (Duckworth, London), date references to both the original article and to the relevant volume of the *Collected Essays*, respectively, are provided. The page reference given, however, is to the *Collected Essays* only.

And what is really meant by the directive to 'start off with a "stylised" view of the facts—i.e. concentrate on broad tendencies, ignoring individual detail'? What is a broad tendency? And why, and in what sense, ignore individual detail? And what exactly does it mean to be uncommitted 'to the historical accuracy, or sufficiency, of the facts or tendencies' described as 'stylised'? Indeed what actually is the relationship between 'stylised facts' and 'broad tendencies'?

In fact, when Kaldor does attempt to throw some light on such issues, more questions tend to be raised than answered. Thus in emphasising his attachment to 'the method of proceeding by collecting "stylised facts" and constructing a hypothesis that fits them' (1985, p. 8) Kaldor adds, as if by way of explanation, that in 'other words, contrary to the prevailing trend, one should subordinate deduction to induction, and discover the empirical regularities first . . .' Now why subordinate? And how? And is the relevant contrast really between deduction and induction? A few lines later Kaldor explains that 'stylised facts' are so called 'because in the social sciences, unlike the natural sciences, it is impossible to establish facts that are precise and at the same time suggestive and intriguing in their implications, and that admit of no exception. (Kaldor, 1985, p. 8). But if 'facts' do admit of exception what exactly is the nature of the generalisations or invariances being emphasised or sought? And so on.

In short, while Kaldor is characteristically explicit about indicating what he believes to be appropriate (and inappropriate) general approaches and features of them, like most other contributors he seems to provide little by way of clear or sufficient methodological explanation or justification of his numerous assertions, directives and stipulations.

In what follows I want to argue that a coherent account of the sort of analytical features and assertions just noted can be provided, and in a relatively straightforward manner, through adopting an explicitly *realist* approach (defined below) to economic analysis. In making this case, I shall also suggest that *realism* represents a serious alternative to the current orthodox approaches to economic analysis and does not suffer from certain of the latter's more obvious limitations. And I shall argue that not only can the realist approach accommodate a coherent interpretation of the notions of abstraction, tendencies and stylised facts, but that the latter form essential elements of such an approach. From this realist perspective, in fact, the sort of general comments made by Kaldor can be straightforwardly interpreted, and the nature of his opposition to the method of economic theory, and to General Equilibrium Theory in particular, explained and justified.

The paper is structured as follows. In Section 2 I set out a brief sketch of the realist position and emphasise how the notion of 'tendencies' fits into the picture. In this section, I also indicate briefly how the realist approach is capable of overcoming certain drawbacks of more orthodox approaches in economics. In Section 3 the notion of 'stylised fact' is examined in the context of developing economic theories. In Section 4 the notion of 'abstraction', and in particular 'inappropriate abstraction', is examined and in Section 5 the conclusions so far reached are brought to bear in a critical way upon Kaldor's favourite target of criticism: formal 'Economic Theory' including General Equlibrium Analysis. It is argued here that although Kaldor's main criticisms warrant a more complete rationale than Kaldor provides, Kaldor's conclusions nevertheless are essentially correct. Some final comments and conclusions are contained in Section 6.

2. A realist approach to analysis

In the context of a scientific activity such as economic analysis (scientific) *realism* asserts the existence of the objects of research as independent of the enquiry of which they are the objects. In other words, according to this doctrine, there is a material and social world that exists independently of any individual conciousness and which is knowable by conciousness—true theories of real entities can be obtained. And a methodological stipulation that needs to be tagged on, here, is that such knowledge, or true theories, should be pursued. It is necessary to emphasise the last step because, in economics, it is not unusual to find accounts which implicitly suppose both that real entities or structures exist and that the truth status of relevant theories can be determined, and yet which argue that theories useful for predictive purposes—including theories acknowledged to be false—are *all* that is required. Indeed in the context of economics the philosophical doctrine most frequently opposed to realism is this peculiar form of 'predictive instrumentalism', and consequently some explicit comparisons of the two doctrines will be made below. Outside economics, however, it is more usual to find adherence to instrumentalism taking an essentially idealist form, whereby theories are not to be regarded as true or false but merely as (better or worse) instruments of prediction.[1] For the purposes of what follows, however, there seems to be little harm in conflating these two versions of instrumentalism. [The significance of the differences between these two versions is discussed in Lawson (1989).] Thus, unless an explicit qualification is made, the term instrumentalism is used here to denote the methodological doctrine that all that is required of analysis (whether or not it is all that is considered to be possible) is a theory that is consistent with the given set of data in question. Clearly these distinctions require some further elaboration in the context of economics and in doing this I draw significantly on some recent contributions in the philosophy of science and social theory, and especially Bhasker (1978).[2]

Realism and tendencies

Consider, first, three conceptual stages or aspects of a possible research analysis. The first involves the identification of some empirical phenomenon of interest, the second involves the construction of a 'model' or 'explanation' which entails (at least 'part' of) the empirical phenomenon in question—clearly these two stages can proceed in any order or simultaneously—and the third stage of the analysis entails subjecting the entities postulated at the 'modelling' or 'explanatory' stage to further/continuous scrutiny.

For the instrumentalist the first two stages are sufficient. The empirical phenomenon in this case is always a presumed empirical regularity. And all that is required is a model that can accommodate it. To the extent that more than one model is sufficient for this task, conventionalist criteria (such as simplicity, parsimony, etc.) can be introduced for choosing between models. There is not even a necessary requirement that a chosen model be plausible—convenient fictions suffice. All that is required is an instrument for the job at hand. A model is accepted by the instrumentalist *merely* if the phenomenon in question is 'as if' it had been generated according to the constructed model.

[1] This version of instrumentalism has been traced, by Popper (1965), back to Bishop Berkeley, for whom theories could not possibly be taken as true descriptions of deeper structures that are real, for such a view would bear the sacrilegious implication that the human intellect, unaided by divine intervention, had uncovered secrets of the world. Thus Berkeley concluded that theories can only deal with appearances, and if they are found to be useful for prediction then they should be treated merely as instruments for this purpose.

[2] In recent years there has been a growth of both an interest in, and of, essentially realist contributions, not just in the domain of the philosophy of science, but also in general social sciences or humanities—(see for example, Bhaskar, 1978; Cartwright, 1983; Chalmers, 1978, Giddens, 1976; Gregory and Urry, 1985; Hacking, 1983; Hesse, 1974; Keohane, 1986; Leplin, 1984; Levy, 1981; Sayer, 1984; and Sayers, 1985). The present paper owes much to this general literature, and most especially—and significantly—to the contributions of Bhaskar.

For the realist, by contrast, while the empirically identified phenomenon may itself warrant re-conceptualisation and further examination (see below), the third stage of analysis is essential. The realist, does also use the 'as if' form of reasoning, but is committed to the view that the entities posited at the modelling stage are or may be real, and are to be further investigated. According to the (essentially Aristotelean) version of realism that is considered here, it is such entities, things, natural kinds or generative structures that lie behind and actually govern the flux of observed phenomena. The object is to construct explanations for, that is to produce knowledge of the mechanisms that generate or govern, some observed phenomenon of interest. If several explanations are put forward and found to be consistent with the phenomenon in question, then these have to be selected amongst on the basis of their power to illuminate a range of empirical findings. In turn some explanation is to be provided as to how any identified mechanism is maintained and so on. In short, for the realist the objective of economics, as indeed with all scientific activity, is to identify and understand real structures or mechanisms that govern the (equally real) phenomena that are experienced.

How, then, does the notion of a *tendency* fit into this realist picture? According to the version of realism being defended here, given things can have powers to act in certain ways in appropriate circumstances by virtue of certain enduring intrinsic structures, or constitutions, or, more generally, natures. In other words, a given thing will have the power or disposition to act in a certain way by virtue of being the sort of thing it is. Often we will have knowledge only of causal powers of something and not of its nature. But if we do have knowledge of what a thing is, then we can deduce its causal powers. Thus once we understand the natures of copper, trade unions and private enterprise, for example, we can deduce their respective powers to conduct electricity well, defend conditions of workers, or seek profits, etc. Now central to this realist view is the notion that powers may be exercised without being (precisely) manifest in actual states of, or happenings in, the world. And in recent realist literature it is this notion of a power that may be exercised and yet unrealised in manifest phenomena that is designated a tendency. Moreover, and in similar *sort* of fashion to the accounts of Marshall, Marx and Mill, for example,[1] it is the ascription of a tendency to a certain kind of thing that is interpreted as a statement of a law.[2]

Why, then, should realists place such emphasis upon notions of generative structures and tendencies (so conceived)? And why, in doing so, should they reject the more orthodox, including instrumentalist, conception of laws as, or as necessitating, regularities amongst events (under some description), in favour of enduring tendencies of things? These questions can be straightforwardly addressed through a consideration of Bhaskar's

[1] Thus Marshall, for example, summarises the content of Section I, III, 3 of his *Principles of Economics* with the observation that 'Nearly all laws of science are statements of tendencies', and he underlines this view by setting out what he thinks social laws and economic laws specifically involve: 'Thus a law of social science, or a *social law*, is a statement of social tendencies; that is a statement that a certain course of action may be expected under certain conditions from the members of a social group. *Economic Laws*, or statements of economic tendencies, are those social laws which relate to branches of conduct in which the strength of the motives chiefly concerned can be measured by a money price' (Section I, III, 4). I do not want to argue for Marshall's particular interpretations of social and economic laws here; I merely cite Marshall to indicate that the idea of laws as tendency statements is not novel. As far as I can discern Kaldor does not explicitly state that he understands laws and tendencies to be one and the same thing, but it is noteworthy that in one of his few explicit references to the nature of laws, Kaldor discusses Marshall's attitude approvingly and at least emphasises that Marshall 'said that "law" in social science is no more than a "statement of social tendencies"' (Kaldor, 1985, p. 59).

[2] For a further discussion of the conception of a law as a tendency see, for example, Baechler, 1971; or Bhaskar, 1978.

(1978) illuminating analysis of the role of experiment in science. Experimental work, of course, is an often central aspect of scientific research—at least in subject-areas where it proves to be possible. Yet, on the whole, it remains relatively unanalysed as a form of scientific activity, despite being frequently emphasised as the ideal to which science, including economics, should aspire. Bhaskar's contribution is to draw out the significance of two readily available observations concerning it. The first observation is that most of the constant conjunctions of events that constitute important results in science, in fact, *only* occur in experimental situations. That is *closed systems*—those in which constant conjunctions of events hold—do not, in general (outside astronomy, at least), occur spontaneously. The second observation is that laws supported in experimental activity are frequently successfully applied outside experimental situations.

Now these observations pose difficulties for accounts which view event regularities as necessary to causal laws. If laws are interpreted as necessitating regularities of the kind 'event (of type) X is *invariably* accompanied by event (of type) Y', then most of the accepted laws of physics, for example, do not hold—for they only hold in conditions of controlled experiment. If, however, this account of laws is then qualified so that laws take the form 'event (of type) X is invariably accompanied by event (of type) Y, under circumstances E', where E is typically those circumstances that obtain only in experimental situations, then other problems follow. First there is the consequence that any actual regularities of events (that the empirical law denotes) do not, in fact, generally occur independently of human intervention—a somewhat counterintuitive result with regard to the notion of laws of *Nature*. But, more seriously, the problem of what governs events outside the experimental situations is left completely without an answer and even unaddressed. And yet, as noted above, experimentally established results *are*, as a matter of fact, successfully applied outside experimental situations—an observation that is apparently without explanation.

As Bhaskar emphasises such problems can be avoided—experimental activity and the application of experimentally determined knowledge outside experimental situations can be rendered intelligible—through invoking an ontology of generative structures and causal mechanisms that lie behind and govern the flux of events. Laws, for the realist, as noted above, are ascriptions of tendencies to certain kinds of things—they describe how generative structures behave. Now such tendencies do not, in general, lead to regularities at the level of events because they will typically be juxtaposed with tendencies of other structures. Thus a breakaway leaf does not fall to the ground in strict conformity with an empirical regularity, for its actual path is influenced by aerodynamic, thermal and other tendencies. Yet its path is still recognised as being subject to the law of fall understood as a tendency, and this explains why the leaf eventually ends up on the ground (when it does). As J. S. Mill put it:

> If indeed every phenomenon was generally the effect of not more than one cause, a knowledge of the law of cause would, unless there was a logical error in our reasoning, enable us confidently to predict all circumstances of the phenomenon . . . Effects [however] are commonly determined by a *concurrence* of causes. If we have overlooked any one cause, we may reason justly from all the others, and only be the further wrong . . .
> . . . [A person's] error generally consists . . . in making the wrong *kind* of assertion: he predicated an actual result, when he should only have predicated a *tendency* to that result—a power acting with a certain intensity in that direction (1844, pp. 160–1).

Or, in the words of J. N. Keynes:

> As a matter of fact, in the instances that actually occur of the operation of a given cause, counteracting

causes sometimes will and sometimes will not be present; and, therefore, laws of causation are to be regarded as statement of tendencies only (1890, p. 218).

On this account, then, experimental activity can be rendered intelligible not as an attempt to effect a law, but as an attempt merely to *identify* it. In other words the objective of experimentation is to intervene in order to isolate a causal mechanism of interest by 'holding off' all other potentially interfering causal mechanisms. The intention is to engineer a closed system in which a one-to-one correspondence between actual outcomes and relevant tendencies can be expected. And, of course, the application of experimentally supported knowledge is an open system—that is outside the conditions of the experimental situation—can also be rendered intelligible through the realisation that, once they are activated, relevant tendencies must necessarily be operative whatever else is going on. Thus, even as I hold a leaf in the palm of my hand, it is subject to the gravitational tendency. The context or milieu under which any mechanism may be operative is not a relevant condition for the laws specification. Once activated the mechanism is operative whatever empirical pattern ensues.

In short, if certain widely accepted features of scientific activity are to be rendered intelligible, the orthodox (empiricist and idealist/rationalist) conception of laws as necessitating a constant conjunction of events should be abandoned. And in place of it, clearly, something like the realist ontology of generative structures and tendencies, that lie behind and govern the flux of observable phenomena, needs to be invoked. On this realist view, the objective is to identify and understand generative structures and the ways in which they can act, in order that events in, and states of affairs of, the world might ultimately be explained.

Social structures and economic analysis

Perhaps some comments need to be made with respect to the possible existence, in the economic sphere, of causal powers and tendencies other than, or in addition to, the powers of human agents. Economists do generally appear to acknowledge human agency as a causal power but often conclude that, because everything that happens in the social world consists of changes in, or brought about by, people, all causal forces are essentially reduceable to individual agency. The point is, of course, that, although dependent on human agency in general, social structures, relations, practices, conventions etc. exist prior to any individual act (at a given point in time and space) and govern it (that is, make a difference to it) by providing limiting and enabling conditions (that are necessary for action to take place). In this sense social structures have causal powers. For example, the highway code, while certainly a social form, exists prior, and is given, to current motorists, and consequently makes a difference to how a person drives from A to B. At the same time, of course, it does not determine the actual trip taken—this conception of generative structures allows the status of human agency to be preserved. Similarly current rules of grammar impose limits upon, and facilitate, speech acts, but do not determine what is said. Usually, numerous different causal structures will bear upon some manifest phenomenon—work-place activities, for example, will be governed by all sorts of norms and conventions as well as male/female, skilled worker/unskilled worker, employer/worker, etc relations. Thus the operation of any given generative structure will be offset by the action of others and is best understood, therefore, as a tendency. But even such a collection of work-place structures as that just noted will not, in combination, determine *all* that goes on—the status of human agency need not be undermined.

Now, as noted, it is true that social structures, in turn, exist only by virtue of human activity, in total. Of course, the contribution of individual agency to the reproduction and transformation of these structures will often (perhaps usually) be unintended, while the bearing that these structures have on individual action will perhaps be only tacitly and incompletely understood—although agents will always have some conception of what they are doing. But the point remains that for any individual action there are social structures that are given to it. In other words, individual agency presupposes social structure just as the latter presupposes individual agency—neither can be reduced to, identified with, or completely explained in terms of, the other. Generative structures, then, whose ways of acting are generally non-empirical (the world is open) and best interpreted as tendencies, are equally at work in the social, as in the natural realm—although, because of their dependence upon human agency, they are likely, amongst other things, to be relatively less enduring than natural tendencies.

3. Theory development and stylised facts

The question yet to be addressed is how analysis proceeds on this realist account, and one issue to be considered specifically here is how Kaldor's notion of stylised facts fits in? For Kaldor the latter concept seems sometimes to be differentiated from, but sometimes conflated with, the notion of a tendency. However, he does usually treat a stylised fact as an empirical claim and with the idea of a tendency now conceptualised as a non-empirical feature of causal structures the notion of a stylised fact has been 'freed-up' to be consistently applied or interpreted as (a conception that is grounded by) some empirical counterpart.

So far it has been argued that, on the realist view, tendencies may be regarded as powers or liabilities of a thing or structure which, because numerous countervailing mechanisms may be operative at the same moment and place, may be exercised without being manifest in the actual economic outcomes. Usually it is only under the sort of closed conditions striven for in experimental situations that a one-to-one correspondence may hold between the exercise of a tendency and its manifestation in actual phenomena. And in economics such a situation typically does not arise. Even so, if certain tendencies or combinations of tendencies are persistently activated over a significant span of time and/or space (or 'time-space'), or if some significant tendencies dominate others, it is not impossible that their effects will be detectable in actual phenomena to some extent. That is, although their effects will frequently be modified or hidden by the operation of irregular countervailing mechanisms and so forth, their persistency coupled with the irregular operation of the countervailing influences may allow their effects to 'shine through'. Thus, to the extent that any manifest phenomenon appears to reveal some degree of uniformity, generality, or persistency, albeit by no means complete in such respects, it would seem to provide a *prima facie* case for supposing that some enduring generative mechanisms are at work. Consequently, such partial regularities—with completely irregular details ignored—are often essential for initiating searches for operative causal mechanisms. And conceptualisations of such partial regularities, of course, are the obvious candidates for representation as 'stylised facts'.

On this view, then, a stylised fact is a conceptualised phenomenon—typically a broad but not universal generalisation about an event regularity—that is interpreted to hold in a way, or to a degree, such that the researcher regards as significant enough, given the context, that *prima facie* an explanation is called for.[1] Thus, to use Kaldor's own examples,

[1] Or, perhaps just as importantly, an exception to such an observed generality may also indicate that some particular causal mechanism of interest is at work, or at least that some explanation is required (see, for example, Lawson, 1981).

a stylised fact may be of the *form*: 'UK productivity growth is usually less than that of otherwise comparable industrial economies'; or 'when output increases in industrial economies so too do *both* employment and productivity'; or 'over different economies the variation in the capital/output ratio is significantly less than the variation in the capital/labour ratio;[1] or 'productivity is procyclical'; and so on. And such 'facts', once identified, can give rise to searches for causal explanations. Now it is clearly this procedure of moving from stylised facts to the search for causal explanations that typifies much of Kaldor's later 'applied' work. Thus he writes:

when we say, for example, that in the course of economic growth the profit rate or the capital/output ratio tends to remain constant, or that productivity varies procyclically whereas the variation in real wages is neither procyclical nor anticyclical, we do not imply that any of these 'facts' are invariably true in every conceivable instance but that they are true in the broad majority of observed cases—in a sufficient number of cases to call for an explanation that would account for them (Kaldor, 1985, p. 9).[2]

The significance of the notion of a stylised fact in this framework, then, is that it may often provide a starting point for the analysis of enduring structures and mechanisms. In short, stylised facts can provide an access to enduring things as indications of possible manifestations of the effects of (possibly a combination of) causal tendencies. As such, stylised facts have a significant role in the realist framework, as marking a point of entry.

Theory development

Perhaps it will be objected, here, that by starting with a 'stylised' view of economic events or manifest phenomena, we are accepting a pre-conceived idea of, and therefore unnecessarily committing ourselves to the possibility of a false or inadequate conceptualisation of, the particular phenomenon of interest.[3] Several points can be noted. The first is the—at first glance, perhaps, apparently unrelated—observation (already touched upon above) that all forms of social activity presuppose certain given materials to work on. This reliance upon an existing 'heritage', in fact, is explicitly acknowledged by Kaldor—in an elucidation of what can be considered as truly exogenous at a given point in time:

The only truly exogenous factor is *whatever exists at a given moment of time*, as a heritage of the past. This includes all material things, whether the products of nature, or man, or a combination of them, i.e., all forms of capital, as embodied in building, factories, or machines; the available supply of labour—workers, managers, scientists, with all kinds of qualifications and skill. All these in existence at the present moment, the heritage of all past history, determine what can be produced or created in the immediate future, say in the next day, and that, together with what exists now, determines the range of alternatives for the day after, and so on. Taking the very near future, anything that can be produced is determined, or rather limited, by the heritage of the past: the stocks of flour at the hands of

[1] Thus Kaldor (1985, p. 67) writes of 'one of the best established "stylised facts" of capitalist development: that while the capital/labour ratio is rising more or less in proportion to productivity, and it is highest amongst the richest nations and lowest among the poorest, the capital/output ratio is much the same as between poor and rich countries—it is no higher in America . . . than it is in India'.

[2] And elsewhere Kaldor (1966B, 1978A, p. 100) observes: 'One of the basic economic facts which has increasingly entered into national consciousness is the relatively slow rate of economic growth of Britain. Thanks to the work of various international organisations, there is now ample material on the comparative growth records of different countries, and in such comparisons Britain appears almost invariably near the bottom of the league tables . . .
. . . As these facts become more generally known, the minds of our economists and men of affairs, and the public generally, have become increasingly preoccupied with finding the basic cause, or causes, of this phenomenon.'

[3] It appears, in fact, sometimes to be supposed or intimated that any use of such a conception reflects suspect or questionable intent.

the bakers today will determine the bread that can be produced tomorrow. The heritage of the past is the one truly exogenous factor . . . (Kaldor, 1985, p. 61).

Implicit in this statement, then, is a transformational view of social activity. Indeed it follows that, since human activity can usually be thought of as work on, and the transformation of, some given objects, transformational activities represent the sort of manifest phenomena of social life that economics sets itself to explain. But the significant point to emphasise here, of course, is that this transformational view of human activity is no less relevant for scientific analysis, including economics. All analysis must start somewhere, with some materials to work on—with some given stock of theories, methods, hypotheses and facts, etc. A recognition of this necessity facilitates an avoidance of the reductionist illusion, typically associated with empiricist (and also with some rationalist) accounts, of believing it to be possible to obtain some absolute and immutable foundations for knowledge through something like perception, intuition or direct experience alone (see Lawson, 1987 on this). Some degree of epistemological relativeness then is always involved—knowledge has both an absolute and a relative dimension (Bradley, 1914; Eaton, 1965; Sayers, 1985; Lawson, 1987). In the first instance (for any social science) the social activity in question will be conceptualised (albeit possibly inadequately) by the relevant agents concerned—as the hermeneutic tradition has continually emphasised. Specific economists, however, will usually be confronted with theoretical redescriptions of these individual experiences—both as produced through the work of 'data collectors' and through the labours of other economists and social scientists in general. Now the point is that there is scope for criticism and redevelopment whatever the level of conceptualisation and redescription, and this, in itself, does not obviate the claim that 'stylised facts', while obviously pre-conceptualised, can mark a relevant point to begin the analysis. Perhaps the first step will *usually* involve some redefinition of the activities and categories involved—what, after all, is typically meant by skilled labour, semi-skilled work, industrial decline, capital, unemployment and so forth? But to acknowledge this possibility, while it clearly suggests that scientific activity must be a demanding process of human labour, is only to be fallibilist about knowledge—which Kaldor clearly was[1]—which is part and parcel of being realist about events and causal things. In short, then, stylised facts may indeed provide a useful point of entry for analysis. The observation that claims about social phenomena are stylised does not, in itself, indicate capricious or suspect, etc. intent on the part of the conceptualiser—although, to repeat, as with all conceptualisations, stylised facts may be susceptible to immediate conceptual criticism.

Modes of inference

A remaining issue to address here is the mode of inference whereby generative structures or mechanisms are 'inferred' from a conceptualisation of some social phenomenon—or stylised fact—in question. Kaldor, to some extent, obscured this issue by arguing for the superiority of induction over deduction, or by asserting the 'subordination' of the latter to the former. Of course, induction and deduction are both necessary to realist analysis although each alone is insufficient. The essential moment of realist analysis, the movement

[1] Thus Kaldor's own reasons for never having attempted to provide a systematic or comprehensive statement of his views was that 'I have never felt that one's understanding of economic processes has reached a stage where it is no longer liable to radical revision and development in the light of new experience' (Kaldor, 1978B, p. xxix).

from a conceptualisation of some manifest phenomenon to a hypothesis about the possible structures which give rise to or govern it, is one neither of induction nor deduction, and is captured by Kaldor only in his reference to 'the "as if method"' involving the construction of 'a hypothesis that could account for these "stylised facts" . . .' (1961, 1978A, p. 2). In fact several terms exist in recent literature to denote this style of inference. The Aristotelean expression for this mode of inference has been translated as abduction (Peirce, 1867; Institutionalists); as retroduction (Peirce, 1867; Hanson, 1958; McMullin, 1984), and it seems also to be referred to as ontological imputation (Quine, 1953; Bausor, 1987) and, in relevant situations, also retrodiction (Bhaskar, 1978). Some discussion on what is involved with this form of inference—which following recent contributions in the philosophy of science I shall term retroduction—is taken up in the following section. At this stage, it is necessary merely to note that Kaldor's opposing of induction to deduction serves as a distraction from the type of inference most central to the analysis. As Peirce (vol. V, 146) puts it:

> [Induction] never can originate any idea whatever. No more can deduction. All the ideas of science come to it by the way of Abduction. Abduction consists in studying facts and devising a theory to explain them. Its only justification is that if we are ever to understand things at all, it must be in that way. Abductive and inductive reasoning are utterly irreducible, either to the other or to Deduction, or Deduction to either of them . . .

In sum, on the realist view, science is concerned with enduring structures, with what kinds of things there are and with what they tend to do. It is by reference to these that the flux of phenomena can be explained. In economics, in particular, such structures may be relatively less enduring. Certainly, once identified, the conditions of their reproduction and transformation will also need to be assessed. But the object of science is above of all to seek structures that do endure to some extent. And if, in the process of coming to understand these structures, a transformational conception of knowledge is necessarily involved, stylised facts, as conceived above, can play a contributory role, by providing a point of entry.

4. Abstraction and realist analysis

For the realist, then, the object of science is to come to grips with the generative mechanisms, with the ways of acting of relatively enduring economic structures, that govern the flux of economic phenomena that we experience. The next question is how does abstraction fit into the picture? As noted above, in an open system observed phenomena will typically be governed by numerous, often countervailing, causal tendencies, and so must first be resolved into their separate causal components. At the same time most economic structures or entities that give rise to or govern such phenomena will also be complex things possessing an ensemble of tendencies, liabilities and so forth. In this context, then, abstraction has a straightforward interpretation that is quite consistent with its traditional one of looking at something in a one-sided manner—of focussing on certain aspects of something to the neglect of others. On this realist view abstractions are made both in the initial analysis of economic phenomena and in the examination of mechanisms which give rise to them. If economic phenomena are conjuncturally determined they can be resolved into their causal components; that is resolved into the different effects of various causal mechanisms. To isolate one or a few such components is to abstract from the original phenomenon. Economic structures too can be abstracted by isolating certain powers or tendencies possessed amongst others. In each case, the abstraction achieved is intended to be *real*—it is not ideal, a convenient fiction, or some such. The aim is to obtain knowledge of *real* structures or mechanisms which give rise to or govern the flux of *real* phenomena of social and economic life.

That which is abstracted *from*—whether conjuncturally determined events or economic structures/systems etc. with causal powers—is the *concrete*. The concrete is a combination of diverse features, components or determinations etc. The point of abstraction is to isolate or individuate these components or attributes and their relationships in order to come to understand them (better). Once such abstractions have been successfully achieved they can then be synthesised into a unity that re-constitutes the concrete, although at this point more clearly and essentially understood. Ultimately then the concrete can be understood as a synthesis.[1]

Now Kaldor refers to forms of abstraction that are not appropriate (1961, 1978A, p. 2); that are the 'wrong kind' (1975, 1978A, p. 202); that are 'highly artificial' (1985, p. 13), and so on. But when exactly a form of abstraction is appropriate, or of the right kind, or non-artificial, rather than the converse, is not something that Kaldor elaborates upon. From the realist point of view set out above, however, some kind of guiding or necessary principles can now, I suggest, be set down. Thus from the realist perspective:

(a) for an abstraction to be appropriate (in the sense of non artificial)—or for a conception to be appropriately termed an abstraction—it must be concerned with the real rather than some ideal, or convenient fiction;

(b) for an abstraction to be appropriate (in the sense of the right kind) it must be concerned with the essential rather than merely the most general.

These suggested 'principles' are now considered in turn.

The abstraction as real

The view that abstraction is concerned with isolating that which is real follows straightforwardly from the account set out above. Realism, by definition, involves a commitment to identifying that which exists. Thus abstractions obtained are held to obtain not only in thought but also in the real world. Thus retroduction—the mode of inference from manifest phenomenon to possible causes—represents an attempt to identify the real, if abstracted, structure or set of structures that actually governs the phenomenon in question. Now retroduction by itself may well lead to a plurality of hypothesises of possible causal mechanisms—if there is one possible explanation consistent with the relevant aspect of the manifest phenomenon in question there will usually be others. Thus, and as noted above, the elimination of some of the various contending hypotheses must now ensue until only one remains—empirically justified through the explanatory power of the hypotheses that can be deduced from it. In other words, the reality of any posited structure or mechanism must itself be subject to empirical scrutiny. In turn, the conditions supporting an identified generative mechanism need also to be examined and explained, and so on. In short, although the mechanism ultimately identified is an abstraction, the intention is that it should be real for all that.

[1] As Marx (1973, p. 101) argues the 'concrete is concrete because it is the concentration of many determinations, hence unity of the diverse. It appears in the process of thinking, therefore, as a process of concentration, as a result, not as a point of departure, even though it is a point of departure in reality and hence also the point of departure for observation [Anschauung] and conception'.

Although this account of abstraction follows easily from a realist perspective, it represents an interpretation that appears to be in sharp contrast to the way the term is usually used in mainstream economics in general. According to the latter, the process of abstraction seems mainly to mean something like forming artificial constructs, or fictionalising. Friedman's (1953) well known methodological essay, at least in certain places, provides a case in point. Thus Friedman sets up an 'abstract model' (p. 24) which posits consciously deliberating, 'rapidly or instantaneously' mobile, sunlight-maximising, leaves as a putative mechanism to explain the (obviously stylised) phenomenon of a greater density of leaves on the (sunnier) southern sides of trees. Clearly, if we did not know the constructed hypothesis to be false—the mechanism posited to be fictitious—Friedman's reasoning could be considered a valid form of retroduction. Certainly the phenomenon in question—the greater density of leaves on the sunnier side of trees—appears, at first sight, to be broadly consistent with the hypothesis, so that the latter could, perhaps, explain why the observed pattern of leaves arises. But on the realist account, as noted, the reality of the posited mechanism must now be further checked. Its explanatory power, or ability to illuminate a range of empirical phenomena, must be examined, and eventually the identified mechanism itself must be explained in terms of other causal mechanisms. Now Friedman's attitude towards such matters is clearly very different. Suppose, for example, that some phenomenon for which the hypothesis bears implications cannot be explained by the hypothesis. Suppose, say, that the sunnier side of a tree is trimmed, but that the remaining leaves fail to adjust 'rapidly or instantaneously' to the newly-created spare positions. For the realist this would be reason to question the hypothesis. For Friedman, however, it seems clear that the causal mechanisms that actually govern the density of leaves is not at issue, for the sort of contradictory observation just noted is to be treated as merely indicative of qualifications that must be appended to the hypothesis—the object being (as Friedman notes in the context of a further example) to specify the conditions in which the hypothesis is found to hold:

> The important problem in connection with the hypothesis is to specify the circumstances under which the formula works [or empirical regularity holds] or, more precisely, the general magnitude of the error in the predictions under various circumstances. Indeed, . . . such a specification is not one thing and the hypothesis another. The specification is itself an essential part of the hypothesis, and it is a part that is peculiarly likely to be revised and extended as experience accumulates (Friedman, 1953, p. 18).

And what about further checking the reality of the posited mechanism through examining the structures which, in turn, govern it? In other words, what is Friedman's attitude to the issue of trying to understand the structures which govern the 'deliberating' and 'seeking' capacities of leaves? Once again Friedman rules out such endeavours by stipulating that his supposedly abstract conception is only to be assessed as empirically adequate with reference to a certain set or *class of phenomena*—in this case with those associations that the hypothesis was explicitly designed to entail:

> Is the hypothesis rendered unacceptable or invalid because so far as we know, leaves do not 'deliberate' or consciously 'seek', have not been to school and learned the relevant laws of science or the mathematics required to calculate the 'optimum' position, and cannot move from position to position? Clearly, none of these contradictions of the hypothesis is vitally relevant; the phenomena involved are not within the 'class of phenomena the hypothesis is designed to explain'; the hypothesis does not assert that leaves do these things but only that their density is the same *as if* they did. Despite the apparent falsity of the 'assumptions' of the hypothesis, it has great plausibility because of the conformity of its implications with observations (Friedman, 1953, p. 20).

In short, real abstractions are not the objective. For Friedman no independent or further assessment of any merely 'as if' hypothesis is being sought over and above its consistency with a typically very restricted set of phenomena that itself falls within an already restricted 'class of phenomena' that the hypothesis is explicitly designed to entail. (See Lawson (1989) for a fuller discussion.)

Now perhaps not all theorising in mainstream economics is as restrictive as this—or so explicitly so. Nevertheless, economic analysis abounds with acknowledged artificial constructs and even fictions (e.g. universal perfect competition, rational expectations, perfect foresight, etc) which play consequential roles in supposed explanatory contexts.[1] As such, the conclusions to be drawn concerning the limitations for serious analysis of theories positing such constructions are essentially just the same. For the realist, the construction of fictions is to be avoided. The object, through abstraction, is instead to identify the *real* causal mechanisms and necessary relations that govern the flux of *real* phenomena of the economic and social world.

Abstracting the essential

The second suggested 'principle'—that abstraction is concerned with identifying that which is essential rather than merely most general—also follows easily from the sketch of realism so far set out. Realism is concerned with the identification and understanding of real structures and mechanisms that govern some phenomenon of interest. The aim is to identify connections and relations essential to the existence and efficacy of some structure of interest—to gauge the stratification and internal complexity of some significant entity. The aim, as Sayer (1984, p. 126) puts it, is to obtain an abstraction 'which isolates a significant element of the world which has some unity and autonomous force, such as a structure'. (And, if certain structures generating social phenomena combine in a 'system'—involving organic totalities of intra-acting structures or externally related interacting ones—then an abstraction, to be adequate, must both identify any necessary connections and avoid isolating a necessary relation from others essental to its existence.)

Now a widely subscribed to alternative approach, in economics, aims instead to seek formal relations of similarity, rather than to abstract the essential. As Dobb (1937, 1972, p. 40), distancing himself from this alternative approach, says of it, the aim is to base 'abstraction, not on any evidence of fact as to what features in a situation are essential and what are inessential, but simply on the formal procedure of combining the properties common to a heterogeneous assortment of situations and building abstraction out of analogy'. Of course, generality of some kind is also a realist objective[2]—to determine non-empirical invariances at the 'deeper' level of necessary relations and tendencies of things. These, however, are unlikely to be uncovered just by adopting the aim of seeking broad generalisations. As Dobb concludes, what this form of 'abstraction gains in breadth it more than loses, as it were, in depth—in relevance to the particular situations which are the focus of interest' (1937, 1972, p. 40).

[1] Thus, in connection with the rational expectations hypothesis, for example, Minford and Peel (1981, p. 3) assert: 'The rational expectations view has been widely criticized as "unrealistic", "not how people behave . . ." The answer is clear: *of course* it is unrealistic, it is meant to be. It is a very powerful assumption for generating predictions. This one assumption is a rich source of restrictions in economic models. The criticism is quite simply irrelevant.'

[2] In Sayer's (1984, p. 218) words: 'Abstraction seeks necessary relations, conditions and properties and does not expect to find successful generalizations at the concrete level; but in abstracting *from* particular contingencies that co-determine particular concrete objects, they inevitably produce a conception characterized by generality'.

It is a characteristic of economic structures, for example, that much of what is essential to the explaining of a form of human activity is highly context-related. Thus, through a process of seeking merely wide generalisations, economic structures can easily be emptied of their context-related, but often essential, content. The employer-worker relationship, for example, may be identified as a transhistorical, pancultural feature of human society. But this observation, in itself, abstracts from the numerous variations in the nature of this relationship across time and space, and it is certainly insufficient, for example, to any understanding or explanation of work practices and activities that exist at a specific stage of human evolution in any particular region or place. Similarly, to note such generalities as that humans have preferences, or beliefs, or the ability to make choices, is to provide insufficient detail of these generative structures or causal powers for explaining any form of human activity they govern.[1]

Now perhaps the greatest danger of seeking merely broad generalisations, of pushing the abstractions so far that they are almost devoid of substantive content, arises from the fact that they then need to be supplemented by other propositions in order to have any explanatory value; for this opens the door to the inclusion of 'highly artificial' or 'bogus abstractions', to the sort of convenient fictions already noted above. In other words, almost contentless abstractions can easily, if unwittingly, be manipulated or 'strengthened' in illegitimate ways to yield conceptions that really are no longer abstractions at all. In orthodox or mainstream economics, for example, such 'assumptions', which may creep in unnoticed, are usually designed to achieve mathematical tractability, system closure or some such thing, rather than an understanding of the real causal mechanisms at work. Now if the original abstractions alone possess little explanatory content then it is the additional 'strengthening' assumptions that do all the work and determine the upshot. And a failure to appreciate this can lead either to an unthinking and erroneous presumption that these assumptions can eventually be replaced with accounts of essential aspects of real generative mechanisms without the whole construction collapsing entirely, or to a misguided attempt to extract more meaning from the constructions than can possibly be legitimate. The latter, again, is a point that Dobb (1937, 1972, p. 41) has emphasised:

> There is the danger of introducing, unnoticed, purely imaginary or even contradictory assumptions and in general of ignoring how limited a meaning the corollaries deducible from these abstract propositions must have and the qualifications which the presence of other concrete factors (which may be major influences in this or that particular situations) may introduce. All too frequently the propositions which are products of this mode of abstraction have little more than formal meaning and at most tell one that an expression for such-and-such a relation must find a place in any of one's equational systems. But those who use such propositions and build corollories upon them are seldom mindful of this limitation and in applying them as 'laws' of the real world invariably extract from them more meaning than their emptiness of real content can possibly hold.

[1] Thus Dobb (1937, 1972, p. 71) notes that if all that is postulated is simply that people '*choose*, without anything being stated even as to how they choose or what governs their choice, it would seem impossible for economics to provide us with any more than a sort of algebra of human choice, indicating certain rather obvious forms of interrelationship between choices, but telling us little as to the way in any situation we behave' (p. 71). (Of course, broad generalisations as descriptions of some manifest economic phenomenon can be useful as marking sites for analysis to begin—indeed this is the rationale for the notion of stylised facts noted above. But such generalisations will typically not be useful as explanatory devices, as statements of economic causes. As Dobb again observes, if 'an economic law is a statement of what actually tends to happen and not a mere statement of a relation between certain implicitly defined variables, then such propositions [as result from such high level abstractions] can surely be precious little guide to the "laws of motion of capitalist society"—or, indeed, to any of the other matters on which they are intended to pass an economic judgement' (p. 42).

In sum, on the realist view, while abstract and concrete analysis always, in practice, accompany each other, abstract analysis is primarily concerned with attempting to understand real causal objects at their own level of being, in terms of their constitutive structures and causal powers, while concrete analysis is an endeavour to examine how the relevant abstractions combine. In this, abstraction is concerned with the real rather than the ideal or fictitious, and with what is essential in any situation rather than what is merely the most general. On this view, abstraction represents a way of understanding some domain of reality rather than a device for avoiding such endeavour. And in this it involves both theory and empirical observation as equally vital elements in the same scientific process.

5. Realism and economic theory

Finally, it is now possible to bring relevant features of the realist approach to bear briefly upon what became Kaldor's favourite target of criticism:[1] formal economic theory in general, including, and indeed as exemplified by, General Equilibrium Theory, in particular; and to examine, from this realist perspective at least, to what extent Kaldor's numerous assertions can be explained and justified. It is, of course, impossible to provide a complete and uncontentious statement of what economic theory consists of here. However, an important, informative and unusually explicit account of the sort of reasoning that is involved has recently been set out by Hahn (1985) in his Jevon's Memorial Fund Lecture, entitled 'In Praise of Economic Theory', and it is this account that will be mainly considered.[2]

[1] It must be born in mind that although Kaldor always perceived his work to be concerned with relevance—with dealing with real world problems, concerns and issues—the more empirically orientated approach examined above only came about gradually during the post-war period. Prior to that Kaldor himself had been significantly concerned with an approach which implicitly emphasised mainly deductive reasoning starting from highly abstract macroeconomic formulations. His change in methodological approach is perhaps most noticeable on comparing the two papers on Growth both published in 1966 (Kaldor, 1966A, 1978A, 1966B, 1978A). In connection with the first of these papers (1966A) Kaldor was later to observe: 'This paper marked the last of a series of theoretical papers on growth theory which proceeded by way of deductive reasoning from macroeconomic axioms of a rather general character. In my subsequent work I followed a different method: I tried to find what kind of regularities can be detected in empirically observed phenomena and then tried to discover what particular testable hypotheses would be capable of explaining the association. I became aware of this more pragmatic approach during the war when it was used by scientists for the purpose of "operational research". It is an approach which in one sense is more modest in scope (in not searching for explanations that derive from a comprehensive model of the system) and also more ambitious in that is directly aims at discovering solutions (or remedies) for real problems' (Kaldor, 1978A, p. xvii).

[2] It is not, of course, even possible to consider here the different historical conceptions of General Equilibrium Theory, although it seems that in each case the sort of issues considered above are highly relevant. Walras, for example, raises the issue of whether his assumptions—such as 'pure competition'—are abstractions or fictions; Jaffe (1980, p. 533) interprets them as 'ideal fictions'; while Walker (1984, p. 467) views them as abstractions. And whatever the realist pretentions of early General Equilibrium Theory, these were largely liberated by Hicks (1939) and Samuelson (1945). And in its more recent development by Debreu (1959) it has supposedly become 'logically entirely disconnected from its interpretations' (p. 5). Thus on this latter view General Equilibrium Theory has been radically emptied of any remaining empirical content. Interpretations are merely to be tagged on after a formal framework has been derived. As Ingrao and Israel (1985, p. 92) observe in their detailed historical study: the 'concepts of the theory are no longer understood as the outcome of a process of abstracting from real phenomena nor as the formalisation of ideas and knowledge relating to a phenomenon . . . Nor do they need empirical verification to prove their validity'. Now the idea that the formal structure of an economy can be entirely disconnected from any interpretations of it seems problematic, and Arrow and Hahn (1971) amongst others have rejected this position and instead interpreted the theory as a formalisation of the 'invisible hand'. Clearly there are many differences involved here in the various accounts. Indeed as the theory has changed, so too have the mathematical methods—shifting from methods of infinitesimal calculus to convex set theory and topological techniques. Even so the *sort* of issues considered and comments set out above would seem to be of relevance throughout.

According to Hahn, economic theorising attempts 'to gain understanding of the particular by reference to generalising insights and in the light of certain abstract unifying principles' (p. 3). Interestingly, the reference to 'understanding' in this phrase is in part intended to indicate that, like the realist, Hahn perceives economic analysis to be 'not directly related to positivist prediction' (p. 3). An equally interesting part of this phrase, however, is the reference to 'abstract unifying principles' or 'abstractions' for short. Hahn proceeds to label these as 'axioms' and to distinguish them from assumptions. The difference between axioms and assumptions is that the former, but not the latter, are thought to be claims about the real world that are universally agreed upon:

> Axioms are not plucked out of thin air and far from distancing the theorists from what somewhat mysteriously is called the 'real' world they constitute claims about this world so widely agreed as to make further argument unnecessary (p. 5).

Now the axioms that Hahn cites, like, for example, 'agents have preferences', are so general as to fall into the category, noted above, of relatively contentless abstractions. As such, they may indeed be widely held as true, and may even be uncontentious. As Kaldor (1972), notes: 'Taken at its purest and most abstract level the pretentions of this equilibrium theory are modest enough' (p. 176). The problem, of course, is that because these axioms are effectively devoid of content very little can be explained by them alone. For the realist, any move from the abstract to the concrete always involves empirical study, as different abstractions are combined and synthesised in the light of knowledge of contingent relations and conditions. But for the practitioner of 'economic theory' the axioms, instead, are to be 'idealized and strengthened' through the addition of extra formal 'assumptions' (Hahn, 1985, p. 7). And, as noted above, if relatively contentless abstractions are combined with powerful assumptions it is the latter that do much of the work. And a significant and consequential feature of economic theory is that the additional assumptions that tend to be made can be regarded as no more than convenient fictions. Consider the examples mentioned by Hahn:

> That people have preferences and try to satisfy them we treat as an axiom while universal perfect competition, for instance, must count as an assumption (p. 10).

> That managers have preferences is an axiom; that they take a particular form, for instance that they are linear in expected profit, is an assumption . . . (p. 11).

> If you want more out you have to put more in, that is you must supplement the axioms with assumptions, e.g. that production functions are Cobb Douglas (p. 13).

Clearly assumptions such as universal perfect competition, linear expected profit functions, Cobb–Douglas production functions, etc. are not intended to capture the mode of operation of real economic mechanisms—indeed they appear, in the main, to be designed merely to achieve mathematical tractability. To put it mildly, and as Hahn on occasion acknowledges, '. . . at the end we shall have to agree that the genuine axiom: persons have some preferences, has been idealised and strengthened by theorists beyond the point at which it commands universal consent' (1985, p. 7).

Now it should be clear that economic theory, so conceived, has little to commend itself to the realist. Hahn, more astute than most economic theory practitioners, expressly acknowledges this, observing that for 'economic theory' the 'aim is not realism' but to understand where it is that the axioms and assumptions that are made logically lead (p. 13). And to the extent that the axioms are almost contentless, to repeat, it is the additional assumptions that do most of the leading. A failure to appreciate this point, however, easily gives rise to the two, apparently widespread, errors already noted above. Thus, first of all, there appears to be a common misconception that, sooner or later, the assumptions can be removed, just as scaffolding is from an otherwise stable construction, leaving the basic results of economic theory intact. This observation, in fact, seems to lie behind a persistent criticism that Kaldor levels at General Equilibrium Theory in particular. Thus, Kaldor writes in this connection:

> The process of removing the 'scaffolding', as the saying goes—in other words of *relaxing* the unreal basic assumptions—has not yet started. Indeed, the scaffolding gets thicker and more impenetrable with every successive reformulation of the theory, with a growing uncertainty as to whether there is a solid building underneath (1972, 1978A, p. 179).

And more than ten years further on Kaldor is still observing the same sort of situation:

> [The] authors [of general equilibrium theory] were motivated by the belief that they were only laying the foundations of an explanation of how a market economy works, an initial stage of the analysis which is in the nature of 'scaffolding': it has to be erected before the permanent building can be built, but will be removed step by step as the permanent building nears completion. However, since Walras first wrote down his system of equations over 100 years ago, progress has definitely been backwards not forwards in the sense that the present set of axioms are far more restrictive than those of the original Walrasian model. The ship is no nearer to the shore, but considerably farther off, though in a logical, mathematical sense, the present system of derived tautologies is enormously superior to Walras's original effort (Kaldor, 1985, p. 13).

And second, associated with a misconstrual of the aims and nature of economic theory, and in particular with a failure to recognise the significant role of assumptions, is a generally held supposition that, because the original, relatively contentless abstractions, or axioms, are intended to capture some domain of reality, the same is also true of the final conception, so that it can therefore be justifiably used for purposes of explanation and policy analysis. Such a supposition, of course, is incorrect. If a general equilibrium, or any other, model is derived in the manner of economic theory, it can be regarded as no more than something like an ideal fiction. It can, of course, be confronted with data and, with suitable qualifications, may even be found to be data-consistent. But this can tell us very little of value. Indeed it tells us no more than what we learn from the example of Friedman's 'deliberating', 'mobile' leaves—that the particular, highly restricted, set of data employed in the relevant exercise are *merely* 'as if' they had been generated according to some version of the particular fiction in question. Or, perhaps more accurately, we should learn that the nature of the data, the criteria of fit, the degrees of freedom in model specification, and so on, are such that a total fiction can be found to 'fit' the specific set of data to hand. We could deduce little more. Certainly such a result does not help us to explain or understand mechanisms or events in the non-equilibrium world in which we live. On this point, in fact, Hahn—in apparent contrast to many other practitioners of economic theory—seems, to a significant extent, to agree:

> [Certain] economists . . . might be taken to be engaged in the following programme: to enquire how far observed events are consistent with an economy which is in continuous Walrasian equilibrium. Such a programme would be of considerable value. For we might find that events which we had explained as due to disequilibrium or indeed to Trade Unions and monopolists could be accounted for without these. That surely would be valuable for understanding. But it would not be true that we understood the events. For we would not understand how continuous equilibrium is possible in a decentralised economy and we do not understand why a world with Trade Unions and monopolies behaves like a perfectly competitive one. Theorising in economics I have argued is an attempt at understanding and I now add that bad theorising is a premature claim to understand.
>
> What has happened in this instance is that 'as if' prediction methodology has taken over. Recall Friedman's example . . . (p. 15).

In sum, the methods of economic theory in general and General Equilibrium Theory in particular *may* have their own rationale even if, as Hahn critically notes, many of their proponents do not carry them through coherently. If a commitment to realism is accepted, however, the whole basic approach seems misconceived. In particular, the two 'guiding principles' set out above are neglected. Thus, by starting from that which is merely most general, that which is essential is lost. And by incorporating a layer of assumptions designed mainly to achieve mathematical tractability, that which is real is emasculated. From this perspective, then, the resulting conceptions, as 'abstractions', can indeed be seen, following Kaldor, as 'inappropriate', 'artificial' or the 'wrong kind'.

The useful alternative, as Kaldor repeatedly emphasises, is to start from a stylised conceptualisation of some manifest phenomenon of interest. And to explain the interesting or stylised it is necessary to abstract the real and essential. On this realist view the objective of science, including economics, is to understand those entities or structures whose causal tendencies give rise to or govern the flux of observed states of affairs and events. And on this realist view, abstraction, tendencies and stylised facts comprise significant and coherent features within the general scientific approach.

6. Final comments and conclusion

On the realist view, science, including economics, is concerned with what kinds of things there are and what they are able to do. The aim is to understand relatively enduring structures, their powers and tendencies, by reference to which the phenomena of the world are explained.

Typically, economic structures will be highly complex possessing an ensemble of powers and tendencies. Similarly, empirical phenomena will be the resultant of numerous causal effects. Thus *abstraction* is a necessary feature of coming to grips with significant causal *tendencies*, while *stylised facts* may provide a pointer from which to start.

On this view it is *not* that deduction is 'subordinated' to induction as Kaldor suggests. Both are essential in realist analysis though each alone is insufficient, for retroduction—the movement from manifest phenomena to the causal tendencies or necessary relations that govern them—is also essentially involved. This step involves, amongst others, the methods of analogy and metaphor applied to existing cognitive materials, and the whole enterprise represents a complicated and demanding process of human labour.

The objective, in short, is to abstract the real and the essential, to identify the real enduring generative structures and mechanisms that govern the flux of actual economic and social events. This is an aim that seems highly compatible with most of Kaldor's numerous methodological stipulations and assertions—although it is not, as such, elaborated within them. It is an objective of coming to grips with the world as it is. It is an aim, however, that formal economic theory cannot justifiably accept. And it may well be for this last reason above others that Kaldor's attitude to economic theory was persistently oppositional and frequently dismissive.

Bibliography

Arrow, K. J. and Hahn, F. H. 1971. *General Competitive Analysis*, San Francisco, Holden-Day

Baechler, J. 1971. *Les Origines du capitalisme*, Paris, Gallimard (English translation Oxford, Basil Blackwell, 1975)

Bausor, R. 1987. 'Ontological imputation and the "hard core",' University of Massachusetts, mimeo.

Bhaskar, R. 1978. *A Realist Theory of Science*, Brighton, Harvester Press
Bradley, F. M. 1914. *Essays on Truth and Reality*, Oxford, Clarendon Press
Cartwright, N. 1983. *How the Laws of Physics Lie*, Oxford and New York, Clarendon Press.
Chalmers, A. 1978. *What is This Thing Called Science?* Milton Keynes, Open University Press
Debreu, G. 1959. *Theory of Value: An Axiomatic Analysis of Economic Equilibrium*, Cowles Foundation Monograph No. 17, New York, Yale
Dobb, M. 1937. The trend of modern economics, in *Political Economy and Capitalism*, Routledge & Kegan Paul reprinted in Hurst, E. N. and Schwartz, J. G. 1972. *A Critique of Economic Theory*, Harmondsworth, Penguin Books. Page references are to the latter
Eaton, J. 1965. Some thoughts about mathematical models in relations to economic theory, in *On Political Economy and Econometrics: Essays in Honour of Oskar Lange*, Oxford, Pergamon Press
Friedman, M. 1953. The methodology of positive economics, in *Essays in Positive Economics*, Chicago, University of Chicago Press
Giddens, A. 1976. *New Rules of Sociological Method: a positive critique of interpretative sociologies*, London, Hutchinson
Gregory, D. and Urry, J. 1985. *Social Relations and Spacial Structures*, London, Macmillan
Hacking, I. 1983. *Representing and Intervening: introductory topics in the philosophy of natural science*, Cambridge, CUP
Hahn, F. 1985. *In Praise of Economic Theory*, the 1984 Jevons Memorial Fund Lecture, University College London
Hanson, N. R. 1958. *Patterns of Discovery: An Inquiry into the conceptual foundations of Science*, Cambridge, CUP
Hesse, M. 1974. *The Structure of Scientific Inference*, London, Macmillan
Hicks, J. 1939. *Value and Capital*, Oxford, OUP
Ingrao, B. and Israel, G. 1985. General Equilibrium Theory: a history of ineffectual paradigmatic shifts, *Fundamenta Scientae*, vol. 6, no. 1, pp. 1–45; and vol. 6, no. 2, pp. 89–125
Jaffe, W. 1980. Walras's economics as others see it, *Journal of Economic Literature*, vol. 18, pp. 528–49
Kaldor, N. 1961. Capital accumulation and economic growth, in Lutz, F. (ed.), *The Theory of Capital*, London, Macmillan. Reprinted in Kaldor, 1978A
Kaldor, N. 1966A. Marginal productivity and the macro-economic theories of distribution. *Review of Economic Studies*, vol. XXXIII, no. 4. Reprinted in Kaldor, 1978A
Kaldor, N. 1966B. *Causes of the Slow Rate of Economic Growth in the United Kingdom*, Cambridge, CUP. Reprinted in Kaldor, 1978A
Kaldor, N. 1972. The irrelevance of equilibrium economics, *Economic Journal*, vol. 82, pp. 1237–1255. Reprinted in Kaldor, 1978A
Kaldor, N. 1975. What is wrong with economic theory, *Quarterly Journal of Economics*. Reprinted in Kaldor, 1978A
Kaldor, N. 1978A. *Further Essays on Economic Theory*, London, Duckworth
Kaldor, N. 1978B. *Further Essays on Applied Economics*, London, Duckworth
Kaldor, N. 1985. *Economics Without Equilibrium*, University College Cardiff Press
Keohane, R. O. 1986. *Neorealism and its Critics*, New York, Columbia University Press
Keynes, J. N. 1890. *The Scope and Method of Political Economy*, London, Macmillan. Page references are to the 4th edition, published in 1930
Lawson, T. 1981. Paternalism and labour market segmentation theory, in Wilkinson, S. F. (ed.), *Dynamics of Labour Market Segmentation*, London, Academic Press
Lawson, T. 1987. The relative/absolute nature of knowledge and economic analysis, *Economic Journal*, vol. 97
Lawson, T. 1989. 'Realism, Closed Systems and Freidman' mimeo, Cambridge University
Leplin, J. (ed.) 1984. *Scientific Realism*, University of California Press
Levy, D. J. 1981. *Realism: an essay in interpretation and social reality*, Carcanet, Manchester
McMullin, E. 1984. A case for scientific realism, in Leplin, J. (ed.) (1984)
Marshall, A. 1890. *Principles of Economics*, 9th variorum edn, London, Macmillan for the Royal Economic Society
Marx, K. 1973. *Grundrisse: Foundations of a Critique of Political Economy* (translated by Nicolaus, M.), Penguin Books in association with New Left Review

Mill, J. S. 1844. *Essays on Some Unsettled Questions of Political Economy*, London, J. W. Parker
Minford, P. and Peel, D. 1981. Is the Government's Economic Strategy on Course?, *Lloyds Bank Review*
Peirce, C. S. 1867. In Hartshorne, C. and Weiss, P. (eds) *Collected Papers of Charles Sanders Peirce*, Cambridge, Mass., Harvard University Press
Popper, K. R. 1965. *Conjectures and Refutations: The Growth of Scientific Knowledge*, New York, Harper and Row
Quine, W. Van O. 1953. On what there is, in *From a Logical Point of View* Cambridge, Mass., Harvard University Press
Samuelson, P. 1945. *Foundations of Economic Analysis*, Cambridge, Mass., Harvard University Press
Sayer, A. 1984. *Method in Social Science: A Realist Approach*, London, Hutchinson
Sayers, S. 1985. *Reality and Reason*, Oxford, Basil Blackwell
Walker, D. A. 1984. Is Walras's theory of general equilibrium a normative scheme? *History of Political Economy*, vol. 16, no. 3
Walras, L. 1874. *Elements d'économie politique pure*, Lausanne, Corbaz, reprinted 4th Edition, Rouge, Lausanne, 1901, English translation: *Elements of Pure Economics*. London, George Allen & Unwin, 1954

Institutional rigidities and economic growth

Geoff Hodgson*

If we object that . . . historicizing, psychologizing and sociologizing are not the business of economics, then we must conclude that the objector thinks that long-term growth theory is not the business of economics. Herbert Simon (1984).

One of Nicholas Kaldor's most notable contributions to economic science is his theory of growth, initially developed to explain the relatively poor performance of the UK economy (Kaldor, 1966). Whilst modifications were made to this argument in the light of debate,[1] his enduring thesis was that differing national growth rates were to be explained by processes of cumulative causation based on 'increasing returns to scale', with the manufacturing sector as 'the engine of growth' (see, e.g. Kaldor, 1972, 1975A, 1985).

Briefly, Kaldor argued that manufacturing output growth promotes further growth in manufacturing productivity and productivity in the economy as a whole. In addition, growing manufacturing productivity helps to promote exports, further stimulating manufacturing output, as well as shifting the balance of payments constraint. This feedback closes a loop and provides a rationale for the notion of cumulative change. Furthermore, as the manufacturing sector grows in absolute terms, in its relative importance in the economy as a whole, and in its average level of productivity, it is deduced that both output and productivity will grow for the entire economy.

Despite the fact that much evidence has been marshalled in its support (see Thirlwall, 1983), Kaldor's theory has not found universal favour. At least two alternative theories have been proposed. The first is the theory of technological diffusion, proposed by Stanislaw Gomulka (1971, 1979). According to this idea, productivity growth is a function of the varying rates of diffusion of technology from lead to laggard nations,

*Newcastle upon Tyne Polytechnic. The author wishes to thank Dick Bailey, Ha-Joon Chang, Mike Dietrich, Robert Gausden, Ian Gough, Neil Kay, Tony Lawson, Lars Mjoset, Richard Nelson, Steven Pressman, Bob Rowthorn, Brian Snowdon, Ian Steedman, Tony Thirlwall, Arthur Walker, Grahame Wright, Nancy Wulwick and two anonymous referees for comments on earlier drafts and other invaluable assistance.

[1] After criticism from Wolfe (1968), Kaldor (1968) retracted his (1966, 1967) view that 'inelasticity in the supply of labour', due to a comparatively rapid and early exhaustion of the supply of labour power from the rural hinterland, was the 'main constraint' limiting the growth potential of the UK economy. Subsequently he was to put greater 'emphasis on the exogenous components of demand, and in particular on the role of exports, in determining the trend rate of productivity growth' (Kaldor, 1975B, p. 896). On this issue see Thirlwall (1978, 1979, 1983).

depending in turn on the 'technological gap' involved. Explicitly rejected by Kaldor (1975A), but viewed more sympathetically by John Cornwall (1976, 1977), Bob Rowthorn (1975A), Bernard Stafford (1981) and others, this alternative theory has been supported by some econometric evidence.

A second alternative can be found in the recent work of the American neo-Marxists Samuel Bowles, David Gordon and Thomas Weisskopf (1985) and their 'social' explanation of the slow growth of productivity of the US economy, again with supportive econometric tests. We are thus faced with an unresolved dispute of central importance both for economic theory and policy.

It will be suggested below that all these rival approaches point to unresolved problems in the underlying theory of the production process. An examination of the theoretical foundations of the different analyses reveals several flaws and suggests a search for a different framework. Fortunately, a promising alternative paradigm has already begun to emerge, based on the work of several economic theorists and historians, which suggests that growth and development are affected by inherited institutional structures and social practices. Whilst faults are found in parts of Kaldor's theory, the emerging alternative endorses some conclusions which are similar to his.

The following section of this article involves a critical discussion of the contending theories. Section 2 introduces an alternative approach with an empirical test of the type of theory that it implies. A conclusion is that an institutionalist model, based on indices of institutional flexibility or rigidity, is at least as successful, in both theoretical and empirical terms, as other available theories.

1. Foundations of the different analyses

Cumulative causation and increasing returns

At the core of Kaldor's analysis of economic growth is the idea of economic success breeding economic success, and failure breeding failure—or the 'survival of the fastest'. This is, of course, a direct challenge to the equilibrium theorising of orthodoxy, where it is often supposed that the market economy contains self-righting mechanisms to bring recovery from any downturn, and an effective price mechanism to compensate for imbalances in development. This central methodological difference accounts in part for the reluctance of orthodox theorists to embrace Kaldor's arguments.

Kaldor acknowledged two major influences on his formulation of this principle of cumulative causation. The first was the work of the institutionalist Gunnar Myrdal,[1] who initially formulated a model of cumulative causation in his *Monetary Equilibrium*, (published in Swedish in 1931) and repeated the idea in his classic studies of racial discrimination (1944) and of uneven regional development (1957).[2]

The second influence was an article by the American economist Allyn Young (1928). Emphasising that economic change 'propagates itself in a cumulative way' (p. 533), Young based this conclusion on the notion of increasing returns to scale. Kaldor seized upon this

[1] Myrdal himself dates his conversion to institutionalism from after the Second World War (Myrdal, 1978). Veblen argued as early as 1898 that the economic process should be viewed in terms of 'cumulative causation' (Veblen, 1919, pp. 64–70). Institutional economists (for example, Kapp, 1976) have typically stressed cumulative causation as an alternative to equilibrium theorising.

[2] As Shackle (1967) has argued, Myrdal's *Monetary Equilibrium* has extensive parallels with Keynes' *General Theory*.

idea, seeing the failure to recognise increasing returns as a crucial weakness of orthodoxy. The main function of markets, argued Kaldor and Young, is not merely to allocate but to create more resources by enlarging the scope for specialisation and the division of labour. Kaldor saw these increasing returns as particularly prevalent in the manufacturing sector, thus providing a justification for regarding manufacturing production as the engine of growth.

Third, there is the parallel between the work of Kaldor and the so-called 'Verdoorn Law' (1949). In his famous inaugural lecture Kaldor (1966) gave two specifications of this law, arguing that both the rate of growth of employment and the rate of growth of labour productivity were both positively correlated with, and functions of, the rate of growth of output. Kaldor saw this as resulting from 'learning by doing' and economies of scale resulting from general industrial expansion and the enlargement of markets. These important propositions have given rise to an enormous literature, and a number of unresolved issues, which are impossible to survey in detail here (see Bairam, 1987; McCombie, 1983; Thirlwall, 1983).

Nevertheless, we may consider briefly some aspects of this work. Following the criticisms of Rowthorn (1975A), Kaldor (1975B) was to argue that output was determined by demand and this should be taken as exogenous. In response, Erkin Bairam (1987) and others have pointed out that this assumption of exogeneity conflicts with the principle of cumulative causation. Furthermore, given that demand itself was a product of growth, single equation estimates of the Verdoorn Law are likely to be biased and inconsistent. A. Parikh (1978) attempted a simultaneous equation approach to the estimation of the Verdoorn Law, but John McCombie (1983) has pointed to some of its serious limitations.

Another line of enquiry has been to examine the underlying structure of the Verdoorn Law (Rowthorn, 1979; Thirlwall, 1980; Verdoorn, 1980; de Vries, 1980). Notably, Verdoorn's original (1949) formulation of the Law is based on neoclassical foundations and features a static Cobb–Douglas production function. There is no disembodied technical change, nor any 'learning by doing'. Clearly this contrasts with Kaldor's idea of 'dynamic economies of scale'.[1]

McCombie (1982) has shown that *if* the foundation of the Law is a production function of the Cobb–Douglas type then the degree of returns to scale from both static and dynamic equations should be equal. In other words, the coefficient relating the levels of productivity and output should be identical to that relating their growth. However, estimates of the static and dynamic Verdoorn coefficients (McCombie, 1982; McCombie and de Ridder, 1984) lead to an alleged 'paradox'. The static specifications give no evidence of increasing returns to scale, whereas there are significant and increasing returns in the dynamic case. Consequently, this evidence suggests that the assumption of an underlying production function of the Cobb–Douglas type is unwarranted.

Of course, Cambridge itself has produced a number of arguments against the aggregate production function, in the famous capital controversy (Harcourt, 1972). Less well-known are the earlier reservations advanced by Alfred Marshall, concerning the notion of increasing returns. In Appendix H of his *Principles*, he noted that increasing returns could undermine the conditions for an equilibrium of supply and demand.[2] An increase in the

[1] Verdoorn (1980, p. 385) has stated that the law that has been given his name now appears 'to be much less generally valid'.

[2] In addition, Marshall anticipates an aspect of Sraffa's famous (1926) critique by noting that under increasing returns 'whatever firm first gets a good start will obtain a monopoly of the whole business of trade in its district' (Marshall, 1920, p. 459n.). On this see Shackle (1967, ch. 3).

scale of production could mean a dramatic reduction in the supply price undermining the established normal or equilibrium price.[1] Notably, in the case of heterogeneous inputs or outputs, without a price framework it is difficult to establish any notion of changing (increasing or decreasing) returns.

Marshall's attempted solution was to make a distinction between 'internal' and 'external' economies of scale. The former related to a single firm, the latter to the gains made from the extension of markets and demand. Whilst Young drew inspiration from the 'external economies' idea, Frank Knight (who, like Kaldor, was one of Young's students) pointed out that they are dynamic in character, accruing in Smithian fashion through the growth of the market. Consequently, it is quite inappropriate to situate them in a static or equilibrium price theory (see Blitch, 1983). Indeed, for Knight, as it was for Piero Sraffa (1926), the very concept of 'external economies' was problematic.

Young's response was to stress the notion of disequilibrium, as consummated in his 1928 article, and in various letters to Knight in that year (see Blitch, 1983). However, Young gave no indication as to how to dispense with the fundamentals of equilibrium price theory. Sadly, a few months later Young was dead, leaving such theoretical problems unresolved to this day.

In addition to this theoretical difficulty, it is sometimes argued that the theory of cumulative causation is incomplete because it lacks a 'first cause': in terms of initial divergences in rates of growth. In Section 2 of this article it will be argued that both initial and persistent differences in growth rates can be partly explained by reference to differences in institutional ossification in the countries concerned.

The productivity enigma

For a long time the orthodox 'production function' model has faced a nagging problem in explaining considerable inter-plant and international differences in productivity. Much of this evidence has been reviewed elsewhere (Hodgson, 1982; Nichols, 1986). Despite productivity growth that is lower than in other developed capitalist countries, absolute US productivity levels are still higher than elsewhere, and in particular still well ahead of those in the UK and Japan (Maddison, 1982, 1987). Even more striking is the evidence for single industries, showing big sectoral productivity gaps between different countries (Prais, 1981).

A typical orthodox response is to suggest that such differences in productivity must be due, in the main, to differences in the inputs of the production function. In fact there is considerable evidence portraying relatively low levels of capital investment in the UK (Blackaby, 1978; Caves and Krause, 1980). However, there are serious problems in isolating these as the main cause of low productivity. For instance, studies show that the average increase in output resulting from a unit of investment expenditure has been much lower in Britain and Japan than in France, Italy, West Germany and the USA (Brown and Sheriff, 1978; Blume, 1980). Pratten (1976) found that differences in the amounts of hardware and other machinery appeared to be responsible for no more than one-fifth of the average difference in productivity found in comparable plants in Britain, the USA,

[1] In fact Marshall had exposed a general logical problem with neoclassical theory: of assuming what it is required to prove. The schedule of 'normal supply prices' which lies behind the supply curve requires some assumption of stability for each price, which in orthodox theory implies some notion of equilibrium for each point on the curve. In other words, the idea of equilibrium is tacit in the reasoning through which it is meant to be established.

Skouras (1981, pp. 202–4) finds a similar argument concerning the logical difficulties of supply and demand analysis in the work of Joan Robinson. For further discussions of this issue see Hodgson (1988, ch. 8; in press).

West Germany and France. Prais (1981, p. 269) argued that low UK productivity could not be attributed to low investment in machinery but to inadequate 'knowledge of how to create and operate modern machinery efficiently'. We are led to the conclusion that varied amounts of capital equipment per employee are not the main factor explaining internationally diverse levels of productivity.[1]

Of course, an inferior labour input could be blamed as well, but the 'production function' model is still in some difficulty in explaining the lack of a clear relation between outputs and capital inputs. Instead of further attempts to fit this awkward evidence into this 'meat grinder' model, where production results from the automatic or mechanical transformation of given inputs, the process of production should be conceived in a different manner. Instead of the orthodox symmetry of 'factors of production', labour should be seen as an active agency with capital goods as passive instruments. Production is a social process involving people with aspirations of their own, in structured social interaction with each other. As Richard Nelson (1981) argues, the firm is a 'social system' and not 'a machine'.

Most importantly, productivity is not mechanically dependent on the number of hours of work that is agreed between employer and employee. Owing to uncertainty and imperfect knowledge, the amount and efficiency of work has to be imperfectly specified in the contract; it depends not only on the given technology but also upon both the motivation and skill of the workforce and the organisation and supervision of management. These, in turn, depend on complex institutional structures and routines and on cultural norms that are inherited from the past. This is not, however, a deterministic view: there is space for the partial indeterminacy of action and will. In particular, the fact that the employment contract cannot be fully specified in advance means that outputs are not completely nor mechanically determined by inputs.

A 'social' model of production

In the 1980s some alternative formal models of the production process have emerged. Bowles's (1985) analysis focuses on the (costly) processes through which employers exercise power over labour, and the ability of workers to resist employer directives. An econometric test of this type of model appears in a study of the US economy by Bowles, Gordon and Weisskopf (1985). They regress productivity growth against several variables including indices of 'employer leverage over workers' and the 'quality of working conditions', using postwar annual US data. These variables are found to be highly significant.

On close inspection the Bowles–Gordon–Weisskopf model is not as radical as claimed.[2] For instance, Bowles's (1985) analysis is virtually identical, in formal terms, to that of Carl Shapiro and Joseph Stiglitz (1984): both employ the standard neoclassical assumption of maximising behaviour to determine an (unemployment) equilibrium

[1] See the further references in Hodgson (1982, 1984). Davies and Caves (1987) found a significant but slight relationship between productivity and the value of gross fixed capital stock per employee. In his comprehensive study Denison (1979) found that 'factor inputs', including capital stock, the educational level of the workforce, and the amount of expenditure on research and development, explained no more than a small fraction of the US productivity slowdown in the 1970s. Note, however, the criticism of the definition of investment in Denison's work by Scott (1981).

[2] Some of the ostensible radicalism of the Bowles–Gordon–Weisskopf account results simply from the use of revolutionary-romantic language. For instance, one of their significant independent variables is the relative cost of nonagricultural crude materials with respect to the price of finished goods. This is described as the level of 'popular resistance', suggesting that the price of oil, for example, has more to do with the struggles of the oilfield workers and less to do with the fortunes of geological exploration and the state of the OPEC cartel.

outcome. Notably, in the Bowles–Gordon–Weisskopf model the role of effective demand in promoting productivity does not have a clear and central place.[1]

An attempt by Weisskopf (1987) to extend this type of econometric analysis to eight OECD countries gives chequered results. He focuses on the level of unemployment which is supposed to increase employer leverage and work intensity. A significant short-run effect of unemployment on productivity is found in three countries only (US, UK and Italy) and a positive long-run effect simply in the case of the US. In four countries (Canada, France, Germany and Sweden) a statistically significant and *negative* relationship between unemployment and productivity growth is discovered, contrary to the Bowles–Gordon–Weisskopf analysis of the US. Weisskopf tries to explain this anomaly by suggesting that the 'threat' of unemployment may not be as effective in Canada, France, Germany and Sweden because of a more developed welfare state. But this auxiliary hypothesis is neither tested nor examined closely.

In addition, despite justified criticism of the neoclassical 'meat grinder' conception of production, the Bowles–Gordon–Weisskopf model replaces this with a 'stick and carrot' conception of the labour process which is only marginally more sophisticated. It relates to the model of management proposed by Frederick Taylor (1911) which has over-influenced Marxists, particularly in the US.[2]

Production, institutions and knowledge

One major reason why Taylorism is of limited efficiency is that 'scientific management' ignores the difficulties and costs involved in gathering and processing the information that is required to monitor and motivate workers. Furthermore, it ignores the importance of the information that the workers may themselves possess, and the fact that their 'practical knowledge' is highly significant but difficult to codify or evaluate. Productivity, especially in a complex process of production, is closely related to both the development of practical knowledge and to the signalling and interpretation of information within the firm.[3]

As Thorstein Veblen has elaborated (see Veblen, 1964; Dyer, 1984; Hodgson, 1988), labour is made up of congealed habits or skills, which may take some time to acquire and depend upon their institutional integument. Later writers have stressed that it is difficult to codify or readily communicate such skills, hence the references of Edith Penrose (1959) to 'unteachable' and Michael Polanyi (1957, 1967) to 'tacit' knowledge. The general social importance of routinised behaviour has been more recently emphasised by Anthony Giddens (1984) and Richard Nelson and Sidney Winter (1982). Contrary to the treatment of 'information problems' by neoclassical theorists, 'tacit' or 'unteachable' knowledge cannot be reduced simply to 'information' because it is partly embodied in routines or unconscious reflexes, and it cannot be reduced to or transmitted in a codified form.

Given that the productivity of an economy is crucially related to the transmission and interpretation of information, and the growth of different kinds of knowledge, there are important consequences for the theory of economic growth. For instance, improvements

[1] See the criticisms of the Bowles–Gordon–Weisskopf model in Nell (1984, pp. 246–7) and the remarks on the relationship between the pressure of demand and productivity by Matthews (1982) and Worswick (1982).

[2] For critiques of Taylor's (1911) theory of 'scientific management' see Vroom and Deci (1970). For Marxist correctives to Braverman's (1974) over-emphasis on Taylorism see Friedman (1977) and Burawoy (1985). Braverman's deskilling hypothesis is criticised in Cutler (1978) and Wood (1982).

[3] Informational considerations should be at the centre of explanations of why worker participation can improve productivity (see Hodgson, 1984; Jones and Svejnar, 1982; Stephen, 1982).

in work organisation are often designed both to facilitate the communication of information and the enhancement and transfer of skills within the plant.[1] Significant increases in productivity can result from better deployment of tasks, a reduction of waste, and improved organisational or other skills. These developments are not necessarily associated with an increase in the intensity of work.

This argument contrasts with a view which is found across the political spectrum: it is the idea that increases in productivity, with given capital goods and technology, are generally associated with enhanced managerial control and subsequent work intensification. As Craig Littler and Graeme Salaman (1982) have argued, the depiction of virtually unqualified managerial control means that the performance of the worker is essentially predetermined, thus removing the major reason for sustaining a distinction between labour and labour-power, and denying many subtleties in Marx's (1976) account of the production process.

Littler and Salaman point out that even under Taylorist managerial regimes, and even with the most menial or routinised jobs, there is a real zone of discretion for the workers, involving alternative courses of action and degrees of conscientiousness or consent. One of the reasons for the existence of this zone is that the gathering together of all relevant information and knowledge in management's hands is, contrary to Taylor, an impossible task.

A consequence is that the behaviour of the firm is not, within the given constraints, entirely determined by, nor entirely subject to, the decisions of its managers. Because much of the 'expertise' of the firm is embedded in the firm's routines and the habitual skills of its workforce, it is neither completely codifiable and communicable, nor completely manageable from the apex of the organisation. As Nelson (1981, p. 1038) puts it: 'management cannot effectively "choose" what is to be done in any detailed way, and has only broad control over what is done, and how well. Only a small portion of what people actually do on a job can be monitored in detail.'

Thus any model of productivity growth which is centred on the application of, and resistance to, 'employer leverage' will give us only part of the picture. As Nelson and Winter (1982) and Veblen (1964) argue, the behaviour of the firm is largely routinised. For this reason economic development can appear, for significant periods of time, with exceptions discussed below, to be subject to inertia. An adequate theory of the development of productive capabilities must take into account both the social culture and institutions within which habits and routines are reproduced, and the conditions which lead to their disruption or mutation.[2]

These considerations give us grounds to reject Kaldor's (1966, pp. 12–13) argument against the possibility that productivity growth may be the driving force behind output growth. He contends that the 'usual hypothesis is that the growth of productivity is mainly to be explained by the progress in science and technology', and points out, quite rightly, that the levels and growth rates of productivity can vary greatly from plant to plant, and

[1] Williamson (1975, 1985) has taken on board some of these points. For differing approaches see Beer (1972), Emery (1977), and Rice (1958).

[2] Note also that the Veblen–Nelson–Winter idea of habits and routines amounts to some 'unity of knowing and doing'. This is incompatible with Braverman's (1974) stress on the 'separation of conception and execution', and his idea that managers appropriate the decision-making process while the worker becomes 'an appendage to the machine'. Capitalism displays elements of both managerial dominance and (limited) worker autonomy, and it would be incorrect, therefore, to put exclusive stress on either idea. As Burawoy (1985, p. 41) puts it: 'Rather than a separation of conception and execution, we find a separation of workers' conception and management's conception, of workers' knowledge and management's knowledge'.

from country to country, even when the plants are controlled by common multinational corporations. But 'these must have had the same access to improvements in knowledge and know-how', so if productivity growth determined output growth we should presumably expect productivity and output to be growing at more uniform rates than are evident.

The error in this argument is clear. Plants cannot have the 'same access to improvements in knowledge and know-how' because much relevant knowledge is 'tacit', 'unteachable', 'parcellised', embodied in habit or routine, and non-codifiable. Furthermore, even codifiable information does not become knowledge independent of the context of its transmission or of the cognitive framework of the receiver.[1] Knowledge and information are not readily storable, nor transmissible from agent to agent as water flows in a pipe.

The diffusion hypothesis

Such considerations lead us directly to Gomulka's (1971, 1979) theory of productivity growth and economic development. He argues that the dominant factor in determining productivity growth is the degree of 'diffusion of innovations' from technologically more advanced countries to the relatively less developed, using productivity levels as a proxy for technological development. In addition, the impact of this diffusion depends upon the 'absorptive capacity' of the country in question. This is allegedly determined by educational levels, the institutional framework and 'a variety of social, cultural, institutional and political factors' (1979, p. 186). Thus, for example, productivity growth in Japan is said to be greater because of its remaining productivity gap with the leading nations, and because of its superior ability to absorb new technology, and its encouragement of, rather than resistance to, innovation and change.

Although the literature on technological diffusion cannot be surveyed here, it can be pointed out that one feature is almost universal; the term 'technology' is related almost exclusively to technical innovations for which there is codifiable knowledge or a 'blueprint'. Thus, given the will to assimilate the technique, there are few remaining barriers other than technical competence and education. Technology is treated as a kind of substance, whose meaning and content is independent of culture, institutions, and cognitive frames. This empiricist and technicist conception of information and knowledge is, however, unacceptable.

Contrary to the assumptions of the diffusion theorists, production does not simply depend upon well-specified innovations such as hybrid corn or the silicon chip. Productive advance is also a matter of countless ways of understanding, interpreting and doing, which are embedded in the social culture and reinforced by its routines. Furthermore, production is a social process, depending on social institutions, relations, customs and rules. Consequently, the level of productivity in a nation is not uniquely nor closely related to its technological development, as an exclusive emphasis on technological diffusion would suggest.

A crucial feature of non-codifiable knowledge is that it is not simply accessible like blueprints in a file; its full acquisition can never be immediate, nor independent of its progressive application in practice. In such instances it is crucial to recognise that knowing and doing are inseparable.

Thus Nelson (1980) has criticised the common idea that 'technological knowledge is in the form of codified how-to-do-it knowledge which provides sufficient guidance so that if

[1] Contrary to the Austrian view, these considerations do not necessarily imply a subjectivist, nor a purely relativist, view of knowledge. See Lawson (1985, 1987) and Hodgson (1988).

one had access to the book one would be able to do it' (p. 63). He rejects also the notion that such knowledge is expanded in volume largely by expenditure on R&D: 'If the salient elements of techniques involve special personal skills, or a personalised pattern of interaction and cooperation among a group of individuals in an important way, then one cannot easily infer how it would work from an experiment conducted elsewhere' (p. 67).

Looked at in this way, the validity of the diffusion hypothesis would depend on considerations such as: (i) the extent to which the lead countries are developing and transmitting codifiable technical knowledge, (ii) the propensity of the laggard countries to absorb the knowledge, and (iii) the extent to which codifiable technical knowledge is representative of skill and technique as a whole.

For example, the hypothesis would be invalid in a situation where the country at the top of the absolute productivity league (say the US) was relying largely on substantial non-codifiable knowledge which had been accumulated and dispersed over the years, and a laggard country (say Japan) was achieving high rates of productivity growth largely by generating its own codifiable knowledge (through R&D or whatever) which had not been brought in from elsewhere. The *prima facie* evidence would then suggest that the diffusion hypothesis was valid, but the main source of advance would not in fact be diffusion itself.

The validity of the diffusion hypothesis depends on the 'balance' between codifiable and non-codifiable knowledge in the economy. Our conclusion must be that the assumed model of technological development in the diffusion hypothesis is too simple, and does too much violence to the complexities of knowledge and technology, and to the conditions of productive advance.

Manufacturing as the engine of growth

A crude distinction between codifiable and non-codifiable knowledge may provide insights regarding different rates of productivity growth in different industries or sectors of the economy. Before we consolidate this point we shall consider alternative arguments as to why manufacturing, in particular, should be regarded as the leading sector of the economy.

Kaldor's (1966) proposition to this effect is partly based on the assertion that it is in the field of manufacturing that the phenomenon of increasing returns is likely to be more prevalent. Other sectors, such as mining and agriculture, are presumed to exhibit diminishing returns. However, as indicated above, there are theoretical problems with this argument, and a strong empirical case for the presumed pattern of returns to scale has yet to be made.

Being influenced by Kaldor, John Eatwell (1982, pp. 52–3) endorses the engine of growth idea, asserting that the income elasticity of demand for manufacturing products remains high, compared, for example, with agriculture. However, whilst there may be limits to the consumption of food, there are no equivalent limits elsewhere, particularly in the service sector. There is no apparent reason why higher incomes should condemn such sectors to relative decline.

Much of Eatwell's remaining argument is based on a false reductionism; he asserts that manufactured goods are essential for other sectors of the economy and concludes that manufacturing thus has a primary importance. However, just as manufactured goods are essential to the agricultural and service sectors, so too are services and agricultural goods essential to manufacturing. To say that X is essential to Y does not necessarily give X primacy, especially if Y is also essential to X. Consequently, a good part of his argument is flawed.

Yet there are reasons for giving manufacturing some distinctiveness. Nelson (1980, p. 67) suggests that differences in productivity growth might be affected by 'hardware versus human organization' which in turn relates to the question of codifiability of knowledge. Codifiable knowledge is likely to be relatively more significant in a highly-mechanised sector than in one depending more on traditional craft skills and routines. Consequently, highly mechanised sectors will be relatively more responsive to R&D initiatives and technological diffusion, even if much knowledge is still non-codifiable in this sector.

Furthermore, manufacturing is generally associated with a compact spatial organisation. Productive activities are often gathered together, with relatively easy communications between the persons involved. In contrast, spatial dispersion is wider in agriculture and communications are inferior. And in services there have traditionally been smaller-scale production units. Thus manufacturing may enjoy the greatest and fastest diffusion of skills and technique.

If this argument is correct, and manufacturing has a higher 'proportion' of codifiable knowledge than other sectors, as well as more compactness facilitating diffusion or communication of skills, then its importance stems not from a causal primacy or structural position in the economy but from its ability to respond to the diffusion or internal generation of codifiable knowledge.

On the other hand, circumstances may arise in which other sectors increase their dependence on modern science and technology, and make more use of codifiable knowledge. The rapidly increasing use of codifiable knowledge in a sector which has traditionally been dominated by embedded habits and skills, may partly explain the higher productivity growth in agriculture since the Industrial Revolution. Currently, productivity in the service sector is increasing as it makes greater use of information technology and compact spatial organisation.

Manufacturing, however, has advantages in these terms which have yet to be surpassed. It still may be potentially more responsive to any development and communication of codifiable technique that is promoted by the policy-makers, and act as a kind of 'engine of growth' for this reason. But in the absence of flows of codifiable knowledge to the manufacturing sector, Kaldor-type or Verdoorn-type relationships would break down. This could occur, for instance, in the country in the technological lead, or in the event of a world slowdown in innovation or demand.

Kaldor's theory may also break down in conditions of recession for another reason. It is widely accepted that one effect of a slump may be to cause a relatively higher bankruptcy rate amongst low-productivity firms. A consequence is 'degenerate' productivity growth, where average productivity is rising but the economy as a whole is contracting in size. It is possible, therefore, for the rates of growth of productivity in both manufacturing and the economy as a whole to be *inversely* related to the rate of change of manufacturing output for a limited period. This would be in defiance of two out of three of Kaldor's laws.[1] Consequently, whilst these laws may find some empirical support in periods of sustained economic expansion, there may be problems in applying Kaldor's theory to periods of recession.

In this survey of ideas and theories concerning economic growth, the role of social institutions, and the transmission of different forms of knowledge, have been highlighted. We now turn to the development and application of this approach.

[1] Some members of the French *régulation* school have suggested that Kaldor–Verdoorn type relationships may have broken down since the oil shock of 1973 (Boyer and Petit, 1981).

2. Towards an institutionalist alternative

This section commences with a discussion of the concept of institutional ossification, followed by an econometric test of the theory outlined here. Although no statistical test should be taken as conclusive, the preliminary results are good.

Since 1960 there has been much research by historians as to the causes of the slow growth of the American and British economies and of much faster growth in France, Germany, Italy and Japan. A prominent theme is to explain much of the difference in growth rates by the different degrees of cultural or institutional ossification of the countries involved.

Institutional ossification

There are two aspects to these processes of ossification. The first is to do with the timing of the industrial revolution in different countries. During this period of rapid economic and social transformation, habits and patterns of work are laid down which endure after industrialisation is accomplished. Hence, in general, the most flexible period for the more rapid development of new skills and routines is during the period at which industrialisation is proceeding at the fastest pace. Consequently, the countries which industrialised some time ago pay 'the penalty of taking the lead', to use Veblen's (1915) phrase.

Marxist historians, amongst others, have initiated much of the debate about the ossification of British political and economic institutions. Thus Perry Anderson (1964, p. 50) sees Britain as 'a sclerosed, archaic society, trapped and burdened by its past successes'. Similarly, Eric Hobsbawm (1969, p. 188) argues that Britain's early industrialisation used 'methods and techniques which, however advanced and efficient at the time, could not remain the most advanced and efficient, and it created a pattern of both production and markets which would not necessarily remain the one best fitted to sustain economic growth and technological change'.

Non-Marxist analysts repeat a similar theme. For example, Ronald Dore (1973, p. 419) argues that: 'The way a country comes to industrialization can have a lasting effect on the kind of industrial society it becomes. It will be a long time before Britain loses the marks of the pioneer, the scars and stiffnesses that come from the searing experience of having made the first, most long-drawn-out industrial revolution'. Also Sir Henry Phelps Brown (1977, pp. 25–26) writes of practical minds that 'became bounded by the processes and products that they mastered in long apprenticeships'. Past success in the old methods, whilst being cossetted by the old imperial trading systems, made managers and administrators reluctant to learn the new. Britain in the twentieth century remained bounded by the methods, processes and products of the nineteenth century.

Perhaps the most extensive development of these ideas to date comes in a collection of essays edited by Bernard Elbaum and William Lazonick (1986) who attribute the relative decline of the British economy in the twentieth century to 'rigidities in the economic and social institutions that developed during the nineteenth century, a period when Britain was the world's leading economic power and British industry was highly atomistic and competitive in organisation'. (p. 2). These institutional rigidities, they argue, obstructed efforts at economic renovation. Examples include entrenched shopfloor unionism (see also Kilpatrick and Lawson, 1980), rigid financial institutions and inflexible corporate structures. Clearly, all these have since undergone considerable change, but in all cases its pace and extent has been affected by the structures which were laid down in the formative years of the nineteenth century.

If the ossification argument is accepted then a country in the throes of industrial revolution will be more flexible and open to new techniques than either a nation which industrialised long ago, or a predominantly agricultural economy which has yet to escape from its immobile traditions and structures. We are not referring here mainly to the advantage that accrues to laggard industrialising nations in their ability to learn or import (codifiable) techniques from the leaders. Instead the emphasis is on the non-codifiable aspects of economic transformation, and to the flexibility that accrues to the country that is experiencing the most disruptive phase in the transition from an agricultural to an industrialised society.

Another aspect of institutional ossification is the extent to which it has been temporarily arrested and reversed by the upheaval of revolution or war, leading to new regimes and institutions, often of a more dynamic or less conservative hue. This theme is also found in historical studies of the reasons for Britain's relative economic decline. For instance, Anderson (1964, p. 37) notes that: 'Alone of major European nations, England emerged undefeated and unoccupied from two World Wars, its social structure uniquely untouched by external shocks or discontinuities.' Whilst Anderson recognises the convulsive and reforming effects of the two World Wars, Britain was not shattered by invasion or revolution on the Continental scale.

Similarly, Phelps Brown (1977, p. 20) sees British institutions, such as trade unions, suffering from 'the extraordinary continuity of their history: they have had no revolution, no defeat in war and no foreign occupation to give them a fresh start'. Consequently, in the British case, advanced institutional ossification was not alleviated by any major disruption on home soil in modern times.

Mancur Olson (1982) proposes that 'countries whose distributional coalitions have been emasculated or abolished by totalitarian government or foreign occupation should grow relatively quickly after a free and stable legal order is established' (p. 75). In contrast, the absence of these disruptions from Britain 'made it easier from the firms and families that advanced in the Industrial Revolution and the nineteenth century to organise or collude to protect their interests' (p. 84). Like many other authors, Olson argues that sweeping radical change, particularly that resulting from internal revolution or defeat in war, has helped to promote economic growth by overcoming the inertia of ossified, growth-retarding institutions.

The two aspects of institutional ossification—relating to the timing of the industrial revolution and the degree of major disruption—are observed most graphically in Britain. Relatively speaking, the United States has enjoyed a superior economic performance. But the prime concern here is to explain differing degrees of dynamism and growth. The US faces the problem of the slowdown in productivity growth and the erosion of its share of world trade. In this case the institutional arguments again seem convincing. The United States was one of the first countries to follow Britain into industrialisation. The American Revolution was two centuries ago, followed later by the Civil War. Consequently, post-industrial ossification is relatively advanced, with few periods of major disruption to increase flexibility.

In contrast, countries such as Belgium, France, Germany and Italy have been disrupted both by several revolutions in the last two centuries and by extensive invasion and occupation. In each of these cases, industrial transformation was later than Britain. Japan's social and economic transformation was later still, developing during a period of fascism, to be greatly accelerated after the foreign occupation of 1945. From the point of view of the timing of industrialisation, Japan's economic institutions should be the most flexible, whereas the degree of disruption has been the greatest in Belgium, France, Germany and Italy.[1]

Much of the historical literature on institutional ossification captures the underlying and more durable features of the institutions and routines in a capitalist country. The particular emphasis and interpretation offered here is on the function of non-codifiable knowledge and deeply-embedded structures and routines. This provides a counterpoint to the theory of technological diffusion which is more relevant to codifiable knowledge and techniques. However, before we proceed to a statistical test of the theories discussed here, it is necessary to evaluate briefly Olson's argument to which the present discussion concerning institutional ossification bears a superficial similarity.[2]

Considerations regarding the creation and transmission of knowledge are not significant in Olson's theory, neither are habits or routines given pride of place. Instead of a focus on the development and mutation of industrial skills, attention shifts onto the allegedly 'growth retarding' effects of 'interest groups' and 'distributional coalitions'. Implicitly, Olson is making the same classical liberal assumptions that lie at the core of much neoclassical theory: that the market is an elemental or natural order, and that institutional rigidities play a largely negative and restrictive role. These assumptions are inconsistent with a perspective which sees markets themselves as institutions, and in which institutions in general have features which enable as well as restrict economic activity. In particular, institutionalised or routinised behaviour provides information on likely outcomes for decision-making agents (see Hodgson, 1988).

In a rather *ad hoc* manner, however, Olson considers the possibility of an 'encompassing' interest group which stands at the pinnacle of society and prevents other feuding interest groups from being formed. In this manner he explains the relative success of social democratic countries such as Sweden. Furthermore, and in conflict with his liberal presumptions, positive virtues have to be given to fascist countries or similar regimes, which have prevented other 'distributional coalitions' from emerging. However, as Frederic Pryor (1983) has shown, a statistical test of Olson's theory with a sample of capitalist and Communist-led countries fails to confirm that the supremely 'encompassing' interest group of a Communist Party has a positive or statistically significant effect on growth. Whilst being useful in its stress on institutions, when applied to capitalist countries Olson's theory ends up being a re-worked argument for the benevolent Hobbesian sovereign: one who will ensure that markets work but will break up interest groups and coalitions whenever they may occur.

Hypotheses for statistical testing

It is rare that theories of economic growth can be applied equally without qualification to both capitalist and non-capitalist countries. Unlike the theories of Kaldor, Gomulka or Olson, the present analysis takes differences in the knowledge-transmitting functions of economic structures and institutions directly into account. Consequently, it is not intended to be applicable, at least not without major modification, to centrally-planned economies. Our statistical test may be applied to capitalist economies only.

[1] This brings to mind the words of Harry Lime in the film *The Third Man*: 'In Italy for thirty years under the Borgias they had warfare, terror, murder, bloodshed: but they produced Michelangelo, Leonardo da Vinci and the Renaissance. In Switzerland they had brotherly love; they had five hundred years of democracy and peace, and what did that produce? The cuckoo clock.'

[2] Critiques of Olson (1982) are found in Barry (1983), Bowles and Eatwell (1983), Kindleberger (1983), Mjoset (1985), Pryor (1983), de Vries (1983), Wallis and Oates (1988) and Whiteley (1986).

Available OECD data reduced the sample to 16 major capitalist countries (namely Australia, Austria, Belgium, Canada, Denmark, Finland, France, Germany, Italy, Japan, Netherlands, Norway, Sweden, Switzerland, United Kingdom, United States). The foregoing discussion of institutional ossification suggests a slow, long-term process, thus cross-section data were used, with periods of more than ten years; namely 1960–73 and 1973–84, i.e. before and after the oil price shock of 1973. Four data sets were thus generated: (i) 1960–73, (ii) 1973–84, (iii) 1960–84 as a whole, and (iv) a composite sample of 32 observations made up by juxtaposing the data from 1960–73 and 1973–84 with the addition of a dummy variable to indicate pre- and post-oil shock conditions.

The OECD data presented a limited choice of dependent variables. The annual rate of growth of real GDP per person employed was selected as an index of productivity growth, and denoted by *PROD* (source: OECD, 1986, Table 3.7).

Four types of hypothesis were tested:

(a) that productivity growth was dependent both on the degree of institutional flexibility—the inverse of ossification—and the degree of institutional disruption. The derivation of these variables is discussed below;

(b) that productivity growth was dependent on the 'technological gap' between each country and the lead country—the United States—measured by the relative productivity levels involved;

(c) that productivity growth was dependent on the level of investment in each country, measured by gross fixed capital formation as a percentage of GDP;

(d) that productivity growth reflected Kaldors' third law, i.e. being positively correlated with the growth rate of the manufacturing sector and negatively with the growth rate of employment outside manufacturing.[1]

The institutional data

The derivation of the institutional data in (a) presents several difficulties and a degree of over-simplification is unavoidable in any such test. A precedent exists in the work of Kwang Choi (1983) but this is built upon Olson's conceptual framework. Choi uses a rising logistic curve to reflect the 'sclerosis' resulting from the growth of interest groups. Cyril Black's (1966) typology and dates are used to provide the timing of the logistic in each case.

Of course, any such periodisation of history is problematic and highly questionable.[2] An advantage of Black's dates is that he demarcates two relevant periods for a large number of countries: that pertaining to the 'consolidation of modernising leadership' followed by the period of 'economic and social transformation'. The former marks the transition into modernity, and the second is taken to represent a number of political, social and economic changes of which industrialisation is a part. Choi chooses the date that is said to mark the beginning of the consolidation of modernising leadership, but in the present study it is suggested that the start of the period of economic and social transformation would best locate the years when socio-economic change was proceeding apace.

Choi's use of a logistic curve reflects the Olsonian assumption that history is progressing from a market-based and interest-group-free 'state of nature' to the sclerosis of a coalition-

[1] The third law is chosen because it has productivity growth as the dependent variable. Note, however, McCombie (1981) where its economic significance is challenged.

[2] Inspired by Rowthorn and Wells (1987), another approach would be to take shifts in employment to or from industry, agriculture and services as time-series indicators of institutional flexibility (*FLX*) for each country. This would peak when the total rate of transition to or from these sectors was at a maximum, and this would substitute for the year *EST*. However, the Rowthorn–Wells data cover 13 countries only.

ridden world. Instead, a curve which would more accurately reflect the arguments concerning institutional flexibility would be hat-shaped. The peak level would correspond to the period when industrialisation was most rapid, when the capacity for promoting and absorbing new routines and skills was highest, and existing routines were at the highest level of malleability.

Once established, routinised actions and non-codifiable knowledge have an inertia of their own. As the pace of transformation declines, the system tends to ossify and reinforce existing routines. Thus for routines it is relevant to consider their 'date stamp', marking the time at which they were derived or laid down. The more ossification, the less the inclination to, and the greater the difficulty of, further transformation and change.

In addition, the older the institutions and routines the less the receptiveness of the system to flows of codifiable knowledge and techniques that are generated elsewhere. For instance, current R&D may not relate to older techniques and practices. Restructuring has to take place to improve the absorptive capacity for new ideas. Consequently, in the absence of major crises or disruptions which would promote the search for, and creation of, new institutions and routines, it is reasonable to assume that their contribution to productivity growth declines progressively through time after the transformational peak.

To present this idea in mathematical terms it was decided not to use a normal frequency function because it tailed off too rapidly at the extremes. Instead, the variable representing institutional flexibility (*FLX*) is defined as follows:[1]

$$FLX(t) = 100/[1 + 0{\cdot}002\,(t - EST)^2]$$

where *EST* is the year at the start of the period of economic and social transformation and *t* is the year.

Choi's measure of disruption is derived from summing the number of 'years of major disruption'. Unfortunately, as well as including revolutions and foreign occupations, Choi assumes that each year under totalitarian government constitutes an instance of major disruption, whereas democracy is given no such accolade. The assumption that simply the presence of fascism and totalitarianism constitute major disruption is consistent with Olson's argument but not the thesis presented here. Contrary to Olson, totalitarianism is normally associated with multiple interest groups and nepotism on a grand scale. Disruptions worth including are revolutions or occupations leading to totalitarianism, and those leading to its removal. During such disruptions, but not the intervening period, new habits and routines can be more easily established.

The conditions here chosen to represent periods of major disruption are more restrictive than Choi's. To qualify, a period of major disruption (*PMD*) must be:

(i) an extensive foreign occupation of home soil, or revolution, or civil war, or year of national independence, in either case leading to significant social changes;

(ii) at least 10 years from any other *PMD*;

(iii) at or after the beginning of the period of 'consolidation of modernising leadership'.

The second criterion prevents over-weighting of single major disruptions which span more than one year. The third excludes disruptions which precede the inauguration of the

[1] The coefficient in the denominator of $FLX(t)$, and that in DIS_i (see below), were both crudely estimated by ordinary least-squares regressions on the institutional data for the 1960–84 period. Experimentation suggested that the results were not over-sensitive to changes in these coefficients. Nevertheless, some arbitrariness inevitably remains. For each period, mid-point values of these functions were used in the regressions. All data are available from the author.

Table 1. *Institutional data*

	EST	*CML*	←	*PMDs*				→
Australia	1901	1801	1901					
Austria	1918	1848	1848	1918	1945			
Belgium	1848	1795	1813	1830	1848	1918	1945	
Canada	1867	1791	1867					
Denmark	1866	1807	1945					
Finland	1919	1863	1918					
France	1848	1789	1789	1814	1830	1848	1871	1945
Germany	1871	1803	1805	1848	1918	1933	1945	
Italy	1871	1805	1805	1848	1860	1922	1945	
Japan	1945	1868	1868	1945				
Netherlands	1848	1795	1795	1810	1945			
Norway	1905	1809	1905	1945				
Sweden	1905	1809						
Switzerland	1848	1798	1803					
United Kingdom	1832	1649	1688					
United States	1865	1776	1783	1865				

Notes: EST: Beginning year of 'economic and social transformation'. *Source:* Black (1966, pp. 90–92); *CML:* Beginning year of 'consolidation of modernizing leadership'. *Source:* Black (1966, pp. 90–92); *PMD:* Period of major disruption, denoted by the last or most crucial year.

modern socio-economic system, which are too early to affect modern institutions and structures. Disruptions, like information, are structure-specific.

Of course, these strict criteria exclude many other disruptions which have had significant effects. However, their inclusion would involve difficult problems of relative weighting. This statistical study is mainly designed to indicate the general value of the approach, so that only the most important disruptions have been included here.

It is argued above that a large-scale disruptive event will generally create the opportunity to recast social relationships and routines and lay down more modern and progressive habits and routines. Disruption on this scale gives the opportunity of ridding the system of many old methods and arrangements and of adopting new ones.

It is assumed that major disruptions would have greater effect the more that economic and social transformation has advanced. Thus disruption in a less-developed country would have less impact than in one which was developed. Each period of major disruption is assumed to have an impact according to the following formula:

$$DIS_i = \exp[0{\cdot}002(PMD_i - EST)]$$

where DIS_i is the degree of disruption resulting from the given *PMD* and exp is the exponential function. The index of total institutional disruption is simply the sum of the appropriate DIS_is for each country. Black's data, and the chosen *PMD*s, are shown in Table 1.

Regressions

To test the technological diffusion hypothesis the following variable was taken from Maddison (1982, p. 212). Where required, an estimate was made by linear interpolation.

RPR = Relative productivity level (GDP per man-hour) as percentage of US level.

The level of investment was captured by the following:

INV = Gross fixed capital formation as a percentage of GDP (source: OECD, 1986, Table 6.8).

Kaldor's third law was tested using these variables:

MAN = Annual percentage change in real value added in manufacturing (source: OECD, 1986, Table 3.5). Data for Switzerland estimated from World Bank sources.

ENM = Annual percentage change in non-manufacturing employment (source: OECD, 1986, Tables 1.7, 1.10 and 2.11).

As a comparative test of a relatively large number of independent variables was involved, a sequential nested testing procedure was chosen, to eliminate insignificant variables one by one. The results, for all variables that are significant at a 10% level, are shown in Table 2. *SHOCK* is a dummy variable that takes the value of 0 for the 1960–73 data and 1 for 1973–84.

The results shown in Table 2 are a confirmation of the institutionalist hypothesis (a) in all four cases. Notably, neither the country with the lowest productivity growth rate (the USA) nor the one with the highest (Japan) is an outlier in the regressions, nor are the results significantly affected by their removal.

The technological diffusion hypothesis is confirmed for 1960–73 and 1960–84, but not for the other two regressions. This could mean that the diffusion of codifiable knowledge has slowed down since 1973. Explanations of productivity growth in terms of levels of investment receive confirmation for the 1973–84 period only; in other cases the investment variable is not significant.

Kaldor's third law receives strong confirmation in 1960–73: the years of economic boom. However, during 1973–84, whilst the *MAN* and *ENM* variables are both significant, *MAN* has the wrong sign. Growth in productivity is thus associated with a contraction of manufacturing. This could be explained in terms of the 'degenerate' productivity growth associated with the post-1973 recession. *MAN* is not significant in the other regressions. It could be that whilst *MAN* and *PROD* are correlated in the period of boom, in the post-1973 recession a Kaldor-type relationship has broken down.

The fourth regression suggests that the overall effect of the 1973 oil shock and its deflationary regressions is to lower the growth rate of productivity by about 2% per year. Arguably, much of the post-1973 growth slowdown is explicable in terms of the contraction in effective demand, as well as supply-side factors.[1]

Concluding remarks

In this paper an important distinction has been made between codifiable and non-codifiable knowledge. The latter is related to embedded skills and routines, and their

[1] The impact of effective demand on productivity growth is endorsed by contributors to the Matthews (1982) volume and by Fagerberg (1987), Lindbeck (1983) and Giersch and Wolter (1983).

Table 2. *Regressions*

1960–73 period ($N=16$)

$$\begin{array}{lllllll} PROD= & 3{\cdot}06 & +\ 0{\cdot}0465FLX & +\ 0{\cdot}172DIS & -\ 0{\cdot}0168RPR & +\ 0{\cdot}242MAN & -\ 0{\cdot}335ENM \\ & (0{\cdot}54) & (0{\cdot}012) & (0{\cdot}057) & (0{\cdot}0076) & (0{\cdot}059) & (0{\cdot}094) \\ & \ast\ast\ast\ast & \ast\ast\ast & \ast\ast & \ast & \ast\ast\ast & \ast\ast\ast \end{array}$$

$R^2=0{\cdot}978$; adjusted $R^2=0{\cdot}967$

1973–84 period ($N=16$)

$$\begin{array}{lllllll} PROD= & -\ 0{\cdot}691 & +\ 0{\cdot}0762FLX & +\ 0{\cdot}225DIS & +\ 0{\cdot}0833INV & -\ 0{\cdot}233MAN & -\ 0{\cdot}324ENM \\ & (0{\cdot}65) & (0{\cdot}027) & (0{\cdot}050) & (0{\cdot}033) & (0{\cdot}094) & (0{\cdot}12) \\ & & \ast\ast & \ast\ast\ast & \ast\ast & \ast\ast & \ast\ast \end{array}$$

$R^2=0{\cdot}897$; adjusted $R^2=0{\cdot}846$

1960–84 period ($N=16$)

$$\begin{array}{lllll} PROD= & 3{\cdot}10 & +\ 0{\cdot}0784FLX & +\ 0{\cdot}327DIS & -\ 0{\cdot}0248RPR \\ & (0{\cdot}39) & (0{\cdot}0069) & (0{\cdot}028) & (0{\cdot}0048) \\ & \ast\ast\ast\ast & \ast\ast\ast\ast & \ast\ast\ast\ast & \ast\ast\ast\ast \end{array}$$

$R^2=0{\cdot}973$; adjusted $R^2=0{\cdot}965$

1960–73 period combined with 1973–84 ($N=32$)

$$\begin{array}{llllll} PROD= & 2{\cdot}92 & +\ 0{\cdot}0885FLX & +\ 0{\cdot}242DIS & -\ 0{\cdot}393ENM & -\ 2{\cdot}12SHOCK \\ & (0{\cdot}27) & (0{\cdot}0090) & (0{\cdot}051) & (0{\cdot}10) & (0{\cdot}17) \\ & \ast\ast\ast\ast & \ast\ast\ast\ast & \ast\ast\ast\ast & \ast\ast\ast & \ast\ast\ast\ast \end{array}$$

$R^2=0{\cdot}936$; adjusted $R^2=0{\cdot}926$

Notes: Method of estimate: ordinary least squares. Standard errors in brackets. Levels of significance (two-tailed test): **** 0·1%; *** 1%; ** 5%; * 10%.

development depends upon the transformation and degress of flexibility of socio-economic institutions. For connected reasons it was argued that both the technological diffusion hypothesis and Kaldor's theory of economic growth must be qualified.

A statistical test has confirmed a very strong relationship between the institutional variables and the rate of growth of productivity. Both the technological diffusion hypothesis and Kaldor's third law fare worse after the oil shock of 1973.

It is interesting to project the regression-generated equations into the future. Taking the third regression, and making the heroic assumption that the coefficients in the model remain fixed, *RPR* is recalculated annually according to the derived productivity growth. The projection suggests that France will overtake the United States in terms of overall levels of productivity in the 1990s.[1] After its steep climb, Japan's relative productivity level reaches a peak of about 76% of the French in about 2006, and then begins to decline. British relative productivity rises, then peaks at about 67% of the French or American level in about 1990.

As *FLX(t)* declines over time, and assuming that no further periods of major disruption ensue, the variable of increasing relative influence is *DIS*. Eventually, countries begin to assume a rank order according to the degree of disruption they have experienced in

[1] Recent data in Maddison (1987, p. 651) suggest that French and Dutch productivity levels exceeded 97% of the US as early as 1984. Japan, still behind the UK, was at 55·6%.

modern times. Having experienced the greatest degree of disruption, France thus emerges as the lead nation, followed by Germany, Italy, Belgium, Austria and the Netherlands.

Of course, these projections ignore variations in performance that may result from changes in effective demand and from the transformation of the socio-economic institutions themselves, as well as the degree of statistical variability that is suggested by the regressions. However, what they do indicate is a process which assumes the form, but not the specific dynamic, of Young–Myrdal–Kaldor models of cumulative causation. Whilst the rank order changes, and some countries overtake others, the gap between the leading and the laggard nations eventually widens in absolute terms. Thus the effect of the institutional variables is to replicate some aspects of the cumulative causation process, and nullify any convergence that is implied by the diffusion hypothesis. We have, to use an old phrase, a process of 'combined and uneven development'.

Regarding policy conclusions, the argument points to an eclectic stance. First, at the international level, it endorses a worldwide expansion in effective demand. There is also some scope for policies to increase investment and to generate and infuse technological knowledge.

Whilst war and revolution may have the effect of increasing institutional flexibility, the first, at least, is not to be recommended. In addition, whilst New Right regimes, such as that experienced in the USA and Britain, may promote some restructuring, including work practices and the ownership of industry, key areas remain untouched, and are protected by a strong residual conservatism. Furthermore, New Right restructuring relies on a crude and misplaced Darwinism and often fails to promote long-term initiatives, in contrast with an interventionist policy in a more favourable economic environment.

Instead, the emphasis must be the kind of 'deep' institutional transformation that is implied by a radical industrial policy, but its outlines will have to await the results of further study.[1] As far as policy recommendations for Britain are concerned, institutional economic integration with more dynamic Continental Europe is a desirable, and perhaps inevitable, outcome.

There is a challenging epilogue. Maddison's sweeping (1982) study of three centuries of capitalist development suggests all too precise correlations between the overall level of productivity within a country and its world hegemonic position in politico-economic terms. We must thus anticipate the political disruption that may result from a loss of economic leadership by the United States, and the shift of the focus of capitalist development back again to its ancient Western European homeland.[2] And if disruption is to result, who can foretell the institutional outcomes? We are condemned, as the Chinese say, to live in interesting times.

Bibliography

Anderson, P. 1964. Origins of the present crisis, *New Left Review*, no. 23, January–February. Reprinted in Anderson and Blackburn (eds) (1966)

Anderson, P. and Blackburn, R. (eds) 1966. *Towards Socialism*, London, Collins

Bairam, E. I. 1987. The Verdoorn Law, returns to scale and industrial growth: a review of the literature, *Australian Economic Papers*, vol. 26, June

Barry, B. 1983. Some questions about explanation, *International Studies Quarterly*, vol. 27, no. 1, March

Beckerman, W. (ed.) 1979. *Slow Growth in Britain: Causes and Consequences*, Oxford, OUP

[1] Interventionist industrial policies are discussed by Best (1986), Carter (1981), Cowling (1987), Gruchy (1984) and Hughes (1986).

[2] This possibility, amongst others, is considered, with some scepticism, in Kennedy (1988).

Beer, S. 1972. *Brain of the Firm*, London, Allen Lane
Best, M. H. 1986. Strategic planning, the new competition and industrial policy, in Nolan and Paine (eds) (1986)
Black, C. E. 1966. *The Dynamics of Modernization: A Study in Comparative History*, New York, Harper and Row
Blackaby, F. (ed.) 1978. *De-Industrialisation*, London, Heinemann
Blitch, C. P. 1983. Allyn Young on increasing returns, *Journal of Post Keynesian Economics*, vol. 5, no. 3, Spring
Blume, M. E. 1980. The financial markets, in Caves and Krause (eds) (1980)
Bowles, S. 1985. The production process in a competitive economy: Walrasian, neo-Hobbesian, and Marxian models, *American Economic Review*, vol. 75, no. 1, March
Bowles, S. and Eatwell, J. 1983. Between two worlds: interest groups, class structure and capitalist growth, in Mueller (ed.) (1983)
Bowles, S., Gordon, D. M. and Weisskopf, T. E. 1985. *Beyond the Waste Land: A Democratic Alternative to Economic Decline*, London, Verso
Boyer, R. and Petit, P. 1981. Progrès technique, croissance et emploi: un modèle d'inspiration kaldorienne pour six industries européennes, *Revue économique*, vol. 32, no. 6, November
Braverman, H. 1974. *Labor and Monopoly Capital: The Degradation of Work in the Twentieth Century*, New York, Monthly Review Press
Brown, C. J. F. and Sheriff, T. D. 1978. 'De-industrialisation in the UK: Background Statistics', NIESR Discussion Paper
Burawoy, M. 1985. *The Politics of Production: Factory Regimes Under Capitalism and Socialism*, London, Verso
Carter, C. (ed.) 1981. *Industrial Policy and Innovation*, London, Heinemann
Caves, R. E. and Krause, L. B. (eds) 1980. *Britain's Economic Performance*, Washington DC, The Brookings Institution
Choi, K. 1983. A statistical test of Olson's model, in Mueller (ed.) (1983)
Coates, D. and Hillard, J. (eds) 1986. *The Economic Decline of Modern Britain: The Debate Between Left and Right*, Brighton, Harvester
Cornwall, J. 1976. Diffusion, convergence and Kaldor's laws, *Economic Journal*, vol. 86 (ed.) no. 2, June
Cornwall, J. 1977. *Modern Capitalism: Its Growth and Transformation*, Oxford, Martin Robertson
Cowling, K. 1987. An industrial strategy for Britain: the nature and role of planning, *International Review of Applied Economics*, vol. 1, no. 1
Cutler, A. 1978. The Romance of 'Labour', *Economy and Society*, vol. 7, no. 1, February
Davies, S. and Caves, R. E. 1987. *Britain's Productivity Gap*, Cambridge, CUP
Denison, E. 1979. *Accounting for Slower Economic Growth*, Washington DC, The Brookings Institution
Dore, R. 1973. *British Factory–Japanese Factory: The Origins of National Diversity in Industrial Relations*, London, George Allen & Unwin
Dyer, A. W. 1984. The habit of work: a theoretical exploration, *Journal of Economic Issues*, vol. 18, no. 2
Eatwell, J. 1982. *Whatever Happened to Britain? The Economics of Decline*, London, BBC
Elbaum, B. and Lazonick, W. 1986. An institutional perspective on British decline, in Elbaum and Lazonick (eds) (1986)
Elbaum, B. and Lazonick, W. (eds) (1986) *The Decline of the British Economy*, Oxford, OUP
Emery, F. E. 1977. *The Future We Are In*, Leiden, Martinus Nijhoff
Fagerberg, J. 1987. A technology gap approach to why growth rates differ, *Research Policy*, vol. 16, nos 2–4, August
Friedman, A. L. 1977. *Industry and Labour: Class Struggle at Work and Monopoly Capitalism*, London, Macmillan
Giddens, A. 1984. *The Constitution of Society: Outline of the Theory of Structuration*, Cambridge, Polity Press
Giersch, H. and Wolter, F. 1983. Towards an explanation of the productivity slowdown: an acceleration-deceleration hypothesis, *Economic Journal*, vol. 93, no. 1, March
Gomulka, S. 1971. *Inventive Activity, Diffusion, and the Stages of Economic Growth*, Aarhus, Aarhus Institute of Economics

Gomulka, S. 1979. Britain's slow industrial growth—increasing inefficiency versus low rate of technological change, in Beckerman (ed.) (1979)
Gruchy, A. G. 1984. Uncertainty, indicative planning, and industrial policy, *Journal of Economic Issues*, vol. 18, no. 1, March
Harcourt, G. C. 1972. *Some Cambridge Controversies in the Theory of Capital*, Cambridge, CUP
Hobsbawm, E. J. 1969. *Industry and Empire*, Harmondsworth, Penguin
Hodgson, G. M. 1982. Theoretical and policy implications of variable productivity, *Cambridge Journal of Economics*, vol. 6, no. 3, September
Hodgson, G. M. 1984. *The Democratic Economy*, Harmondsworth, Pelican
Hodgson, G. M. 1988. *Economics and Institutions: A Manifesto for a Modern Institutional Economics*, Cambridge, Polity Press
Hodgson, G. M. (in press). Post Keynesianism and institutionalism: the missing link, in Pheby (ed.) (in press)
Hughes, A. 1986. Investment Finance, Industrial Strategy and Economic Recovery, in Nolan and Paine (eds) (1986)
Jones, D. C. and Svejnar, J. (eds) 1982. *Participatory and Self-Managed Firms*, Lexington, Mass., Heath
Kaldor, N. 1966. *Causes of the Slow Rate of Economic Growth in the United Kingdom: An Inaugural Lecture*, Cambridge, CUP. Reprinted in Kaldor (1978)
Kaldor, N. 1967. *Strategic Factors in Economic Development*, New York, Cornell University Press
Kaldor, N. 1968. Productivity and growth in manufacturing industry: a reply, *Economica*, vol. 35, no. 4, November. Reprinted in Kaldor (1978)
Kaldor, N. 1972. The irrelevance of equilibrium economics, *Economic Journal*, vol. 82, no. 4, December. Reprinted in Kaldor (1978)
Kaldor, N. 1975A. What is wrong with economic theory?, *Quarterly Journal of Economics*, vol. 89, no. 3, August. Reprinted in Kaldor (1978)
Kaldor, N. 1975B. Economic growth and the Verdoorn Law: a comment on Mr Rowthorn's article, *Economic Journal*, vol. 85, no. 4, December
Kaldor, N. 1978. *Further Essays on Economic Theory: Collected Economic Essays Vol. 5*, London, Duckworth
Kaldor, N. 1985. *Economics Without Equilibrium*, Cardiff, University College Cardiff Press
Kapp. K. W. 1976. The nature and significance of institutional economics, *Kyklos*, vol. 29, Fasc. 2
Kennedy, P. 1988. *The Rise and Fall of the Great Powers: Economic Change and Military Conflict from 1500 to 2000*, London, Unwin Hyman
Keynes, J. M. 1936. *The General Theory of Employment, Interest and Money*, London, Macmillan
Kilpatrick, A. and Lawson, A. 1980. On the nature of the industrial decline in the UK, *Cambridge Journal of Economics*, vol. 4, no. 1, March
Kindleberger, C. P. 1983. On the rise and decline of nations, *International Studies Quarterly*, vol. 27, no. 1, March
Lawson, T. 1985. Uncertainty and economic analysis, *Economic Journal*, vol. 95, no. 4, December
Lawson, T. 1987. The relative/absolute nature of knowledge and economic analysis, *Economic Journal*, vol. 97, no. 4, December
Lindbeck, A. 1983. The recent slowdown in productivity growth, *Economic Journal*, vol. 93, no. 1, March
Littler, C. R. and Salaman, G. 1982. Bravermania and beyond: recent theories of the labour process, *Sociology*, vol. 16, no. 2, May
Maddison, A. 1982. *Phases of Capitalist Development*, Oxford, OUP
Maddison, A. 1987. Growth and slowdown in advanced capitalist economies: techniques of quantitative assessment, *Journal of Economic Literature*, vol. 25, no. 2, June
Marshall, A. 1920. *Principles of Economics: An Introductory Volume*, 8th edn, London, Macmillan
Marx, K. 1976. *Capital*, vol. 1 (translated by B. Fowkes from the fourth German edition of 1890), Harmondsworth, Pelican
Matthews, R. C. O. 1982. Introduction: A Summary View, in Matthews (ed.) (1982)
Matthews, R. C. O. (ed.) 1982. *Slower Growth in the Western World*, London, Heinemann
McCombie, J. S. L. 1981. What still remains of Kaldor's laws? *Economic Journal*, vol. 91, no. 1, March

McCombie, J. S. L. 1982. Economic growth, Kaldor's laws, and the static-dynamic Verdoorn Law paradox, *Applied Economics*, vol. 14, pp. 279–94
McCombie, J. S. L. 1983. Kaldor's Laws in retrospect, *Journal of Post Keynesian Economics*, vol. 5, no. 3, Spring
McCombie, J. S. L. and de Ridder, J. P. 1984. The Verdoorn Law controversy: some new empirical evidence using the US state data, *Oxford Economic Papers*, vol. 36, no. 2, June
Mjoset, L. 1985. The limits of neoclassical institutionalism, *Journal of Peace Research*, vol. 22, no. 1
Mueller, D. C. (ed.) 1983. *The Political Economy of Growth*, New Haven, Yale University Press
Myrdal, G. 1939. *Monetary Equilibrium*, London, Hodge
Myrdal, G. 1944. *An American Dilemma: The Negro Problem and Modern Democracy*, New York, Harper and Row
Myrdal, G. 1957. *Economic Theory and Underdeveloped Regions*, London, Duckworth
Myrdal, G. 1978. Institutional economics, *Journal of Economic Issues*, vol. 12, no. 4, December
Nell, E. J. 1984. Conclusions—cowboy capitalism: the last round-up', in Nell (ed.) (1984)
Nell, E. J. (ed.) 1984. *Free Market Conservatism: A Critique of Theory and Practice*, London, George Allen & Unwin
Nelson, R. R. 1980. Production sets, technological knowledge, and R&D: fragile and overworked constructs for analysis of productivity growth?, *American Economic Review (Papers and Proceedings)*, vol. 70, no. 2, May
Nelson, R. R. 1981. Research on productivity growth and productivity differences: dead ends and new departures, *Journal of Economic Literature*, vol. 29, September
Nelson, R. R. and Winter, S. G. 1982. *An Evolutionary Theory of Economic Change*, Cambridge Mass., Harvard University Press
Nichols, T. 1986. *The British Worker Question: A New Look at Workers and Productivity in Manufacturing*, London, Routledge & Kegan Paul
Nolan, P. and Paine, S. (eds) 1986. *Rethinking Socialist Economics*, Cambridge, Polity Press
OECD 1986. *Historical Statistics, 1960–1984*, Paris, OECD
Olson, M. 1982. *The Rise and Decline of Nations: Economic Growth, Stagflation, and Social Rigidities*, New Haven, Yale University Press
Parikh, A. 1978. Differences in growth rates and Kaldor's laws, *Economica*, vol. 45, no. 1, February
Penrose, E. T. 1959. *The Theory of the Growth of the Firm*, Oxford, Basil Blackwell
Pheby, J. (ed.) in press. *New Directions in Post Keynesian Economics*, Aldershot, Edward Elgar
Phelps Brown, H. 1977. What is the British predicament?, *Three Banks Review*, no. 116, December. Extracted in Coates and Hillard (eds) (1986)
Polanyi, M. 1957. *Personal Knowledge: Towards a Post-Critical Philosophy*, London, Routledge & Kegan Paul
Polanyi, M. 1967. *The Tacit Dimension*, London, Routledge & Kegan Paul
Prais, S. J. 1981. *Productivity and Industrial Structure: A Statistical Study of Manufacturing Industry in Britain, Germany and the United States*, Cambridge, CUP
Pratten, C. F. 1976. *Labour Productivity Differences in International Companies*, Cambridge, CUP
Pryor, F. L. 1983. A quasi-test of Olson's Hypothesis, in Mueller (ed.) (1983)
Rice, A. K. 1958. *Productivity and Social Organization: The Ahmedabad Experiment*, London, Wiley
Rowthorn, R. E. 1975A. What remains of Kaldor's Law?, *Economic Journal*, vol. 85, no. 1, March
Rowthorn, R. E. 1975B. A reply to Lord Kaldor's Comment, *Economic Journal*, vol. 85, no. 4, December
Rowthorn, R. E. 1979. A Note on Verdoorn's Law, *Economic Journal*, vol. 89, no. 1, March
Rowthorn, R. E. and Wells, J. R. 1987. *De-industrialization and Foreign Trade*, Cambridge, CUP
Scott, M. F. 1981. The contribution of investment to growth, *Scottish Journal of Political Economy*, vol. 28, no. 3, November
Shackle, G. L. S. 1967. *The Years of High Theory: Invention and Tradition in Economic Thought 1926–1939*, Cambridge, CUP
Shackleton, J. R. and Locksley, G. 1981. *Twelve Contemporary Economists*, London, Macmillan
Shapiro, C. and Stiglitz, J. E. 1984. Equilibrium unemployment as a worker discipline device, *American Economic Review*, vol. 74, no. 3, June
Simon, H. A. 1984. On the behavioural and rational foundations of economic dynamics, *Journal of Economic Behavior and Organisation*, vol. 5, no. 1

Skouras, A. 1981. The Economics of Joan Robinson, in Shackleton and Locksley (1981)
Sraffa, P. 1926. The laws of returns under competitive conditions, *Economic Journal*, vol. 36, no. 4, December
Stafford, G. B. 1981. *The End of Economic Growth?: Growth and Decline in the UK Since 1945*, Oxford, Martin Robertson
Stephen, F. H. (ed.) 1982. *The Performance of Labour-Managed Firms*, London, Macmillan
Taylor, F. W. 1911. *The Principles of Scientific Management*, New York, Harper
Thirlwall, A. P. 1978. The UK's economic problem: a balance of payments constraint, *National Westminster Bank Quarterly Review*, February
Thirlwall, A. P. 1979. The balance of payments constraint as an explanation of international growth rate differences, *Banca Nazionale del Lavoro Quarterly Review*, no. 128, March
Thirlwall, A. P. 1980. Rowthorn's interpretation of Verdoorn's Law, *Economic Journal*, vol. 80, no. 2, June
Thirlwall, A. P. 1983. A plain man's guide to Kaldor's growth laws, *Journal of Post Keynesian Economics*, vol. 5, no. 3, Spring
Veblen, T. B. 1898. Why is economics not an evolutionary science? *Quarterly Journal of Economics*, vol. 12, no. 3, July. Reprinted in Veblen (1919)
Veblen, T. B. 1915. *Imperial Germany and the Industrial Revolution*, New York, Macmillan
Veblen, T. B. 1919. *The Place of Science in Modern Civilisation and Other Essays*, New York, Huebsch
Veblen, T. B. 1964. *The Instinct of Workmanship*, New York, Augustus Kelley
Verdoorn, P. J. 1949. Fattori che regolano lo sviluppo della produttività del lavoro, *L'Industria*, 1
Verdoorn, P. J. 1980. Verdoorn's Law in retrospect: a comment, *Economic Journal*, vol. 90, no. 2, June
Vries, A. S. W. de 1980. The Verdoorn Law revisited, *European Economic Review*, vol. 14
Vries, J. de 1983. The rise and decline of nations in historical perspective, *International Studies Quarterly*, vol. 27, no. 1, March
Vroom, V. H. and Deci, E. L. (eds) 1970. *Management and Motivation*, Harmondsworth, Penguin
Wallis, J. J. and Oates, W. E. 1988. Does economic sclerosis set in with age? An empirical study of the Olson hypothesis, *Kyklos*, vol. 41, Fasc. 3
Weisskopf, T. E. 1987. The effect of unemployment on labour productivity: an international comparative analysis, *International Review of Applied Economics*, vol. 1, no. 2, June
Whiteley, P. 1986. *Political Control of the Macroeconomy: The Political Economy of Public Policy Making*, London, Sage
Williamson, O. E. 1975. *Markets and Hierarchies: Analysis and Anti-Trust Implications: A Study in the Economics of Internal Organization*, New York, Free Press
Williamson, O. E. 1985. *The Economic Institutions of Capitalism: Firms, Markets, Relational Contracting*, London, Macmillan
Wolfe, J. N. 1968. Productivity and growth in manufacturing industry: some reflections on Professor Kaldor's inaugural lecture, *Economica*, vol. 35, no. 2, May
Wood, S. (ed.) 1982. *The Degradation of Work? Skill, Deskilling and the Labour Process*, London, Hutchinson
Worswick, G. D. N. 1982. The relationship between pressure of demand and productivity, in Matthews (ed.) (1982)
Young, A. A. 1928. Increasing returns and economic progress, *Economic Journal*, vol. 38, no. 4, December

Third World competition and de-industrialisation in advanced countries

Ajit Singh*

1. Introduction

Nicholas Kaldor was an apostle of the rapid industrialisation of the Third World since, in his view, this was the only means by which the developing countries could improve the standard of living of their people. He was also very concerned about de-industrialisation in advanced countries and was among the first to call attention to this phenomenon in the UK.[1] He claimed to have coined the term 'de-industrialisation' which the government ministers used in the mid 1970s to highlight the contraction of manufacturing capacity and employment which had been taking place in the UK economy. The central purpose of this paper is to examine how these two phenomena—the industrialisation in the Third World and de-industrialisation in advanced countries—are related, and to analyse some of the implications of this relationship.

Industrialisation of the Third World, the socialist countries of Eastern Europe, and Japan has been an outstanding feature of the world industrial economy during the last four decades. In a very short span of time, the global industrial map has changed beyond recognition. In the light of Japan's present industrial might, it is easy to forget that as late as the early 1950s, Japan produced annually only about 5 million tons of steel and 50,000 passenger cars. At the time, US steel production was approximately 100 million tons and the country produced nearly 6 million cars annually. Significantly, the Japanese costs of producing steel in the mid 1950s were almost twice the world price of steel. Yet it took Japan no more than about two decades to become the lowest-cost steel producer in the world and to produce as much steel as the US. By the late 1970s, Japan was producing more cars than the US and in the process capturing a significant share of the US market.

A major question is whether in the next two decades South Korea and the other newly industrialising countries will be able to emulate the Japanese example. And if they do, what will be their impact on the product and labour markets of the developed countries including those of Japan? As Heilbronner (1987) observes

> the Four little Dragons—South Korea, Singapore, Taiwan and Hong Kong . . . were all unequivocally 'backward' as recently as the 1960s. Today, there is no commodity that has not been made in

*University of Cambridge. An earlier version of this paper, Singh and Craypo (1988), was presented at the Notre Dame Conference on Economic Development and Labour Market Segmentation, held at the University of Notre Dame in April 1988. In writing it, I have borrowed passages from Singh (1987)

[1] For Kaldor's views on the role of manufacturing in economic development, see, for example, Kaldor (1967). For his analysis of the problems of the UK manufacturing industry and the question of de-industrialisation, see among others Kaldor (1966), Kaldor (1971) and Kaldor (1979).

these countries, from television sets and integrated circuits to steel and automobiles, and none that cannot be made. If the story of Taiwan and South Korea can sooner or later be duplicated in Turkey and Egypt, Nigeria and Indonesia, Argentina and India—and why should it not be?—the present industrial core of capitalism would face a challenge of unprecedented magnitude (p. 100).

Thus, one of the main issues addressed in this paper is to what extent, if any, 'de-industrialisation' of the older industrial countries is being, or can in future be, caused by industrialisation of the developing countries. There is, however, a prior analytical question which also needs to be considered. Does de-industrialisation—in the sense of an absolute decline or a falling share of manufacturing in output and employment—matter? Singh (1977), in one of the first papers on de-industrialisation, put this issue as follows:

What is so special about industry that one should be concerned about de-industrialization? There has also been a considerable loss of employment from agriculture, but not much has been said, at least by economists, about 'de-ruralization'. In other words, an important issue is whether de-industrialization can be regarded simply as a normal response to changing technology and tastes, or does it signify some structural disequilibrium in the economy as a whole with unfavourable overall consequences?

2. The post-war global industrial economy and Third World competition in manufactures

Table 1 summarises the main structural changes in the world industrial economy during the period 1960–80. Three points deserve attention. Firstly, the lower third of the table shows that the Third World's share of world manufacturing production, though still quite small, increased appreciably (by nearly 50%) over the two decades.[1] Similarly, there was rapid industrialisation of the socialist countries of Eastern Europe, whose share of world manufacturing also increased by about 50% during this period, starting from a much higher initial level. There was a corresponding reduction in the proportion of manufacturing output produced in the deeveloped market economy countries (DMEC).

Secondly, the middle part of the table indicates that there was a significant transformation of the internal economic structure of the developing countries. The contribution of manufacturing to GDP in these countries increased from an average of 13·4% in 1960 to nearly 20% by 1980. Moreover, there is evidence (not reported in Table 1) of positive qualitative changes in the structure of manufacturing itself in the Third World over this period. Starting from an extremely low level, there was an enormous expansion of capital goods production in the developing countries. Disaggregated data show that the latter's share of world manufacturing increased significantly not only in consumer goods industry but also in most branches of capital goods industry (Singh, 1984; UN, 1982).

Thirdly, the last part of the table indicates that in the 1970s the rate of growth of manufacturing production slowed down considerably in the OECD countries, from nearly 6% per annum to less than 4% per annum. However, there was no such slow-down in the pace of expansion of manufacturing in the Third World; if anything, the growth of manufacturing in the developing countries in the 1970s was slightly faster than in the 1960s.

Tables 2 and 3, which do not include the socialist countries of Eastern Europe, bring the story up to the mid 1980s.[2] Table 2 shows that, despite the severe world economic crisis

[1] China is not included in the data reported in Table 1. China's share of world manufacturing production in 1980 was approximately 4% (see UN, 1982).

[2] The composition of 'developing countries' in Tables 2 and 3 (which are based on the World Bank data bank) is different from that in Table 1 (whose source is UNCTAD). This does not, however, affect the broad trend movements over time portrayed in these tables.

Table 1. *Structural changes in the world industrial economy: 1960–80 manufacturing output (value added) for major economic groups*

	1960	1970	1980
Value added (billions US dollars at 1975 prices)			
Developing countries	49	101	218
DMEC[a]	533	942	1358
Socialist countries	119	283	574
Total	701	1326	2150
Contribution to GDP (%)			
Developing countries	13·4	15·7	19·7
DMEC[a]	24·3	26·5	27·8
Socialist countries	24·6	30·7	36·7
Total	23·1	25·9	23·4
Share in world manufacturing output (%)			
Developing countries	6·9	7·6	10·2
DMEC[a]	76·0	71·1	63·2
Socialist countries	17·1	21·3	26·6
Total	100·0	100·0	100·0

	1960–70	1970–80
Average annual growth (%)		
Developing countries	7·6	8·0
DMEC[a]	5·9	3·7
Socialist countries	9·0	7·3
Total	6·6	4·9

Source: UNCTAD, *Trade and Development Report*, 1981, New York, 1981.
[a]Developed market-economy countries.

of the 1980s, which has had a devastating effect on the economies of many developing countries, the latter's share of world manufacturing production has continued to increase. Table 3, however, indicates that the rate of growth of manufacturing production in the Third World has slowed down considerably in the 1980s. Significantly, the two tables also show that, over the last decade, the developing countries' performance with respect to manufacturing exports has been much better than with respect to production. These countries' share of world manufacturing exports increased to only a relatively small extent betwen 1965 and 1973, from 7·3% to 9·9%; however, between 1973 and 1985, the share has almost doubled. Table 3 shows that, whereas there has been a sharp trend decrease in the rate of growth of manufactured exports from the industrial market economies during 1973–85 compared with 1965–73, the developing countries have recorded a trend increase in their growth of manufacturing exports over the corresponding periods. This is a very

Table 2. *Shares of production and exports of manufactures by country group, 1965, 1973, and 1985* (%)

	Share in production			Share in exports		
Country group	1965	1973	1985	1965	1973	1985
Industrial market economies	85·4	83·9	81·6	92·5	90·0	82·3
Developing countries	14·5	16·0	18·1	7·3	9·9	17·4
low-income	7·5	7·0	6·9	2·3	1·8	2·1
middle-income	7·0	9·0	11·2	5·0	8·1	15·3
High-income oil exporters	0·1	0·1	0·3	0·2	0·1	0·3
Total	100·0	100·0	100·0	100·0	100·0	100·0

Source: World Development Report (1987).

Table 3. *Growth in production and exports of manufactures by country group, 1965–73, 1973–85, and 1965–85* (%)

	Growth in production			Growth in exports		
Country group	1965–73	1973–85	1965–85	1965–73	1973–85	1965–85
Industrial market economies	5·3	3·0	3·8	10·6	4·4	6·8
Developing countries	9·0	6·0	7·2	11·6	12·3	12·2
low-income	8·9	7·9	7·5	2·4	8·7	6·0
middle-income	9·1	5·0	6·6	14·9	12·9	13·8
High-income oil exporters	10·6	7·5[a]	8·4[a]	16·2	11·5	16·0
Total	5·8	3·5	4·5	10·7	5·3	7·4

Source: World Development Report (1987).
[a]End period is 1984 instead of 1985.

important point for our subsequent analysis and can be put in a more striking way as follows: during 1965–73, the rate of growth of manufacturing exports of the developed countries was much the same as that of the developing countries; however, between 1973 and 1985, the former's exports grew only at 4·4% per annum, whilst the latter's increased at an incredible 12·3% per annum. Moreover, much the larger part of the Third World's manufactured exports continued to go to the industrial countries. Further, Table 4 shows that the developing countries are exporting not only the traditional labour intensive and resource-based products, but are also recording very fast growth in the exports of a variety of products of capital goods industries.

It is necessary to enter an important caveat with respect to the above generally favourable long-term record of Third World industrialisation and exports. The data in Tables 1 to 4 refer to the developing countries as a whole. Clearly, there has not been a uniformly good industrial performance in all parts of the Third World. In particular, it is worth emphasising that the relatively good overall performance of the developing countries in

Table 4. *Structure of manufactured exports from developing countries, 1970–84*

Description	Share of developing countries' exports[a]		Growth rate[b]
	1970	1984	1970–84
Traditional manufactured exports			
Labour-intensive			
Textiles and apparel (84 and 65)	31·3	24·8	11·8
Footwear (85)	1·8	2·9	18·2
Other labour-intensive (61 and 83)	2·9	2·3	11·6
Total	36·0	30·0	12·4
Resource-based			
Wood and cork (63)	3·6	1·5	6·9
Paper manufactures (64)	0·8	1·1	17·6
Other resource-based (52 and 56)	0·8	0·9	14·5
Total	5·2	3·5	12·2
Nontraditional manufactured exports[c]			
Electrical machinery (72)	16·1	16·7	14·1
Chemicals (51)	8·3	9·9	15·3
Nonelectrical machinery (71)	4·2	8·7	20·1
Transport equipment (73)	2·6	5·2	20·0
Iron and steel (67)	6·2	6·5	14·2
Other nontraditional[d]	21·4	19·5	12·9
Total	58·8	66·5	15·1
Total	100·0	100·0	14·0

Source: World Development Report (1987).
Note: Figures in parentheses are the SITC categories for the respective product group.
[a]Developing countries' exports of the listed product as a share of developing countries' total exports of manufactured products defined as SITC categories 5, 6, 7, and 8, less 68.
[b]The rate of growth of developing countries' exports of the listed product during 1970–84 in constant dollars.
[c]Total manufacturing exports less traditional manufactured exports.
[d]Rest of nontraditional exports.

the economic crisis of the 1980s is basically due to the superior record of the Asian countries, not just the four little Dragons, but also India and China. Latin American and Sub-Saharan African manufacturing industry has generally suffered a set-back in the 1980s.[1] For example, in Mexico during the oil boom years 1977–81, manufacturing industry was growing at a rate of about 6% per annum. In 1982, manufacturing production fell by 4% and in 1983 by a further 8%. By 1984, average real wages in Mexico had fallen by nearly 50% compared with 1982. Similarly in Tanzania, as a consequence of a balance of payments crisis, by the mid 1980s industrial capacity utilisation had fallen to a bare 20%. Nevertheless, because of the necessity to service their huge debts, the manufacturing export performance of the Latin American countries in the 1980s has been relatively much better than their record in production.

It is, however, also essential at this point to draw attention to the *immense potential* for ever-increasing competition from the Third World in industrial products in the future.

[1] For a fuller discussion, see Singh (1984, 1986A).

This potential arises from the fact that rapid industrialisation is a compelling social imperative for the developing countries. As Singh (1979A) has argued, if the Third World countries are (a) to meet the minimum basic needs of the people for food, shelter, education and health, and (b) to provide sufficient employment for their fast-expanding labour forces (at a rate of approximately 3·5% or more per annum in many countries), the GDP in these countries must increase by nearly 6 to 7% per annum. Given the present very low level of average GDP per capita in the developing countries, this implies, on the basis of past empirical relationships, a rate of growth of manufacturing production in the Third World of nearly 10% per annum.[1] If such a fast expansion of manufacturing output in the South is realised, it could *in principle* pose a continuing competitive problem to Northern industry.

3. 'De-industrialisation' in advanced countries: stylised facts

The most important long-term changes which have taken place in industrial output and employment in advanced countries in the post-war period may be summarised as follows:[2]

First, in the first decade or so of the long post-war boom (1945–73), the *share* of manufacturing in total *employment* increased in almost all industrial countries, including old industrial countries like the UK which already had a large proportion of their labour force employed in manufacturing. (As long ago as 1860, 33% of the UK labour force was employed in manufacturing: Feinstein, 1972.) The manufacturing employment share reached its peak (36·1% of civil employment) in the UK in 1955, but since then, it has been in decline. The share fell marginally over the next decade (it was 34·8% in 1966), at a somewhat faster rate to 32·3% until 1973, and at a much faster rate since then (the 1981 figure was 26·48%). In countries like Belgium and Sweden, the pattern of change in the proportion of labour force employed in manufacturing was broadly similar to that of the UK, i.e. a slow decrease up to 1973 and an accelerated decline subsequently as the world economy slowed down after 1973. However, it is significant that in France and Germany there was no evidence of a trend decline in manufacturing industry's share of employment until 1973, although since then the share has fallen markedly in both countries. In Italy and Japan, the share actually expanded up to 1973, but even in these countries there has been a trend decline since then. In the US the proportion of the labour force employed in manufacturing fell from 28·5% in 1955 to 24·8% in 1973 and to 21·7% in 1981.

Second, in relation to the *numbers* employed in manufacturing and their rate of growth, manufacturing employment increased in all industrial countries (including the UK) in the post World War II period up to the mid 1960s. Between 1966 and 1973, although it fell in a few countries (e.g. the UK, the Netherlands, Belgium), manufacturing employment continued to grow in most OECD countries, including the US, Japan, Italy, France and Germany. However, during the decade 1973–83, manufacturing employment has fallen in almost all industrial countries, the rate of decline ranging from 0·04% per annum in Japan and the US to a massive 3·1% per annum in the UK and 3·4% per annum in Belgium. Thus, in the UK, the numbers employed in manufacturing industry have fallen from their

[1] For a full elaboration of this argument, see Singh (1979A, 1984); see also ILO (1976).

[2] This summary is based on the following works: Blackaby (1979), Martin and Rowthorn (1986), Singh (1977, 1982) and Matthews and Bowen (1987).

Table 5. *The excess of rate of growth of manufacturing over the rate of growth of GDP, leading OECD countries 1950–73, 1974–84 (annual percentage growth rates)*

	1950–73	1973–84
UK	0·2	−2·4
France	1·3	−1·7
W. Germany	1·1	−1·1
Italy	4·2	−0·5
US	0·8	−0·1
Japan	5·7	−1·3

Source: Matthews and Bowen (1987).

historical peak of 8·4 million workers in 1966 to 5·4 million at the end of 1984, a drop of 35%, half of which occurred in the five-year period 1979–84.

Third, turning to manufacturing *production*, the share of manufacturing in total production at *constant prices* did not show any trend decline in most industrial countries, including the UK, during the period of the long boom (1950–73). However, in almost all the leading OECD economies, manufacturing industry's share at constant prices appears to have reached its peak in 1973. Between 1973 and 1984, the GDP in these countries has expanded at an appreciably faster rate than manufacturing production, thus indicating a fall in the share of manufacturing in GDP over this period (see Table 5). The abysmal record of UK manufacturing industry again stands out. Despite the slowdown in the world economy after 1973, all the leading industrial countries other than the UK managed to expand their manufacturing production during the decade 1973–83, albeit at a far slower rate than before. However, manufacturing output in the UK in 1983 was 18% lower than it was a decade earlier.[1]

Fourth, in contrast to the behaviour of manufacturing in constant prices, when the share of manufacturing in total production is measured at *current* prices, it shows a trend decline in a large number of industrial countries even before 1973. In the UK, the share fell from 36·1% in 1960 to 31% in 1973; in the US the corresponding decline was from 28·4% to 24·9%. The main reason for this difference in the constant and current prices shares of manufacturing lies in the fact that in many advanced countries, because of the faster growth of productivity in manufacturing than in services, the terms of trade tended to move in favour of the latter.

In short, the empirical evidence indicates that before 1973 there was a small decline in the proportion of the labour force employed in manufacturing in some of the advanced countries. However, no country showed a trend decline in the share of manufacturing in output at constant prices. Since the slowdown in world economic growth in 1973, the share of manufacturing in both output and employment has fallen to a greater or smaller degree in most industrial countries.

[1]Since the trough of 1982, there has been a more or less sustained expansion of manufacturing production in the UK. However, even in 1985, the level of manufacturing outout was 5·5% lower than in 1979 and 5% lower than in the first quarter of 1974 when the 'three day week' was in operation (Coutts *et al.*, 1986). Manufacturing production is expected to reach its previous peak level of 1973 in 1988 (*Financial Times*, 16 August, 1988).

4. Third World competition and de-industrialisation in advanced countries: conceptual issues

The common perception among many business leaders and trade unions in industrial countries, that cheap labour imports from the Third World are responsible for the de-industrialisation of their economies, is given a rigorous expression in Beenstock (1984). Beenstock argues that for a variety of reasons (e.g. product cycles, transfers of technology) the comparative advantage in a wide range of industries has shifted from the North to the South, leading to a re-allocation of capital from Northern industry to other economic sectors in the North as well as to Southern industry (via multi-national investment). The loss of manufacturing employment in the North therefore stems from the rise of industry in the South and the liberalisation of world trade in manufactures. Beenstock regards this as a temporary phenomenon, a problem of 'mismatch' between the jobs which are lost in manufacturing and the new jobs which may be created elsewhere.

However, to establish an empirical link between de-industrialisation in advanced countries and Third World competition there are a number of conceptual issues that need to be clarified. First, a contraction of manufacturing output and employment in either an absolute or a relative sense may indeed not be significant from a macroeconomic standpoint if it does not lead to increased overall unemployment and is simply a reflection of changing technology and market conditions.[1] The shedding of the industrial labour force could in fact lead to a rise in productivity if, for example, there was previous overmanning in industry.

Second, and more importantly, de-industrialisation may be a structural feature of all economies during the course of economic development. As numerous studies have shown, as per capita income rises, the share of output and employment in agriculture (A) falls and that in manufacturing (M) rises until a very high level of per capita income is reached. Subsequently, the share of services (S) in employment (but not necessarily in output) expands at the expense of manufacturing.[2] There are good analytical reasons for these observed empirical regularities. They arise essentially from differences in (a) the income elasticity of demand, η, and (b) the rate of growth of productivity, $\dot{P}$, in the different sectors of the economy. The value of η in agriculture (η^A) usually tends to be much less than that in manufacturing (η^M); η^M is however normally somewhat smaller than η^S but, since the prices of manufactured products usually rise at a slower rate than those of services, the long-run rates of growth of demand in manufacturing and services may be more or less the same. However, $\dot{P}^M$ is usually greater than $\dot{P}^S$, which makes it the main factor responsible for the contraction of manufacturing employment as economic development in industrial countries proceeds.[3]

Nevertheless, it may also be the case that for any particular country, the extent of the loss of industrial employment may be greater than is warranted at its level of per capita

[1] However, 'gross job' losses can and often do cause enormous social distress even if there is equivalent employment created elsewhere and there is no net contraction of jobs in the economy as a whole. The new service sector jobs may often pay less and may be relatively unprotected by union rights and other benefits compared to the manufacturing jobs which disappear. Bluestone and Harrison (1982) called particular attention to this phenomenon. See also Singh and Craypo (1988).

[2] For a fuller analysis of the issues, see Singh (1987); Rowthorn and Wells (1987); Fuchs (1968, 1981).

[3] If these postulates about the relative values of η and $\dot{P}$ in different sectors of the economy hold, in the limit, most of the labour force would be employed in services and hardly any in manufacturing or agriculture. However, the share of manufacturing in production may not fall much even in the limit. It is of course possible to argue that in the very long run, people's preferences and technology may change in such a way that these postulates about η and $\dot{P}$ no longer hold.

income. Moreover, the contraction of manufacturing employment or output may also denote a structural disequilibrium in the economy in the sense that the country is consequently unable to reach its long-term growth potential or a full employment of its resources. For all these reasons, in Singh (1977) I argued that whether de-industrialisation should be regarded either as benign or alternatively as a manifestation of a long-term structural disequilibrium of the economy, cannot be properly considered in terms of the characteristics of the domestic economy alone. As a minimum, I suggested, for an open economy these questions can be sensibly analysed only in the context of the interactions of the economy with the rest of the world, i.e. in terms of its overall trading and payments position in the world economy. Since trade in manufactures is a major determinant of the current account balance of most advanced countries (usually much more important than the trade in services), an analysis of de-industrialisation necessarily entails an examination of the performance of the country's manufacturing sector in the international economy.

With these considerations in mind, to give precision to the concept of structural disequilibrium, I there defined an efficient manufacturing sector in the specific case of the UK economy, in the following terms: *Given the normal levels of the other components of the balance of payments*, an efficient manufacturing sector is one which (*currently as well as potentially*) not only satisfies the demand of consumers at home at least cost, *but is also able to sell enough of its products abroad to pay for the nation's import requirements.* This is, however, subject to the qualification that an 'efficient manufacturing sector' must be able to achieve these objectives *at socially acceptable levels of output, employment and exchange rate.* The latter restrictions are extremely important, since at low enough levels of output and employment, or more arguably at a sufficiently low exchange rate, almost any manufacturing sector may be able to meet this criterion of efficiency. (The exchange rate should be regarded here as an indicator of the socially acceptable levels of inflation and inequality of income distribution.) It is also necessary to emphasise the significance of the condition that, to be efficient, the manufacturing sector must be able to fulfil the above requirements not merely currently, but also in the long run.[1] For instance, a windfall gain to the balance of payments (e.g. from the discovery of North Sea oil) may put it temporarily into surplus (at desired levels of output, employment etc.), although manufacturing industry may be incapable of ensuring this when 'normal' conditions return. Cairncross (1979) has rightly pointed out that an implication of this conception of an efficient manufacturing sector is that even when 'manufacturing output was actually growing in proportion to GDP (as on one measure it did up to 1973), or even when manufacturing employment was growing in proportion to total employment', there may be a structural disequilibrium in the sense of a progressive failure to achieve sufficient exports to pay for full employment level of imports at a 'reasonable' exchange rate.[2]

Thus to establish that Third World competition has an unfavourable impact on industry and the overall UK economy, it is essential to investigate the following causal chain:

(1) Is the economy in long-term structural disequilibrium in the sense outlined above?

[1] The emphasis here is on the long-term or structural factors which may prevent an economy from achieving its full potential, rather than on temporary disturbances which may easily be self-correcting. The disequilibrium becomes structural in the sense that it cannot correct itself through the normal market mechanisms. This is either because, for institutional reasons, there is not adequate wage/price flexibility in the economy (e.g. because of the workings of the labour market, it is not possible to achieve a large enough real devaluation without risking inflation), or even to the extent that there is wage/price flexibility, it cannot restore competitiveness because the latter has very important non-price dimensions (the quality of the products, technical progress, delivery dates, etc). See further Singh (1977, 1986B). See also below.

For footnote 2 see next page.

(2) If so, is this disequilibrium due to trade in manufactures rather than, for example, to trade in services?

(3) If the structural disequilibrium is, indeed, because of the trade in manufactures, is this due to competition with the Third World or with other advanced countries (e.g. Japan)?

A quantitative examination of these questions should also make it possible to estimate the *size* of the efect of Third World competition in manufacturing on output and employment in the UK economy.[1]

At a more general level, it should be emphasised that the expansion of industry in one part of the world need not necessarily be at the expense of industrial development in another part of the world. Sayers (1965) made a useful distinction between 'complementary' and 'competitive' aspects of world economic expansion for any particular country or region. Economic growth elsewhere is 'complementary' to the extent that it raises demand for the country's exports, but it becomes 'competitive' insofar as it leads to the

[2] In a recent paper, Professor Sir James Ball (1988) in his extended comments on Singh (1977) has objected to the above definition of an 'efficient manufacturing sector' on the grounds that 'in a neo-classical world with fully flexible prices and capital mobility, there is no such thing as *the* "full employment level of imports" ' (emphasis and quotes in the original, page 9). However, in Singh (1977) (as indeed here), I was concerned with the real world rather than with the neo-classical 'world of perfect adjustments' (Professor Ball's phrase, page 25). I wrote: 'However, even assuming wage-price flexibility, whether the market forces can restore equilibrium depends crucially on the nature and adequacy of the response of entrepreneurs in bringing about the required changes in the productive structure, as well as the magnitude of the relevant elasticities for exports and imports, and in a dynamic world on the speed of these adjustments. Now if, in addition, for institutional reasons, real wages and exchange rate are not sufficiently flexible*, there cannot be any presumption that market forces will on their own be able to correct the disequilibrium' (Singh, 1977, pp. 119–120). (The footnote indication is in the original). The first sentence of the footnote noted that: 'The nature and degree of wage price flexibility in the real world are essentially empirical questions'. The rest of the footnote provided a critique of Frankel and Johnson (1976) for their 'theoretical justification for the assumption of wage flexibility'.

Sir James also suggests that I regarded the balance of payments constraint on the UK economy as a problem arising from deficiencies on the demand side. This is not correct since I specifically stated that this was a supply-side phenomenon. I wrote: 'To sum up, the evidence outlined here suggests that there are serious weaknesses on the supply side in UK manufacturing, which make it increasingly difficult for it to meet foreign competition in either home or overseas markets. It is these facts, when considered in conjunction with the reduction in the labour force in manufacturing, which make 'de-industrialization' a matter of serious concern. In view of the sluggish rate of investment, low growth and high unemployment, it is difficult to see how such deficiencies, which pertain to the dynamic factors in the production system, can be remedied. The evidence suggests that, left to itself, the situation may continue to deteriorate in the manner postulated by Myrdal's theory. The relative absence of these dynamic factors (which manifests itself in slower technical progress, product innovation and ability to respond to demand changes as compared with competitors) may continue to lead to growing inroads by competitive imports, poor export performance and hence balance-of-payments difficulties and low growth' (pp. 132–133). Like Sir James, Singh (1977) also emphasised the importance of the non-price factors in determining competitiveness (see also Singh (1979B) for a further analysis of these issues). However, where Sir James and I obviously disagree is on what are the best ways to improve the supply side. In the present context, it is also relevant to mention that Sir James's article also contains an interesting and insightful commentary on Professor Kaldor's views on the role of manufacturing, the balance of payments constraint, the exchange rate and economic growth.

[1] An alternative approach to estimating the effects of Third World competition on de-industrialisation in advanced countries relies on the following equation

$$dE = \frac{1}{P_t}(dD + dX - dM - E_{t+1}\,dP)$$

where E = employment, D = domestic demand, X = exports, M = imports, P = productivity, t, $t+1$ are the time periods being considered, and d indicates the change between t and $t+1$. This model has been widely used in the literature—see for example Cable (1977), Foreign and Commonwealth Office (1979), Frank (1977), UNIDO (1979). Although the empirical estimates based on this equation are not unreasonable, there are serious conceptual and methodological objections to the underlying model (see Singh, 1987).

development of alternative sources of supply. So, from the point of view of a country or a region, the development of the world economy may be characterised by a changing balance between 'complementarity' and 'competitiveness'. During 1960–80, not just the South, but the Socialist countries of Eastern Europe, industrialised very fast; as seen in Section 2, the latter's share of world industrial production increased from 17% to 27% over these two decades. Nevertheless, it would be difficult to maintain that East European industrialisation was achieved at the expense of the older industrial countries of Western Europe. On the contrary, most observers would agree that, if anything, West European industrial development was most probably positively helped by industrial demand from the East. Put in these terms, the question remains whether industrialisation of the South and, in particular, of the NICs has been more 'competitive' rather than 'complementary' to the North and, hence, responsible for the loss of manufacturing or other jobs in the advanced countries.

5. Third World competition in manufactures and the UK economy

This section (based on Singh, 1982) will report on an empirical analysis of the impact of Third World competition in manufactures on output and employment in the UK economy, in terms of the concepts outlined in Section 4. The analysis covers the period 1964–78 which preceded the advent of Mrs Thatcher's government in 1979 as well as the availability of North Sea oil to the UK economy. Both the radically different economic policies of the Thatcher administration and North Sea oil have had a major impact on the UK industry and economy.[1] Between 1973 and 1979, the UK manufacturing employment fell by nearly 700,000; over the next seven years, the job losses in manufacturing were more than twice as high.[2]

However, there is a large body of evidence that, even before 1979, UK manufacturing industry was not only 'inefficient' in the sense outlined above (i.e. characterised by long-term disequilibrium), but more importantly, this disequilibrium was growing worse over time.[3] Between 1964 and 1978, the UK's share of world manufacturing exports was nearly halved, whilst the industry suffered a huge increase in import penetration in its own home market. Significantly, this was despite the fact that, over this period, UK costs and prices, expressed in terms of a common currency, had *fallen* relative to those in the competitive countries. Mainly because of this decline in the performance of UK industry in the world economy, there was, during the 1970s, a trend deterioration in the country's current account balance at full employment. To illustrate, in 1965–66, the UK was able to achieve a rough balance on the current account although there was near full employment (rate of unemployment of 1·5%). A decade later, in 1975, although nearly 4% of the labour force waxs unemployed, there was a current account deficit of £1,700 million. Part of this was, indeed, due to the effects of the rise in oil prices in 1973. However, as CEPG (1976) showed, even assuming that the terms of trade had remained constant at the pre-1972 level, there would have been a current account deficit of £2,000 million at full employment

[1] These events have arguably led to a different 'economic regime' than the one which prevailed before 1979. In order not to further complicate the analysis by an examination of these regime changes, the following discussion in the text concentrates on Britain's industrial experience before Mrs Thatcher and before North Sea oil.

[2] For an analysis of the UK industry and economy since 1979, see among others Singh, 1987; Barker, 1988; Coutts *et al.* 1986; Rowthorn and Wells, 1987; Ball, 1988.

[3] See Blackaby (1979); Singh (1977, 1979 and 1986B); CEPG (1976–82).

in that year. By 1977, the UK's current account deficit at full employment had soared to nearly £6,000 million.

Disaggregated analyses show that the main reason for the above disequilibrium did not lie in the UK's trade in services or invisibles, but in visible trade in finished manufactures. In the present context, the important question is to what extent, if any, this deficit arose from the UK's manufacturing trade with the Third World, particularly the newly industrialising countries (the NICs) rather than with the other advanced economies. To examine this issue, Table 6 reports on the UK's trade balance in finished manufactures (SITC 7 and 8) with the world as a whole, with the NICs and with the advanced countries.[1] To avoid aggregation bias, different sub-groups of NICs have been considered, since it is quite possible that a single NIC trading partner of the UK (in particular, Iran during this period) may have a major influence on its trade balance. The average annual trade balance over three successive three-year periods is shown to indicate long-term trends. Table 6 indicates that whereas the annual balance with the world increased by approximately £500 million between 1964–66 and 1970–72, over the next six years there was a much larger increase of almost £1,500 million. This is in striking contrast to the picture with respect to the advanced industrial countries. For example, in the case of the original six members of the European Economic Community (EEC), the trade balance in finished manufactures *declined* by over £100 million between 1964–66 and 1970–72, and at an accelerated pace over the subsequent six years. The negative time-trend in the balance with certain individual industrial countries, such as Japan and West Germany, was equally significant.

As far as the newly industrialising countries are concerned, the pattern is similar to that for the world, i.e. a growing increase in trade balance over time. Although, during the 1970s, there was a particularly large increase in the balance with Iran, the broad picture remains unaltered, even if Iran is excluded from the NICs. Various sub-groups of NICs identified in the table (Mediterranean and Israel, Eastern Europe, Latin America) also show approximately similar trends except for East Asia (i.e., Korea, Hong Kong, Singapore, Malaysia, etc.). The last three columns of Table 6 indicate that, inclusive of Iran, the NICs accounted on average for nearly 22% of UK trade balance in finished manufactures during 1964–66, and for about a third in 1977–78; without Iran, the corresponding figures are 20·6 and 21·7% respectively. Parenthetically, it should be noted that if the UK's trade balance is considered in relation to the Third World rather than the NICs, the picture will be even more favourable. The main reason for this is that the great bulk of Third World imports of finished manufactures into the UK emanate from the NICs; further, many of the countries included amongst the NICs here (e.g. Poland, Spain, etc.) are not generally regarded as developing Third World nations.

There is one potentially serious weakness of the analysis presented in Table 6. It may legitimately be objected that in the examination of the UK's manufacturing trade with the NICs, SITC categories 7 and 8 are too restrictive. In particular, under SITC category 6, there are a number of industries where the developing countries are known to have made striking inroads in advanced countries' markets (e.g. textiles); it is conceivable that the

[1]Many different definitions of 'NICs' have been used in the literature. We have here followed the practice of Foreign and Commonwealth Office's (1979) influential study in including a relatively large number of countries in the list of NICs. The 24 countries, constituting the group of NICs, whose trade data has been analysed in this study, are: Argentina, Brazil, Mexico, Philippines, S. Korea, Hong Kong, Taiwan, Singapore, Malaysia, Thailand, India, Bangladesh, Pakistan, Iran, Romania, Hungary, Poland, Israel, Turkey, Greece, Yugoslavia, Malta, Spain, Portugal. This list is more or less the same as that of the Foreign and Commonwealth Office (1979).

Table 6. *UK trade balance in finished manufactures (SITC 7 and 8) with NICs and other regions and countries, 1964–1978*

	£m, current prices			As % of world balance		
	1964–66	1970–72	1976–78	1964–66	1970–72	1976–78
World	1501·4	2014·7	3525·2	100·0	100·0	100·0
EEC (original six)	78·6	−41·6	−1377·7	5·24	−2·06	−39·08
Japan	2·7	−55·0	−655·5	0·18	−2·73	−18·59
W. Germany	−46·9	−149·0	−1005·5	−3·12	17·40	−28·52
US	2·7	−30·2	−412·8	0·18	−1·50	−11·71
NICs	328·1	512·1	1159·6	21·85	25·42	32·89
NICs-Iran	309·3	455·2	765·1	20·60	22·59	21·70
Med. + Israel[a]	115·5	200·4	462·5	7·69	9·95	12·10
E. Europe[b]	14·4	35·4	57·9	0·96	1·76	1·64
India	106·0	78·2	149·4	7·06	3·88	4·24
E. Asia[c]	43·2	48·6	−101·9	2·88	2·41	−2·89
Latin America[d]	30·2	92·5	233·2	2·01	4·59	6·62
Iran	18·8	56·9	394·5	1·25	2·82	11·19

Sources: Overseas Trade Accounts; Overseas Trade Statistics of the UK; Annual Statement of Trade of the UK.

[a]Portugal, Spain, Malta, Yugoslavia, Greece, Turkey, Israel.
[b]Poland, Hungary, Romania.
[c]Thailand, Malaysia, Singapore, Hong Kong, Philippines, Taiwan, S. Korea.
[d]Mexico, Brazil, Argentina.

inclusion of such industries might change the results significantly. To examine this hypothesis, Table 7 presents corresponding information to that for Table 6, but with a broader commodity coverage. In addition to products in SITC categories 7 and 8, it also includes those under SITC sub-groups 62 (rubber manufactures); 65 (textiles); 66 (non-metallic mineral manufactures); and 69 (metal manufactures).[1] The table shows that with the inclusion of additional commodities, the UK's trade balance with the world becomes larger, over $8 billion (equivalent to about £4·66 billion) on average during the years 1975–77 (the corresponding figure in Table 6 being £3·5 billion). However, the data also indicate that as far as the time-trends in trade balance for the various groups of countries are concerned, they are broadly similar to those in Table 6. Expressed in sterling, the UK's average annual trade balance with NICs for this larger group of commodities increased by approximately £200 million between 1963–65 and 1969–71, and by about £750 million over the subsequent six years.

It was noted earlier that the UK economy was becoming increasingly balance-of-payments constrained during the 1970s. Since the country's trade balance with the NICs was improving over time, the results of Table 6 and 7 therefore suggest that, despite the fast pace of industrialisation in the NICs and a large increase in their manufactured exports to the UK, the UK's trade with the NICs was leading overall to an *increase* in domestic output and employment rather than a reduction. In contrast, the data in these tables also indicate that manufacturing trade with the Japanese, the West Germans and with the other advanced countries, by contributing to a further tightening of the balance of

[1]The UK statistical sources do not provide a consistent source going beyond 1970 for category 6. Table 7 is therefore based on OECD figures expressed in dollars.

Table 7. *UK trade balance in manufactures [SITC(R) 62, 65, 66, 69, 7 and 8] with NICS and other regions and countries, 1963–77*

	$m, current prices			As % of world balance		
	1963–65	1969–71	1975–77	1963–65	1969–71	1975–77
World	4739·9	5764·4	8818·4	100·0	100·0	100·0
EEC (original six)	276·5	295·7	−1188·9	5·83	5·13	−13·48
Japan	15·9	8·2	−887·3	0·34	0·14	−10·06
W. Germany	−99·6	−271·9	−1437·8	−2·10	−4·72	−16·30
USA	29·1	9·9	−332·6	0·61	0·17	−3·77
NICs	962·4	1340·3	2514·4	20·30	23·25	28·51
NICs − Iran	911·6	1223·3	1798·2	19·23	21·22	20·39
Med. + Israel	400·8	601·6	1136·4	8·46	10·44	12·89
E. Europe	43·6	90·1	161·0	0·92	1·56	1·83
India	255·0	125·4	215·4	5·38	2·18	2·44
E. Asia	120·0	158·4	−155·4	2·53	2·75	−1·76
Latin America	92·3	247·7	440·7	1·95	4·30	5·00
Iran	50·8	117·0	716·2	1·07	2·03	8·12

Sources: OECD Statistics of Foreign Trade, Series C, Annual
Note: For definitions of the country groups, see Table 6.

payment constraint, was causing losses in jobs and production. Singh (1982) provided some rough, back-of-the-envelope, quantitative estimates of the effects of the UK's manufacturing trade with the NICs during 1972 to 1978 on output and employment in the economy. On the basis of the CEPG (1977) estimate of the value of foreign trade multiplier of about three in the UK economy in this period, it was calculated that at a macroeconomic level trade in manufacturing products with the NICs generated annually 65,000 jobs during the mid 1970s. This was no more than a very crude estimate intended merely to provide some broad idea of the order of magnitudes involved. It did, however, take into account the *composition* effects of the changes in an advanced country's output resulting from the changes in its trade with a Third World economy. A number of studies have shown (see for example OECD, 1979) that, because of these effects, a *balanced* increase in manufactured trade between industrial and developing countries has a small negative impact on employment in the former since imported products tend to be more labour-intensive than the exports from the industrial countries.

However, although during the 1960s and 1970s the UK had an increasing trade balance in manufactures with the newly industrialising countries, with an overall small positive impact on domestic employment, this does not by any means tell the whole story. For the data also contained evidence that in the case of a number of the NICs, *there was likely to emerge over time, imbalances in trade of a kind similar to the UK's trade with Japan and other advanced countries*, although that had not happened up to the late 1970s. In general, it is entirely possible for a country's trade balance to improve for a period in absolute terms, while its trade performance was deteriorating in the sense that its trend rate of growth of exports was lower than its trend rate of growth of imports.

Figure 1 shows UK trade performance ratios (defined as the net trade balance as a proportion of total trade) in finished manufactures (SITC 7 and 8) over the period

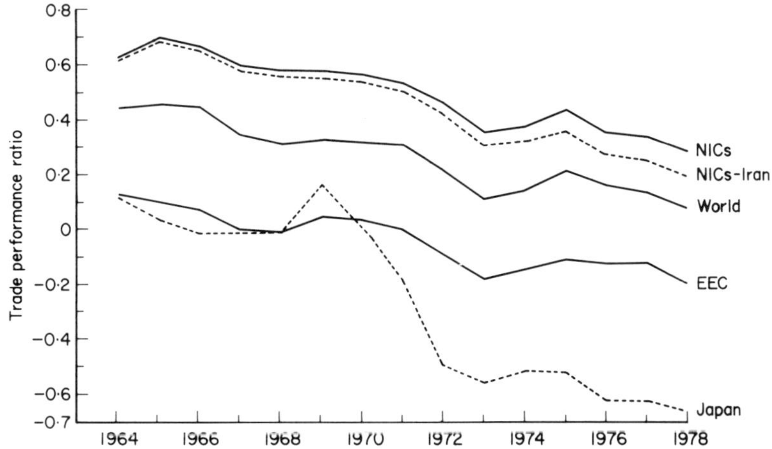

Fig. 1. *UK trade performance ratios in finished manufactures (SITC 7 and 8), 1964–78 with NICs, EEC, Japan and the World. Source:* see Table 6. See text for definition of the variable.

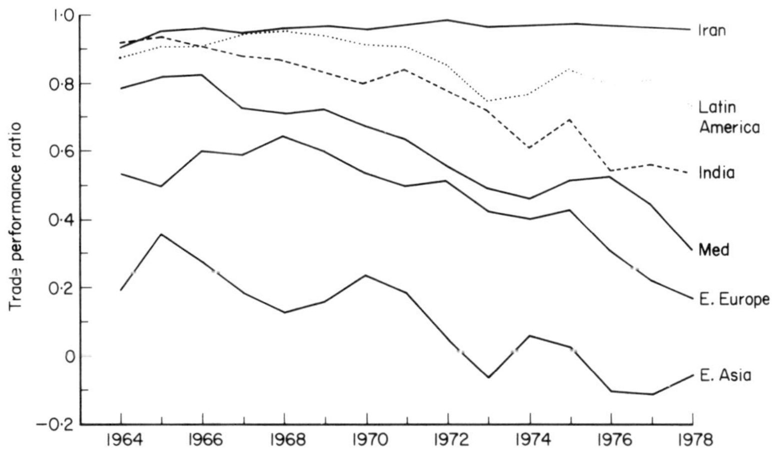

Fig. 2. *UK trade performance ratios in finished manufactures (SITC 7 and 8), 1964–78 with various groups of NICs, India and Iran. Source:* see Table 6.

1964–78, with the NICs, the EEC (the original six), Japan and the World; trade ratios for various sub-groups of NICs are shown in Fig. 2. Figure 1 indicates that, although UK trade ratios with the NICs and the world were positive throughout 1964–78, they were subject to negative long-run trends. Trade ratios with the EEC and Japan, which were a little above zero at the beginning of the period, had become persistently negative throughout the 1970s, the negative values being particularly large in the case of Japan. Figure 2 shows that apart from Iran, the UK's trade ratios with the various individual as well as sub-groups of newly industrialising countries, although still mostly positive, suffered a continuing decline throughout the period.

In order to compare more precisely changes over time in UK trade ratios with the various groups of countries, Table 8 gives trend rates of change obtained by regression

Table 8. *UK trade performance ratios in finished manufactures (SITC 7 and 8) with NICs and other regions and countries, 1964–78: trend rates of change*[a]

Region or country	Trend rates of change b	Standard error of b	R^2
World	−0·0578**	0·0057	0·8887
USA	−0·0117	0·0076	0·1540
Japan	−0·1432**	0·0175	0·8381
W. Germany	−0·0249	0·0063	0·5453
EEC	−0·0422**	0·0052	0·8335
Med. + Israel	−0·1140**	0·0095	0·9170
E. Europe	−0·0661*	0·0118	0·7085
Iran	0·0246	0·0216	0·0909
India	−0·1635**	0·0100	0·9536
E. Asia	−0·0576**	0·0087	0·7704
Latin America	−0·1054*	0·0258	0·5619
Total newly ind.	−0·0761**	0·0068	0·9055
Total newly ind. – Iran	−0·0881**	0·0066	0·9317

*t value > 4; **t value > 6.

[a]Given by the coefficient 'b' in the table, obtained by fitting the regression curve:

$$\log (X/M) = \log a + bt + \log e$$

where X and M refer to values of exports and imports respectively. Note that correction for serial correlation does not alter the above results.

analysis.[1] The striking feature of this table is not only that all the 'b' coefficients (except for Iran) are negative, but that the trend decline in UK trade ratios with the newly industrialising countries (with or without Iran) was *greater* than that with the EEC and West Germany.[2] Thus, although during 1964–78 the UK trade balance with the newly industrialising countries was increasing whilst that with the industrial counties was decreasing, trade *performance* with respect to the former was deteriorating faster than in relation to the latter. The apparent anomaly here is entirely due to the fact that the initial absolute level of the UK's trade ratio with NICs was much larger than that with the EEC countries. This analysis suggests that, although up to the late 1970s the increasing trade balance with the NICs had a positive impact on domestic UK employment, if the observed adverse trends in trade performance continued, the long-term effect would become negative (as had already happened with the EEC and other advanced countries).

Turning very briefly from the UK to the industrial countries in general, the OECD (1978) study for a group of advanced countries and a sub-set of NICs found that OECD's trade balance in manufacturing with NICS increased over the period 1970–77. This suggests that even if in some balance of payments constrained advanced countries, manufacturing trade with NICs had become disequilibriating in the 1970s, it is likely in

[1]As the ratio, $(X-M)/(X+M)$, assumes negative values, it is not possible to fit logarithmic time trend regression equations to this variable. Instead the equations fitted were:

$$\log (X/M) = a + bt + e.$$

A negative value of 'b' indicates that the trend rate of growth of imports was greater than that of exports.

[2]Much the same results are obtained if the analysis is done on the basis of the wider commodity coverage, i.e. the data set corresponding to Table 7.

general to have been a far smaller source of disequilibrium than the trade among the industrial countries themselves. However, as in the case of the UK, there is no reason to believe that this will necessarily continue to be the case over time.

6. Conclusion

Rapid industrialisation in the Third World during the last three decades as well as the continuing extremely fast expansion of Third World manufacturing exports to the advanced countries has raised the question whether these have, or will in future, lead to 'de-industrialisation' in advanced countries. Will Third World industrialisation become 'competitive' with industry in the North, as Japanese post-war growth appears to have been, or will it be 'complementary', as in the case of East European industrial development *vis à vis* Western Europe? There is a complex chain of causation, linking industrialisation in the Third World to 'de-industrialisation' in the advanced countries and this paper has focused on elucidating and clarifying a number of conceptual issues which are involved here. In an empirical analysis of 'de-industrialisation' in the UK economy in the period before Mrs Thatcher's government and the advent of the North Sea oil, it has been argued that the UK's manufacturing trade with the newly-industrialising countries was if anything responsible for *increased* overall output and employment during the 1970s rather than a decline. There was, however, evidence of certain negative long-term trends which suggested that, in the future, the country's trade with the NICs could well become disequilibriating. The large trade surpluses which economies like Taiwan and South Korea are presently running with the United States suggests that the same may also be true for some other advanced countries.

If the world economy were again to expand at the rates that were achieved during the Golden Age (1950–1973) and there were near full employment in the advanced countries, the fast growth of the manufactured exports from the growing list of NICs could clearly be much more easily accommodated. However, in a slow growing world economy with high levels of unemployment in many industrial countries, such an accommodation is far more problematical and leads to ad hoc calls for protection against the Third World (as well as the Japanese and other countries') products. As there are powerful reasons for thinking that the world economy is unlikely to resume its Golden Age growth path and will continue to expand at its much slower post 1973 rate in the foreseeable future,[1] Kaldor's proposals for managed or planned trade (including commodity price stabilisation agreements) are timely and deserve serious consideration.[2]

Bibliography

Ball, J. 1988. 'Manufacturing Industry, Economic Growth and the Balance of Payments', An essay in honour of Professor Dennis Coppock's 65th birthday, mimeo
Barker, T. S. 1988. International trade and the British economy, in Barker, T. S. and Dunne, P., *The British Economy after Oil: Manufacturing or Services?* London, Croom Helm
Beenstock, M. 1984. *The World Economy in Transition*, London and Boston, Allen and Unwin
Blackaby, F. (ed.) 1979. *Deindustrialisation*, London, Heinemann Educational Books
Bluestone, B. and Harrison, B. 1982. *The De-industrialization of America*, New York, Basic Books
Cable, V. 1977. British protectionism and imports, *ODI Review*
Cairncross, A. 1979. What is deindustrialisation? in Blackaby (1979)

[1]For a full examination of these issues, see Glyn, Hughes, Lipietz and Singh (forthcoming).

[2]The essential argument here can be put as follows: the resumption of the Golden Age growth path is the first best solution to the present problems of the world economy; if this is not feasible, planned, coordinated trade is a second best solution, much to be preferred to the current unsatisfactory state of ad hoc protectionism which can easily degenerate into a negative sum game. See further Singh (1986B).

CEPG 1976–82. *Cambridge Economic Policy Review*, Cambridge, Department of Applied Economics, various issues

Coutts, K. J., Godley, W. A. H., Rowthorn, R. E. and Ward, T. S. 1986. *A Cambridge Bulletin on the Thatcher Experiment*, Cambridge, Department of Applied Economics

Feinstein, C. 1972. *National Income, Expenditure and Output of the United Kingdom, 1855–1965*, Cambridge, CUP

Frank, C. R. Junior, 1977. *Foreign Trade and Domestic Aid*, Washington, Brookings Institution

Foreign and Commonwealth Office 1979. *The Newly Industrialising Countries and the Adjustment Problem*, London, Foreign and Commonwealth Office

Frankel, J. A. and Johnson, H. G. 1976. *The Monetary Approach to the Balance of Payments*, London, Allen and Unwin

Fuchs, V. R. 1968. *The Service Economy*, New York, National Bureau of Economic Research

Fuchs, V. R. 1981. Economic growth and the rise of service employment, in *Towards an Explanation of Economic Growth: Symposium 1980*, (ed.) H. Giersch, Tubingen, J. C. B. Mohr

Glyn, A., Hughes, A., Lipietz, A. and Singh, A. Forthcoming. The rise and fall of the Golden Age, in Marglin, S. A. (ed.), *The End of the Golden Age*, Oxford, OUP

Heilbronner, R. 1987. Hard Times, *The New Yorker*, 4 September

ILO 1976. *Employment Growth and Basic Needs: A One World Problem*, Geneva, ILO

Kaldor, N. 1966. *Causes of the Slow Rate of Economic Growth of the United Kingdom*, Cambridge, CUP

Kaldor, N. 1967. *Strategic factors in Economic Development*, Ithaca, Princeton University Press

Kaldor, N. 1971. Conflicts in national objectives, *Economic Journal*, vol. 81

Kaldor, N. 1976. Inflation and recession in the world economy, *Economic Journal*, vol. 86

Kaldor, N. 1979. Comment, in Blackaby (1979)

Martin, R. and Rowthorn, R. (eds) 1986. *The Geography of De-industrialisation*, London, Macmillan

Matthews, R. C. O. and Bowen, A. 1987. Keynsian and other explanations of post-war macro-economic trends, paper prepared for *Keynes General Theory After Fifty Years* Conference held at the National Economic Development Office, London, September

Norton, R. D. 1986. Industrial policy and American renewal, *Journal of Economic Literature*, March

OECD 1979. *The Impact on Newly Industrialising Countries on Production and Trade of Manufactures*, Paris, OECD

Rowthorn, R. E. and Wells, J. R. 1987. *De-industrialization and Foreign Trade*, Cambridge, CUP

Sayers, R. S. 1965. *The Vicissitudes of an Export Economy: Britain since 1880*, Sydney, University of Sydney Press

Singh, A. 1977. UK industry and the world economy: a case of de-industrislisation? *Cambridge Journal of Economics*, vol. 1 no. 2, June

Singh, A. 1979A. The 'basic needs' approach to development and the new international economic order: the significance of Third World industrialization, *World Development*, June

Singh, A. 1979B. North Sea Oil and the reconstruction of the UK industry, in Blackaby (1979)

Singh, A. 1982. *Structural Changes in the UK Economy: a Long-Term Structural Analysis of the UK's Trade with Less Developed Countries and its Impact on the UK Economy*, Vienna, UNIDO

Singh, A. 1984. The interrupted industrial revolution of the third world: prospects and policies for resumption, *Industry and Development*, no 12

Singh, A. 1986A. The great continental divide: the Asian and Latin American countries in the world economic crisis, *Labour and Society*, September

Singh, A. 1986B. The long-term structural disequilibrium of the UK economy: employment, trade and import controls, in Sjostedt, G. and Sundelius, B. (eds) *Free Trade—Managed Trade? Perspectives on a Realistic International Trade Order*, Boulder, Colorado, Westview

Singh, A. 1987. Manufacturing and Deindustrialization, in the *New Palgrave*, London, Macmillan

Singh, A. and Craypo, C. 1988. Restructuring of the Domestic and the Global Economy and Labour Market Segmentation, paper presented at the Conference on Labour Market Segmentation and Economic Development held at the University of Notre Dame, 18–20 April

UN 1982. *World Industry in 1980*, UNIDO, ID/269

UNIDO, 1979A. *World Industry since 1960: Progress and Prospects*, New York, United Nations

UNIDO, 1979B. The Impact of Trade with Developing Countries on Employment in Developed Countries, Vienna

Kaldor as a policy adviser

A. P. Thirlwall*

Introduction

What made Kaldor so fascinating as an economist was his sparkling originality, his wide diversity of economic interests, and the many facets of his long and distinguished career which sometimes took him out of academic life into the public domain and into political controversy. Even within academe he was a controversial figure, holding unorthodox views on a variety of subjects. He was not only a first rate theorist and applied economist, but he was also involved in policy making at the highest level in the United Kingdom and in many other countries. Kaldor followed Keynes from King's College to Whitehall, and they had many other characteristics in common. Both treated economics as a moral science—as a branch of ethics in the Cambridge tradition of Marshall, Pigou and Sidgwick—as a means to the end of attempting to make the world a more humane and civilised place. Both men shared the urge to protest against stupidity and injustice. Keynes described graphically in his Essay to the Memoir Club (Keynes, 1933) his own 'impulse to protest, to write a letter to *The Times*, call a meeting in the Guildhall etc. etc. I behave as if there really existed some authority or standard to which I can successfully appeal if I shout loud enough.' Kaldor was the most prolific letter writer to *The Times* of any economist this century, airing his views and leading campaigns on a wide variety of economic, social and political issues. Both men shared the over-optimistic, but naïve and frequently mistaken, view that rational argument and the power of intelligence would triumph over prejudice and ignorance and could solve any problem. Both were adept at devising new and ingenious schemes to improve the functioning of the economy, with an intuition about events and behaviour often ahead of their theoretical understanding. As Keynes said in his obituary memoir of Marshall, 'it was an essential truth to which he held firmly that those individuals who are endowed with a special genius for the subject of economics and have a powerful economic intuition will often be more right in their conclusions and implicit presumptions than in their explanations and explicit statements. That is to say their intuition will be in advance of their analysis and their terminology' (Keynes, 1933). A lot of Kaldor's economics and advice, I believe, falls into this category. Keynes and Kaldor both held official and unofficial advisory positions for long periods, and exerted a considerable influence on the direction of economic policy both overtly and behind the scenes. Finally, both men aroused passions. Keynes fundamentally revolutionised the way economists thought about economic behaviour at the macro-level, and assigned a role to the State to compensate for market failure. Keynes wanted to save liberal capitalism

*University of Kent at Canterbury. This essay draws heavily on Thirlwall (1987). I am grateful to Professor Brian Reddaway for helpful comments on an early draft of this paper.

but, for many, his policy conclusions smacked of the thin edge of the wedge of socialism. Kaldor was a professed and committed Socialist and this generated hostility amongst those of *laissez-faire* persuasion and in the Conservative press which revelled in portraying him as a dangerous subversive intent, by his tax advice, on squeezing the capitalist class. His Hungarian background added colour and credence to the image. Truth and image can be very different, however. He believed passionately that the tax system should be made more equitable, but he was a reformer and a democrat, never a revolutionary, who in the last resort agreed with Keynes 'that it is better that a man should tyrannise over his bank balance than over his fellow citizens' (Keynes, 1936, p. 374).

From a young age, as a schoolboy in Hungary, and as a student in Berlin and London between 1925 and 1932, Kaldor took a keen interest in politics and public affairs. He was an accredited journalist in Berlin and in London, working for the Hungarian newspapers, Pester Lloyd and Magyar Hirlap, as well as the London General Press. He never contemplated standing for political office, but his deep concern for the underdog and for social justice attracted him to the left of the political spectrum and he found his natural political home in the British Labour Party. The London School of Economics (LSE), where he taught from 1932 to 1947, was deeply divided politically. The left-wing image of the School, largely attributable to its historical origins and to Harold Laski in the politics department, contrasted with the generally rightwing complexion of the economics department dominated by the Austrian, libertarian thinking of Lionel Robbins and Friedrich von Hayek. Economists to the left of centre were in a minority. The Keynesian revolution, to which Kaldor was one of the first LSE converts, further widened the schism in the economics department. Most of Kaldor's writing during the 1930s, however, was theoretical.

Kaldor's involvement in public policy started with the Second World War. For the purposes of this essay, I interpret Kaldor's role as a policy adviser to include his influence on economic policy not only in an official capacity, but also in an unofficial capacity, such as, for example, his evaluation of government Reports on important matters or his evidence to Royal Commissions or Select Committees of the House of Commons—research and advice which has influenced the course of economic policy and history. From 1939 on, he was rarely out of the public eye in one capacity or another. His advisory role spanned, therefore, nearly fifty years; rather longer, in fact, than Keynes', whose influence stretched from 1913, when he was a member of the Royal Commission on Indian Currency and Finance, to his death in 1946. Kaldor's work during the war on various aspects of war economics, and on preparations for the peace, was done in a private capacity, but was highly influential nonetheless. After the war, he was heavily involved in aspects of post-war reconstruction, particularly following his appointment as Director of the Research and Planning Division of the Economic Commission for Europe in Geneva in 1947. On his return to Cambridge in 1949, he was appointed in 1950 as one of two economists on the Royal Commission on the Taxation of Profits and Income, out of which came his powerful *Memorandum of Dissent* which laid the basis for the future tax strategy of the Labour Party. His tax expertise led to a flood of requests to serve as a tax adviser in developing countries, starting with India in 1956. With the election of a Labour government in the United Kingdom in 1964, he became Special Adviser to the Chancellor of the Exchequer, first to Mr Callaghan and then to Mr Jenkins, and then in 1969 he was appointed as a Special Adviser to Mr Crossman at the Department of Health and Social Security. Out of office between 1970 to 1974, he gave evidence to various Select Committees and became active in the campaign against the entry of the UK into the EEC on the terms proposed. When the Labour government was returned to power in 1974, he again became

Special Adviser to the Chancellor, this time to Mr Healey, but resigned in 1976, disillusioned with the course of economic policy, and took his seat in the House of Lords, having been given a peerage in 1974. Throughout the 1950s and 1960s and into the 1970s and 1980s, he was also advising formally and informally on a number of specific economic issues in this country and abroad, particularly relating to international monetary reform and the conduct of monetary policy. He was an economic consultant to the Economic Commission for Latin America in 1956 and 1963; a consultant to the Food and Agricultural Organisation in 1952; an adviser to the Indian Planning Commission in 1967; a crucial witness before the Radcliffe Committee on the Working of the Monetary System in 1958, and before the Treasury Select Committee on Monetary Policy in 1980—and so on. He had the ear of Prime Ministers, Finance Ministers, and politicians across the globe in several countries, in a manner unique among contemporary economists. This essay will be structured around these epochs and themes.

The war years 1939–45

Many of Kaldor's professional contemporaries made their contribution to the war effort by becoming civil servants in the various Ministries concerned with physical and financial planning. Because of his foreign extraction, Kaldor was excluded, although he had become a naturalised British subject in 1934. He was eligible for call-up, but opted instead to continue teaching and research, with the LSE evacuated to Peterhouse, Cambridge. He devoted his research energies to aspects of the war effort in Britain, and to the study of the problems of post-war reconstruction. He also took a keen interest in the war effort of Germany, and followed closely the economies of the Allied countries. The three areas in which he was particularly influential related to the finance of the war effort; national income accounting; and, perhaps most important of all, the political acceptance of the two Beveridge Reports on Social Insurance (Beveridge, 1942) and Unemployment (Beveridge, 1944).

From the onset of the war, Kaldor was communicating with Keynes on a regular basis over various aspects of war finance and national income accounting. In an early paper in *The Banker* (Kaldor, 1939) he laid down two major principles which he believed should govern war finance: first, that the aggregate real burden should be kept as small as possible and, second, that the distribution of the burden should be equitable. If resources are unemployed, the government should borrow rather than tax to finance expenditure. He believed borrowing of £1000 million to be justified in the prevailing circumstances. Kaldor sent his estimates of war finance to Keynes who in reply gave his classic statement of what he meant by an inflationary gap: 'the amount of purchasing power which has to be withdrawn, either by taxation or primary savings, in order that the remaining purchasing power should be equal to the available supplies on the market at the existing level of prices'. Keynes had in mind a compulsory savings scheme, and Kaldor made several practical suggestions on how the scheme might be made operational. He also helped to clarify and improve the papers that Keynes was writing on the estimation of national income, which became an essential exercise for calculating the resources available for war. Keynes worked in net terms, while Kaldor preferred the concept of Gross National Income. Kaldor felt that using estimates of net investment and net income might considerably understate the resources available since depreciation is arbitrary, and therefore net income is a much vaguer concept than gross income. He also insisted that calculations should be net of indirect taxation. When the first White Papers on National Income appeared, Kaldor was sent them to review for the *Economic Journal* (see Kaldor,

1941, 1942; Kaldor and Barna, 1943). His detailed critical dissection of their contents had a considerable influence on future procedures in the UK and abroad. Tibor Scitovsky wrote from America: 'your articles on the two British White Papers on War Finance are regarded as classics in this country . . . everybody regards them as a model on which the corresponding estimates in this country are being based'. *The Manchester Guardian* (2 October 1943) described the reviews as a 'welcome annual habit'. In the review of the first White Paper,[1] Kaldor pointed to what he regarded as deficiencies in the presentation of the accounts, some of which were subsequently remedied, and others he attempted to rectify himself. For example, in the second White Paper, in contrast to the first, the data relating to war finance and national income now covered the same time period; subsidies and transfer payments were deducted from government expenditure, and estimates were given of the tax burden among different classes of the population—all of which Kaldor suggested. For some time, however, the estimates continued to be presented in money terms, and Kaldor made his own estimates of real income.

Kaldor's detailed understanding of national income accounting, and his experience with forecasting trends, made him an ideal person to calculate the financial implications of the 1942 Beveridge Report on Social Insurance. Kaldor's careful analysis of the costs was extremely important in putting the financial burden in perspective, making it easy for the more extravagent claims over cost, and that the Plan could not be afforded, to be refuted. (Kaldor, 1943A and B). Under the proposed scheme, everyone would be covered for all needs by a single weekly contribution, with the underlying principle that benefit should be in return for contribution, with risks pooled. The immediate political response was that the Plan would be too costly; that the proposed Exchequer contribution would mean excessive tax increases, and that the increased employers' contribution would so raise costs as to price British goods out of export markets. Armed with estimates of post-war national income and government expenditures, Kaldor showed the cost to be trivial: '10 pence on income tax or 6 pence on income tax and a penny a pint on beer'. He thus concluded: 'the argument that the Beveridge Plan would make the financial burden on the taxpayer unbearably heavy is just nonsense—for neither is the aggregate tax burden excessively large, nor does the Beveridge scheme make any appreciable difference to the size of the burden'. The estimated cost would amount to just under 1·6% of average disposable income—'a very moderate sacrifice indeed for the abolition of want'. Kaldor campaigned publicly and vociferously, as did Beveridge himself, for the implementation of the Plan. He wrote several letters to the press and broadcast on the radio on the theme of 'The Cost of Social Security'[2] in the BBC series 'The World We Want' edited by Joan Robinson.

The sequel to Beveridge's *Report on Social Insurance* was his 1944 *Report on Full Employment* which helped to lay the foundations for the post-war government commitment to full employment, which was largely honoured for three decades and then effectively abandoned in 1979 (to be replaced by a commitment to stable prices, apparently at any price). Kaldor also played a major role in the political and public acceptance of this second Report, with his examination (assisted by Tibor Barna), in the now famous Appendix C, of the revenue and expenditure implications for the government of pursuing a fiscal policy to maintain full employment (Kaldor and Barna, 1944). Beveridge's definition of full employment was 'more vacant jobs than unemployed men' with the

[1] *Analysis of the Source of War Finance and Estimates of the National Income and Expenditures in 1938 and 1940*, London, HMSO, 1941.

[2] *The Listener*, 4 November 1943.

additional proviso that the jobs should be 'at fair wages, of such a kind, and so located that the unemployed men can reasonably be expected to take them'. The acceptable 'full employment' level of unemployment was put at 3%. The full employment policy had three main components: the maintenance of total expenditure; the control of industrial location, and organised labour and mobility. Kaldor concentrated on the implications of maintaining total expenditure, and on the different ways of financing increased expenditure, the conclusion being an estimated 6% increase in 1938 tax rates for the budget to be balanced at full employment in 1948. There turned out to be errors in the forecasts, but this was the first attempt to make comprehensive and consistent estimates of income, taxation and other variables from a large number of separate forecasts and assumptions within the framework of a consistent 'econometric' model. Kaldor's contribution to the *Report* was widely acclaimed. Alvin Hansen wrote from America: 'I think you did a wonderful job on Appendix C'. Colin Clark wrote from Brisbane: 'I should like to congratulate you on a most effective piece of work'. John Hicks in *The Manchester Guardian* (17 November, 1944) described Appendix C as 'one of the most important and fascinating chapters of the book.' David Worswick, writing in the paper *Socialist Commentary*, described Kaldor's contribution as a 'brilliant essay in applied economics'. On the question of budgeting for full employment, Kaldor argued the case elsewhere for two separate budgets, one for current expenditure financed by taxation and a second capital budget to be financed by loans.[1] Keynes wanted the same (see Wilson, 1982).

When the war ended, Kaldor wanted a continuation of war-time controls. In responding to criticism of his optimistic calculations of national income in the 1944 *Beveridge Report* he remarked:

> the conclusion to be drawn is not that we 'can't afford' major schemes of national improvement without a drastic curtailment of consumption but that we cannot afford to do without planning. Provided that the idea of budgeting the use of national resources in accordance with a scheme of priorities is carried over into peacetime, and the necessary controls are retained, there is little danger of the post-war reconstruction plans having to be curtailed for lack of means. (Letter to *The Economist*, 3 March 1944)

In retrospect, there was a consensus that after the First World War controls were abolished too quickly, with the result that there was a short-lived boom followed by a collapse of the heavy industries. In a pamphlet with M.F.W. Joseph (Kaldor and Joseph, 1942), Kaldor argued for the retention of consumer rationing and price controls, with maximum prices set sufficiently low for only the most efficient firms to survive. Raw materials should be allocated according to the urgency of needs. Import controls should continue in order to secure the most essential imports, and controls over capital flows abroad should also continue. He was also strongly in favour of the continuation of utility production, in order to reap maximum economies of scale (as in effect the Americans had done with their car industry)[2] particularly for the stimulation of exports, and for key industries to be taken into public ownership.

Post-war reconstruction at home and abroad, 1945–9

By the end of the war, Kaldor was regarded as one of the most incisive applied economists of his generation. As a result, he received a flood of requests from newspapers, and various

[1] *The Times*, 25 and 26 March 1943 in two (anonymous) articles as part of a series of ten on the theme of full employment.

[2] In the US, ten leading car producers with 88% of sales produced only 15 engine types. In Britain, eight leading makers, also with 88% of sales, produced 39 engine types. Output per man hour was 3·4 times higher in the US than in the UK.

organisations at home and abroad, to write articles, to undertake research, and to advise on a wide range of economic problems. On the domestic front, he was for a short time economic adviser to the Air Ministry and Ministry of Supply (with the rank of Brigadier General) to assist the British Bombing Survey Unit with the construction and comparison of the output series of the British and German armaments industries. He contributed regularly to *The Manchester Guardian*, writing articles on aspects of post-war reconstruction.[1] He carried on his campaign for planning, and severely criticised the Labour government for attempting to run a planned economy without a Plan.[2] When Stafford Cripps became Chancellor of the Exchequer in 1947 a more serious approach to planning was taken, but Kaldor still criticised the undue neglect of the external balance. He wanted production targets for exports. Following the devaluation of 1949, he was critical of the budget in 1950 for not being austere enough to meet the external challenge, so that Britain could be free of American aid.[3] Kaldor himself played a role in the 1949 devaluation decision. The Chancellor, Stafford Cripps, was ill in hospital in Zurich, and a decision had to be taken in his absence. Kaldor came to London from Geneva specifically to advise on the devaluation issue. He met Hugh Gaitskell and Douglas Jay on the 13 July, and they were unanimous that devaluation was the wisest course. Three days earlier, Kaldor had written an influential letter to *The Times* under the pseudonym 'Exile' in which he argued that if the City had made up its mind that sterling was over-valued, the attempt to hold the pound would have increasingly costly effects on Britain's foreign trade and financial reserves.

Abroad, Kaldor accepted three important advisory roles, before becoming in 1947 the first Director of the Research and Planning Division of the newly created Economic Commission for Europe (ECE) in Geneva. He was Chief of the Planning Staff of the US Strategic Bombing Survey in Germany (1945); an adviser to the Hungarian government (1946), and assisted Jean Monnet at the French Commissariat Général du Plan in preparing a plan for the financial stabilisation of France (1947).

The purpose of the US Strategic Bombing Survey was to investigate the military and economic effects on Germany of bombing by the Allied forces. The US airforce wanted confirmation that they had won the war. Kenneth Galbraith had overall responsibility for the Survey, and he recruited what he later described as 'one of the most diversely talented groups of scholars ever brought together for a single research task' (Galbraith, 1981). As Chief of the Planning Staff, Kaldor interviewed many of the German generals, including Halder, who had been Chief of the General Staff of the German army in 1938. As well as confiding that there was a *putsch* planned to arrest Hitler in Berlin on the very day that Chamberlain announced his intention to come to Munich, he and the other Generals exposed the myth of a ruthless German war machine, with the whole economy made subservient to the needs of war. More pertinent to the Survey, it was revealed that German war production continued to expand despite US bombing. It was not the US airforce but the ground troops that proved decisive (see US Strategic Bombing Survey, 1945; Kaldor, 1945).

In Hungary after the war, a new coalition government was elected including Communists and Socialists. The Communists had produced a new Three Year Plan under the direction of Eugene Varga. The Socialists employed Kaldor to produce an alternative

[1] See, for example, 'The Washington Settlement', 11 and 12 December 1945 and his review of the Treasury's *Economic Survey 1947*, 10 and 11 March 1946.

[2] See a series of letters in *The Times*, 25 February, 15 March and 3 April 1947.

[3] In a BBC broadcast. See *The Listener*, 11 May 1950.

Plan, which he did with the aid of thirty staff in the space of six weeks using the technique of material balances.

The invitation in 1947 to assist in the preparation of a Plan for the financial stabilisation of France came from Robert Marjolin, who was Jean Monnet's right-hand man at the Commissariat Général du Plan. France was in the process of implementing a new five-year plan, and the task was to ensure monetary stability without jeopardising investment. Kaldor (assisted by Pierre Uri) proposed a whole new series of taxes to restrain consumption and to bring the tax ratio close to that of other European countries ('A Plan for the Financial Stabilisation of France', in Kaldor, 1980C). The tax proposals formulated then are interesting because they were very similar to those he later proposed for many developing countries when he commenced his role as a tax adviser in 1956.

Kaldor was not happy at the LSE after the war. He disliked the right-wing atmosphere of the institution and the petty attitude of Robbins towards him, which bordered on hostility. He was more than receptive to attractive new job offers. In 1947 the Economic Commission for Europe was created, designed to organise Europe on a collaborative basis for the purposes of European recovery, bringing together both East and West. Indeed, it was the original intention that the ECE should administer Marshall Aid to Europe.[1] Gunnar Myrdal, Minister of Commerce in the Swedish government at the time, was appointed Executive Director and offered Kaldor the post of Director of Research. He had no hesitation in accepting and resigned from the LSE which had been his academic home for twenty years. His main brief was to prepare an annual *Economic Survey of Europe*. He set about the task with relish. With his own budget, he created the Research and Planning Division from scratch, recruiting between fifteen and twenty economists and assistants to work on various sections of the *Survey*. Among the young and energetic staff, later to achieve distinction as professional economists, were Robert Neild, Esther Boserup, Helen Makower, Albert Kervyn, Hans Staehle, Hal Lary, Tibor Barna, and P. J. Verdoorn. When the Surveys appeared, they were treated as the authoritative account of the economic conditions and trends in Eastern and Western Europe, and attracted widespread international interest in official circles and the press.[2] Kaldor wrote the first two *Surveys* for 1947 and 1948 virtually single-handed, and co-authored with Hal Lary the 1949 *Survey* before leaving the Commission to become a Fellow of King's and Lecturer in Economics at the University of Cambridge. The first *Survey* concentrated primarily on the tasks facing Europe in the wake of war-time devastation; in particular, the recovery of production and trade, and the restoration of balance of payments equilibrium to reduce dependence on the US. Europe's current account deficit totalled $7·5 billion, of which $5·4 billion was with the US. The tone of the second and third *Surveys* was less grave, but the current account of the balance of payments continued to be a major problem.

While Kaldor was in Geneva as a United Nations official, he participated in several special assignments, including acting as an adviser to the UN Technical Committee on Berlin Currency and Trade in the winter of 1948–9, and serving on a UN Expert Committee in 1949 to prepare a Report on national and international measures for full employment. In 1948 the Soviet Union blockaded Berlin, and the Soviet condition for lifting the blockade was that a common currency should be restored. The UN Technical

[1] In the event, owing to the political intrigue and infighting between East and West over the Marshall Plan, the Organisation for European Economic Cooperation (OEEC), established in 1948, took on this role.

[2] The first Survey was printed beforehand by the US Congress as an Official Document: *A Survey of the Economic Situation and Prospects of Europe* (US Government Printing Office, Washington, 1948).

Committee was set up to examine the matter, and Kaldor was a member of the Committee's Secretariat with the formidable task of cross-examining representatives of the big-Four powers. Sidney Dell, also a member of the Secretariat, recalls Kaldor's performance as 'brilliant' and 'one of the most fascinating experiences of my entire career' (personal correspondence). Kaldor drafted the Report recommending the Soviet mark as the sole currency for Berlin. The Report was overtaken by events, however, when Stalin eventually lifted the blockade unconditionally.

The UN Experts Committee's *Report* (1949) identified the balance of payments as the major constraint on the return to full employment in Europe. Other members of the Committee were J. M. Clark of Columbia University, Arthur Smithies of Harvard, Pierre Uri of the French Commissariat Général du Plan, and Ronald Walker of the Australian Department of External Affairs. The *Report* was largely drafted by Kaldor, and its adoption by the United Nations owed much to his verbal dexterity. Sidney Dell wrote to him afterwards saying that his influence in uniting inter-governmental interests had been 'without parallel' and conjectured that 'it would have been a wishy-washy Report of no international consequence if you hadn't been there and worked like hell!' In the press, the *Report* was generally well received. Interestingly, it envisaged a role for the newly created World Bank in recycling American surpluses. But at a meeting of the UN Economic and Social Council in 1950 to discuss the *Report*, at which Kaldor was present, spokesmen from the World Bank and the IMF were hostile to such a proposal, and this role for the World Bank never materialised. The interest that the *Report* generated in Europe led the Committee on Economic Questions of the Council of Europe to request the Secretariat-General to prepare a study of how the measures recommended should be applied to Europe. A Working Party was set up, chaired by Kaldor, and prepared a Report entitled *Full Employment Objectives in Relation to the Problem of European Co-operation* (1951). Amongst other things, it recommended a European Advisory Board to oversee national efforts to promote full employment; a European Investment Bank to promote development of underdeveloped regions of Europe, and import controls rather than deflation to secure simultaneous internal and external equilibrium.

It was Kaldor's work for the United Nations and Europe on full employment that impressed the future Labour Chancellor of the Exchequer, Hugh Gaitskell, who then appointed Kaldor to the Royal Commission on the Taxation of Profits and Income. This important assignment ushered in another phase of Kaldor's life, which later opened up unexpected doors in high places in Britain and overseas.

Taxation

Kaldor's appointment to the Royal Commission on the Taxation of Profits and Income in 1951, and his immersion in tax matters for the next four years, turned him into one of the world's leading experts on tax theory and policy. The only other academic economist appointed to the Commission was John Hicks who was much more conservative in his outlook. Fundamental differences of opinion caused Kaldor, with Mr H. L. Bullock and George Woodcock, to produce a lengthy Memorandum of Dissent (Minority Report) to the Commission's Report, which became a minor classic in the literature on taxation. So, too, did Kaldor's book *An Expenditure Tax* written at the same time on a subject precluded by the Commission's terms of reference. Kaldor was deeply concerned with the inequities in the British tax system, and believed, more strongly than any economist of his generation, in the power of taxation to alter economic welfare and performance for the better. He was not persuasive in determining the final recommendations of the Commission, but the Minority Report, which he largely drafted, became very influential within Labour Party circles, and formed the basis of tax reform when the Labour Party assumed office in 1964 with Kaldor as Special Adviser to the Chancellor of the Exchequer.

For most of the time, the Commission worked under the Chairmanship of Lord Radcliffe, whom Kaldor came to respect and admire. But there emerged major differences between himself and most other members of the Commission on issues of principle relating to the taxation of capital gains; the treatment of expenses under Schedule D and E, and the taxation of company profits. If a tax system is to be fair between individuals according to ability to pay, the first requirement is a just and comprehensive definition of income. However comprehensively income is defined for tax purposes, however, it remains an inadequate measure of ability to pay because it ignores taxable capacity that resides in property as such. For Kaldor, this constituted an argument for measuring ability to pay by spending power. The question then becomes whether there is a definition of income which can measure an individual's spending power better than his actual spending, and whether a tax on expenditure would be more equitable than one based on income, however income is defined. Kaldor was not allowed to address these issues in the Minority Report. Instead, attention had to be confined to how existing inequities in the taxation of income might be reduced, and to the reform of company taxation. The Majority Report did not propose widening the existing legal definition of taxable income to include capital gains. Kaldor regarded this as inexcusable, not only because capital gains increase an individual's capacity to spend or save like any other form of income, but the exemption of capital gains from taxation also gives the owners of capital the opportunity to avoid income tax by converting taxable income into capital appreciation. The Minority Report therefore recommended a flat rate capital gains tax on *net* realised gains, with no distinction between short and long term gains.

The Majority Report also failed to get to grips with the inequitable treatment of income as between Schedule D and E taxpayers. Schedule D earners (essentially the self-employed) were allowed many more expenses to offset against taxable income; under Schedule E, only 'unavoidable' expenses were allowable. The Majority wanted to relax the Schedule E expenses rule, while the Minority wanted to tighten up the Schedule D allowances. Nothing of significance happened, and inequities still exist, except that it is now only possible for Schedule D earners to offset losses against income from the same source. This was one of the recommendations of the Minority Report to reduce tax avoidance.

On the matter of company tax, the Minority Report was strongly in favour of the separation of personal and company taxation, and this was adopted as offical Labour Party policy before the 1959 General Election, and was implemented in 1965. The Majority Report rejected a uniform corporation tax on technical grounds relating to the desire to avoid the double taxation of dividends. The Majority was also against tax discrimination in favour of undistributed profits on the grounds that it artificially depresses the market value of shares, and the market knows best how to allocate investment resources. The Minority dissented: discrimination should continue at least until the introduction of a capital gains tax.

When work on the Commission ended in 1954, Kaldor turned his attention to an expenditure tax. His book by the same title (Kaldor, 1955) received wide acclaim. Alan Peacock in *The Manchester Guardian* described the book as 'one of the most stimulating post-war books on Public Finance'.[1] Arnold Harberger, the American public finance

[1] 23 December 1955.

expert, praised it as 'one of the best books of the decade in public finance ranking with the classic works of Edgeworth, Pigou, Simons and Vickrey',[1] and Richard Musgrave remarked 'the book . . . excels in a high idea-to-page ratio. It makes a splendid contribution to rethinking of the traditional principles of taxation. Like the tracts of old, it may even have an effect on the actual course of legislation'.[2]

Kaldor's tax expertise led to his advice being sought all over the world, particularly by developing countries. The political storms and intrigue associated with his various missions to developing countries have become legendary, although like all legends the stories have increasingly departed from the facts. Two major themes recur in his advice on tax reform in developing countries. The first is the desirability of broadening the tax base, but at the same time reducing the high marginal rates of tax. The second is the importance of a comprehensive reporting system to reduce evasion and avoidance. In most of the countries he visited, the politicians accepted the advice and tried to implement his proposals, but as Kaldor said in his own retrospective reflections on his role as adviser ('Introduction' to Kaldor, 1964B) it became clear that the power behind the scenes of the wealthy property-owning classes was much greater than the political leaders suspected. Kaldor believed firmly, however, that the economic adviser must stick to his brief of advising to the best of his knowledge and competence, and leave it to the politicians to sort out the implications: 'Progressive taxation is, in the end, the only alternative to complete expropriation through violent revolution.' The experience is discussed in some detail elsewhere in this volume, by Chakravarty, by Palma and Marcel, and by Toye (see also Thirlwall, 1987, ch. 5).

Economic adviser to Labour Governments

When the Labour Party was elected to office after thirteen years in opposition, Kaldor was appointed Special Adviser to the Chancellor of the Exchequer on the Social and Economic Aspects of Taxation Policy. That was his official title. He was a natural choice. He was the Party's foremost academic economist with a particular expertise in tax matters; he had been prominent in Labour Party circles for many years, and Harold Wilson was anxious to keep Gaitskell's pledge to appoint him to an advisory post in government.[3] He served first James Callaghan from 1964 to 1967, and then Roy Jenkins for a brief period between 1967 and 1968. He then transferred to the Department of Health and Social Security as adviser to Richard Crossman from 1968 to 1970. His Hungarian compatriot, Thomas Balogh, was appointed at the same time as Adviser on Economic Affairs to the Cabinet, and they were depicted together in press cartoons and photos as if a sinister Eastern European experiment was about to be launched on the British people. The 'Hungarian mafia', 'Terrible Twins', and 'B and K' (after Bulganin and Kruschev) were typical descriptions. Some of the unfortunate episodes in developing countries were resurrected and used to malign Kaldor. John Chown of the *Sunday Telegraph* (6 December 1964) recalling the events of British Guiana, wrote an article 'The Kaldor System in Operation' including the cryptic rhetorical question 'It couldn't happen here—or could it?' (see Thirlwall, 1987, pp. 147–151). And James Macmillan of the *Daily Express* wrote 'wherever [Kaldor] has proffered advice, from India to Ghana, from Turkey to Ceylon, it has been followed by revolution, inflation and toppling governments' (24 May 1966). The

[1] *Journal of Political Economy*, February 1958.
[2] *American Economic Review*, March 1957.
[3] Hugh Gaitskell died in 1963 while leader of the Labour Party.

City was extremely hostile to Kaldor's appointment. Harold Wincott in the *Financial Times* (15 December 1964) likened Kaldor's Minority Report of the Royal Commission on Taxation, and its influence on Labour's tax policy, to Hitler and *Mein Kampf*. Wincott questioned Kaldor's academic credentials and urged Callaghan to 'send him back to Cambridge . . . and rely on your own good common sense'.

At the beginning he worked part-time in the Inland Revenue headed by Alexander Johnson and then, after his elevation to a Chair in Cambridge at the end of 1965, he became full-time and moved to the Treasury building closer to the centre of power. His friend Robert Neild was Chief Economic Adviser to the Treasury. They made a formidable pair, with Kaldor sparking off ideas and Neild steering them through the Treasury machine. In government, the principal intermediary between advisers and the Minister is the Permanent Secretary, and Kaldor saw the Permanent Secretary of the Treasury, William Armstrong, on a regular basis. Kaldor held both the Inland Revenue and the Treasury in high regard, and the respect was mutual, not the least because, as Sir Douglas Wass has remarked, 'he was the only economic adviser to government that I have worked with who studied the administrative system and sought to fashion his ideas to what the system could bear' (see Thirlwall, 1987, Foreword). It is never easy to gauge the impact on policy of one man working within a large organisation, but Kaldor's innovative mind and the sheer force of his personality makes his contribution easier to evaluate than most. As we shall see, his name is clearly associated with major policy initiatives and innovations particularly in the tax field.

Apart from the intricacies of tax reform, for much of the time he was concerned with the general economic situation, and in this respect he worked as a straightforward Treasury official sitting on the appropriate committees. The first months of the Labour government were dominated by concern over the huge balance of payments deficit left by the Conservatives, and whether the pound should be devalued. Harold Wilson and his Cabinet ruled out devaluation virtually the day after taking office, but this did not stop discussion, and the problem of the balance of payments remained. The government's advisers were divided. Kaldor was in favour of some form of floating, and against other forms of expenditure-switching policies such as tariffs or quotas. Balogh, by contrast, in the Oxford tradition of Henderson and Harrod, was always sceptical of exchange rate adjustment and wanted quantitative controls on imports. He frequently castigated Kaldor for being 'a free trader'! Kaldor was in favour, however, of tighter controls on direct investment overseas, and held the view that a causal relation existed between the budget deficit and the current account of the balance of payments: what came to be called the 'New Cambridge view' that budgetary policy should be used to achieve external balance, while the exchange rate should be used for internal balance—an apparent reversal of Keynesian demand management techniques. Kaldor therefore wanted taxes raised in the first budget, coupled with devaluation. Instead, a 15% surcharge on imports of manufactures and semi-manufactures was imposed. Despite this, and other measures, sterling remained vulnerable largely owing to pressure on the capital account. The response was tighter exchange controls and deflation, but no currency adjustment. Robert Neild resigned as the Treasury's Chief Economic Adviser; Kaldor was approached by Callaghan to take Neild's position, but he was out of sympathy with the stance of policy and effectively talked himself out of the job. Further pressure on sterling in 1967 made devaluation inevitable, and on 18 November sterling's value was reduced from \$2·80 to \$2·40. Kaldor's view was that this was insufficient, particularly since it would be political suicide to devalue again.

During this period, however, Kaldor's major preoccupation was not international economic affairs but tax policy, where his views and advice were extremely influential. Firstly, there was the introduction in 1965 of a comprehensive capital gains tax for which he had campaigned for many years. The previous government had already introduced a short-term gains tax in 1962, and questions such as the definition of a capital gain had already been thrashed out in the Inland Revenue before Kaldor arrived. When the 1965 Finance Bill was introduced, Kaldor would not have discriminated between short-term and long-term gains, but the Revenue persuaded him otherwise. Both Kaldor and the Revenue were united against the Treasury, however, that capital gains on gilt-edged securities should be taxed, and won the argument. They also agreed that capital gains tax should be levied on death and this prevailed until 1971.

Secondly, there was the introduction of corporation tax in the same year, which followed closely Kaldor's thinking. It was also he who pressed the government, against the wishes of the Treasury, to introduce both new taxes at the same time. The new corporation tax introduced the so-called classical system which separated the tax liability of companies from the tax liability of shareholders. The rate of corporation tax was set at 40%. Kaldor wanted the rate to be gradually reduced to 30%, but in fact it was later raised. Kaldor had campaigned for the reform of company taxation for many years and the Inland Revenue were broadly in support. By favouring the retention of profits, the classical system discriminates against equity finance since dividends are, in effect, taxed twice, once as profit and again as the income of shareholders. When the Conservatives came to power in 1970 they were pledged to change the system in favour of the imputation system, which gives shareholders credit for tax paid by the company, which is used as an offset against tax liability. A Select Committee of the House of Commons was set up to which Kaldor gave evidence (see Kaldor, 1980B) arguing strongly against the change, but to no avail. The new system was introduced in 1973 and survived the Labour administration of 1974 to 1979.

In addition to his influence behind capital gains and corporation tax, Kaldor was responsible for the invention and introduction of the completely new Selective Employment Tax (SET), which proved to be not only an efficient revenue raiser but also gave a major boost to productivity in the service sector, with no loss of consumer surplus. The motives behind the tax and its effects are discussed in some detail in Reddaway's contribution to this volume (see also Thirlwall, 1987, ch. 9).

Kaldor also played a part in many other fiscal initiatives during his period as adviser. The differentiation of SET by region in the form of the Regional Employment Premium, to revive lagging regions, was his idea. In 1966 he was instrumental in the overhaul of the investment incentive system, which for the first time introduced investment grants for manufacturing industry differentiated on a regional basis. He would have liked the grants also to be industry-specific, for particular plant and equipment identified by technological working parties, but the Inland Revenue resisted. Measures to combat tax avoidance were also uppermost in his mind, and he played a major role in convincing the Revenue and the Treasury to withdraw various anomalous tax concessions such as stock options, entertainment allowances, covenants, and the deductability of interest payments on personal loans.

The achievements were many, but there were also disappointments. Very little was done to improve the equality of tax treatment between Schedule D and E taxpayers, and the proposal for a wealth tax never got beyond the drawing board. The Revenue resisted the wealth tax owing to the workload, and the government used the excuse that it had more important priorities. The truth is that the Chancellors of the Exchequer in both administrations 1964–70 and 1974–9 were thoroughly orthodox, dominated by a conservative

Treasury, and apprehensive at antagonising the wealth-owning class. The even more revolutionary idea of an expenditure tax was never seriously mentioned.

After sterling was devalued in November 1967, Callaghan resigned as Chancellor to be succeeded by Roy Jenkins. Jenkins wanted to distance himself from Kaldor, who moved from the main Treasury building to Palace Chambers across the road. Kaldor was fully involved in the Spring budget of 1968, but in September 1968 he decided to return to Cambridge full time, remaining in the Treasury as an unpaid consultant working on various research projects with a small research staff including Roger Tarling, Francis Cripps and Christopher Allsopp. At the same time, he started to give advice on an unofficial basis to Richard Crossman at the Department of Health and Social Security. This role was formalised in November 1969, when he was appointed as a Special Adviser to the Department with an office in Alexander Fleming House. He was involved in discussions relating to deferred retirement; a negative income tax; new pension proposals and contracting out of the State scheme; earnings related National Insurance contributions and benefits, and a scheme for minimum earned income relief in order to reduce the burden of tax in the lower income ranges. He was responsible for persuading the government to increase family allowances and to 'claw back' some of the increase through the tax system—a measure to benefit poor families relative to the rich.

In office, Kaldor was confined to giving advice to the government, and was precluded from pronouncing publicly on matters of economic policy. When the Conservatives came to power under Mr Heath in 1970, Kaldor relished his freedom. In letters to *The Times*, newspaper articles and through other means, he was a vociferous critic of Conservative economic policy which started as one of economic *laissez-faire* and ended in crisis with runaway inflation, a huge balance of payments deficit, and a miners' strike which eventually brought the government down. He was particularly critical of the uncontrolled expansion of credit (following the introduction of Competition and Credit Control); of the indifference to consumption-led growth to the neglect of the foreign trade sector (which was the theme of his 1970 Presidential Address to Section F of the British Association) (Kaldor, 1971), and of the clumsy handling of wages and prices policy. But it was the deceitful campaign to bring the UK into the EEC, based on what he regarded as a false prospectus, that angered him most of all and occupied most of his attention. He lent his name to Douglas Jay's Common Market Safeguards Campaign, and campaigned vigorously against the UK's entry on the proposed terms.

From the UK's first application to join the EEC in 1961, he had been sceptical of the alleged economic benefits and preferred a wider European free trade area without a Customs Union (or common external tariff) or a common agricultural policy (CAP). Between 1970 and 1973 he wrote over twenty letters to *The Times* alone, in addition to several articles in newspapers, magazines and pamphlets, warning of the costs of entry and the dangers to the UK's competitive position if the country accepted the Community's CAP and the arrangments governing each country's contribution to the Community's budget. Many of his worries have proved to be well-founded, and many of his prognostications materialised, particularly in relation to the costs of entry and the demise of Britain's manufacturing industry. The promised 'dynamic benefits' of entry, which Kaldor scathingly dismissed in a devastating *New Statesman* article (12 March, 1971) are nowhere to be seen. A fierce attack on Community farm policy delivered at the International Press Institute in Paris in January 1970 was also published in the *New Statesman*, (3 April, 1970) which was one of Kaldor's main outlets of protest. He received extensive press coverage for his Jeremiah forecasts that the UK might become the 'Northern Ireland of Europe' if she entered the Community on the wrong terms. The pro-market press, however, believed that Kaldor exaggerated the costs. *The Economist* (13 March 1971) carried a photo of Kaldor captioned 'soberly wrong'. Andrew Shonfield argued in *The Times* (1 April 1971) that the EEC would not allow Britain to be weakened economically, and Dick Taverne in the *Guardian* (12 March 1971) argued that once inside, Britain would be able to control EEC food prices. The Labour Committee for Europe placed a full-page advertisement in the *New Statesman* chiding Kaldor for being so pessimistic and not appreciating the opportunities to be seized. The country itself was deeply divided. Kaldor wanted a referendum to decide the issue, reminding Edward Heath of his promise in 1970 that he would not take Britain into the Community without the full-hearted consent of Parliament and the British people. Britain formally joined the Community on 1st January 1973, but when the Conservative government fell in 1974, the Labour government renegotiated terms and these were put to a national referendum in June 1975. Kaldor voted 'no' along with eight million others, but fifteen million voted 'yes'. Kaldor then accepted UK membership as a *fait accompli*. He continued to press, however, for institutional reforms, and opposed the commitment to full monetary union and fiscal harmonisation before political union and fiscal integration, because, like free trade between unequal partners, this too would strengthen the strong at the expense of the weak.

When the Labour Party was returned to power in 1974, Kaldor was again appointed as a Special Adviser to the Chancellor of the Exchequer, this time Denis Healey. In the same year, he was elevated to the Peerage as Baron Kaldor of Newnham in the City of Cambridge. The Chief Economic Adviser to the Treasury was Bryan Hopkin, and the Permanent Secretary, Douglas Wass. Kaldor did not see eye to eye with Hopkin on economic policy, but had a good working relationship with Wass. Kaldor sat on all the main Treasury Committees, including the Fiscal Policy Committee and the Short Term Economic Policy Committee, consisting of all Heads of Department, and he attended all important meetings with Healey present, but his influence on the Chancellor was minimal. Healey accepted the orthodox advice of the more conventional economists in the Treasury such as Hopkin, Michael Posner, Andrew Britton and Hans Liesner, despite the mounting economic difficulties facing the country with respect to inflation, the balance of payments and the size of the Public Sector Borrowing Requirement (PSBR). Kaldor stuck to the 'New Cambridge' view that a necessary condition for the balance of payments deficit to be reduced was a reduction in the PSBR, but the resulting unemployment could not be prevented by devaluation. The experience of floating exchange rates since 1972 caused him to lose faith in currency depreciation as an effective weapon to achieve simultaneous internal and external equilibrium. He began to preach the doctrine of the Harrod trade multiplier, that it is income which adjusts to bring imports into line with an exogenously determined level of exports. Hence import controls of one form or another are required. The need for import controls dominated his policy advice during this period as Special Adviser. Without controls, he predicted, the IMF would eventually have to be called in, and dispense medicine even more draconian. His warnings turned out to be prophetic. Many forms of import controls were considered under the code name 'Delve Exercise'; for instance: quotas to curtail inessential imports; a dual exchange rate system applying to manufactured exports and imports; and a voucher system to balance exports and imports.[1] Kaldor made no impact, however. The Treasury continued to pin its faith on the orthodox combination of currency depreciation and deflation. By 1976, as the balance of payments crisis worsened, Kaldor called for a 200% import deposit scheme to

[1] He later prepared a detailed plan on these lines at the specific request of the French Government in 1982.

be applied to manufactures plus a special car tax surcharge, to avoid the only alternative of further drastic deflation. In a memo to the Principal Private Secretary he expressed the fear 'that the Chancellor does not see clearly enough that he is being driven into a course of action that will destroy him and the Labour Party with the inevitableness of a Greek tradegy'. The comparison was drawn with Philip Snowden's measures of 1931 which destroyed the first Labour government.

There were attempts to cut the PSBR in 1975 and 1976, but not enough in Kaldor's view. The level of consumption was far too high. He urged the reintroduction of SET or a payroll tax to yield some £3 billion, and for a rise in indirect taxes with their effect on prices excluded from the retail price index to avoid money wages responding *pari passu*. Despite successive doses of deflation, there was continued speculation against sterling and a problem of massive short-term capital outflows. By 1976 sterling had already depreciated by 50% against its 1972 Smithsonian parity, but there continued to be a huge need for official financing. Kaldor advised controls over capital flight. All his advice for emergency measures went unheeded, and in the end, as he had predicted, the government went cap-in-hand to the IMF seeking credits of $4 billion over two years. The *quid pro quo* was a drastic deflationary package and targets set for domestic credit expansion, which ushered in the first phase of 'monetarism' in the UK—later intensified by Mrs Thatcher's Conservative government in 1979. Before the 'IMF budget' was imposed, Kaldor had already resigned from the Treasury, dispirited and disillusioned.

While Kaldor failed to have any impact on the broad thrust of macroeconomic policy, he did have some success and influence on specific policy changes in the tax field, but not nearly so extensively as between 1964 and 1970. One notable achievement was his idea of stock appreciation tax relief which gave relief to industry of close to one billion pounds and saved several companies from bankruptcy (see below, p. 149).

Another fiscal change which he strongly supported was the replacement of death duties by a capital transfer tax, although it was levied on the donor, and not on the recipient as he advised. Unrealised capital gains on death were also to be taxed again. In addition, he was instrumental in strengthening the general attack on tax avoidance. In the field of corporation tax, he wanted a return to the classical system. He had the support of the Treasury officials, but the Inland Revenue resisted on advice from the Confederation of British Industries that another change in company taxation would be too disruptive. The Treasury took the Revenue's advice and nothing was done. Likewise no action was taken to implement a wealth tax which had been promised in the March 1974 budget.

Social Security reform was also on the political agenda at this time. The Conservatives had floated proposals to introduce tax credits in place of tax allowances and various discretionary social security payments (HM Government, 1972). In evidence to the House of Commons Select Committee on Tax Credits in 1973, Kaldor had written a long critique of the proposals, arguing that the whole scheme would be highly regressive (Kaldor, 1980A). He also gave oral evidence to the Committee. So powerful was his tirade against the proposals that the Chairman of the Committee, William Clark, described the Professor as having left the Committee speechless! Kaldor showed that for the low income groups, the benefits of the tax credits would have been more than offset by the loss of supplementary benefits and other social security payments, and that the net cost of the scheme of £1·3 billion could be attributed entirely to raising tax allowances and had nothing at all to do with the 'generosity' of the new tax credit system itself. Kaldor convinced the Labour Party to reject the scheme. Instead, he proposed a unified system of family endowment which would replace family allowances and tax allowances for children with a system of tax free age-graduated allowances payable to the mother. Child benefits were duly instituted by the Child Benefits Act of 1975.

After his resignation as Special Adviser in 1976, Kaldor continued his political life in the House of Lords. He chose to stay on the Labour back benches, but this did not silence him or diminish his impact as a trenchant critic. He used his new platform to great effect, with a series of pungent and witty speeches on economic issues of the day. The waste of oil revenue, the scourge of unemployment, the demise of British manufacturing industry and the bankruptcy of the doctrine of monetarism were all the subject of his indignation. Some of his best early speeches were published in a booklet *The Economic Consequences of Mrs Thatcher*,[1] which remains unequalled as an economic commentary on the times.

Monetarism

I have told in detail elsewhere the story of Kaldor's intellectual assault on the doctrine of monetarism as preached in theory, and as practised in the UK (see Thirlwall, 1987, ch. 12; also Desai's contribution to this volume). His masterly Memorandum of Evidence to the Treasury and Civil Service on Monetary Policy in 1980,[2] represents one of the most devastating critiques of the doctrine of monetarism ever written. Over twenty years earlier, he had given influential evidence to the Radcliffe Committee on the Working of the Monetary System.

Kaldor was not a monetary economist in the sense that money infused the whole body of his theoretical work as an economist, as it did for Keynes and Robertson, for example. In the 1930s he had theorised about interest rate determination, and the role of money in trade cycle analysis, but not until he gave evidence to the Radcliffe Committee in 1958 did he take an active interest in monetary policy. His evidence was important because, as Harrod noted in reviewing Kaldor's *Essays*,

> there appears to be a certain family resemblance between Mr Kaldor's point of view on certain central questions and that of the Radcliffe Report, and it is possible that the Kaldor memorandum had an important influence on the Radcliffe Report (Harrod, 1965).

Kaldor's first major attack on the doctrine of modern monetarism, associated with Milton Friedman and the Chicago School, was in a public lecture at University College, London in March 1970.[3] It was not until 1980, however, in his Select Committee evidence, that he put some of the core propositions of monetarism, as applied in the UK, to the empirical test. For Kaldor, monetarism was a pernicious doctrine; a synonym for deflation masquerading as science. It worked, if at all, through the deliberate intensification of unemployment; a reactionary movement which must be resisted in every way. Much of his energy in the last years of his life was devoted to a denunciation of the doctrine in letters to the press; speeches in the House of Lords; lectures throughout the world, articles in journals, and in a magnificent polemic, *The Scourge of Monetarism*, reminiscent in its topicality, style and righteous indignation of Keynes's *Economic Consequences of the Peace*. Kaldor lost the policy battle in the UK, but won the theoretical war. It came to be recognised, as he had the intuition and insight to realise all along, that in the real world industrial countries live on a wages standard and money is endogenous. Monetarism in the UK was effectively abandoned when the government first imposed wage controls in the public sector and then abandoned monetary targets.

[1] Fabian Society, 1983 and Duckworth, 1983.

[2] (London, HMSO, 17th July, 1980). Reprinted in *The Scourge of Monetarism* (Oxford University Press, 1982).

[3] Published as 'The New Monetarism, *Lloyds Bank Review*, July 1970.

International issues

Kaldor did not confine himself to the domestic economic stage. I have already noted his controversial role as a tax adviser in developing countries. He was equally concerned with reform of various aspects of the international monetary system for the benefit of both poor countries and the world economy as a whole. He was, for example, a frequent adviser to the Economic Commission for Latin America and United Nations bodies, and when the role of the dollar in the international monetary system was problematic, he did not hesitate to send unsolicited advice to his American friends in positions of influence. Like Robert Triffin, he foresaw the collapse of the Bretton Woods system based on the gold exchange standard, which was largely inevitable because of the inherent contradiction that for confidence in the system the dollar should be strong, but for international liquidity, the United States should run a payments deficit. Throughout the 1950s he believed the dollar to be overvalued and warned of the excessive increase in dollar liabilities. In 1960 he wrote to Walter Heller, the Chairman of the US Council of Economic Advisers, arguing for a devaluation of the dollar. In 1968 he issued the same advice to Arthur Okun occupying the same post. His worry over the inherent fragility of the Bretton Woods system led him to devise various plans to replace the gold exchange standard with a commodity backed international money independent of the US dollar. One such scheme was the proposal he devised in a Report for UNCTAD in 1964 co-authored with Albert Hart and Jan Tinbergen, and presented to the World Trade Conference in Geneva (Hart *et al.*, 1964). The suggestion was that the IMF should establish its own currency (bancor) convertible into both gold and a bundle of, say, thirty principal commodities in world trade. The IMF would maintain parity between bancor and the price of gold so as to maintain parity between gold and the bundle of commodities. The precise details of the scheme were unnecessarily complicated (in particular, the details relating to the composition of the commodity bundle), but the scheme possessed a number of attractive features and still does. It would considerably enhance the stability and smooth functioning of the world economy, by stabilising the price of commodities and ensuring that any increase in primary product production generated an equivalent demand for industrial goods, therefore keeping the two sectors in balance. A new international monetary unit, Special Drawing Rights (SDRs), was introduced in 1969, but not backed by commodities. Nor have SDRs replaced the dollar as the reserve asset of the system, and there is no provision for the automatic increase in the supply of SDRs as the need arises. The SDR does not fulfil the functions that Keynes envisaged at Bretton Woods of a truly international money (bancor) issued by a world Central Bank to serve international collectively agreed purposes. When the British Chancellor of the Exchequer, Mr Barber, proposed in 1971 that the world should move towards an SDR standard, Kaldor wrote to *The Times* (1 October 1971) reiterating the importance and superiority of a commodity backed standard. The only modification he made in later years to his 1964 proposal was for there to be buffer stocks for individual commodities, and for 'bancor' to be convertible into individual commodities as opposed to a basket of commodities. The buffer stocks would be financed by SDRs. In effect, he endorsed Keynes's Commod Control scheme proposed in preparation for Bretton Woods but which never went forward for consideration (see Moggridge (ed.), 1980).

Kaldor's concern over commodity prices dated back to 1952, when he was employed as a Consultant to the FAO in Rome with specific reference to the International Wheat Agreement which was due for renewal (Kaldor, 1952). In 1963, on one of his advisory visits to ECLA, he expressed concern not only over the instability of primary product prices, but also over the long-run trend deterioration of the terms of trade of primary commodities (Kaldor, 1964; see also the paper by Spraos in this volume). He argued then for restriction schemes. In 1977 he wrote to Charles Schultze, the Chairman of the Council of Economic Advisers in America, proposing an initiative to stabilise the world price of wheat. He received a sympathetic reply, but to no avail. The world still lacks the requisite international agreement and institutional structures to control the instability of primary commodity prices which causes so much damage to individual exporting countries and periodically upsets the equilibrium of the world economy as a whole. Kaldor attached the utmost importance to reforms in this sphere for a more stable world economy.

Conclusion

There is no need for a long conclusion. I have outlined the major episodes of Kaldor's life in which he assumed an advisory role and influenced the direction of economic policy and thinking. He revelled in the cut and thrust of political and policy debate, and he loved strutting the world stage, flying here and there to tackle whatever task was given him. He was an important figure; of that there can be no doubt. The sharpness of his mind, and his ability to write clearly and concisely, were the envy of all those with whom he came into contact. His advice was always to the point, and he never compromised his professional integrity or convictions to win favour or praise. His charisma and oratory, delivered in heavily accented English, made him a highly persuasive man. In Ghana, his hold over Dr Nkrumah was likened to the captivating powers of the Ju Ju magicians! He was maligned by the Conservative press, but those in the Civil Service with whom he worked knew a different man, who was moderate in his views and who cooperated well with others. He was passionately concerned with the plight of Britain, his adopted country that he loved so much. Like so many European emigrés, he was more English than the English, and to witness the relative decline of the British economy, and British influence in the world, was, for him, a galling experience. Much of his later academic work and advice was motivated by a desire to arrest the decline. He was particularly critical of the British middle class and of its supporting institutions—the divisive educational system, the City of London, and the anti-industrial culture of the professional classes. Of the professional economists working in Britain outside the Civil Service, Kaldor assumed a role in public life second only to Keynes this century. Future economic historians will judge him, I have no doubt, not only as a brilliant and original academic economist, but as a public servant of the first rank, who gave himself freely in the service not only of Britain but of countries around the world.

Bibliography

Beveridge, W. 1942. *Beveridge Report on Social Insurance and Allied Services*, Cmnd. 6404, London, HMSO

Beveridge, W. 1944. *Full Employment in a Free Society*, London, George Allen & Unwin

Galbraith, J. K. 1981. *A Life in Our Times*, Boston, Houghton Mifflin

Harrod, R. F. 1965, *Economic Journal*, December

Hart, A., Kaldor, N. and Tinbergen, J. 1964. *The Case for an International Commodity Reserve Currency*, Geneva, UNCTAD

HM Government 1972. *Proposals for a Tax-Credit System*, Cmnd. 5116, London, HMSO

Kaldor, N. 1939. Principles of emergency finance, *The Banker*, August

Kaldor, N. 1941. The White Paper on National Income and Expenditure, *Economic Journal*, June–September

Kaldor, N. 1942. The 1941 White Paper on National Income and Expenditure, *Economic Journal*, June–September
Kaldor, N. 1943A. The Beveridge Plan's real cost, *Manchester Guardian*, 10 and 11 February
Kaldor, N. 1943B. The Beveridge Report II: the financial burden, *Economic Journal*, April
Kaldor, N. 1945. The German war economy, *Review of Economic Studies*, vol 13, no. 1 (also in *Manchester School*, September 1946)
Kaldor, N. 1952. *A Reconsideration of the Economics of the International Wheat Agreement*, Commodity Policy Studies No. 1, Rome, FAO
Kaldor, N. 1955. *An Expenditure Tax*, London, George Allen & Unwin
Kaldor, N. 1964A. Stabilising the terms of trade of underdeveloped countries, *Economic Bulletin for Latin America*, March
Kaldor, N. 1964B. *Essays in Economic Policy I, Collected Economic Essays*, vol. 3, London, Duckworth
Kaldor, N. 1971. Conflicts in national economic objectives, *Economic Journal*, March
Kaldor, N. 1980A. Tax credits: a critique of the Green Paper proposals, in *Reports on Taxation I, Collected Economic Essays*, vol. 7, London, Duckworth
Kaldor, N. 1980B. The economic effects of alternative systems of corporation tax, in *Collected Economic Essays*, vol. 7, London, Duckworth
Kaldor, N. 1980C. *Reports on Taxation II, Collected Economic Essays*, vol. 8, London, Duckworth
Kaldor, N. and Barna, T. 1943. The 1943 White Paper on National Income and Expenditure, *Economic Journal*, June–September
Kaldor, N. and Barna, T. 1944. The quantitative aspects of the full employment problem in Britain, Appendix C in Beveridge (1944)
Kaldor, N. and Joseph, M. F. W. 1942. *Economic Reconstruction After the War*, Association for Education Citizenship, English Universities Press
Keynes, J. M. 1933. *Essays in Biography*, London, Macmillan
Keynes, J. M. 1936. *General Theory of Employment, Interest and Money*, London, Macmillan
Moggridge, D. (ed.) 1980. *The Collected Writings of J. M. Keynes: Vol XXVII: Activities 1940–1946 Shaping the Post-War World: Employment and Commodities*, London, Macmillan
Thirlwall, A. P. 1987. *Nicholas Kaldor*, Brighton, Wheatsheaf Books
UN Experts Committee 1949. *Report on National and International Measures for Full Employment*, Geneva, United Nations
US Strategic Bombing Survey 1945. *The Effects of Strategic Bombing on the German War Economy*, Washington DC, US Strategic Bombing Survey
Wilson, T. 1982. Planning for the war and for the peace, in Thirlwall, A. P. (ed.), *Keynes as a Policy Adviser*, London, Macmillan

Tax reform in the United Kingdom

Brian Reddaway*

Nicky Kaldor worked on a vast variety of economic subjects, and what he had to say was always worthy of careful consideration—whether he 'said' it in print, or in a lecture, or in personal discussions. My role is to cover his work on taxation in the United Kingdom, and my problem arose far more from the vast amount of material than from any lack of interesting things about which to write.

Within the field of UK taxation, I shall confine myself mainly to what appears in two books, although I must clearly also include something about the *actions* which were taken by Labour Governments to which he acted as Official Adviser under one title or another.

The first book was published in 1955 under the title *An Expenditure Tax*: its coverage is much wider than its title might suggest, because Nicky was essentially making a case for an expenditure tax as a replacement for surtax, and his arguments involved a complete review of many problems associated with income taxes of all kinds, including corporation tax. This book was, indeed, written primarily because the Conservative Chancellor of the Exchequer ruled that an expenditure tax was outside the terms of reference of the Royal Commission on the Taxation of Profits and Income, to which Nicky had been appointed when it was set up by the previous Labour Government. Consequently, Nicky was unable to include in the Memorandum of Dissent which he drafted his views about the desirability of switching to an expenditure tax as at least a partial substitute for taxes based on income. He therefore worked on his book on the expenditure tax at the same time as the work of the Royal Commission continued, so that it could appear shortly after the publication of the Report: in order to make the book comprehensible in itself, he had to go over a great deal of the criticisms of income as an exclusive basis for direct taxation, even though he had dealt with many of the points (in a rather less academic style) in the Memorandum of Dissent.

Finally, I may perhaps be forgiven for making one special personal reference to this book, since its preface expresses his thanks to me for 'clearing his mind on a number of intricate points' (although these were in fact rather narrow ones, which were the subject of a neighbourly discussion in my garden): very rightly, the preface gives pride of place to Hugh Gaitskell, who first gave him the idea that the expenditure-tax principle might be explored in specific relation to surtax.

The second book, which is indispensable for an understanding of Nicky's writings about taxation, is Volume VII of his *Collected Economic Essays*, entitled *Reports on Taxation I* (*Reports on Taxation II* relates to taxes in countries other than the United

*Clare College, Cambridge.

Kingdom). This book was published in 1980 and has the great advantage, firstly, of reflecting his own choice of articles to which he wished to draw special attention, and, secondly, of incorporating an Introduction which reflects his later views about some of them, as well as putting them into perspective. It has the special merit (to which I shall revert later) of including an article written in 1978 entitled 'The Economics of the Selective Employment Tax', which for the first time sets out the 'theoretical model' that prompted his advocacy of that tax; and the final article is entitled 'A New Look at the Expenditure Tax (1979),' which is a useful complement to his 1955 book.

Direct taxation: analysis

As Nicky makes plain at the outset of the Introduction to his Report on Taxation, his special interest in that field developed largely in consequence of his appointment in 1950 as a member of the Royal Commission on the Taxation of Profits and Income. The Commission worked extremely hard over a period of some four years, and Nicky took his duties very seriously. This involved the reading of many memoranda from very diverse sources, as well as discussions within the Commission.

Nicky pays a generous tribute in his Introduction to the work of Lord Radcliffe, who became the full-time Chairman of the Commission after the resignation of its first Chairman. Thanks to this, the Commission 'was able to work as a team in reasonable harmony in consideration of a large number of complicated matters, the solution of which did not raise important issues of policy or class interest' (Kalder, 1980, p. ix), and to produce some 'unanimous' interim reports which had no more than a few reservations on particular issues. But when it came to a Final Report, Nicky and two trades unionists did not sign it and produced a 45,000-word Memorandum of Dissent, which is reproduced in the *Reports on Taxation I*.)

The Memorandum of Dissent

The Memorandum of Dissent ends with a 'Summary of Recommendations', which begins with paragraph 217 (page 105 of the *Reports on Taxation I*). This is divided into three sections:

1. The Recommendations made by the Minority.
2. The Recommendations of the Majority which the Minority wished to endorse.
3. The specific Dissent from the Majority views which the Minority wished to put on record.

The Dissents consist of only ten items, most of which are rather small matters, and their main underlying theme might be said to be a desire to avoid the erosion of the tax base by specific concessions to particular interests. The shortness and nature of this list thoroughly bears out the comment which Nicky makes, that the real dividing line between the Majority and the Minority was that the latter wished to do a thorough revision of the basic ideas behind the income tax, whilst the former were content with relatively minor 'improvements'.

This view is strengthened by a consideration of the twenty-one specific Recommendations of the Majority, which the Minority wished to endorse. These show clearly that Nicky had paid a good deal of attention to matters of detail, and again a common theme of many of the Recommendations is a desire to strengthen the tax base.

The thirty positive Recommendations put forward by the Minority naturally also reflect this desire to widen the tax base, and to cut down on special concessions. They start with sections bearing the titles which became 'operational' when the Labour Government came to power in the 1960s, i.e. 'capital gains' and 'corporate taxation'. The third section, entitled 'earned income relief', which also deals with expense allowances under Schedule D and Schedule E, reflects Nicky's concern about equitable treatment between recipients of different types of income.

These concluding recommendations are, however, less interesting than the analysis of the whole problem of direct taxation which formed their basis. The keynote of the argument mostly appears as early as paragraph 2 of the Dissent, which starts from the point made by the Majority that a graduated tax differentiated according to personal circumstances is necessarily a tax on persons according to their respective total incomes, and not a tax on a 'body of income as such', considered impersonally under some system of classification. Hence equity between persons cannot be secured unless the tax base itself (i.e. the definition of income for tax purposes) provides a measure which is uniform, comprehensive and capable of consistent application to all individuals. It is impossible to 'compensate' for an unsatisfactory definition of taxable income by elaborate graduation of tax rates or meticulous differentiation to allow for differences in personal circumstances (e.g. number of children). Hence the crucial starting point is to define what should be regarded as the 'true conception of income', regarded not as an accounting concept but as a measure of taxable capacity or 'ability to pay'.

The Minority claimed (paragraph 5) that 'no concept of income can be really equitable that stops short of the comprehensive definition which embraces all receipts which increase an individual's command over the use of society's scarce resources—in other words, his "net accretion of economic power between two points of time" '. At the same time, they recognise (paragraph 8) that receipts which cannot administratively be taxed at all efficiently (e.g. gambling winnings) are best left outside the definition, even though they obviously provide a net accretion of economic power. The problem of inheritances received in the year, or indeed of gifts generally, is not tackled, but one must, I think, assume that they were intended to be excluded also.

The Minority had little difficulty in showing the illogicality of the existing definition of income for taxable purposes, and the circularity with which legal dicta had said that income tax is a tax on income, but also 'the word income means such income as is within the Act and taxable under the Act'. This lack of an underlying principle had clearly led to erosion of the tax base by both legislators and the judiciary.

The most important conclusions from the analysis (the merits of which can only be properly assessed by a full reading of it) are that realised capital gains should be brought within the field of the income tax, and that a tougher view should be taken about expenses claimed (particularly under Schedule D) so as to prevent what was really, at least in part, personal consumption masquerading as a business expense, or expenditure on the build-up of assets (including intangible assets) being treated as a current expense.

A whole section of the Dissent is devoted to a careful consideration of the arguments for and against the taxation of capital gains, in the course of which the arguments put forward by the Majority are effectively demolished. One important conclusion from the analysis is that the capital gains element of 'income' should be subject only to *income tax*, and not to *surtax*. In 1955 these two taxes, although closely related, were in fact assessed separately, with slightly different rules about what income should be covered, so that this distinction was a simple way of ensuring that capital gains were subject only to a flat rate of taxation, and not to what we would now call 'higher rates'. This had enormous advantages from the point of view of administration and of equity (since a large capital gain in a single year would be taxed far more heavily than the same gain spread over ten years, if surtax were charged). The Minority were, however, also much impressed by the need to avoid the disastrous effect on risk-taking which might come from taxing capital gains at 95%; naturally, they had no use for the view of the Majority that the gains should either be taxed at the full progressive rate or not at all.

One point on which the Dissent is insistent is that all disposals of capital assets (including those made at death, or as gifts) should count for capital gains tax purposes as if they had been made at the market value of the day. This was clearly important for the calculation of the probable revenue from the tax, on which the Minority expressed well-justified scepticism about the estimates made by the Inland Revenue: if tax can be avoided by the owner of an asset retaining it until he dies, the yield to the Treasury will not merely be postponed (as the Minority's proposal would imply), but actually forgone.

Corporation Tax. Income tax on individuals involved the addition of each person's income from what might be a wide range of different sources—e.g. a salary, fees for consultancy, interest on Government Stock, dividends on shares, etc. There remains, however, a type of 'income' which does not naturally feature in any individual's return—i.e. company profits which are not distributed. The classic British formula for dealing with company profits was to tax them at the standard rate, and to allow the company to deduct the standard rate from all dividends which it distributed; the shareholder would then show the *gross* amount of the dividend, but would get credit for the tax which had been deducted—and possibly claim a refund, if he were not liable to tax (e.g. because of charitable status). If he were liable to surtax, he would pay this on the gross amount of the dividend. In effect, undistributed profits would be taxed at the standard rate for income tax. This had a considerable degree of logic in the days when income tax was at a flat rate, but with the addition of surtax (or any other form of progressive taxation) *logic* would have called for each shareholder to receive a 'notional' income representing his share of the undistributed profits, on which he would be liable to pay surtax (and perhaps to claim a refund, if he were not liable to taxation). Nobody, however, suggested that logic should be pursued to this extreme (although with accumulating unit trusts the shareholder does in fact receive a voucher showing how much undistributed income has been added to his capital, after deduction of the standard rate of tax, and the procedure is then as indicated here).

At the time of the Commission, Britain was still imposing a special 'profits tax' on the whole profit earned by a company, over and above the income tax due under the rules sketched above. This system had been introduced during the war, and the rate at which it was levied was much higher for distributed profits than for undistributed. The Majority of the Commission recommended the immediate abolition of this discrimination against dividends in the profits tax—a proposal from which the Minority expressed explicit dissent.

For their own proposals, however, the Minority adopted a more radical approach. They argued that there should be a complete separation between a tax on company profits and the tax on personal incomes, so that a dividend paid to a shareholder would be liable to full personal income tax, even though the profits from which it was paid had already paid corporation tax; conversely, company profits would not be liable to income tax at all, but only to the new corporation tax. The Minority's proposals were linked very closely with the introduction of a capital gains tax, which would mean that *in the long run* profits retained by the company would raise its share price, and there would, *in the long run*, be a capital gains tax (at the basic income tax rate) imposed on this increased share price when the shares were next realised. *If* the capital gains tax were introduced, then the rate for the corporation tax should be lower than the basic rate of income tax, but the difference envisaged was not very great.

Personally, I find the combination of a corporation tax at this sort of rate with full taxation of dividends and a capital gains tax somewhat excessive. It does not seem to hold the balance between an enterprise run by a company and a possibly similar enterprise run by an individual or a partnership, though I recognise that the adoption of company status with limited liability is a privilege. Whilst I regard the proposals made for a capital gains tax as thoroughly desirable, I confess to a possibly old-fashioned objection to what I still regard as the double-taxation on dividends which was proposed.[1]

Expenses. The Dissent has a good deal to say about the items which were allowed as expenses in computing taxable income and especially about the difference in the treatment of those assessed under Schedules D and E. Perhaps the most interesting point is that the Minority came out firmly for the retention of the very 'austere' rules about what could be regarded as an expense for the earner of a wage or salary, which required that it should 'necessarily' be incurred if he continued to get that income. This was in conformity with the Minority's praiseworthy desire to prevent the erosion of the tax base, and was one of the reasons which they advanced in support of earned income relief (for which they found other important justifications as well). Their proposal for Schedule D income was, however, that earned income relief should only be granted to taxpayers who voluntarily agreed to have their expenses assessed according to the rules used for Schedule E.

Personally, I find the idea of assessing expenses of a businessman working for himself on Schedule E principles very difficult, and it is perhaps significant that the Labour Government whom Nicky subsequently advised did not attempt to adopt this proposal (although they did take action against certain types of expense, such as entertainment of customers). If one is working on a salary, then the employing organisation provides and pays for many of the expense items which the salary-earner uses, so that the question whether these are deductible does not arise. But if the businessman is working on his own account, it seems to me impossible to draw a line between expense items which are absolutely 'necessarily' incurred if the business is to continue, and those (like the business telephone) which merely facilitate the business.

To my mind, the attack on the privileges of people taxed under Schedule D has to be a rather messy business of defining particular types of expenses which will not be allowed, especially where personal expenditure is disguised as business expenditure, rather than the pronouncement of a general principle of equality with the treatment of salary-earners under Schedule E.

Finally, the Dissent examines a wide range of provisions in the existing income tax whereby people owning property and investments are able to take advantage of concessions which are much less available to people without such possessions, even if the latter knew about the various legal loopholes which existed. The Minority rightly deplored the existence of extremely high nominal rates of surtax, which were accompanied by a miscellaneous collection of devices by which richer people could

[1] In my more lighthearted moods, I confess to a sneaking desire to have the undistributed profits of companies notionally distributed for tax purposes to the shareholders, in the way discussed above.

legally (or sometimes illegally) escape from making the payments which an innocent person might think were due from him. The final paragraph rightly stresses that the adoption of a more comprehensive definition of income as the tax base with fewer loopholes should be accompanied by a more moderate schedule of rates—and that this would, nevertheless, inaugurate a more truly progressive and equitable system of taxation.

An expenditure tax

As explained above, Nicky's full analysis of the reform of UK direct taxation really appeared in his book *An Expenditure Tax*, published in 1955: this looked at the whole subject without being inhibited from recommending that the basis of personal taxation should be partially shifted to *expenditure*, rather than income. The book considers many of the points covered by the Memorandum of Dissent—e.g. on incentives to work, save, take risks, etc., as well as basic matters of equity, but with what one might call the benefit of an added dimension: it is a real *tour de force*, to which it is impossible to do proper justice in the limited space available to me.

Very briefly, Nicky saw the main advantages of basing a progressive system of direct taxation at least partially on expenditure as coming under three headings:

(a) As between one individual and another expenditure provides, on the whole, a *fairer* or *more equitable* measure of relative 'taxable capacity' than does income: it measures what each person has in fact been able to *take* from the general supply of goods and services without regard to the means by which he paid for it.[1]

(b) The measurement of income involves logical problems over depreciation, inventory valuation and the like, which could be avoided by measuring consumption instead—quite apart from the controversial question of capital gains (realised or unrealised), which certainly add to a person's spending power. If one takes consumption as the basis, each person can take such heed as he thought right of the extent to which such gains in his case 'justified' extra spending.

(c) On the whole, the incentive effects of a consumption base are preferable—not merely for saving (where it had long been objected that an income tax involves double taxation of saving) but also on the incentive to undertake risky enterprises and probably to work.

The book states clearly that a person's expenditure on consumption cannot be recorded as such, so as to serve as the basis for progressive taxation. Instead, one would have to start from a somewhat simplified version of income (with no allowance for depreciation, for example) and record various forms of capital transaction which would hopefully be readily identifiable, *plus* some outgoings (and incomings) which the government might wish to exclude (or include) in calculating consumption: these items, with an allowance for any change in cash held, would give what was deemed to be consumption expenditure for tax purposes.

One apparently formal point needs rather careful attention: how is the payment of direct taxation to be brought into these calculations, and how exactly is the rate of taxation on expenditure to be expressed? This is the main matter on which Nicky and I tried to clarify our minds in my garden when he had almost finished his book; and understandably (in

[1] Basing direct taxation on expenditure calls, however, for great care in dealing with the differing circumstances of particular families (e.g. the number of dependent children), to which Nicky devoted much attention.

view of his deadlines) he did not go back to reflect the outcome of those discussions in earlier passages or in the Memorandum of Dissent.[1]

If direct taxation is treated as part of personal consumption, then the progressive tax rates used for income tax and surtax, if 'carried over' to the expenditure tax, will mean much the same tax payment under both systems for an honest taxpayer who neither saves nor dis-saves: an (average) tax rate of 50% means that in each case he spends half his pre-tax income. If, however, the base for the expenditure tax *excludes* what was paid in direct taxes (which is perhaps the most natural meaning to attach to 'expenditure'), then to get the same result the average rate for the expenditure tax will have to be 100%. Moreover, the contrast for *marginal* rates will be dramatic—on p. 235 Nicky highlights this by taking marginal rates at the top end of those prevailing at the time—i.e. 90% on the gross basis, which implies 900% when expressed net.

To my mind, Nicky seriously underestimated the effects of the 'net' method of expressing the tax on the incentive to tax avoidance and evasion. His analysis on p. 235 deals only with *a single act of concealment*: it shows that if a taxpayer whose income is, for simplicity, assumed to be stable 'dresses up £100 of personal expenditure as a business expense', then his tax bill next year will be reduced by £900 on the net basis but only £90 on the gross (this latter figure being the same as would happen with the income tax). If his true personal expenditure is not increased, but the 'dressing up' ceases after that one year, then the tax bill for the succeeding year will, on the net basis, be restored to the proper amount; but on the gross basis there will again be a saving—this time of £81—because the tax base includes the tax paid in the previous year, which was 'short' by £90. Hence the gross basis gives a (declining) series of tax savings (likened by Nicky to the 'multiplier' process), which yields a total saving of £900.

Nicky points out that the net basis gives a greater incentive to tax avoidance, because the saving is immediate, but he plays the difference down. What seems to me crucial, however, is to examine the consequences if the evasion *continues*. The answer is simple: on the net basis, there is a tax saving of £900 in every year from the assumed 'dressing up' of £100 p.a. of personal expenditure as business expenses, but on the gross basis the saving starts at £90 and gradually rises over the years until it also stabilises at £900. Since it is only in the fifth year that the gross basis yields even *half* the tax saving produced on the net basis, and since people are always more impressed by visible immediate results than by the theoretical outcome of calculations based on assumptions of stable income etc., there can be no question that the net basis is enormously more provocative to tax fiddles of all kinds. A 'tax consultant' would be able to claim very large savings indeed from the adoption of his formulae, and the unaided tax payer would be sorely tempted to save £900 per year from a small manipulation of £100 of expenditure, or from a similar forgetfulness of £100 of fees earned.

These somewhat nightmarish visions of the tremendous incentives to tax avoidance or evasion by rich people, even on the gross basis, were considerably weakened by Nicky's conclusion, essentially for other reasons, that only *surtax* should be based on exenditure, with income tax at the standard rate applying to all taxable income above the appropriate exemption limits. The basic reason for this excellent proposal was that income would have to be the starting point for the expenditure assessment, and the existing administrative

[1] In paragraph 6 of that Memorandum, for example, it is stated firmly that 'writers on public finance' all agree in regarding income as the sum of personal consumption and net capital accumulation. Since 'income'—the thing to be taxed—must be regarded as *pre-tax* income, this implies that direct taxation has to be regarded as part of personal consumption. When taxes are based on the income of a previous year and income fluctuates greatly, this has some odd consequences, but they are not of anything like as great importance as with an expenditure tax, since the rate of taxation is naturally applied to *pre-tax* income.

machinery (PAYE, dividends taxed at source, etc.) makes it unnecessary for there to be any end-year adjustments for the vast majority of the population in relation to income tax. The expenditure tax, however—even if self-assessment of income on the US basis were introduced—would call for end-year adjustments to take account of capital transactions etc., and it seemed clear that it would be administratively impossible to do these for more than the relatively small number of people 'in the surtax class'. Moreover, they would be largely pointless, since in most cases the adjustments would be relatively trifling—although there might be a number of cases where they were enormous.

Two further points need to be made about the proposal to put 'surtax' on an expenditure basis, but retain the basic income tax as a tax on income:

(a) *Company profits and capital gains.* If the *whole* of personal direct taxation had been put onto an expenditure basis, Nicky concluded (p. 171) that taxation of company profits should cease and that a capital gains tax would be unnecessary: expenditure by shareholders would 'reflect' company profits and capital gains, which would not need to be separately taxed.

However, with only surtax on an expenditure basis, he concluded on the same page that realised capital gains should be subject to income tax, and a small corporation profits tax (separate from personal income tax) would also be appropriate.

(b) *Form of the expenditure tax.* In calculating 'taxable consumption' it would clearly be necessary to subtract personal payments of income tax from gross income. Nicky's view (p. 237) was that he would then opt for the net system of expressing the expenditure tax (with a possible top marginal rate of 266·2/3%). His reasons were 'more psychological and political than economic or technical in character' (p. 237): he hoped that these high rates would impress the electorate that there really was to be a great increase in the tax-burden *actually borne* by property owners and other wealthy people, and would also restrain their desire to raise *nominal* rates to absurd levels (as had happened with surtax).

I cannot help wondering whether Nicky would have stood by the political assessment given above if he had rewritten his book in 1980, when he recorded on page xxiii of his *Reports on Taxation I* that he had 'become far more sceptical of the possibilities of improving the distribution of income and wealth through taxation or of introducing effective reforms when these are perceived, in anticipation, as affecting adversely the interests of the property-owning classes'. The visible severity of tax rates expressed on a net basis would have stimulated the pressure for 'specific concessions or exceptions', even if they did not prevent the expenditure tax from reaching the Statute Book altogether. Personally, I find the stimulus to tax fiddling created by the net basis so horrifying that I would opt for the gross basis, even if the expenditure tax applies only to the 'surtax zone'.

Direct taxation: action

As Economic Adviser to the Labour Government in the 1960s, Nicky played a large role in securing the simultaneous inclusion of the capital gains tax (CGT) and the corporation tax in the 1965 Budget against the advice of the Inland Revenue Department, which thought that the work of introducing two major changes simultaneously would prove too burdensome.

Essentially, the CGT followed Nicky's ideas as expounded in the Minority Report, except that the Government decided to retain the provision introduced by the Conservative Government in 1962, whereby *short-term* gains (i.e. those realised within one year) were liable to the full marginal rate of income tax for the person concerned, whilst other gains were to be taxed at 30% under a new capital gains tax (against 41·75% as the standard rate of income tax). On other points, Nicky's views were followed—e.g. on the all-important rule that CGT should be applied at death, on the basis of market prices then prevailing, and also on the inclusion of capital gains secured on gilt-edged securities (in the interests of uniform treatment).

Although the 1965 Budget Speech envisaged a series of further reforms in later years, these were not in fact attempted. In particular, no attempt was made to shift to an expenditure tax, and very little was done to improve the equality of tax treatment of people coming under Schedule D and Schedule E respectively. Some 'tidying up' was effected on tax loopholes, such as entertainment allowances; but there was a serious backsliding (on Nicky's view) in 1969, when the scope of CGT was narrowed by the exclusion of gilt-edged securities held for more than one year, because the Treasury argued that the market needed strengthening.

One change was made which had Nicky's strong support, when the investment incentive system was reformed in 1966 by the introduction of investment *grants*, rather than investment allowances: as he put it to me orally, these would be available to new and expanding firms, whether or not they had profits on existing activities against which the allowances could be set. There was also a big differentiation in favour of schemes in the Development Areas.

Under the Conservative Government of 1970–4 the capital gains tax was seriously weakened by the abolition of a tax at death—but simplified by the sensible abolition of the special tax on short-term gains which the Conservatives had themselves introduced in 1962. The Corporation Tax was largely emasculated by the introduction of the 'imputation system', whereby shareholders received a tax credit in respect of income tax at the standard rate which was 'deemed' to have been deducted by the company, so that they could claim a refund if they were not liable to taxation. The equivalent of this credit had to be paid over in cash to the Treasury as 'advance corporation tax', whether or not the company had any taxable profits for that year.

When Labour returned to power in 1974, Nicky may well have hoped that these inroads into the capital gains tax and corporation tax, as introduced in 1965, would be reversed, and possibly that further advances (e.g. towards an expenditure tax) might be undertaken. Although he was again an Adviser, however, no such action was attempted. There was, on the other hand, a measure which doubtless appealed to his sense of equity, in the introduction of the capital transfer tax, under which gifts *inter vivos* were effectively brought under what one might call 'advance death duties', thereby reducing the effectiveness of the well-known loophole for avoiding the latter.

Nicky was also very directly involved in a piece of 'emergency action' to deal with the formidable financial problems which had arisen for many companies as a result of the rapid inflation of prices in 1974. Under the provisions of the corporation tax, these created large 'paper profits' for companies which had sold their goods at prices based on historic costs, and replaced their raw materials and work in progress with goods costed at the much higher levels now prevailing. The stock appreciation represented by the higher prices of stocks at the end of the year, as compared with the beginning, was fully taxable (a provision which the Minority Report had indeed approved in 1955). But with inflation on the 1974 rate, and with industry suffering from many other handicaps which limited its borrowing power, payment of taxes on these paper profits would have produced a financial squeeze of the first water and probably bankruptcies.

Nicky's proposal did not attempt to deal with the inflation element in the increased value of stocks as such, since this would have raised formidable measurement problems. Instead, he suggested that companies should be given relief on increases in the book value of stocks during their financial year which exceeded 10% of the company's trading profits (which might broadly be regarded as the amount of trading profits which could be devoted to raising the value of stock held). This provision could be introduced without any technical problems, and reduced the tax payable by companies in 1975/1976 by well over £1 billion.

Indirect taxation

In the field of indirect taxation, Nicky's outstanding contribution was his 'invention' of a completely new tax—the selective employment tax (SET). Perhaps one should also add the major role which he played in getting this new tax enacted by the Labour Government in 1966, in the face of difficulties raised by the Inland Revenue and other parties, notably about the administrative problems which the tax was thought to involve. As with so many taxes, one has to accept some imperfections in the practical application: for my part, having spent five years or so working on the effects of SET (see below), I have no hesitation in saying that these 'rough edges' (some of which were smoothed away with the benefit of experience) left an enormous credit balance in favour of the tax's introduction.

The basic principle of this new tax was to impose on most of the service trades in the country (and on construction) an obligation to pay what was initially £1·25 per week for every man employed (with lower rates for women, boys and girls). This obligation was enforced by raising the general level of the national insurance stamp in each age-and-sex category by the amount of the tax, and allowing employers in the 'exempted' industries (or with exempt status as, for example, Local Authorities) to claim a refund each quarter. The tax rates were increased in 1968 and again in 1969, and from 1967 partial refunds were permitted for elderly or part-time workers in the trades which were really liable to SET.

The object of the new tax was in the first instance to raise revenue (in furtherance of the Government's policy of reducing over-heating in the economy and improving the balance of payments) and, secondly, to do this by a tax which would, in itself, have beneficial effects on the working of the economy—notably by raising productivity in the service trades and improving the labour supply available to manufacturing industry.

Nicky himself suggested, towards the end of 1967, that an 'impartial assessment' of the effects of the tax should be undertaken and, as Director of the Department of Applied Economics at Cambridge, I was asked to organise such an investigation. I must confess that, whilst I was in no doubt that the Department should undertake the investigation, nevertheless I quailed at the thought of the immense difficulties which it would involve. The more formidable ones may be briefly listed as follows:

(a) One is *not* concerned simply to compare the position in (say) 1968 or 1969 with the position in 1965. This 'historical record' is of interest in itself, but the *effect* of SET has to be assessed by comparing the actual position in 1968 with what might reasonably have been expected to exist if SET had not been imposed. On productivity, for example, there had been a rising trend for many years, with deviations reflecting (for example) cyclical movements in the economy; and it was necessary to establish what level of productivity might have been expected in 1968 on the basis of 'pre-SET rules', given the external circumstances which existed in 1968.

(b) By bad luck, SET was introduced shortly after a process of banning resale price maintenance had been launched, so that this 'abnormal new factor' was operating at much the same time as SET appeared. This was of great importance for the distributive trades, and we found it impossible to produce a statistical rule which would separate out the effects of the two new factors.

(c) SET was, even at its highest rate, a low tax, so that its effect on retail prices, even if it were completely passed on, would only be of the order of 1%. Hence one was looking for very small differences between the 'actual' outcome and what might have been expected.

(d) On top of this, the statistical basis in most of the service trades was extremely poor, so that it was difficult to establish the pre-SET historical record, let alone deduce from it the 'rules' which would govern the movements in (say) retailers' margins or profits. We had, indeed, to establish what had happened since the introduction of SET by special enquiries, but it would have been quite impossible to carry these back over a sufficiently long previous period to deduce the crucial 'rules'.

(e) One had to expect that the 'effects' of SET would be different in the short run and in the long run, and the fact that the rates for the tax were changed twice made attempts at disentangling these even more difficult.

In view of these and other difficulties I feared, on undertaking the job, that, however hard we worked, the margins of error in any conclusions which we reached would be so large that one would have little or no confidence in them; moreover, any of the statistics might be hopelessly contradictory either as to what had happened, or as to the conclusions to be drawn.

The need for an impartial assessment was, however, clear, and the work involved in attempting to arrive at one was certain to be interesting, even if it might become frustrating after a time. Consequently, we set about tackling the problems trade by trade, including the collection of a great deal of new information from each separate trade. Academic purity suggested that, ideally, we should not release any results until we had covered the whole field: then we would consider the entire collection of results simultaneously, with the possibility of forming useful generalisations (or perhaps getting a warning against over-confident remarks about the effects in one trade, if very different ones appeared in another and there were no obvious explanation). Practical considerations, however (notably the understandable desire of the Government and the officials concerned for early results) led us to deliver the preliminary results for the distributive trades (our first venture) in January 1970 (see Reddaway, 1970): we did, however, stress the fact that some of the results might well need reconsideration when we got more up-to-date official statistics to combine with our own data, and also the fact that various points were being held over to a Final Report, when we would have results from other trades as well.

Fortunately, the results which emerged from our investigations on productivity, margins and profits in distribution showed a degree of statistical consistency which far exceeded my most optimistic hopes. Broadly speaking, moreover, the figures vindicated Nicky's expectations, although we had to stress that we could not divide (say) the productivity gain (relatively to pre-SET expectations) between the effects of SET and those of the progressive reduction of resale price maintenance.

This Report made no attempt to give a systematic theoretical explanation of *why* the results should have been what they actually were. This was essentially because I could see a number of different causal mechanisms, all of which might have made some contribution, and I could see no empirical way of determining how much of the outcome might come from one factor rather than another.

From my personal point of view, the unexpected 'success' of the investigation of retailing was a bit embarrassing, because it seemed to imply that I would spend most of the remaining ten years before my retirement in repeating the exercise (with substantial variations, and, very probably, with much less 'statistical success') on the numerous other industries which were liable to SET. We had already started work on a number of services (hotels, restaurants, motor traders, hairdressers and shoe repairers) which called for separate investigations, but which we thought could reasonably be covered by a single report on 'near-distribution'. But we knew that there would be a major job in tackling the construction industry, and there were many other industries about which we had not even begun to think, but which would clearly need separate treatment.

This personal dilemma was resolved for me by the election of the Conservative Government in 1970. As that Government was pledged to repeal SET, we were told that it would provide us only with a limited amount of further grant to cover our responsibilities to staff already appointed. We decided, therefore, that we would aim at producing one further Report, which would have to be published by the DAE, since HMSO would take no further action (see Reddaway *et al.*, 1973). We decided that this Report would deal with 'near-distribution' properly, since we had collected the data, and would do what seemed possible from published data on such of the remaining industries as that data enabled us to tackle, even partially. One major object of the Final Report would, however, be to carry the analysis of the distributive trades forward to later years, in so far as that could be done from published statistics (which meant largely dealing with productivity, but not margins or profits).

This productivity analysis could be extended to include an attempt to assess the effect of SET (and RPM) on what was loosely called 'the number of shops' (although in practice one needs a measure which takes heed of the size of the shops as well as their number). This seemed useful because it would throw some light on the theory that SET would raise productivity by reducing 'the number of shops' below what might otherwise have been expected, and that each shop would work nearer to capacity and so have a higher volume of sales per worker.

Neither the statistics nor the methodology was very good, but the conclusion of our analysis was that it did not provide any convincing evidence that SET as such, even with the aid of the RPM changes, had reduced the growth of the capacity used in retailing. One might hold that belief on a priori grounds, and the statistics are not strong enough to refute it convincingly; but if one stands by the belief, it will be *in spite of* the statistics, not because of them, since if anything they pointed to an increased rate of growth. The analysis went on to say that, even if one believed that there was some small SET effect on 'the number of shops', one cannot possibly believe that this is the *sole* way in which SET/RPM affects productivity, since it is clear that the effect on employment was greater than the effect (if any) on the number of shops. This automatically implies that the number of workers per shop (or more strictly, per unit of retailing capacity) has *fallen*, and such a result must be due to something other than the direct effect of a reduction in the retailing capacity. The 'number of shops' theory implies that SET reduced the number of shops, and enabled each of them to work nearer to capacity, without taking on any extra labour; it does not give a reason for *reducing* the labour in the remaining shops.

In the light of the above, I feel bound to criticise the paper which Nicky wrote in 1979 about the 'theoretical model' that prompted his advocacy of SET. Essentially, this paper sets out (in extremely elegant prose) the 'number of shops theory', arguing that the nature of imperfect competition in the retail market will prevent retailers from passing on SET in the form of higher margins; this will kill off marginal shops and prevent new entry, so that the remaining smaller number of shops can work nearer to capacity. This is a plausible a priori argument, which I believe may have contributed *something* to the productivity gain (despite the fact that the statistics on shops point in the other direction!), but it cannot be the sole explanation. The argument is, in any case, entirely in terms of comparative statics, with all the difficulties which that entails when one tries to use it to explain historical developments in which other factors besides SET were clearly working (with which this particular factor may 'inter-act').

Nicky is also open to criticism in saying (1980, p. xx) that I 'resolutely refused to go into the question of explanation' of the results which emerged. I did not set out the sort of analysis given in his paper because, after examining the empirical results, it seemed to me clear that other factors were not only involved, but also much more important than the 'number of shops hypothesis'. Our Final Report includes, however, a chapter 'Some Concluding Reflections', which reviews SET and the results of our analysis from many points of view, and ends with five pages on 'reasons for SET effect on productivity'. These are not set out in the sort of elegant style which Nicky uses in his paper, but they do have the merit of being related to empirical results; and, above all, they take account of dynamic developments through time, instead of being entirely in terms of comparative statics. 'Acceleration of Trends', for example, reflects what was repeatedly impressed on us by trade witnesses—i.e. that SET induced an acceleration of the processes of improving productivity which were taking place slowly without it. 'Comparative statics' has no room for that kind of argument.

Similarly, the fact that SET has a differential effect on inefficient traders is explored in a wider context than the simple assumption that SET will reduce the number of shops. In the first place, the inefficient traders may be pushed by the fear of bankruptcy into a special effort to improve their productivity; and if in fact the inefficient shop is closed, the premises are likely to be taken over by a more efficient management, so that there is a gain in productivity without any reduction in the number of shops.

These criticisms should not, however, be allowed to detract in any way from the very favourable assessment which our impartial investigation led us to make of the effects of SET, or my admiration for the man who invented it. Our Report's chapter of 'concluding reflections' is one which, if I had been the inventor of the tax, I would have been proud to receive from an impartial assessor.

In that respect, I feel that Nicky is decidedly unfair to himself and to SET when he says (1980, p. 224) 'the tax must be adjudged to have been a failure—not because it failed to operate in the expected manner, but because the general economic situation of the country did not conform to the conditions . . .' SET produced a real gain in productivity, and what was a failure was the general management of the economy.

The Regional Employment Premium

Finally, I would like to pay tribute to Nicky for his part in securing the introduction of the Regional Employment Premium in 1967. This idea belongs to the same family as the SET scheme, but was aimed at giving a differential stimulus to manufacturing in the development areas. The 'impartial assessment' which was made of its effects by Moore and Rhodes (1976) showed these to be beneficial, although not perhaps as sensational as one might have hoped.

And I would like to add a sort of 'postscript' to this article by recommending readers to study the foreword by Sir Douglas Wass to A. P. Thirlwall's book *Nicholas Kaldor*, in which Sir Douglas gives his first-hand impressions of Nicky as a consultant helping the officials in the Treasury or elsewhere.

Bibliography

Kaldor, N. 1955. *An Expenditure Tax*, London, George Allen & Unwin

Kaldor, N. 1979. The economics of the Selective Employment Tax, in Kaldor (1980)

Kaldor, N. 1980. *Reports on Taxation I*, London, Duckworth

Moore, B. and Rhodes, J. 1976. A quantitive analysis of the effects of the Regional Employment Premium and other regional policy instruments, in A. Whiting (ed.), *The Economics of Industrial Subsidies*, London HMSO

Reddaway, W. B. 1970. *Effects of the Selective Employment Tax. First Report. The Distributive Trades*, London, HMSO

Reddaway, W. B. *et al.* 1973. *Effects of the Selective Employment Tax: Final Report*, DAE Occasional Paper 32, Cambridge, CUP

Thirlwall, A. P. 1987. *Nicholas Kaldor*, Brighton, Wheatsheaf Books

The macroeconomics of protectionism: the case of Britain in the 1930s

Michael Kitson* and Solomos Solomou*

Introduction

The use of protection as an instrument for economic revival in a flexible exchange rate regime remains a controversial policy issue. The experience of the UK in the 1930s offers an excellent opportunity for testing the hypotheses that discouragement of imports through tariffs was an effective way of reducing the propensity to import, and that the effective demand for the products of UK industry was significantly increased as a result.

During the period 1932–37, GDP and manufacturing production showed unprecedented annual growth rates of 4·7 and 8·2% respectively. In a long-term historical perspective the peak-to-peak cycle of 1929–37 showed signs of trend acceleration in economic growth. Whilst manufacturing production grew at 1·6% per annum during the period 1900–29, this more than doubled to 3·6% per annum during the 1929–39 cycle; similarly, GDP grew at 0·7% per annum during 1913–29 and 2·0% during 1929–37.

The problem we address in this paper is whether the policy shift to protection in 1931/2 *contributed significantly* to this cyclical and trend recovery of the economy. Most economic historians have agreed that the impact of the tariff on economic growth was negligible, if not negative (Richardson, 1967; Capie, 1978). These studies have sought to quantify the impact of the 1932 tariff by focusing on the possible substitution effects, considering the advantage to individual industries from the imposition of an import tariff on competing goods. Studies that have viewed tariffs as a macroeconomic policy instrument have shown that some positive output effects are observed (Foreman-Peck, 1981; Eichengreen, 1979 and 1981). This paper is drawn from a larger study on the sectoral and macroeconomic impact of the tariff during the period (Kitson and Solomou, forthcoming). Here we focus exclusively on the macroeconomic impact, analysing the historical evidence from a theoretical perspective different to that proposed by Foreman-Peck or Eichengreen. The disaggregated analysis of the impact of tariffs will be analysed elsewhere.

The paper is divided into three parts. First, we evaluate the theoretical issues concerning tariffs as an instrument of macroeconomic policy. Second, we present an empirical

*University of Cambridge. Much of this paper is based on research funded by the ESRC (grant BOO230075) and directed by the late Lord Kaldor. His involvement was immense and is sadly missed. A major contribution was also made by John Rhodes who provided critical help in the development of many ideas contained in this paper. We also received valuable comments from Derek Aldcroft, Alec Cairncross, Forrest Capie, Barry Eichengreen, Peter Fearon, Charles Feinstein, James Foreman-Peck, Tim Hatton, Alfred Maizels, Nick Von Tunzelmann, three anonymous referees and the Editors of this journal. The usual disclaimer of course applies.

analysis of the imposition of a general tariff in Britain in 1932, illustrating the macroeconomic processes arising from this policy shift and attempting to disentangle the effects of devaluation from those of the tariff. Finally, we provide an overview of other influences on the 1930s recovery and place our views on the impact of the 1932 tariff in a broader context.

1. The macroeconomics of protection

The first major contribution to the analysis of tariffs as a macroeconomic policy under a system of flexible exchange rates is given in Mundell's (1961) seminal paper. Mundell recognised that under fixed exchange rates, and in the absence of extensive retaliation, a tariff may generate higher output and employment. However, under flexible exchange rates, the appreciation of the real exchange rate, resulting from the imposition of tariffs, will render commerical policy ineffective. Mundell's results relies on the Laursen–Metzler (1950) hypothesis that saving will increase with improved terms of trade, owing to an improvement in real disposable income. However, the Laursen–Metzler effect is not a clearly established empirical or theoretical result. The final effect of a terms-of-trade shift will depend on direct price effects, wealth effects and intertemporal substitutions, so that a non-retaliatory tariff can have expansionary macroeconomic effects as long as the restrictive Laursen–Metzler assumption is dropped from Mundell's model (Ford and Sen, 1985).

The model can also be extended to allow for monetary and portfolio considerations under flexible exchange rates (Boyer, 1977; Chan, 1978; Eichengreen, 1981; Krugman, 1982). These extended models also suggest that tariffs will affect output only in the short run (Eichengreen, 1981), but depend for this result on the use of the quantity theory of money or the Cambridge equation of money demand.[1] Thus, the idea that under flexible exchange rates commercial policy will be rendered ineffective does not hold as a general result; even within a standard macroeconomic framework, tariffs can have positive output and employment effects.

Our intention here is to indicate further plausible mechanisms by which tariffs may have had a favourable effect on economic performance. Our perspective is a Kaldorian one, incorporating the Harrod foreign trade multiplier (Harrod, 1933). Kaldor (1970, 1982) saw the importance of the Harrod foreign trade multiplier within a 'stylized facts' perspective, noting that the British trade cycle reflected fluctuations in export demand. Investment is best modelled not as exogenous but as an induced component of aggregate demand, being determined by the income changes which are, in turn, induced by the Harrod foreign trade multiplier.[2]

Kaldor argued that the Ricardian rationale for free trade is dependent on the assumption of constant returns to scale. The existence of economies of scale in manufacturing, however, means that a nation that is successfully competing in foreign trade can expect that the advantage of an expanding market will increase its competitiveness. Similarly, a

[1] Ford and Sen (1985) show that the effects of tariffs depends on the specification of the money demand function and that accommodatory changes in the money stock, such as were observed in the 1930s, can improve the chances of a general tariff having positive output and employment effects.

[2] In the most simple terms the Harrod foreign trade multiplier can be expressed as

$$Y=(1/m)X$$

where Y = Income; X = Exports; m = marginal propensity to import. For extensions see Kennedy and Thirlwall (1983).

nation with a poor performance in international trade can expect a trend of deteriorating competitiveness and declining markets. Thus, while not explaining the causes of initial imbalances in international trade, the existence of economies of scale indicates why such imbalances may generate virtuous or vicious circles of growth.

The existence of economies of scale and the process of cumulative causation led Kaldor to stress the importance of trends in foreign trade, in particular trade in manufactures, for demand management. In analysing British post-war economic policies, Kaldor (1971) argued that the poor economic performance was due to insufficient demand. This was not in the sense of an excessive propensity to save relative to the opportunities to invest but of an excessive propensity to import relative to the ability to export.

The importance of the idea of export-led growth gave rise to a policy debate on the best means for securing full employment. While exchange rate adjustment seemed the most applicable method, its efficiency was called in question, particularly after the limited impact of the 1967 devaluation. It was argued that a nominal devaluation may not have a large impact on the real exchange rate, and thus on competitiveness, owing to the effect of rising import prices, particularly of wage goods. Devaluation is a non-selective policy and raises the prices of all imports, not just competitive ones. Consequently, any attempt to generate a substantial and long-term improvement in competitiveness through the exchange rate may require a large reduction in the nominal rate, with repercussions for inflation, real income and economic stability.

This led Kaldor and others to argue that some form of protection of competitive manufactures would be superior.[1] On the other hand, since protection acts solely on imports (whereas devaluation acts on both sides of the trade account) it has been argued that protection cannot promote export-led growth. Strictly speaking this is true; however, by encouraging import substitutes, protection can expand the domestic traded-goods sector. In terms of the Harrod foreign trade multiplier, the means of expansion operates through reducing the propensity to import, so reducing the leakages from the domestic economy. As Kaldor pointed out in 1951, the objective of protection in an underemployed economy would be to reduce the propensity to import competitive goods, not to reduce the volume of such imports. If the policy was successful, the rise in domestic incomes should encourage more imports of complementary and subsequently competitive goods.

This superiority of protection over devaluation applies more to quotas or other forms of quantitative restrictions than to tariffs. Tariffs, like devaluation, act on relative prices, so their effect may be limited if price elasticities are low or non-price factors dominate. They work best when applied selectively on competitive rather than complementary imports, discriminating between sectors producing import substitutes and those dependent on imported inputs.

[1] Although Kaldor's perspective influenced the Cambridge Economic Policy Group (CEPG) in the 1970s the two approaches are rather different. The CEPG proposed the use of tariffs as an expenditure switching policy to be combined with fiscal reflation. The tariff would alleviate the balance-of-payments constraint on fiscal policy and would prevent demand expansion from generating an unsustainable trade deficit. A tariff was preferred to devaluation for many of the reasons discussed above; most importantly the CEPG argued that in Britain the process of free collective bargaining combined with real wage resistance would prevent a significant improvement in competitiveness through exchange rate adjustment. The CEPG saw fiscal policy as providing the stimulus to demand with the tariff alleviating the balance-of-payments constraint. Our approach, derived from Kaldor, is to view the tariff as the means for expansion. By improving domestic competitiveness it will stimulate the production of import substitutes generating increased profits and wages which will subsequently expand the demand for all products (domestic and foreign) via the kind of mechanisms discussed below.

Thus, in this simplified Kaldorian framework, the main determinants of a rapid recovery inthe 1930s could have arisen from two sources: an exogenous increase in exports or a fall in the propensity to import. Since the world economy was constrained by slow growth of aggregate demand, the main catalyst for recovery must have arisen from a fall in import propensities caused by tariffs and/or devalution.

These statements can only be understood in the context of an overall economic perspective: they do not represent the makings of a complete model of an economy. The Harrod multiplier simply indicates that a fall in import propensity can increase domestic demand and stimulate output. The mechanisms by which this may come about are:

(i) *Increased competitiveness*
A tariff makes domestic products cheaper relative to foreign products in the home market, encouraging import substitution in consumption and production.

(ii) *Income effects*
The resulting increase in domestic incomes stimulates higher demand that extends beyond the protected manufacturing sector. Some of the increase in domestic incomes will leak abroad in the form of an increased demand for imports. Hence, given constraints on world exports, the *ex post* trade balance need not improve with the imposition of tariffs.

(iii) *Increasing returns effects*
The more favourable conditions for manufactures and the wider domestic market allows the manufacturing sector to expand along a path of increasing returns. Since the process of import substitution induces a higher level of domestic investment, increasing returns also arise from improved vintages of capital.

(iv) *Institutional and psychological effects*
Given a world of uncertainty, a major policy shift aimed at guaranteeing a higher level of domestic demand for home producers may increase investment by far more than can be explained by relative price and output shifts. Thus, tariffs may be viewed as an institution aimed at reducing uncertainty for home producers, as may devaluation and rationalisation schemes.

2. The case of the 1930s

Between 1932 and 1939 the UK share of world manufacturing trade stabilised, halting the downward trend which had persisted since 1870, but the substantial decline in world trade in the 1930s meant that the volume of manufacturing exports never reached the levels which had prevailed in the 1920s. Thus, export performance was not responsible for the observed improvement in economic growth. Our attention must therefore focus on the shift in import propensities.

The measure of import propensity used here is imports expressed as a proportion of domestic expenditure (gross output *minus* exports *plus* imports).[1] Table 1 shows, for

[1] The import propensity (m) can be calculated as

$$\frac{M}{N-X+M}$$

Where M=Import Volume, N=Volume of Domestic Output and X=Export Volume. No allowance has been made for changes in stocks.

Table 1. *Import propensity of manufactures (volume), 1924–38*

Year	%
1924	9·9
1925	10·8
1926	11·9
1927	11·9
1928	12·3
1929	12·6
1930	12·7
1931	13·4
1932	9·2
1933	8·9
1934	9·3
1935	9·1
1936	8·9
1937	9·3
1938	8·7

Sources: Trade data: Board of Trade *Journal* (various editions, 1924–38). Output data: Feinstein (1972), Tables 9 and 51.

Notes: The index shows manufactures imports expressed as a percentage of domestic demand for manufactures; gross output figures were estimated by grossing up the 1924 value from the *Census of Production* using the Lomax index for 1924–38. This gives a series for gross output at constant (1924) prices. The published trade data were also assembled to form a consistent series at constant (1924) prices.

each year between 1924 and 1938, the import propensity (m) for UK manufacturing industry as a whole. Between 1924 and 1931 m increased steadily from 9·9% to 13·4%. During 1932–38, m fell by almost one-third despite very rapid output growth.[1] Since the General Tariff on manufacturing imports was introduced in 1932, there is a prima facie case for the new policy having contributed to these trend changes.

The other component of GDP accounting for the aggregate trends was food, beverages and tobacco (Matthews *et al.*, 1982, p. 432). In current price terms, imports of this sector fell from 14·7% of GDP in 1924 to 9·2% in 1937. Given that this component of expenditure was not directly influenced by the tariffs of 1932, it may be argued that a fairly large part of the aggregate propensity shift was not policy-induced.[2]

[1] The fall in import propensities was observed in most industries, the largest reductions being experienced in the vehicle industry, textiles, iron and steel, clothing, electrical goods and chemicals (Kaldor and Kitson, 1986). Only in the raw material based industries of timber and paper did any significant fall in m fail to occur. Such a disaggregated picture suggests that import propensity changes were observed both in the newly protected sectors of 1931–2 and the industries that were already protected. Hence, the tariff cannot be seen as the only influence on sectoral import propensity changes.

[2] Although some protection was afforded to the domestic agricultural and manufactured food sectors, its scope was limited by Imperial Preference and by the fact that most of British trade in agricultural products was conducted in the sterling bloc.

Table 2. *Import ratio for food, drink and tobacco: current and constant prices*

Year	Constant (1938) prices (% of GDP)	Current prices (% of GDP)
1924	11·2	14·7
1925	10·6	13·9
1926	11·2	13·7
1927	10·8	13·2
1928	10·5	12·9
1929	10·8	12·7
1930	11·0	12·8
1931	11·5	10·8
1932	10·3	10·0
1933	9·9	9·0
1934	9·2	8·6
1935	8·9	8·5
1936	8·7	8·7
1937	8·5	9·2
1938	8·6	8·7

Sources: Imports of food, drink and tobacco from B. R. Mitchell, *Abstract of British Historical Statistics* (1988), p. 457. The GDP series are taken from Feinstein (1972).

In the case of food imports there are clearly a number of influences on the changed import propensity. First, the differences between the value and volume figures (see Table 2) show that a major part of the fall in the import propensity for this component of expenditure is due to a relative price shift between the price of food imports and the GDP deflator. On average, the differences between 1924–31 and 1932–38 suggest that over two percentage points of the fall can be accounted for by a relative price shift. Second, there was a fall in the level of food imports in the 1930s compared to the 1920s, which may imply a change in competitiveness due to devaluation. Finally, given that the rate of growth of food imports was below the trend growth rate of GDP throughout 1924–37,[1] some of the fall has to be explained in terms of the relatively low income elasticity of demand for food. This meant that as growth picked up between 1932–37 there was an endogenous beneficial effect on income from a reduced food import ratio. Thus, to the extent that the tariff stimulated the manufacturing sector and the aggregate economy, it also had a repercussion effect on the food import propensity.

Although the trend in the propensity to import food is only very indirectly linked to tariffs, the impact of protection on the manufacturing sector needs to be considered. We evaluate this by considering the evidence on changes in manufacturing competitiveness in the 1930s. Table 3 shows a number of different indicators of exchange-rate behaviour during the period 1924–38. The sterling–dollar rate shows considerable stability during the 1920s, reflecting Britain's return to the Gold Standard in 1925. This stability is also evident when account is taken of movements in other currencies; columns 3 and 4 show the

[1] During 1924–29 constant (1938) price food imports increased by 1·4% per annum while during 1929–37 they fell by 1·2% per annum.

Table 3. *Sterling exchange rate measures*

	(1) Sterling–dollar	(2) Sterling effective exchange rate	(3) Sterling average exchange rate	(4) Sterling manufacturing exchange rate
1924	91·0		84·6	83·0
1925	99·5		93·5	91·4
1926	100·1		102·3	101·6
1927	100·1		100·0	100·1
1928	100·2		100·0	100·0
1929	100·0	100·0	100·0	100·0
1930	100·1		99·6	100·1
1931	93·4	100·1	93·7	94·8
1932	72·2	86·7	75·2	75·7
1933	87·3	91·3	77·0	83·8
1934	103·8	95·9	75·4	86·0
1935	100·1	95·4	74·5	85·5
1936	102·4	97·5	77·7	88·5
1937	101·8	100·8	84·7	94·3
1938	100·7	105·1	86·9	100·3

Sources: column (1) Svennilson (1954), pp. 318–19; column (2) Redmond (1980), appendix; column (3) Dimsdale (1981), tables 3 and 9; column (4) Svennilson (1954), pp. 318–19, LCES (various editions) and Board of Trade (1929 and 1939). Countries covered are USA, France, Germany, Belgium, Netherlands, Canada, Australia and India. Weights are average share of UK manufacturing trade for 1928 and 1935.
Notes: 1929 = 100 except for the sterling effective exchange rate where 1929–30 = 100.

movement in sterling against a basket of currencies for trade in manufactures.[1] Considering the manufacturing exchange rate (column 4) as the best indicator, there was an average devaluation of nearly 15% for the period 1932–37 compared to 1929.

To compare the impacts of this devaluation with that of tariffs it is necessary first to consider the scale of the tariff introduced. The Import Duties Act 1932 provided a base rate on newly protected imports of 10%, but one which could be raised subsequently on the recommendation of the newly established Import Duties Advisory Committee. On the Committee's recommendation, most rates were soon raised to 20% and for a more limited category of commodities (which included steel and chemicals) to $33\frac{1}{3}\%$. There were

[1] The average exchange rate of Dimsdale (1981) uses each country's share in world trade as weights while the manufacturing exchange rate is constructed using shares in UK overseas trade. There are also small differences in the countries covered. The sterling effective exchange rate shown in Table 3 (column 2) was constructed by Redmond (1980) using shares in bilateral and multilateral trade as weights. It indicates an average sterling devaluation of approximately 5% in the period 1932–37 compared with the 1929–30 level. The average exchange rate (column 3) and the manufacturing exchange rate (column 4) show a greater devaluation, 22·6% and 14·4% respectively, compared with 1929. As both these indicators are based on manufacturing trade they are influenced by the European gold bloc currencies which were comparatively overvalued against sterling. Thus they indicate a higher devaluation for manufacturing trade, as opposed to the effective rate which is influenced by the currencies of raw material and food exporters. A striking point is the difference between the average exchange rate and the manufacturing rate. In part this can be explained by coverage and alternative weighting procedures. The major divergence however arises after 1933 and is primarily due to our decision to allow for a 35% devaluation of the German exchange rate for the period 1933–38. Germany operated a complex multiple exchange rate régime during this period with an effective devaluation of the official rate for trade in manufactures (Kindleberger, 1956, p. 116).

Table 4. *Manufactures dutiable only under the Import Duties Act, 1932*

Rate of duty %	Value of imports from all countries in 1930 £m
0	17·5
10	38·9
15	12·1
20	57·9
25	6·6
30	4·3
$33\frac{1}{3}$	17·0
Over $33\frac{1}{3}$	1·8
Total	156·1

Source: Leak (1937), p. 569.

further increases in 1934 and 1935. Assessment of the incidence of the tariff is dependent on the volume of manufacturing imports charged duty at each rate. Table 4 gives this information based on the value of imports in 1930. By using a base year prior to the introduction of the tariff it is possible to calculate the rate of duty that would have been levied on the pre-protection volume of imports. This method thus takes into account those imports that were discouraged by the tariff as well as those that were imported with the duty levied. Calculations are complicated, as many products were liable to specific or mixed rates of duty. Allowing for these difficulties an average rate of duty of 17·2% can be calculated from Table 4 for 1932. Leak (1937, p. 589) estimated that the average rate of duty was 18·5% in 1933, rising to 19·4% in 1934 and declining to 19·3 and 19·1% respectively in the subsequent years.

It is also necessary to consider changes in domestic and world prices. A number of alternative indicators are presented in Table 5. The real sterling index in column 1 is derived from the manufacturing exchange rate in Table 3 adjusted for movements in relative wholesale prices. This shows that following the return to the Gold Standard in 1925 there was an effective depreciation of the real exchange rate owing to a relative decline in UK prices. It is questionable, however, whether this depreciation led to increased competitiveness of manufactures or to higher real income in sectors providing exports and import substitutes (Dimsdale, 1981, p. 320). Following the supsension of the Gold Standard, the real exchange rate depreciated by some 16% in 1932, but by 1937 this improvement in competitiveness had been eroded. The average real depreciation for manufactures was only 6% for the period 1932–37 compared with the 1929 level. The rise in UK wholesale prices served to diminish its impact on competitiveness.

The use of the real exchange rate as a measure of competitiveness is limited by a number of factors (Durand and Giorno, 1987). As we are analysing trade in manufactures, the use of wholesale price indices as deflators for the nominal index is undesirable since they include the prices of non-manufactures, but indices for manufactures do not exist for the countries included in our index. A second problem is that the real exchange rate does not

Table 5. *Measures of competitiveness*

	(1) Real sterling manufacturing exchange rate	(2) Export competitiveness	(3) Import competitiveness
1924	106·7	98·1	103·6
1925	109·6	101·7	105·0
1926	104·3	98·7	105·9
1927	101·2	100·4	106·4
1928	100·0	98·1	102·8
1929	100·0	100·0	100·0
1930	100·7	102·7	96·6
1931	96·9	103·4	102·3
1932	83·4	91·2	90·2
1933	91·8	95·1	92·9
1934	94·6	97·9	91·1
1935	90·5	98·1	91·2
1936	96·4	100·8	94·8
1937	106·4	101·9	94·0
1938	106·0	104·6	97·9

Sources: column (1) column 4, Table 3 adjusted for differences in wholesale prices (from Mitchell, 1980, 1982 and 1983); column (2) Lewis (1952) and Board of Trade *Journal* (various editions). Index shows unit value of manufacturing exports divided by world price of manufactures, both measured in gold; column (3) Feinstein (1972), BSO (1978), Board of Trade *Journal* (various editions) and Leak (1937). Index shows price of home sales of manufactures divided by unit values of imports adjusted for an average duty payable of 17·2%.

allow for differences in pricing strategy following a change in the nominal exchange rate. To overcome this deficiency we have calculated separate indices for export and import competitiveness, the latter including the impact of the tariff. The former (column 2, Table 5) shows the unit value of UK manufacturing exports relative to the world price of manufactures, both measured in gold. This index shows a similar trend to the real exchange rate in the period 1932–37, although the average depreciation is only 2·5% relative to 1929.

On the import side, the index (column 3, Table 5) shows the price of home sales of manufactures relative to the unit value of manufacturing imports adjusted for an average duty payable of 17·2% (see above), both measured in sterling. This index shows an average improvement in the competitiveness of domestic manufactures following the imposition of import duties and devaluation of 7·6% compared with 1929, and over 10% if comparison is made with the alternative policy period of 1925–31.

Thus, the competitive advantages of a substantial nominal devaluation were significantly reduced by the induced increase in prices, so that there was only a small increase in competitiveness for UK manufacturing exports. There was however a major improvement in the competitiveness of domestic manufactures relative to imports. This was primarily due to the imposition of the tariff, with devaluation also making a (smaller) contribution.

Implicit in the preceding analysis has been the assumption that exchange depreciation and the tariff can be considered as independent policies. While this is a simplfying assumption, we believe that the widely accepted idea that tariffs and devaluation counteract each other is not applicable to the UK during the 1930s. It is commonly contended that if a tariff is imposed it will generate a trade surplus through discouraging imports. This will consequently cause the exchange rate to appreciate to restore a trade balance. In the UK during the 1930s, however, the exchange rate was not allowed to float. It was a managed currency with intervention particularly through the Treasury and the newly created Exchange Equalisation Account. More importantly, even if the exchange rate had been allowed to float it would not have eliminated the tariff's expansionary impact owing to the prevailing conditions of unemployment and excess capacity. The primary effect of the tariff was to increase the level of economic activity. While it may have reduced total imports in the very short term, the increase in income and output induced a rise in imports in the medium term. Thus, the balance of trade in the 1930s was not significantly different from that in the 1920s.[1]

An additional consideration is that the tariff may have led to a revaluation of the *real* exchange rate. Our contention is that the nominal devaluation did increase domestic costs and the prices of manufactures, but the impact of the tariff is less conclusive. As the devaluation did not discriminate between complementary and competitive imports it increased directly raw material costs and the price of wage goods. The tariff, however, was directed at competitive goods and thus should have had a limited impact on costs (of course, the scope of the tariff did mean that it raised the prices of some inputs, most notably iron and steel). It could also be argued that the imposition of a tariff would lead domestic producers of import substitutes to raise their prices by the amount of the tariff. Leak (1937) shows that domestic producers' pricing responses to tariffs were not systematic and suggests that many firms were able to decrease prices owing to economies of scale. Thus the increase in profits during the period most probably came from increased sales, and not from higher margins.

Both devaluation and import duties were important in altering the long-term trends in trade which constrained UK growth in the inter-war period. The devaluation of 1931 has featured prominently in the literature as a major cause of recovery in the period 1932–37. Our evidence suggests, however, that the resulting improvement in competitiveness was significantly eroded by the increase in domestic prices and costs. On the export side the evidence suggests that devaluation did help to halt the long-term decline in the UK share of world manufacturing exports, but only for a relatively short period of three to four years. Britain's manufacturing exports had become seriously uncompetitive by 1930, and effective devaluation was necessary to restore competitiveness to a more 'normal' level.

Import propensities for manufactured goods had been rising up to 1931 and we would expect devaluation to have helped halt such a rising trend. But in 1932 there was a sharp fall in the import propensity of UK manufactures of about one-third, and this was sustained from 1932 through to 1938. This fall was not matched by a sustained parallel increase in export share. There must be a strong presumption, therefore, that the large fall in import propensities was caused largely by the improved competitiveness of domestic manufacturing industry following the extension of tariffs in 1931–32, on top of the benefits of a 'corrective' devaluation.

3. Tariffs and economic revival: an overall perspective on the 1930s

For a complete analysis of the success of the British economic revival after 1932 we need to look beyond changes in trade performance. This recovery is usually discussed within the

[1] The deficit on the balance of trade averaged £261 million annually for the period 1924–29 and £236 million for the period 1932–37.

context of a 'natural recovery' versus a policy-induced recovery, with stress being placed on monetary and fiscal policy as well as on exchange rate and tariff policy. Devaluation freed monetary policy from its role in defence of the exchange rate, making possible the 'cheap money' policy of 1932–37. Devaluation may also have benefited the economy via labour market mechanisms; by inflating the domestic price level, devaluation helps to account for the lower rate of growth of real wages observed after 1932–33. This, in turn, generated a redistribution of income towards profits favouring investment.

The 'cheap money' policy was initially concerned with debt management but it has also been seen as a permissive policy for economic revival. The problem is to document a convincing transmission mechanism. The Bank Rate remained at the low level of 2% throughout 1932–39 compared to an average level of over $4\frac{1}{2}$% in 1925–31. However, there was no increase in bank advances to industry until 1935. Cheap money could have stimulated recovery by stimulating consumption and housing, but here too the mechanism is not obvious.[1] Even if such a link between monetary policy and the housing boom could be established, the contribution of housing to the revival of the 1930s is limited. A sectoral decomposition of growth shows that the relative contribution of building and contracting declined in the 1930s relative to the 1920s. During 1924–29 this sector accounted for 12·5% of the overall GDP growth rate, a contribution which fell to 8·7% during 1932–37. In contrast, manufacturing industries accounted for 35·6% and 46·6% of the GDP growth rate in the two periods respectively. This suggests that manufacturing industry played a dominant role in the acceleration of the overall rate of growth after 1932 (Kaldor and Kitson, 1986, p. 11).

This is not to deny the critical role of housing in the early stages of recovery. Although housing accounted for only 3% of GDP it accounted for 17% of the *change* in GDP between 1932–34; in terms of employment, building accounted for 7·5% of total employment but for 20% of the *rise* in employment between 1932–35 (Worswick, 1984). However, to emphasise such leading sector characteristics only in the early stages of recovery fails to place the role of this sector in the overall context of revival in the 1930s.

On the fiscal policy side the balanced budgets of the 1930s have created the impression that fiscal policy was fairly neutral in the recovery. However, studies of the fiscal stance of the government, as measured by the constant employment budget balance, suggest that fiscal policy imparted a significant deflationary impact that was destabilising to recovery between 1932–34. During 1934–38 the fiscal grip was loosened by 1% of GDP per annum, providing a small expansionary effect sustaining the recovery (Middleton, 1981). This fiscal expansion was increasingly dominated by the rearmament policy after 1935; by 1938 the rearmament policy accounted for 30% of government expenditure.

In our view, the imposition of tariffs on an extensive scale by Britain in 1932 was a major policy shift that could help account for the observed shift in the growth path of the economy (and its sectoral characteristics) via the impact of the Harrod foreign trade multiplier. Fiscal, monetary and exchange rate policies in themselves cannot explain the extent and timing of the recovery.

Of course, the improvement in the growth performance of the economy could be viewed as a supply-side shift, unrelated to any policy. The idea of a natural recovery can be

[1] Two mechanisms have been suggested with respect to housing. First, falling interest rates gave rise to a reallocation of saving towards housing investment owing to more stable returns. Second, building society shares became more attractive to savers, giving the societies an excess of funds which resulted in favourable mortgage items. The evidence, however, shows building society deposits grew faster in the 1920s than in the 1930s, so that the availability of funds in the 1930s is mainly due to the favourable conditions of the 1920s, not the monetary policy shift of 1932 (Humphries, 1987).

interpreted in a number of ways. First, British economic growth was 'catching up' in the 1930s. During 1899–1929 a large technological gap had arisen with respect to the fast growing economies. Britain could borrow technology and follow existing demand patterns very easily. There is no doubt that there was such a catching up process in the 1930s, but it cannot explain the timing and extent of the revival. Policy may have been acting in favourable initial conditions, but it is hard to believe that recovery would have occurred without such initiatives being implemented.

A second potential source of natural recovery was the favourable shift in the terms of trade during 1929–32. In this period the collapse of world primary commodity prices improved Britain's terms of trade by 20·8%. Moreover, given the small size of the domestic primary producing sector and the collapse of world trade, the beneficial effects on domestic aggregate demand more than compensated for any adverse effects. Thus, consumer real wages rose rapidly between 1929 and 1932, sustaining aggregate consumption and moderating the depth of the depression. The beneficial macroeconomic effects of the terms-of-trade movements have already been noted above in our discussion of the import ratio for food, drink and tobacco. The relative price effect sustained a low import ratio for food throughout the 1930s. However, these beneficial effects need to be kept in perspective. Most of the fall in the import ratio for food in current prices was observed during 1924–31; moreover, from 1933–37 the terms of trade deteriorated by approximately 10%.

A third source of natural recovery which has been emphasised recently is the claimed moderation of real wages between 1932–37 induced by structural shifts in the labour market (Bank of England, 1984; Beenstock and Warburton, 1986). According to this view, the rise in unemployment during the 1929–32 depression was due partly to increased unwillingness to work caused by too high 'real benefits' and partly to excessively high real wages, induced by unanticipated price-falls. After 1932 this process is assumed to have gone into reverse.

Consumer and producer real wages or incomes can be measured in terms of various wages and price series. Dimsdale (1984) calculated a variety of indicators for the period 1920–38. Only when wages are deflated by wholesale prices does the series peak in 1932. In general, the various measures are not consistent with recovery occurring in 1932. Moreover, during the two cycles of 1924–29 and 1929–37 consumer and producer real wages grew on the same trend path of 1·0% and 0·7% per annum respectively.

A final potential source of natural recovery is the technological and demand structure of the 1930s, which supposedly generated a supply-side shift through the relative decline of the traditional staples and the rapid growth of new industries such as motor cars, precision instruments, dyestuffs, synthetic chemicals and consumer durables. Such industries are thought to form a self-contained 'new development bloc' with complementarity of demand and strong input-output links between them. Since many of these industries were not subject to the change in commercial policy in 1932 (being already protected as new industries) the tariffs of the 1930s could not account for economic revival.

A study of these industries using the detailed industry tables of the *Censuses of Production* for 1924, 1930 and 1935 reveals that they were indeed growing rapidly when compared to other industries. Between 1924 and 1930 output growth in these industries averaged 4·5% per annum as against 1% in other industries. Between 1930 and 1935 the modern industries grew even faster, at an average rate of 7·8% per annum. However, although these industries were growing rapidly, their small share in industrial production—only 10% of manufacturing output in 1924 and still below 20% in 1935—limited their overall impact. Hence, most of the acceleration of growth in the 1930s resulted from the established traditional industries.

A more important criticism of the new development bloc idea is that, according to the input-output tables for 1930 and 1935, the backward linkages from the new industries ran predominantly to the old staples rather than to other new industries (von Tunzelmann, 1982). Hence, any policy shift that stimulated the old staple industries would have major effects on overall economic performance.

This review of potential natural recovery sources suggests that many of the arguments are empirically invalid or that by themselves they are not capable of explaining adequately the characteristics of economic revival in the 1930s. There is no doubt that some supply conditions were favourable to growth. But it is their *interaction* with a new trade policy (and other favourable policy measures) which is the most plausible explanation of the success of the British economy in the 1930s.

Conclusion

The evidence presented in this paper suggests that at a macroeconomic level of analysis the policy shift to protection in 1932 benefited the British economy by generating a major fall in the manufacturing sector's import propensity. Through the Harrod foreign trade multiplier, such a change is important in explaining both the cyclical and relative trend recovery of the economy. Though tariffs by themselves cannot account for all the characteristic of economic revival in the 1930s—other policies and factors were also important—they were a major source of recovery which has been underemphasised in the past.

Such a conclusion does not necessarily imply that the tariff of 1932 generated an industrial structure that was beneficial to economic growth after the Second World War. To the extent that tariffs gave a new life to the old staple sectors, they may have actually prevented the necessary structural change that could have benefited long-term economic growth in the 1950–73 boom. Nevertheless, in the uncoordinated economic environment of the 1930s tariffs were successful in achieving a period of adjustment and pushing the British inter-war economy onto a higher long-term growth path.

Bibliography

Bank of England 1984. 'The U.K. Economic Recovery in the 1930s', Panel Paper No. 23, April

Beenstock, M. and Warburton, P. 1986. Wages and unemployment in interwar Britain, *Explorations in Economic History*, vol. 23

Board of Trade (various years). *Journal*, London, HMSO

Boyer, R. 1977. Commercial policy under alternative exchange rate regimes, *Canadian Journal of Economics*, vol. 10

BSO 1978. *Historical Record of the Census of Production, 1907–70*

Capie, F. 1978. The British Tariff and Industrial Protection in the 1930s, *Economic History Review* vol. 31

Capie, F. 1983. *Depression and Protectionism: Britain Between the Wars*, London, George Allen & Unwin

Chan, K. 1978. The employment effects of tariffs under a free exchange rate regime, *Journal of International Economics*, vol. 8

Dimsdale, N. H. 1981. British monetary policy and the exchange rate 1920–38, in Eltis and Sinclair (eds), *The Money Supply and the Exchange Rate*, Oxford, OUP

Dimsdale, N. H. 1984. Employment and real wages in the inter-war period, *National Institute Economic Review*, vol. 110

Dowie, J. R. 1968. Growth in the interwar period: some more arithmetic, *Economic History Review*, vol. 21

Durand, M. and Giorno, C. 1987. Indicators of international competitiveness: conceptual aspects and evaluation, *OECD Economic Studies*, no. 9, Autumn

Eichengreen, B. J. 1979.'Tariffs and Flexible Exchange Rates', unpublished Ph.D. dissertation, Yale University

Eichengreen, B. J. 1981. A dynamic model of tariffs, output and employment under flexible exchange rates, *Journal of International Economics*, vol. 11

Feinstein, C. H. 1972. *National Income, Expenditure and Output of the United Kingdom, 1855–1965*, Cambridge, CUP

Ford, J. L. and Sen, S. 1985. *Protectionism, Exchange Rates and the Macroeconomy*, Oxford, Basil Blackwell

Foreman-Peck, J. S. 1981. The British tariff and industrial protection in the 1930s: an alternative model, *Economic History Review*, vol. 34

Harrod, R. 1933. *International Economics*, Cambridge, CUP

HMSO 1934. *Final Report on Fourth Census of Production of the United Kingdom (1930); Part V General Report*, London, HMSO

Humphries, J. 1987. Inter-war house building, cheap money and building societies: the housing boom revisited, *Business History*, vol. XXIX, no. 3

Kaldor, N. 1951. Employment policies and the problem of international balance, *Review of Economic Studies*, vol. XIX, no. 1

Kaldor, N. 1970. The case for regional policies, *Scottish Journal of Political Economy*, November

Kaldor, N. 1971. Conflicts in national economic objectives, *Economic Journal*, March

Kaldor, N. 1977. The nemesis of free trade, in Kaldor, N., *Further Essays on Applied Economics*, Duckworth, London

Kaldor, N. 1982. Limitations of the 'General Theory', *Proceedings of the British Academy*, vol. LXVIII

Kaldor, N. and Kitson, M. 1986. 'The Impact of Import Restrictions in the Interwar period', Report to the ESRC, Department of Applied Economics, Cambridge

Kennedy, C. and Thirlwall, A. P. 1983. Import and export ratios and the dynamic Harrod trade multiplier. A reply to McGregor and Swales, *Oxford Economic Papers*, vol. 35

Kindleberger, C. P. 1956. *The Terms of Trade: A European Case Study*, New York, MIT

Kitson, M. and Solomou, S. 1988. 'The Macroeconomics of Protectionism: A Case Study of Britain in the 1930s', Department of Applied Economics, Working Paper No. 882

Kitson, M. and Solomou, S. forthcoming. *Protectionism and Economic Revival: The British Economy in the 1930s*, Cambridge, CUP

Krugman, P. 1982. The macroeconomics of protection with a floating exchange rate, in vol. 16, *Carnegie-Rochester Conference Series on Public Policy*, Amsterdam, North-Holland

Laursen, S. and Metzler, L. 1950. Flexible exchange rates and the theory of employment, *Review of Economics and Statistics*, vol. 32

Leak, H. 1937. Some results of the Import Duties Act, *Journal of the Royal Statistical Society*, vol. C. part IV

Lewis, W. A. 1952. World production prices and trade 1870–1960, *The Manchester School*, vol. XX, no. 2

Lewis, W. A. 1978. *Growth and Fluctuations 1870–1913*, London, George Allen & Unwin

Lomax, K. S. 1969. Growth and productivity in the United Kingdom, in Aldcroft, D. H. and Fearon, P. (eds), *Economic Growth in 20th-Century Britain*, London, Macmillan

London and Cambridge Economic Service (various dates) *Monthly Bulletin*, London, LCES

Matthews, R. C. O., Feinstein, C. H. and Odling-Smee, J. C. 1982. *British Economic Growth 1856–1973*, Oxford, OUP

McCombie, J. S. L. 1985. Economic growth, the Harrod foreign trade multiplier and the Hicks super multiplier, *Applied Economics*, vol. 17

Metzler, L. A. 1949. Tariffs, the terms of trade, and the distribution of national income, *Journal of Political Economy*, vol. 62

Middleton, R. 1981. The constant employment budget balance and British budgetary policy, 1929–39, *Economic History Review*, vol. 34

Mitchell, B. R. 1980. *European Historical Statistics 1750–1970*, London, Macmillan

Mitchell, B. R. 1982. *International Historical Statistics: Africa and Asia*, London, Macmillan

Mitchell, B. R. 1983. *International Historical Statistics: The Americas and Australasia*, London, Macmillan
Mundell, R. A. 1961. Flexible exchange rates and employment policy, *Canadian Journal of Economics*, vol. 27
Obsfeld, M. 1982. Aggregate spending and the terms-of-trade: is there a Laursen-Metzler effect? *Quarterly Journal of Economics*, vol. 97
Persson, T. and Svensson, L. E. O. 1984. 'Current account dynamics and the terms of trade: Harberger-Laursen-Metzler two generations later', Institute of International Economic Studies Seminar Paper No. 277
Redmond, J. 1980. An indicator of the effective exchange rate of the pound in the nineteen-thirties, *Economic History Review*, vol. 33
Redmond, J. 1981. 'More effective exchange rates in the nineteen-thirties: North America and the Gold Bloc', Discussion Paper Series D, no. 8, Faculty of Commerce and Social Science, University of Birmingham
Redmond, J. 1984. The sterling overvaluation in 1925: a multilateral approach, *Economic History Review*, vol. 37
Richardson, H. W. 1967. *Economic Recovery in Britain, 1932–9*, London, Weidenfeld and Nicolson
Solomou, S. N. 1987. *Phases of Economic Growth 1850–1973: Kondratieff Waves and Kuznets Swings*, Cambridge, CUP
Svennilson, I. 1954. *Growth and Stagnation in the European Economy*, Geneva, Economic Commission for Europe
Thirlwall, A. P. 1979. The balance of payments constraint as an explanation of international growth rate differences, *Banca Nazionale Del Lavoro Quarterly Review*, vol. 128
Thirlwall, A. P. 1982. The Harrod trade multiplier and the importance of export-led growth, *Pakistan Journal of Applied Economics*, vol 1
Tunzelmann, G. N. 1982. Structural change and leading sectors in British manufacturing 1907–68, in Kindleberger and di Tella (eds), *Economics in the Long View*, vol. III; London, Macmillan
Worswick, G. D. N. 1984. Economic recovery in the 1930's, *National Institute Economic Review*, vol. 110 no. 4

The scourge of the monetarists: Kaldor on monetarism and on money

Meghnad Desai*

I regard "monetarism" as a terrible curse, a visitation of evil spirits, with particularly unfortunate, one could almost say devastating, effects on our own country, Britain (Kaldor, 1981, p. 3).

This is an essay whose main concern is Nicholas Kaldor's writings, undisguisedly critical and hostile, on monetarism. There is much else in his work that touches on monetary issues which is deliberately ignored here. Primary among these issues is Kaldor's writings on international monetary issues, especially his scheme for a commodity reserve currency (see Thirlwall, 1987, ch. 11 for some discussion). I also ignore Kaldor's 1939 paper in which he discussed the theory of interest rates. This is because nothing in his subsequent writing on monetarism refers to that paper. On a more positive note, this paper deals with Kaldor's critique of monetarism. As a background to this I take up his evidence before the Radcliffe Committee, since by his own admission this contains the germ of his later theory. He was not the only prominent economist to submit evidence to the Committee but his evidence was the most influential. In his Radcliffe Lectures at the University of Warwick in 1981, Kaldor mentions this as a personal note with some pride. Harrod is cited as having explicitly pointed to the influence Kaldor's evidence had on Radcliffe, but surely Nicky was only quoting Harrod for seeing the obvious! (1982, p. 2). The second and much more active phase of Kaldor's work on monetarism began with the public lecture given at University College London in March 1970 and published in the *Lloyds Bank Review* later that year. Kaldor showed in this that unlike most other senior British economists he was much more aware of the danger that the revival of the Quantity Theory posed. From then on, and especially after 1979, he paid increasing attention to monetarism. He used every platform available—academic articles, public lectures, evidence to Select Committees, speeches in the House of Lords—to battle aginst the theory and the practice of monetarism. His writings in this period contain evocative phrases such as the scourge, the façade, the nonsense of monetarism. Tobin in the USA and Kaldor in the UK were the two senior Keynesians who were not overawed either by the statistical-polemical onslaught of Friedman and Monetarism Mark I nor by the mathematical-econometric attack of Lucas and Monetarism Mark II and who kept up the anti-monetarist fight.

In this paper I shall concentrate on the later episodes. Kaldor's strictures against monetarism were linked to his Radcliffe evidence and there was a single framework informing these two episodes. But in some ways the anti-monetarist stance is also extended to an attack on the simplistic monetary model in *The General Theory*. Kaldor took his views

*London School of Economics.

against Fisher–Friedman to opposing the Cambridge Marshall–Keynes views as well. Not given to exegetical pursuits he did not explore the differences in Keynes's view as between the *Treatise on Money* and *The General Theory* nor yet the difference within *The General Theory* as between the better known Marshallian treatment in Chapter 15 and the novel argument sketched out in Chapter 19, which became known as the Keynes Effect. In arguing the case for the endogeneity of money, Kaldor condensed a complex argument into a few equations to make his theory comparable to those of Friedman and Keynes. But it could be said that he did himself an injustice. The theory of the endogeneity of money needs to be linked to the developments in the literature on the finance motive. Indeed, the works of Minsky, Davidson and Chick supplemented by the issues raised by Kaldor could be said to contribute the beginnings of a monetary Keynesianism (Chick, 1986; Davidson, 1972; Minsky, 1975). Such an approach alone could counter fully the monetarist approaches of Friedman and Lucas which caricature Keynesianism as well as monetary theory. These aspects which relate to the future relevance of Kaldor's work will be touched upon towards the end of this paper, but not fully developed into a theory.

Section 1 outlines the major propositions of Kaldor's theory. I summarise the many separate statements scattered in his writings. Some of these propositions are theoretical and others empirical. I indicate their connections with the Radcliffe evidence and then develop Kaldor's sketch of the endogenous money issue. Section 2 takes up the validity of Kaldor's critique of monetarism. I summarise the current monetarist stance on those matters raised by Kaldor's sketch of the endogenous money issue. In Section 3 I turn to the positive task of developing the insights offered by Kaldor which help in building a new theory.

1. Kaldor's critique of monetarism

Through a number of writings (see bibliography for details) between 1958 and 1985 Kaldor's opposition to the Quantity Theory of Money was explicit and direct. His scepticism about the relevance of money supply either as an explanatory or as a policy variable in macroeconomics was total. Perhaps the best way to deal with this large body of writing is to summarise the basic themes which run through it.

(*a*) *The ratio of money to nominal income—the income velocity of money—shows a great deal of variation across countries.* At various times Kaldor cites the intercountry variation in the level of (M/PY). For instance, for 1975 he quotes the ratio as 0·67 in West Germany, 0·34 in UK and 1·25 in Switzerland: thus the velocity was variable across countries (Kaldor, 1983, pp. 37–8).

(*b*) *Over time, rates of growth of money stock and the rate of inflation diverge considerably across countries.* Thus for 1973–8, Kaldor claims that M_3 growth was 10% for four countries whose inflationary experiences were very different. These countries with their rates of inflation were UK (15%), West Germany (4·5%), Belgium (9%), and Switzerland (4·5%). Thus $\dot{m}$ could not be causing $\dot{p}$ if there was such a wide scatter. (Lower case denote log in terms of upper case letter variables. · denotes d/dt. Thus $\dot{m} = dm/dt \equiv d\log M/dt$ etc.)

(*c*) *The idea that growth in M_3 could be controlled by fixing PSBR is false.* In this matter Kaldor claimed that he had discovered the $\dot{M}_3$/PSBR relation in 1970 (Kaldor, 1981). But with the advent of the Conservative Government and the first bout of deregulation in the shape of Competition and Credit Control, this relationship was undermined. Subsequently, there was no stable correlation between the two variables. In this respect, he proudly cited a regression that he had run on the Cambridge computer with data for the 1970s which showed an R^2 of 0·4 (10^{-4}). 'It is only an uneducated person, or a person who is not in the least familiar with the subject, who would not know that since 1970 there has ceased to be any connection between the borrowing requirement and the change in money supply' (1983, p. 39).

(*d*) *In a commodity money economy, money supply is precisely definable and (though he was never explicit on this) in principle, controllable. In a credit money economy, money supply is demand determined and not controllable:* 'In an economy where money consists of an immense credit pyramid and not a commodity like gold, you cannot control the money supply because beyond a certain point, any such control leads to the collapse of the credit pyramid—which is pretty well the same thing as the collapse of the capitalist system' (Kaldor, 1983, p.17). *In a credit economy, money supply is demand determined.* It is unusual in such an economy for individuals to have undesired excess money balances since they can always retire their debts by getting rid of such an excess. Thus it is a mistake to seek the transmission of money on real variables via a real balance effect operating through a stable money demand function. The transmission mechanism as outlined in (*e*) below is the nominal interest rate.

(*e*) *It is the variation in the rate of interest that transmits the impact of monetary policy on real variables.* This was a constant theme in Kaldor's monetary theory, articulated for the Radcliffe committee and continued to his last writing: 'Yet it is through the consequential changes in interest rates that we must look for the effects of changes in the money supply or the demand for goods and services' (Kaldor, 1958, p.147).

The mechanism is the same as that described by Thornton in his *Paper Credit*. It is the difference between the rate of profit on investments (in fixed capital, in inventories, in financial assets) and the rate of interest on money loans that is the crucial determinant. But for Kaldor the interest elasticity of fixed investments is quite small. The various reasons for this—low elasticity of long rates relative to the short rate, capacity constraints being more important than other considerations in investment decisions, the large absolute margin between the rate of profit and the long-term rate of interest—are described in the Radcliffe evidence. Typically for a 1950s document, the effect of interest rate variations on hire purchase is thought to be the only effective channel of control of real activity.

But given the low interest elasticity, large variations would be required in interest rates to 'fine tune' the economy and this was not advocated since it would make interest rates unstable. When in later years the government made a fetish of money supply and its control, Kaldor knew that the only way this could be achieved would be via large variations in interest rates. Even before MTFS was adopted, or the various external shocks that are now cited as reasons for the failure to control money supply happened (for a litany of excuses see Matthews and Minford, 1987), he warned:

> The only weapon at the disposal of the monetary authorities ... is to keep on raising the rates of interest in the hope that there is some rate which is high enough—perhaps 50 or 60 per cent—at which sufficient economic activity becomes unprofitable or a sufficient number of business firms go into bankruptcy, to create a level of unemployment at which the resistance of trade unions is broken, partly because the nation will be in such a state of poverty that it will no longer be possible to afford social services such as unemployment pay, which undoubtedly stiffen trade union resistance at the present time. But nobody knows when, if ever, that point will be reached, or how much loss of production and employment and how much misery will be required. Will there be 3 million or 5 million unemployed? (1983, p. 17).

This was said in 1979 and, while the interest rate did not go to 50 or 60%, the rest of the transmission mechanism—decline in investment, bankruptcy, reduction in union resistance, cutting of unemployment benefits—was very accurately predicted.

(*f*) *Perhaps the most surprising aspect of Kaldor's theory was the desirability of inflation for a capitalist system; no hyperinflation but definitely a steady rate of mild inflation.* This is urged in the Radcliffe evidence. The idea is that the margin between the rate of profit and the rate of interest is large, about 6 to 10 percentage points gross of tax and 3 to 5 percentage points net of tax. Investment shrinks if the margin falls below this. When the rate of inflation is positive as it often is in a growing economy, high profit rates can be expected with relatively high interest rates with the margin at an adequate level. But price stability would reduce the rate of profit drastically. Implicitly, interest rates are not similarly flexible downwards. Thus price stability would squeeze the margin and cause investment activity to cease. Since this is a rather startling idea in the current discussion about inflation, it may be worth elaborating it formally. Kaldor assumes here that the slope of the rate of profit with respect to the rate of inflation given by the reciprocal of the proportion of profits reinvested is greater than one. If $\dot{q}$, $\dot{p}$ are rates of growth of real output and price level respectively, the rate of profit and ρ the proportion of profits saved, we have

$$\rho = S_{\pi}^{-1}(\dot{q}+\dot{p}) \qquad (1)$$

This is a result derived in his 1957 *Economic Journal* paper which is cited in the Radcliffe evidence. By contrast, the nominal rate of interest has a floor below which it will not fall. The slope with respect to inflation though not mentioned explicitly is less than or equal to one. Let R be the nominal rate. Then we would say

$$\begin{aligned} R &= \overline{R}+\beta\dot{p} \qquad 0<\beta\leqslant 1, \overline{R}>0, \dot{p}\geqslant 0 \\ &= \overline{R} \qquad \dot{p}<0 \end{aligned} \qquad (2)$$

Now investment reacts to the margin between p and R but with a rather large reservation constant. Let k be the growth rate of capital stock

$$\dot{k} = \delta_0 + \delta_1(\rho - R) \qquad (3)$$

If σ is the capital output ratio, then

$$\dot{q} = -\dot{\sigma} + \dot{k} \qquad (4)$$

Putting these simple equations together, we can illustrate the desirability of inflation for growth as

$$\dot{q} = \frac{\delta_0 - \dot{\sigma} + S_{\pi}^{-1}\delta_1\dot{p} - \delta_1 R}{(1-\delta_1 S_{\pi})} \qquad (5)$$

Equation (5) is the reduced form for growth of output. We see that the impact of inflation is positive and equal to $\delta_1/(1-\delta_1)S_{\pi}$. Notice the crucial role played by the parameter S_{π}. If S_{π} is set equal to one, then one gets the neoclassical result where the real rate of interest is the crucial variable, i.e.

$$\dot{q} = \frac{\delta_0 - \dot{\sigma} - \delta_1(R-\dot{p})}{(1-\delta_1)} \qquad (5a)$$

There are several features worth noting about equations (1)–(5a). Firstly, while Kaldor did not specify such a model explicitly in his Radcliffe evidence (hardly an appropriate place), it is possible to argue that this set of equations captures the implicit model therein. Secondly, note that by embedding the neoclassical result (equation (5a)) as a special case, Kaldor's formulation is more general. Thirdly, of course, (5) or (5a) by itself is incomplete since there are variables such as $\dot{\sigma}$, $\dot{p}$ and R which would need to be explained to complete the model. Nothing is lost by setting $\sigma=0$. If one were to specify a process for the determination of the rate of inflation $\dot{p}$, taking $\overline{R}$ as being policy determined, then the model would be complete. Kaldor did not do this himself (see however Skott, 1988 for an attempt along such lines). He merely drove home the lesson of this exercise by saying,

> The moral of this is that it is dangerous for a weekly progressive economy to aim at a regime of stable prices (let alone at a regime of falling prices!) since when the rate of growth of production is low (on account of a stagnant working population, also rate of technical progress, or both) stable prices are only consistent with low rates of profit which may be insufficient to maintain the inducement to invest unless the latter is stimulated by measures which cut down the ratio of investment to output and thereby reduce still further the rate of growth of production (1982, p. 148).

Extending the critique to Keynes' monetary theory

Once this is said, Kaldor comes to reject Keynes's theory of liquidity preference as well as Friedman's demand for money function. 'However, once we realise that the supply of money is endogenous (it varies automatically with the demand at a given rate of interest), "liquidity preference" and the behaviour of the velocity of circulation cease to be important' (1982, p. xvii). He regretted that Keynes presented his solution of the determination of interest rate, 'Unfortunately . . . as a *modification* of the quantity theory of money, not its *abandonment*' ibid., p. 21). In the Radcliffe lectures from which this quotation is taken, Kaldor treats this similarity between Keynes and Fisher in a simple way. He writes the two equations as

$$M=L(Y,R)=k(R)Y \qquad \text{Keynes} \quad (6a)$$

$$Y=MV(R) \qquad \text{Fisher} \quad (6b)$$

In these equations, Y is nominal income, V and k are the velocity and Cambridge k. In the Cardiff lectures there is a more elaborate treatment of this argument. Kaldor writes down a five-equation model comparing his position with the Keynes–Fisher position.

$$P=MV/Q=M/kQ \qquad (7)$$

This is the standard Fisher Equation. Q is real output. An equation for price can be written down following Pigou's amendment to the Quantity Theory in his Theory of Unemployment.

Let $Q=f(L)$ be the short-run production function. Then the Pigou equation is

$$P=(1+\eta)W/f' \qquad (8)$$

Here η is the reciprocal of the elasticity of demand for the product of the representative firm $f'=\partial f/\partial L$. Kaldor suggests a 'modern version' of (8) in terms of average rather than marginal product of labour and a cost plus mark up (μ) pricing rule.

$$P=(1+\mu)W(L/Q) \qquad (8a)$$

Now (7) and (8) (or 8a) jointly determine P and Q given M and W:

> And though formally the two equations *jointly determine both* P and Q, it will depend on the elasticity of the short period cost function, i.e. the variability of [f'] or simply (L/Q) which changes Q—whether P is *mainly* determined by [equation (7)] and Q *mainly* determined by [(8)] or vice versa (1981, p. 9).

The more inelastic the cost function the more likely it was that P is determined by equation (7) and so on.

Now according to Kaldor, Keynes added two equation to this Fisher–Pigou theory.

$$MV \equiv D \equiv Y = (1-c)^{-1}I \tag{9}$$

$$M = L(Y,R) \tag{6}$$

$$= Y/V(R) \tag{6a}$$

Equation (9) is the multiplier but in terms of nominal income. Equations (6) or (6a) are money demand equations

> It then [i.e. given equation (9)] becomes possible depending only on the elasticity of the $V(R)$ function that effective demand and its fluctuations should be determined more or less independently of monetary changes; and conversely that changes in the money supply M should fail to be a significant factor in determining monetary demand (1981, p. 13).

It was this invariance of Y (or D) to changes in M that became Friedman's characterisation of Keynes as saying that 'money is an unimportant quantity'. But Friedman's findings were in no sense a test of the importance of M. 'When I first heard of Friedman's empirical findings in the early 1950s, I received the news with some incredulity, until it dawned on me that Friedman's results must be read in *reverse*; the causation must run from Y to M, and not from M to Y' (Kaldor, 1982, p. 22). While this recalls Tobin's arguments in his 'Post Hoc' critique of Friedman, Kaldor went further: '(T)he Friedman findings do not "refute" the Keynesian theory—or rather they "refute" it only on the hypothesis that M is an exogenous variable, which is determined independently of the demand for money (which latter varies with Y)' (1981, p. 15).

Thus in modern parlance one would say that the issue is not Granger causality as between M and Y but exogeneity. M would have to be 'non-Granger caused' by Y and also be exogenous in the sense that the parameters determining M are distinct from those determining Y (see Engle, Hendry and Richard, 1983; also Desai, 1987). But Kaldor thought the exogeneity of M an unlikely possibility:

> Since credit money has no supply function in the production sense (since its costs of production are insignificant if not actually zero); it comes into existence as a result of bank lending, and is extinguished through the repayment of bank loans. At any one time, the volume of bank lending or its rate of expansion is limited only by the availability of credit-worthy borrowers (1981, p. 15).

Kaldor unfortunately did not elaborate this mechanism of demand for money caused by the action of credit-worthy borrowers. He could have linked here the investment decision as in equation (3) above with the demand for money as supplied by banks. But he chose to leave this vital bit unspecified. This is where the connection with Keynes's finance motive would have come in and have led him to reject simplifications such as equations (6) or (6a) and to elaborate a connection between I (nominal investment) and credit (a larger concept in the Radcliffe spirit than M). He chose in the Cardiff lecture a somewhat reductionist strategy and claimed that what was needed was to close the model with a fifth equation (recall Friedman's complaint about the missing equation in Keynes). This was the exogeneity of the interest rate

$$R = \overline{R} \tag{10}$$

'where [$\overline{R}$] is the short-term interest rate (MLR if you like) determined by the monetary authorities' (1981, p. 21).

Thus Kaldor had arrived in the course of his critique of monetarism at a critique of the Keynesian demand function for money. But as I shall argue below he never fully developed this 'positive' side of his monetary theory. His primary interest in the last ten years of his life was to combat monetarism. In this battle, he used economic theory which was his best weapon and also debated the empirical evidence but he knew all the time that theoretical and empirical structure of monetarism that he was challenging was a massive diversion. He saw clearly the issues of class and power which lay at the heart of the battle.

The true rationale behind this policy—it is not as stupid as I make it appear—lies in the belief that it is only through a great deal more unemployment that inflation can be brought to a halt. Though official doctrine makes inflation solely a matter of the money supply, or else solely a matter of the borrowing requirement, I believe this is only a façade. The causal chain, in which everybody—the government included—really believes, runs from cost increases of all kinds, whether they are due to rises of oil prices or rise of wages, to price increases and from price increases to further wage increases.

The belief in the efficacy of monetary controls resides not in any direct influence over prices, but on their supposed effect on unemployment. As unemployment rises, the bargaining power of trade unions diminishes, and wage settlements become less inflationary. There must be some level of unemployment at which this bargaining power disappears altogether. It is then, and only then, that a policy of 'squeezing inflation out of the system' can be successful. This, I take it, is what the strategy really is: it is obviously not what it is said to be (Kaldor, 1983, p. 42).

2. Assessing Kaldor's critique of monetarism

How has Kaldor's critique of monetarism fared? In this assessment, one must bear in mind that a critique of monetarism had to aim at a moving target. To use again an analogy I have already employed in this context, it is not a straight shoot-out between hypothesis and fact, which naive falsificationism leads us to believe is the way theories are tested, but a guerilla warfare where things change over time—repeatedly rejected hypotheses reappear as maintained hypotheses in subsequent debates (e.g. the absence of money illusion in the wage bargain or the Fisher proposition about real interest rate as being the difference between the nominal rate and inflation—actual or expected, adaptively or rationally), definitions change (of 'money' for instance), one side takes over the ideas of the opposition, etc., etc., (Desai, 1981). Through all this Kaldor's critique summarised as propositions (*a*), (*b*) and (*c*) above remained unaltered. Since monetarists were pretending to be econometrically sophisticated, Kaldor's strictures sounded naive and simplistic. But that does not mean he was not right. Now that monetarism has been officially abandoned by the US and UK governments, it is amazing to see how long it took the profession to accept (to the extent that it has done so) the fragile nature of the evidence offered by the monetarists.

Thus, we now know that the demand for money function is not stable and has not been so for the US since early 1970s (Judd and Scadding, 1982). Despite this, Friedman and Schwartz tried to repeat their earlier triumph with UK as well as US data. When examined carefully, their econometric findings collapse (Friedman and Schwartz, 1982). (For the econometric demolition, see Hendry and Ericson, 1983.) An escape was sought from the collapse of the old-fashioned demand for money function in the buffer stock theory of money (Carr and Darby, 1981; Laidler, 1984). But here again a proper econometric test has found the hypothesis rejected (Cuthbertson and Taylor, 1986).

Another strand of monetarism was the Sargent–Wallace government policy ineffectiveness proposition (Sargent and Wallace, 1975). Much was made of this by Barro (1977; 1978). But here again subsequent work has shown that the econometric equations fitted by Barro were misspecified and his technique of estimation inappropriate. Once a proper approach is made, the ineffectiveness proposition finds no support (see Leiderman, 1980; Mishkin, 1982; Pesaran, 1982). Sims had originally lent much support to the money income causal nexus suggested by Friedman (Sims, 1972). This result had used the Granger bivariate definition of causality. Sims found that once he extended his basic set of variables from money and income to include the nominal rate of interest, the latter dominates money quantity in its explanatory power (Sims, 1980). Note that this result bears out Kaldor's faith in the interest rate as the crucial variable. In fairness, one should mention that the argument has now shifted to the real rate of interest. Of course, as I said above, the Fisher equation of the real interest rate fails to hold in the data. But if one maintains it as true, then the real rate seems to be exogenous and the world is more classical than Keynesian (Litterman and Weiss, 1985). Of course, an exogenous real rate does not give any room for money supply regulating policies.

Lastly, one should mention that even in a multiequation model, a central proposition of new classical macroeconomics *viz*, the independence of the real economy from the nominal variables, has been rejected. This was in the context of Sargent's 1976 model of the US economy (Sargent, 1976; Cuddington, 1980). There is some evidence for the UK economy of non-neutrality of money but under the assumption that money is exogenous (Desai and Weber, 1988).

Thus Kaldor's intuition about the nature of empirical support for monetarist theories was entirely sound. He expressed it in terms of the stability of the velocity of circulation and a lack of coherence, to say nothing about causality, between changes in the money stock and changes in the price level. The proposition about change in M_3 and PSBR which he had himself established and then abandoned was made much of in the early phase of MTFS. But while PSBR was brought under control, M_3 growth targets were violated in six out of seven years of MTFS (Desai, 1986). Eventually M_3 was abandoned as a target in favour of M_1 and then M_0. In the meantime new measures of liquidity had been established (PSL_1 and PSL_2) all of which only goes to vindicate the Radcliffe view on money supply.

3. Kaldor's critique of Keynesian monetary theory

Kaldor's critique of Keynesian theory and the positive side of his argument need some careful treatment. As I said above, Kaldor was not given to scholarly exegesis. He does not deal with Keynes's monetary theory but merely the textbook treatment of the Keynesian money demand function. Kaldor knew Keynes's theory of interest, as his 1939 paper demonstrates, but in his later writing which emphasised interest rates, he never discussed either the *Treatise on Money* or *The General Theory*. Although the literature on Keynes's monetary theory is large, certain points of comparison can be made concerning areas of Keynes's thought relevant to but neglected by Kaldor.

(a) In Chapter 17 of *The General Theory*, 'The Essential Properties of Interest and Money', Keynes asserts that the two peculiar features of money are low elasticity of production and the lack of close substitutes. In discussing the low elasticity of production, Keynes was confining himself to the private sector. But this is obviously applicable only to metal standard based currency and cannot be true of credit. Kaldor nowhere takes up this part of Keynes's theory which was clearly inconsistent with the finance motive part of Keynes's discussion on investment. The notion of low elasticity is also empirically false once financial innovations occur (Desai, 1983).

(b) In Chapter 19, Keynes outlines a demand for money theory which is in total constrast with that in Chapter 15. Here the demand for money is by *producers* to cover the prime costs of output and it is this which leads Keynes to speak of money in wage units as a measure of effective ('real') money supply. The *Keynes Effect*, as it is now called, works via the effect of M/W on the rate of interest and hence on investment and output (Desai and Weber, 1986). Now this idea whereby one could integrate the price/cost equation (equation (8), (8a)) above with the demand for money was never explored by Kaldor. He seems entirely unaware of the Keynes Effect.

(c) Kaldor was quite a conventional (i.e. Hicks–Hansen) Keynesian in asserting the interest inelasticity of investment and hence the necessity of large movements in interest rates to control output. But in this he misses out Keynes's argument about the diversity of opinions in the market. As long as there is a wide spread of opinion then a small change in interest rates will elicit responses in the money quantity side (Desai, 1983). Whether the UK money markets in the 1950s (or even later) had sufficient diversity of opinion is an open question but to assert that large interest rate swings would be necessary is to assume that there was little diversity. Kaldor offered no evidence for this of either a quantitative or qualitative character. This is perhaps why in the quotation above he says interest rates of 50 to 60% may be required to affect economic activity sharply. In the event, nominal interest rates never had to exceed 20% at the worst stage of the depression induced by MTFS.

But these consideration having been mentioned, there remains a bigger gap on the positive side of Kaldor's theory. This is in the area of a theory of credit. Having emphasised the endogeneity of money and asserted that the supply of credit is limited only by the availability of borrowers, Kaldor did nothing to develop this further. Thus he did not specify a model with bank lending and investment demand which could have bridged the vast gap between the 'M' of equation (6) or (6a) and the supply of credit that he was speaking of. It is clearly not possible in a paper such as this to perform this task of supplying a complete theory of endogenous money in a macroeconomic setting. One would need a theory of the demand for credit which would link the theory of investment behaviour and the financing of investment together. On the supply of credit side, we need a theory of bank behaviour. No such complete theory exists for either of the two relationships, but two suggestive avenues are explored in the work of Victoria Chick and Hyman Minsky. I sketch them here briefly.

(1) Chick (1986) has demonstrated in a paper how, with the evolution of the banking system, the relationship between bank deposits, reserves and loans changes. This suggests a way of developing a theory of supply of credit. This if D is deposits, RR reserves and L loans, several stages of evolution towards a credit economy can be traced in a simple fashion. To begin with we have small and geographically scattered banks with limited use of bank liabilities as means of payment. In such a world, the causal link will run from deposits via reserves to loans.

$$\Delta D \rightarrow \Delta RR \rightarrow \Delta L$$

where arrows indicate the direction of causality and Δ indicates change.

In the next stage there are fewer but larger banks and they have a clearing mechanism.

Bank liabilities circulate as means of payment and deposits arising from loans are not lost to the banking system. In this system, we get

$$\Delta RR \rightarrow \Delta L \rightarrow \Delta D = 1/r(\Delta RR)$$

where r is the required reserve ratio. In the next stage, we have a central bank functioning as a lender of last resort. In this stage, 'banks are further emboldened: lending may now expand beyond the reserve capacity of the system, . . . if they expect the expansion to be profitable' (Chick, 1986, pp. 115–6). This leads to

$$\Delta L^d = \Delta L \rightarrow \Delta D \rightarrow \Delta RR$$

At this stage loan demand L^d drives the system. This seems to be the sort of world Kaldor was thinking of in his Radcliffe evidence and later. Chick however goes on to suggest that with liability management and abolition of formal reserve requirement, we enter a 'stage of aggressive expansion':

$$\Delta L^s = \Delta L \rightarrow \Delta D \rightarrow \Delta RR$$

In this last stage, banks supply loans seeking borrowers in an aggressive fashion. Once borrowers are found, their activity provides the required deposits and asset management will ensure the required reserves.

This evolutionary sketch is very much in the spirit of Kaldor's thinking about the banking system.

For a full model of credit creation by the banks, one would need to specify the micro-economic profit function of banks as they act under changing macroeconomic constraints, e.g. as the economy shifts from a situation where asset management is the right strategy to one where liability management is more appropriate. At the macroeconomic level, we have to account for changing monetary policy as well as any external shocks that the economy may suffer. Once these extensions are made to the Chick model, we have a theory of credit supply in place. What is needed then is a theory of credit demand, i.e. the forces that shape the availability of credit-worthy borrowers.

(2) Minsky (1975, 1986) has over a number of years provided a theory of investment with attention to the financing of the investment. Whether financed by equity or bond issues or by bank loans, the financing of investment will create the demand for credit for the financial system. In his 1975 book, *John Maynard Keynes*, Minsky developed a theory of investment distinguishing between borrower's and lender's risks. He also distinguishes between the price of the capital goods already installed (P_k) and the price of new investment goods (P_I). If a firm has an expected internal cash flow (i.e. profits π) then it can finance $\pi = P_I I_I$ amount of investment internally. Beyond that point, the firm needs to borrow and incurs borrower's risk. The greater the borrower's risk, the more steeply would it expect the market to revalue the price of its installed capital (P_k) downwards. The lender's risk rises steeply beyond the point where the firm has to start borrowing. This risk element makes the supply price of finance rise faster than the supply price of the investment goods. If expectations are buoyant both borrowers and lenders are sanguine and a lot of borrowing will take place. If not, the firms may become so bearish that they become net lenders rather than net borrowers.

Minsky thus develops a relation between investment expenditure $P_I I_I$ and profits π which is mediated through borrowing/lending risks and the supply conditions in the investment goods producing industry. The lender's risk function in his model fits into

Kaldor's theory of banks looking for credit worthy borrowers. It is the demand for credit that is driven by investment dynamism (animal spirits) which reflects realised profits and borrower's expectations.

It is not my intention here to develop a fully integrated model. Minsky has also a theory of bank behaviour which is very much along the lines that Kaldor would have liked. It remains for future work to put together elements of these developments and embody the Kaldor ideas in a fully articulated model. If that is done, it will be a lasting tribute to Nicky's crusade against monetarism and for a better monetary theory.

Bibliography

Barro, R. 1977. Unanticipated money growth and unemployment in the United States, *American Economic Review*, vol. 67, no. 1, March

Barro, R. 1978. Unanticipated money, output and price level in the United States, *Journal of Political Economy*, vol. 86, no. 4, August

Carr, J. and Darby, M. R. 1981. The role of money supply shocks in the short run demand for money, *Journal of Monetary Economics*, vol. 8

Chick, V. 1986. The evolution of the banking system and the theory of saving, investment and interest, *Economies et Societés*, pp. 111–126

Cuddington, J. 1980. Simultaneous equations test of the natural rate hypothesis, *Journal of Political Economy*, June, pp. 539–549

Cuthbertson, K. and Taylor, M. 1956. Monetary anticipations and the demand for money in the UK: testing rationality in the shock-absorbers hypothesis, *Journal of Applied Econometrics*, vol. 1, pp. 355–365

Davidson, P. 1972. *Money and the Real World*, London, Macmillan

Desai, M. 1981. *Testing Monetarism*, London, Frances Pinter

Desai, M. 1983. Monetary theory and monetary policy in the general theory, (published as Teoria Monetaria y politica Monetaria en la Teoria General), in *Información Commercial Española*, Keynes Centenary Number, January 1983. English Version, LSE unpublished

Desai, M. 1986. *Is Monetarism Dead?* (De Roos Lecture at the Free University of Amsterdam, September 12, 1986), Amsterdam, Nederlands Institut voor het Bank-en Effecten bedrijf

Desai, M. 1987. Endogenous and exogenous money, in Eatwell, J. *et al.* (eds), *New Palgrave Dictionary of Economics*, London, Macmillan

Desai, M. and Weber, G. 1986. Money inflation and unemployment, LSE DEMEIC Discussion Paper, No. A59

Desai, M. and Weber, G. 1988. A Keynesian macroeconomic model for the UK, 1955–84, *Journal of Applied Econometrics*, January

Engle, R., Hendry, D. and Richard, J.-F. 1983. Exogeneity, *Econometrica*, vol. 51, March

Friedman, M. and Schwartz, A. 1982. *Monetary Trends in the United States and the United Kingdom: Their Relationship to Income, Prices and Interest Rates 1867–1975*. Chicago, University of Chicago Press

Hendry, D. F. and Ericson, N. 1983. 'Assertion without Empirical Basis: An Econometric Appraisal of Monetary Trends in ... the United Kingdom' by M. Friedman and A. Schwartz, Oxford, Nuffield College, mimeo

Judd, J. and Scadding, J. L. 1982. The search for a stable money demand function: a survey of the post-1973 literature, *Journal of Economic Literature*, September

Kaldor, N. 1939. Speculation and economic stability, *Review of Economic Studies*, October. Reprinted in *Essays on Economic Stability and Growth*

Kaldor, N. 1957. A model of economic growth, *Economic Journal*, vol. 67, December

Kaldor, N. 1958. *Memorandum of Evidence submitted to the Committee on the Workings of the Monetary System: Principal Memoradum of Evidence*, vol. 3, HMSO, 1960

Kaldor, N. 1970. The New Monetarism, (lecture given at University College London, 12 March 1970), *Lloyds Bank Review*, July

Kaldor, N. 1981. *Origins of the New Monetarism* (The Page Fund Lecture Delivered at University College Cardiff on Dec 3, 1980), University of Wales

Kaldor, N. 1982. *The Scourge of Monetarism:* comprising; (i) The Radcliffe Report and Monetary Policy (The Radcliffe Lectures at the University of Warwick, 1981), (ii) Evidence before the House of Commons Select Committee on Treasury and Civil Service. (First Ed 1982, Second Ed 1985)

Kaldor, N. 1983. *Economic Consequences of Mrs Thatcher*, (ed. N. Butler), London, Duckworth

Kaldor, N. 1985A. Has Monetarism Failed, *Challenge*, May–June

Kaldor, N. 1985B. Lessons of the monetarist experiment, in Van Ewijk, C. and Klant, J. J. (eds), *Monetary Conditions for Economic Recovery*, Dordrecht, Martinus Nijhoff

Laidler, D. 1984. The buffer stock notion in monetary economics, *Economic Journal*, AUTE (1983) Conference Supplement

Leiderman, L. 1980. Macroeconometric testing of the rational expectations and structural neutrality hypothesis for the United States, *Journal of Monetary Economics*, January

Litterman, R. B. and Weiss, L. 1985. Money, real interest rates and output: a reinterpretation of post-war US data, *Econometrica*, vol. 53, January

Matthews, K. and Minford, P. 1987. Mrs Thatcher's economic policies 1979–87, *Economic Policy*, October

Minsky, H. 1975. *John Maynard Keynes*, New York, Columbia University Press

Minsky, H. 1986. *Stabilising An Unstable Economy: A Twentieth Century Fund Report*, New Haven, Conn, Yale University Press

Mishkin, F. S. 1982. Does unanticipated monetary policy matter? an econometric investigation, *Journal of Political Economy*, vol. 90, pp. 22–51

Pesaran, M. H. 1982. A critique of the proposed tests of the natural rate rational expectations hypothesis, *Economic Journal*, vol. 92, September

Sargent, T. 1976. A classical macroeconomic model for the US, *Journal of Political Economy*, vol. 84, June

Sargent, T. and Wallace, N. 1975. 'Rational' expectations, the optimal monetary instruments and the optimal money supply rate, *Journal of Political Economy*, vol. 83, April

Sims, C. 1972. Money, income and causality, *American Economic Review*, vol. 62, pp. 540–552

Sims, C. 1980. Comparison of inter-war and post war cycles: monetarism reconsidered, *American Economic Review*, vol. 70, 250–257

Skott, P. 1989. *Effective Demand and Class Struggle*, Cambridge, CUP

Thornton, H. 1802/1939. *An Inquiry into the Nature and Effects of the Paper Credit of Great Britain.* Edited with an Introduction by F. A. Hayek, London, George Allen & Unwin

Nicholas Kaldor and tax reform in developing countries

John Toye*

Introduction

Professor A. P. Thirlwall has recently published a fascinating intellectual biography of Nicholas Kaldor. It provides both an opportunity and (in part) the means to look again at the problems which tax reformers face in developing countries. Kaldor, when at the height of his powers as an economist, advised in succession no less than eight developing countries on taxation policy—India, Sri Lanka (then Ceylon), Mexico, Ghana, Guyana (then British Guiana), Turkey, Iran and Venezuela. In most cases, he had been invited to advise by, and continued to have access to, the very top of the national leadership in the developing country where he worked. Yet Kaldor's own verdict on his efforts was that they

> earned me (and the governments I advised) a lot of unpopularity, without, I fear, always succeeding in making the property-owning classes contribute substantial amounts to the public purse (CEE 3, xviii).

Recent evaluations of Kaldor's life and work leave plenty of scope for further assessment of his efforts towards developing country tax reform. Thirlwall discreetly overlooks the actual results of these efforts in his final summing up of Kaldor's permanent contribution to the economics profession (1987A, pp. 330–1). He merely says that 'there were few economists in the world, and no one in Britain, so concerned with the reform of taxation in the interests of equity and efficiency as Kaldor was'. The *New Palgrave* entry on Kaldor does not specifically discuss tax reform in developing countries at all (Wood, 1987).

Central to Kaldor's conception of the role of taxation in developing countries were three propositions: (a) that the degree of inequality in income distribution was probably greater in developing countries than in developed; (b) that property-owning as a source of income and inequality in wealth distribution was probably more important in developing than in developed countries; (c) that the elite has a higher propensity to consume out of income in developing than in developed countries. These propositions were combined with his belief, developed in the UK context, that a major criterion by which any tax system must

*Institute of Development Studies at the University of Sussex. An earlier version of this paper was presented at seminars at the LSE and Manchester University in January and February, 1988. For helpful comments, I am much obliged to Ehtisham Ahmad, Hans Singer, Nicholas Stern, Frances Stewart, Tony Thirlwall and Adrian Wood. Citations of Kaldor refer to his *Collected Economic Essays* (1980) (indicated as CEE) unless otherwise stated.

be judged is its degree of equity, both vertical and horizontal. Publication of Kaldor's central ideas occurred after the majority of his overseas tax reform missions had been undertaken, but they crystallise in the context of poor countries the same concern with equality between income-earners with differing asset endowments and different income sources which animated his Minority Report to the UK Royal Commission on the Taxation of Income and Profit (1951–54). They flow directly from the *fons et origo* of Kaldor's taxation expertise, his membership of this Royal Commission.

If equity has a special and primary importance as an objective of a Kaldorian tax reform, it was far from being his exclusive goal. Unlike some later fiscal proposals which built on Kaldor's idea of an expenditure tax (e.g. Mathur, 1975), Kaldor himself never reduced the problem of tax design by eliminating the other policy objectives of taxation, namely revenue, economic efficiency and administrative simplicity. Indeed, his outstanding skill was his ability to identify the trade-offs between these four objectives in any tax design. At the same time, it is possible to argue that his judgement of the weight which ought to be accorded to each was sometimes at fault—specifically, that too low a weight was placed on administrative simplicity in the first phase of his tax reform activities in the 1950s. It may be that Kaldor began with a naïve view that tax administration in developing countries *must* be less complicated than in industrial countries since the population contains fewer potential taxpayers and a smaller proportion of taxable enterprises. But this, as he came to discover, was only part of the story, and not the most important part.

The sources of Kaldor's tax reform ideas

The proposition that, at least in the 1950s, Kaldorian tax reforms derived from analytical brilliance rather than a strong sense of the problems of tax administration in developing countries is substantiated when the sources of his recommendations are examined. They did not derive from long familiarity with the institutions and circumstances of the economies for which he was prescribing. He had no prior acquaintance with any of the countries where he worked, and never could stay in them for very long. His tax recommendations are not, at least until his visit to Turkey in 1962, explicitly tied in with his analysis of the 'stylised facts' of economic development and the essential components of a development strategy.

From what sources then were his recommendations matured? Kaldor himself notes that he assumed the role of a tax specialist 'rather belatedly and unexpectedly, as a result of the Minority Report of the (1951) Royal Commission on Taxation and my book *An Expenditure Tax*' (CEE 3, xviii). Before this change of professional direction, his intellectual formation had been as a pure theorist. But, significantly for his conception of the *efficiency* of taxation, Kaldor had abandoned welfare economics. He became an economic policy adviser in the UK and Europe in the 1940s. But he had not been connected with the emerging sub-discipline of development economics. Although Kaldor had largely written the UN Report on 'National and International Measures for Full Employment' in 1949, he had not been involved with the 1951 UN Report on 'Measures for the Economic Development of Under-Developed Countries', authored by Arthur Lewis, T. W. Schultz, D. R. Gadgil and others. This report crystallised what later became the conventional wisdom on capital accumulation in a labour-surplus economy (Meier, 1984, pp. 12–13).

Rather than embryonic development economics, Kaldor's approach to taxation was imprinted by his experience as a member of the UK Royal Commission on Taxation of Profits and Income. It is hard for an academic economist who has not been involved from the inside in a deep examination of a major government policy issue to realise (a) how much complex real-world detail has to be taken into account and (b) how intellectually stimulating it is *not* to share the political-constitutional-administrative framework of thought which constrains most insiders' conceptualisation of this detail. Working on the Royal Commission, Kaldor achieved a quite unusual mastery for any non-official person of the structure and peculiarities of the UK direct tax system. This in turn prepared him to understand many of the features of the British colonial tax systems which he later advised on. Apart from the Majority Report of the Commission, in which Kaldor was fully involved, the Minority Report (which he authored) succeeded in outlining a policy programme for the British Labour Party which lasted for twenty years, while *An Expenditure Tax* represented the academic distillation of his Royal Commission experience, looking back to Hobbes, Mill, Pigou and Keynes and forward to the tax debates of the 1970s, for example those surrounding the work of the Meade Committee (1978).

The circumstances of Kaldor's assumption of the role of tax specialist gave him an initial approach to tax analysis that was very intense, but very narrowly focused. His contribution was to achieve the brilliant illumination of a small part of the whole field of tax theory and policy. This part—the equitable direct taxation of those well-endowed with economic capacity—remained during the first phase of his tax advisory work in developing countries rather detached from broader considerations of economic policy, such as trade and exchange rate policy, or public sector pricing and investment policy. Again, this self-contained specialisation was encouraged by the form of his first developing country assignment, in India. Here he was invited along with at least a dozen other distinguished foreign economists to the Indian Statistical Institute. Each was asked to make a contribution to Indian planning on the basis of his own specialist expertise—direct taxation policy in Kaldor's case (Rosen, 1985, p. 59).

At this time, Kaldor had published only one paper on economic development (CEE 2, pp. 233–242). Interestingly enough, he points to the critical importance for economic development *not* of the standard ingredients of economic growth models—capital accumulation, population growth and technical change—but of 'changing human attitudes to risk-taking and profit-making'. This is not the remark of a man indifferent to the impact of taxation on incentives. He also argues that 'a true theory of economic growth will require far broader consideration of the purely sociological aspects . . . than is usual in writings on economic theory'. It is perhaps true to say that the full force of this insight with respect to taxation had still to come home to him. Apart from these brief but penetrating comments and his 1956 paper on the economic problems of Chile (CEE 4, pp. 233–87), Kaldor had little else to say about development (as contrasted with formal models of economic growth) until 1962–3, when he relates the problems of tax reform to the economic structure of developing countries—their income structure, the dominance of agriculture, and the need for the socio-economic infrastructure to expand (CEE 3, pp. 225–65; cf. Thirlwall, 1987B, p. 28).

Kaldorian tax reform starts from the principle that taxation should be related (not proportionately, but with a mild degree of progression) to the taxable capacity of the individual. How was the individual's taxable capacity to be measured for the practical purpose of taxation? The problem is that the different forms in which income accrues—wages, salaries, dividends, interest, gifts, social security payments and realised capital gains—are indicative of different taxable capacities. That is because each of these types of income flow will be associated with differences in the stock of wealth owned by the recipient, and it is the total stock of wealth plus income accruals which measures taxable capacity. As Kaldor put it: 'a man earning £5000 a year by way of salary cannot be presumed to have the same spending power as a man who obtains £5000 a year from property worth £100,000' (Kaldor, 1955, p. 31). To him it was clear that 'the sources of spending power are numerous, and the nominal accruals arising from different sources cannot be reduced to a common denominator, except on some highly arbitrary basis'. Therefore, 'no definition of Income, which is a plausible one for purposes of tax assessment, can measure taxable capacity' (1955, pp. 46–7). On the other hand, everyone judges for himself or herself what his or her spending power is (and hence indicates a corresponding taxable capacity) when choosing the lavishness of personal lifestyle. An expenditure tax is thus a tax based on a self-chosen indicator of taxable capacity, and the result will be less arbitrary than an income tax, however taxable income is defined.

Kaldor recognised that this was still a second-best solution, in that an injustice remains in allocating the tax burden as between misers and spendthrifts, although he doubted that such differences in tastes and temperaments would be empirically very significant (CEE 7, pp. 235–6).

The second step of Kaldorian tax reform is the insight (picked up from Henry Simons and Irving Fisher in 1935–6) that every individual's capital transactions, income, windfall receipts and thus *his implied expenditure* can all be represented in a set of self-consistent annual accounts. So a comprehensive return would make concealment of economic capacity harder than does the return for 'income', however defined, alone. It also creates the possibility of cross-checking information on sales and purchases of assets from the returns of both buyer and seller, in a situation where it could not be in their mutual interest to collude to defraud the exchequer.

A switch from income-based to expenditure-based taxation, administered through a comprehensive return, had previously been seen to have distinct economic benefits, but to be unworkable in practice. As Alfred Marshall put it,

> There is general agreement that a system of taxation should be adjusted in more or less steep graduation, to people's incomes: or better still to their expenditures . . . [But] taxes, and especially graduated taxes on expenditure in general, present great technical difficulties to the tax collector . . . (Marshall, 1961, p. 802).

Keynes thus was only repeating Marshall when he declared to the Colwyn Committee that an expenditure tax was 'perhaps theoretically sound, [but] it is practically impossible'. The objection from practice has been repeated again in response to the publication of Thirlwall's book: 'the technical and political difficulties associated with such a transition [to expenditure taxation] are simply too great to be contemplated even in advanced countries' (Prowse, 1987). Kay and King (1986, pp. 101–6), who believe that a transition *is* possible in the UK over the longer term, stipulate that the complete computerisation of the existing income tax returns is a pre-condition of success—and this has not yet been achieved.

It was partly in deference to the difficulty of acquiring the necessary information from taxpayers that Kaldor decided *not* to recommend a complete transition to an expenditure tax either in India or Sri Lanka, but a 'belt and braces' combination of the expenditure tax *and* its logical alternative, a constellation of personal taxes on income, wealth, gifts and capital gains. Expenditure tax then became one star in the constellation, confined to very few with large incomes, a substitute for existing surtaxes. Indian tax reform was a blend of the classic Expenditure Tax with the package of direct taxes which Kaldor had put forward in his 1947 'Plan for the Financial Stabilisation of France'. The package had been devised originally by the French trades union confederation (CGT). The details of the original CGT reform plan are not included in the *Collected Economic Essays* (CEE 8, p. 22), but the very close resemblance between CGT and Kaldor on tax reform is presented in Appendix 1.

The rationale for using 'belt and braces' was twofold. It would be easier to gather the required information if it were in support of a number of different taxes, rather than just one. It would also ease the transitional problems of moving away from existing income taxes (CEE 7, pp. 236–7). Even if a proportional expenditure tax were—as some assert, and as others equally distinguished deny—part of an ideal tax scheme for a just society, movement towards any ideal in an unjust society can only be governed by rules of prudence, which tend to echo the advice of Hippocrates to doctors attempting to cure illness: judgement is uncertain and experiment dangerous (Rawls, 1971, pp. 278–9; Friedrich, 1949, p. 428).

The melding of expenditure tax with other taxes in a multiple-criteria system created puzzlement among Indian fiscal economists e.g. Chelliah (1969, pp. 132–5) who asked some awkward questions:

(i) If the income-tax department is hopelessly in arrears with existing cases because of staff shortages, does it make sense to introduce a complex new untested tax?

(ii) In India much saving is done in unproductive forms, e.g. the hoarding of gold. Will not this economically anti-social behaviour be encouraged (as well as 'productive' saving) by a switch from income to expenditure taxation?

(iii) Given the small number of likely assessees, approximately 6000, is the impact of expenditure tax on saving likely to be worth the effort of setting up the new tax?

(iv) Is not too much effort directed to the reduction of inequalities among the business and professional elites in the urban areas, without a similar reduction being sought among those who enjoy feudal incomes from the land?

In the subsequent debate, none of these criticisms was answered by Kaldor with great persuasiveness. In response to (iv), it could be pointed out that he did in fact invite the Indian government to consider a fivefold increase in land taxation as one of a set of 'disagreeable decisions' which would have to accompany a Rs10,000 Crores plan (CEE 4, p. 305). But Chelliah's other criticisms were not deflected, and (i) and (ii) taken together add up to a serious problem of enforcement, because the proposed new comprehensive return could be side-stepped by those adept at concealment and willing to hold their 'black money' in the form of gold, jewellery and cash. In 1963, Kaldor was still reluctant to accept the force of this argument. Instead, he argued that 'with aid of modern business machines, it would be possible to keep a record of the ownership of all property . . . and to keep a running check on changes in the personal balance sheet of all wealthy individuals'. Far from accepting that less thorough tax administration would have to be accepted in developing countries than in developed, he persisted in expecting something better, arguing that:

> In advanced countries, such investigations are made sporadically, as a spot-check on returns or in cases where fraud is suspected; *there is no reason* why they should not be made systematically in countries where taxpayers are less honest or compliant. (CEE 3, p. 263, emphasis added).

This does now seem like the triumph of faith in technical virtuosity over the experience of persistent and frustrating failure. It does so particularly because the enforcement problem extends beyond lack of information and incompetent tax officials to outright corruption and obstruction from the government itself when tax officials try to collect taxes due from its political associates.

Kaldorian tax reform: style, content and reception

Before we can offer an interpretation of Kaldor's contribution, it is essential to try and summarise his activities as a developing country tax adviser, and their apparent consequences. A minimum of information about Kaldor's work in this area is given in Table I. This presents, for each of the eight developing countries where Kaldor worked, the timing of his involvement, the nub of his recommendations, whether they were adopted or not and the concomitant political and economic events, according to Kaldor's own assessment. This Table is essentially an ultra-condensed version of Chapter 5 of Thirlwall's (1987A) biography, to which those seeking additional detail are recommended to turn.

Even from the very sparse information in this Table, some salient features of Kaldor's career as a tax adviser in developing countries become obvious.

(i) With regard to *timing*, Kaldor spent relatively little time in each developing country where he worked. In extreme cases, e.g. Guyana and Iran, it was as little as eight or ten days. His longest stay was his three months in India, and here and in Sri Lanka Kaldor was able to absorb much more local detail. His modal visit was about three weeks or a month. The shortness of time between starting to learn about an economy and its problems and the offer of a prescription is one characteristic of what Albert Hirschman has called 'the visiting economist syndrome'—the quickfire giving of advice which can be politically naïve, socially explosive and economically counter-productive in the longer run (Hirschman, 1984, pp. 88–94). Any economist who agrees to give policy advice after a brief visit to a country, having no prior knowledge of its political economy, clearly risks the visiting economist syndrome. Kaldor was happy to take the risk.

(ii) Kaldor's *policy recommendations*, however, do not carry that typical sign of the visiting economist—the standard remedy, deduced from and validated by universal economic principles and claimed to be appropriate to all, or nearly all, circumstances and policy-making contexts. Kaldor certainly came close to this in the period 1956–60, when his recommendations for India, Sri Lanka and Mexico exhibit a very close family resemblance, albeit with the expenditure tax being omitted from the Mexican package. But there is a break in this pattern after 1960. The recommended packages became much more heterogeneous and diversified, and a new element appears—the compulsory saving scheme. The expenditure tax proposal does not recur in mission proposals of the 1960s, and played no part at all in the visits to Ghana, Guyana and Turkey. This break came in response to various factors: some disappointment with the results of the initial standard remedy; recognition of differences in the economic circumstances of the earlier countries visited from the later ones; and the simple fact that the terms of reference given to him differed from mission to mission. Kaldor's terms of reference included general economic advice in Ghana and Guyana, while his final mission to Venezuela in 1976 was quite atypical in that an elaborate fiscal reform package was already under discussion, and Kaldor's role was to comment and suggest relatively minor amendments rather than to design his own package.

(iii) There are also clear differences in the *reception* of Kaldor's advice by the government which he was advising. Some governments simply decided not to take the prescribed

Table 1. *Summary statement of Kaldor's developing country tax reform activities*

Country	Timing	Recommendations	Published?	Legislated?	Enforced?	Political impact	Economic impact	Repeal?
India	January–March 1956	Personal taxation based on income, wealth, capital gains, gifts and expenditure. Lower marginal inc. tax rates. Comprehensive tax return. Wealth tax on companies; with lower profit tax	Yes	Yes, but 'riddled with loopholes'; 'truncated and emasculated'; 'a joke' CEE 7, p. 238	Only partially; tax evasion condoned by officials	Marathon budget debate	Very small sums of additional revenue, less than anticipated Wealth tax = R.10 covers up to 1966 Gift tax = R1·5cr Exp. tax = R4·5cr	Expenditure tax repealed in 1962 welcomed by NK CEE 7, p. 238
Sri Lanka	1958	Personal taxation based on income, wealth, capital gains, gifts and expenditure. Lower maginal inc. tax rates. Comprehensive tax return	Yes, in 1960 by successor government	Yes	Not enforced effectively by successor govt to Mr Bandaranaika	Slight	Slight	[Yes, expenditure tax repealed in 1970s]
Mexico	September 1960	As India and Sri Lanka, but with *no expenditure tax*	No, despite promise to contrary	In 1962, some simplification of income tax	na	na	na	na
Ghana	April, June, October 1961	Single, progressive income tax; action against company transfer pricing; *compulsory saving scheme*	No published report	Yes	Yes, though administration was badly thought out	General strike; labour and employers turn against govt	Rising food prices, due to a 66·5% tax on lorries *not* due to NK.	NK involved in advising further emergency measures
Guyana	11–21 December 1961	Exchange controls. New taxes of gifts, property and capital gains. *Compulsory savings scheme*. Presumptive basis for business taxation. PAYE for income tax with reduced allowances	Not clear whether published in 1961	Virtually all proposals contained in January 1962 Budget	Yes, partially	Budget debate delayed; 6-day general strike; riots put down by 500 British troops		No, but original proposals greatly 'softened' by Sidney Dell in early 1962
Turkey	April 1962	Land tax based on potential output. Minor proposals for business taxes. Misc. new taxes	No; for confidential use of PM	No	na	Cabinet opposition to PM led to resignation of 4 officials of State Planning Organisation	None	na
Iran	1967 (8 days)	*Compulsory saving scheme for civil servants*. Flat rate VAT; sales tax; urban property tax	No	?	?	?	?	?
Venezuela	December 1976	Various minor changes suggested in an existing plan of fiscal reform	Yes, in March 1977					

Source: Thirlwall (1987A), Chapter 5.

remedy, because it opened up divisions within the government between the political figure who had sponsored Kaldor's visit and his senior colleagues. (Indeed the point of entry of an economic adviser is perhaps the largest single determinant of the fate of his or her advice.) In Mexico, the Finance Minister could not persuade the President, while in Turkey, the Prime Minister could not persuade his Cabinet. Other governments were less divided, but still were not able to translate the reforms properly into legislation, because although the executive was united, it failed to control adequately the legislature. India is the prime example here. Finally, when governments were united in accepting Kaldor's advice *and* would have had sufficient parliamentary control to legislate it into being, they often faced powerful and effective extra-parliamentary opposition—the dramatic strikes and riots of the Ghana and Guyana episodes.

The hostile caricature of Kaldor's activities in British Conservative newspapers of the 1960s was that, *wherever* in developing countries Kaldor had given advice on tax reform, 'it had been followed by revolution, inflation and toppling governments' (Thirlwall, 1987A, p. 157). Although this was plainly factually wrong, it was further used to suggest that Kaldor's advice was responsible for, or the cause of, revolution, inflation and toppling governments. The political motive for putting such a suggestion about was to dislodge him as an official Adviser to the Labour Governments of 1964–70 and thus frustrate a move towards a more equitable tax system.

This tactic helped to create a myth which still lives on in the minds of some people, not excluding professional economists. So perhaps it is necessary to point out two fallacies embodied in the caricature. When Kaldor's proposals were rejected, they could hardly have been the cause of any subsequent disaster. When they were accepted, they were never the sole influence on subsequent events, and in those cases where the subsequent events were most disastrous (Ghana and Guyana) so also were the initial economic and political circumstances most threatening. The very presence of Kaldor was sometimes itself an indicator of severe pre-existing economic distress and political instability in the developing country to which he had been invited.

It is probably too much to hope that elementary logic will have much impact on the myth of Kaldor the tax adviser who started revolutions. It is a piece of right-wing ideology, and ideologies actually require adherents to believe three impossible things before breakfast, like the Red Queen in *Alice in Wonderland* (Gellner, 1979, pp. 117–32). But let us be clear that this is indeed an impossible interpretation of what Kaldor did in the area of tax reform.

A milder caricature of Kaldor's approach to tax reform is also still in circulation. It is that he advocated a large public sector, and saw increased taxation as the means to make this possible, regardless of its impact on personal and business incentives. Although there are some grains of truth here, there are also considerable distortions, and it is worth trying to separate out the one from the other.

Did Kaldor advocate a large and expanding public sector? He believed that development would not take place unless the quantity and quality of real physical resources per head devoted to the socio-economic infrastructure—the education, health and communication systems—expanded steadily. He also believed that such infrastructure would have to be largely financed out of general taxation, since its financing by fees and charges was not practical on a large scale. For him, *these categories* of public expenditure would have to expand as a proportion of gross domestic expenditure if development were to occur. This was intrinsic to development, and not a political choice: it would occur 'irrespective of the prevailing ideology or the political colour of particular governments' (CEE 3, p. 225). In this regard, Kaldor's position bears a striking resemblance to that of R. H. Tawney:

> No individual can create by his isolated action a healthy environment, or establish an educational system with a wide range of facilities, or organise an industry in such a manner as to diminish economic insecurity, or eliminate the causes of accidents in factories and streets (Tawney, 1971, p. 127).

Kaldor's approach to public expenditure drew directly on this doctrine of public goods, which is at the heart of much mid-twentieth century English socialism. It merits a better response than the jibe of profligacy, and of a supposed unthinking willingness 'to go on throwing money at social problems'.

The unsatisfactory results of attempts of the early 1980s to promote development via macroeconomic adjustment and pricing reform alone are bringing informed opinion back to the view that health and education systems are central to development and need to be properly funded out of taxation. Kaldor would understand immediately why the new policy emphasis on 'adjustment with a human face' has arisen: it addresses a fundamental issue which price reform policies have proved incapable of manipulating. It is noteworthy that in Ghana, the most successful example yet of structural adjustment, the World Bank adopted a much stronger pro-public expenditure stance than Kaldor's, arguing that expansion of *all* categories of spending other than defence would be beneficial to development (World Bank, 1985). Kaldor never went so far, nor was he an advocate of public expenditure *as such*. He was perfectly well aware that 'many underdeveloped countries suffer, not only from lack of revenue, but also from an irrational scale of priorities in the allocation of public funds' (CEE 3, p. 227).

Kaldor favoured increased taxation both to finance more current government expenditure on health, education and communications and to raise the economy's overall saving rate to permit increased investment in these and other sectors. The aim of raising the saving rate by raising taxes has been questioned. Are extra savings socially beneficial? Can savings be raised by increasing taxes?

Kaldor was clear that extra savings might be frittered away by foolish governments in unproductive uses. He specifically warned against the expansion of taxation to finance fanciful defence 'needs', ostentatious public buildings and lavish life-styles for developing country diplomats abroad. He also recognised that ill-judged interventions by developing country governments could induce misguided industrial investment (although he certainly did not think that *all* government interventions were ill-judged—witness his praise of the Chilean Corporacion de Fomento (CEE 4, p. 237)).

He was perhaps not so clear about the 'Please Effect', the failure of extra taxes to be translated into extra savings. Extra tax receipts can simply be matched by additional government consumption expenditure. In fact, in India at least, they were so matched in the decade after Kaldor's mission (Prest, 1985, p. 17). Kaldor does not seem to have been particularly alive to this danger.

The use of taxation to raise savings also requires that a rise in budget surplus is not offset by reductions in private saving of an equivalent amount. To claim that Kaldor favoured using taxation to raise revenue regardless of its consequences for personal and business incentives is a travesty of his genuine concern for incentives. He was indeed sceptical of the rash of special tax concessions to firms or groups of people (i.e. what are now called 'tax expenditures') which tend to be justified as 'incentives'. This was for various reasons:

(i) their use in practice is often arbitrary, one concession's purpose being at variance with the objectives of other concessions in the tax system;

(ii) even when coordinated at the national level, there is an unresolved problem of international coordination, e.g. in respect of tax concessions designed to attract foreign investment (CEE 3, pp. 248–9). (This scepticism has been well justified by later studies such as Shah and Toye, 1978 and Lim, 1983);

(iii) firm empirical evidence of the economic effects of tax incentives is very scarce.

Kaldor's scepticism is now very widely shared. A recent survey of the literature on taxation and development found that 'most empirical studies of the effects of tax policies on savings or investment have failed to find strong incentive effects' (Gemmell, 1987, p. 281). The World Bank has also advised that 'it makes sense to reduce the number of investment incentives' (World Bank, 1988, pp. 95–6).

Notwithstanding the above, Kaldor was indeed centrally concerned with the *overall* incentive effect of tax systems. One area of his concern was the balance between direct and indirect taxation. As Stern has pointed out (Newbery and Stern, 1987, p. 43), in simple models, the disincentive effects of both kinds of taxation may be identical, either because distorting consumer prices or distorting the price of labour can have an identical excess burden; or because a switch from direct to indirect taxation can (in the absence of intertemporal choices and expectations) have a neutral effect on the incentive to work. Kaldor, however, was explicitly considering the distortion of intertemporal choice of consumption, when he argued that income taxes were inferior to commodity taxes because the latter avoided creating a disincentive to saving. He believed that in post-war Britain, the decline of saving resulted from the extensive taxation of income in itself, and not from the progressivity of the income tax schedule, as was commonly alleged (Kaldor, 1955, pp. 91–4).

Such concern for the discouragement of saving by taxing income might seem odd, coming from an economist whose famous growth model showed savings adjusting (through changes in the share of profits) to whatever level was required to match exogenously-determined investment—but the implications of the growth theory for taxation cannot be usefully drawn out unless the growth model is disaggregated to the point where it includes separate foreign trade and government sectors. Kaldor did not attempt this, so that any suspicions of inconsistency remain unproven.

A final example of Kaldor's concern for the incentive effects of taxation is the fact that he argued passionately *against* the 'moral and intellectual dishonesty' involved in the pseudo-egalitarianism of very high marginal tax rates (CEE 8, pp. 47–9). 'Can anyone seriously believe', he asked, 'that [a 100% marginal tax rate] could be made to serve the elimination of anything but desirable social incentives?' (CEE 8, p. 47, n.2). For progressive taxation to have significant effects on savings, resource allocation and incentives, it must have some in-built counter to tax evasion and avoidance. Kaldor insisted the marginal tax rate had to be kept relatively moderate—45%—a recommendation which was ignored in India.

However, to reject these misrepresentations of Kaldorian tax reform is not the same as laying to rest all criticism. With respect, some aspects of the tributes which have been paid to Kaldor as a tax adviser must be challenged. For example, Sir Douglas Wass, Permanent Secretary of the Treasury 1974–83, described Kaldor (Thirlwall, 1987A, p. xii) as 'the epitome of Baconian empiricism' who 'heeded the objections of those concerned with the practical and administrative implications of what he wanted to do'. This seems a little exaggerated, and somewhat misleading about the nature of Kaldor's special genius. In economic theory, he was indeed a rare and committed exponent of the inductive approach, but it will be argued here that his practice as a tax adviser had a strong element of apriorism. As one senior administrator expressed it, 'Kaldor was endlessly persuasive (though not himself readily open to persuasion)' (Pliatzky, 1982, p. 69).

If the UK's Selective Employment Tax (SET) is taken as his greatest policy success, its genesis in early 1966 did not really indicate much concern for practicalities, and advice on its administrative implications was not sought before its surprise announcement in the Budget. Some of the otherwise inexplicable features of SET, e.g. the fact that employers who had no *net* liability to pay it nevertheless had to pay it, and then have it elaborately returned to them in full, become understandable only when it is realised that the administrative mechanisms of the tax had to be virtually invented *ab initio* after the imposition of the tax had been announced. In fact, there was minimal consultation either with Treasury officials or with Cabinet ministers before SET was decided on (Crossman, 1979, pp. 203–4). The Inland Revenue were opposed to its introduction, so collection was via the National Insurance mechanism, while repayment fell to the Ministry of Labour. The modalities of taxing and repayment had not been properly investigated in advance and led to a series of anomalies (Pliatzky, 1982, pp. 70–71; Reddaway, *et al.* 1973, pp. 172–5). It was obviously a last minute idea which Kaldor successfully got past the administrators' collective defences.

While responsibility for this state of affairs lay with the ministers concerned, Kaldor at least seemed willing to cooperate with this manner of introduction for his taxation brainchild. Failure to consult adequately on administrative issues is, however, not inconsistent with willingness to heed warnings of administrative infeasibility when they are given with sufficient force. On subsequent occasions, advance planning for tax changes was much more in evidence, useful exchanges between economists and administrators did take place, e.g. on proposals for a negative income tax. But on these occasions nothing emerged at the time in finished legislative form (Thirlwall, 1987A, p. 255). There was a later impact on Conservative Government tax reform, and Edward Heath apparently formed an excellent opinion of Kaldor because of this (personal communication). Clearly there is as real a problem for the tax innovator in the UK where officials are highly conservative, sometimes for bad reasons and sometimes for good. Anyone promoting rapid reform thus has a strong inducement *not* to consult.

If one had to emphasise one special skill or quality that Kaldor displayed as a tax adviser, it would not be his sensitivity to administrative issues. Rather it was his superb ability—superb both in terms of speed and approximate accuracy—to manipulate the complex interdependencies in a scheme of tax reform. Not only was he able to estimate the approximate trade-offs between revenue, equity, efficiency (defined admittedly by neglecting excess burden) and administrative ease for alternative designs of a single tax. He could also estimate the approximate trade-offs between objectives for alternative versions of complex tax systems, for example, his favourite set of income, expenditure, capital gains, wealth and gift taxes. It was to match this ability, as well as to supply the required administrative detail, that Inland Revenue officials attended meetings with Kaldor in the same way that policemen enter no-go areas—in groups of six.

These recollections relate to Kaldor's period as Special Adviser to the Chancellor of the Exchequer during the 1964–70 Labour Government. Thus they post-date most of his overseas forays as a tax adviser. But it is reasonable to infer that, if anything, the balance between analytical brilliance and administrative sensitivity would have been weighted even more heavily in favour of the former during the overseas missions. In the 1950s, he had less hard first-hand experience of the effect of administrative constraints; and the changing pattern of his tax proposals—away from the comprehensive tax return and towards presumptive bases for individual land and business taxes—seems to reflect a real loss of confidence that the administrative problem was one of specifying what information the taxman needs rather than one of what to do in the absence of the required information.

Kaldor may have been partly the victim of his own deserved reputation for intellectual brilliance. It may well be that officials in developing countries with whom he had to deal were so dazzled by his analytical ability that they did not feel able to discuss fully with him the mundane realities of tax administration. The very fact that he was the honoured guest of the top figures in the national leadership of the developing country may have sheltered him more from critical debate than would have been the case in the UK, and thus deprived him of the vigorous feedback which would have caused him to think again. Hans Singer at the time remarked to a fellow UN official that sending Kaldor to advise developing countries on tax reform 'was like asking Keynes to write an economics textbook for first-year undergraduates' (personal communication).

Kaldor on the realities of power

By 1978, Kaldor was ready to agree that his tax reform proposals had lacked sufficient awareness of the political and sociological problems of closing tax loopholes and thus were based on an inappropriate comparison. 'A highly distorted and loophole-ridden income tax is compared with an expenditure tax . . . free of . . . anomalous concessions resulting from political pressures' (CEE 7, p. 238). It is 'the realities of power' that set the limits to effective tax reform in developing countries. These political realities included:

(i) *Division of opinion* within the central leadership of the government;

(ii) *Simple vested interest,* such as that of the Turkish landowners who used their Cabinet positions to defeat Kaldor's proposed land tax;

(iii) *Peculiar class alliances* which appear 'strange and unexpected' from a British or European perspective. In both Ghana and Guyana, the moneyed interest was able to manipulate labour unions very effectively. In their strikes against tax changes, Kaldor noted that union demands often included demands that not only would not benefit the average worker, but which would benefit the business interest, and sometimes even foreign business interests. Unions were, on the one hand, powerful in the mobilisation that they could achieve in urban areas but, on the other hand, puppets whose strings were pulled by capital. Thus Kaldor explained the paradox that the tax reforms which he justified on the basis of their benefit to social cohesion created class unity only in order to ensure their defeat!

(iv) *Fragile political institutions* failed to play their normal (European) role in legitimating social change (including tax reform). Parliaments with multiple parties and regular elections do not in developing countries act as an instrument for producing the peaceful accommodation of class interests. Instead, 'power remains in the hands of certain dominant groups, irrespective of whether one party or another is in office or whether there is an elected government or a dictatorship of some kind' (CEE 3, pp. 264–5). Parliaments and parties are as much puppets as the trades union movements;

(v) *Corruption* can entrench itself in the central political leadership. Kaldor did not despair of curing 'ordinary' corruption, in those developing countries where it was a mere by-product of a clumsy bureaucratic system. His standard recommendation was the creation of a permanent elite corps of highly-paid tax inspectors, along the lines of the

French Inspecteurs des Finances or the Chinese Maritime Customs (CEE 3, p. 262). But he also noted a kind of super-corruption, where official discretion was legislated into the tax system in order to create wide scope for arbitrary assessment and the subsequent 'buying off' of tax officials. Iran was singled out by Kaldor as a country where corruption was the 'cement' which gave coherence and solidity to the ruling regime (CEE 8, p. xv). He recognised that this kind of corruption would not yield easily, even to a new model army of tax inspectors.

What are the lessons for 1980s policy reform?

Since Kaldor's pioneering work in the field of developing country tax reform, the world has not lost interest in the matter. The World Bank (operating in conjunction with the IMF) has made a rising share of its loans to developing countries conditional on their agreement to undertake a variety of policy reforms. An interesting statistic in this connection is that some 70% of World Bank structural adjustment loans include conditions which relate to budgetary or taxation reform (Mosley, 1987, p. 5). The failure of many developing countries to build rational and effective tax systems remains a matter of widespread and urgent concern, at least to development economists and international development agencies. At the same time, the problem is no longer generally perceived in the same way as it was perceived by Kaldor. Tax policy is now seen as much less of a self-contained specialism, and much more as one important element in an inter-related nexus of economic policy issues which include the choice of foreign trade régime and the pricing and investment policy in the public sector.

This broadening of vision has taken place as part of the revival of applied welfare economics. Kaldor had briefly but effectively contributed to welfare economics, but had become convinced that it was normatively empty unless there is some authoritative way to specify a social welfare function. Thus, although in giving tax policy advice he remained concerned with who gains and who loses, and how equity should be traded off against efficiency (as all prescriptive economists must be), he no longer defined 'efficiency' by reference to the optimal properties of a static competitive equilibrium. He was, therefore, little exercised by the problem of the excess burden of indirect taxation, the loss of welfare arising from the alteration in the chosen consumption bundle which indirect taxation can bring about. Despite a strong concern with the impact of taxes on the incentive to work, to save and to take risks, Kaldor paid little attention to the tax impact on the pattern of consumption and the utility loss thereby occasioned.

His reasons for this deliberate neglect were many. Kaldor himself attributes his 'basic distrust of abstract systems, *per se*' to his initial economics education at the LSE, and specifically to the influence of Allyn Young. To the end of his professional career, he criticised the neoclassical economist because

> when it comes to judging the effects of particular policy measures—whether these relate to unemployment, foreign trade, *the incidence of taxation*, exchange rates, etc.—he applies conclusions derived from the theory of general equilibrium to the real world without hesitation: that is to say, without investigating how far his results are dependent on implied or explicit assumptions that are manifestly contrary to experience (CEE, 1, p. x, italics added).

One of the commonest assumptions required for the existence of a competitive equilibrium is constant or decreasing returns to scale. Kaldor had been convinced by Young that increasing returns to scale were a real world phenomenon of the greatest economic importance.

Apart from that, each different income distribution may produce a different competitive equilibrium, so that some *further* normative principle is required to select the best among them. This is the social welfare function, which Kaldor believed that it was impossible to specify (CEE 1, pp. 145–6). The revival of competitive equilibrium welfare economics in the field of taxation in the 1970s and 1980s has produced a range of possible ways of specifying a social welfare function, but its practitioners do not feel obliged to defend any one possible interpretation as being definitely preferable to another (Newbery and Stern, 1987, pp. 46–9). The question of *how* the economist 'discovers' the social welfare function is left up in the air. So the further question of the sense in which any particular social welfare function constitutes a *normative* principle, rather than the fiat of madmen in authority, also remains unresolved in the modern, post-Kaldor theory of taxation.

The interpretation of the social welfare function as a set of values that is, in some sense, iteratively 'negotiated' between a government and an economically-trained policy adviser is one of the offered resolutions. It seems clear that a social welfare function negotiated in this way might well be consistent and fairly precise, but what is less clear is why the product of a developing country government's negotiation with its economic adviser should be either desirable or morally binding on those excluded from the negotiation. The government and its advisers may be out of step with the values of the governed in either direction. Either they may agree together to be more egalitarian (the case of Nehru and Kaldor in India of the 1950s) or they may agree together to be less egalitarian (the case of the UK in the 1980s). But such negotiated welfare functions would remain essentially contestable, and indeed contested.

The 'negotiated' social welfare function conveniently coheres with the new 1980s practice of policy dialogue between a developing country government and some advisers (usually donors of foreign aid). It is thus an explicit rejection of the 'Santa Claus' method of giving policy advice. With this, the foreign tax adviser appeared like Santa Claus, a benign person on a brief flying visit who departs leaving behind a large handsome package of tax reform proposals. (Kaldor conformed to this stereotype less in India and Sri Lanka than he did on some later missions.) Interpreting the social welfare function as negotiable (or seeing tax advisers as ends–means instructors) manifestly puts more stress on the need for continuity in the relationship between a tax adviser and the government being advised, for a genuine mutuality of dialogue and even (in the former case) for tactical collusion in handling the political aspects of a tax reform process (Harvey, 1986).

Accompanying the revival of applied welfare economics has been a growing sense that heavy emphasis, in the style of Kaldor, on redistribution by means of the tax system is misdirected. Nowadays a greater scepticism reigns about how much income redistribution any tax system can achieve. The cutting edge of redistribution is seen as public expenditure, used to give poor people access to goods and services which their privately acquired incomes would not afford them. Tax revenue is seen as the major means to finance this public expenditure. The equity aspects of the tax system should aim merely to support the redistributive effects of the public spending which it finances. The World Bank, for example, concludes that 'it is public finance broadly defined—taxes and spending together—that matters for equity, not the structure of taxation alone' (1988, p. 85). One should really go even more broadly, to take account of the inflation rate and its tax-like impact on distribution.

Perhaps the most striking change in tax reform in developing countries over the last thirty years has been the massive shift in focus from direct to indirect taxation. Kaldor devoted very little of his attention to indirect taxes. Partly this was for personal and institutional reasons: his seminal experience was with the Inland Revenue, and in the UK indirect taxation is collected by the Customs and Excise Department. But Kaldor also had definite views about the limitations of indirect taxes in improving the equity of taxation. Although (following the CGT) he included a value-added tax in his 1947 fiscal proposals for France, he was lukewarm about a switch to VAT in the UK in the early 1960s—despite its elegant self-checking features—because its equity effects would be less egalitarian than the existing profits tax and purchase tax (CEE 3, pp. 269–82). In developing countries, indirect taxes normally fall on items of mass consumption, and Kaldor wrongly took this to imply that a tax system which relied heavily on indirect taxes could never achieve much by way of progressivity (CEE 3, pp. 238, 257 and 260).

Even fairly basic empirical research (e.g. Toye, 1976) showed that this was an exaggerated view. Progressivity did not depend merely on the ability to impose higher rates of indirect tax on more luxurious goods, although that was certainly important. It also depended importantly on a combination of exemptions from tax and the structure of household expenditure at different levels of income. Exemptions for very basic items like food grains, firewood and coarse cloth, which figure heavily in the budgets of those with very low incomes, can create considerable progressivity even with a single-rate tax. One close observer of South Asian tax reform in the 1960s and 1970s went so far as to claim (privately) that 'many public finance economists have done great harm by emphasising the potential revenue raising capacity of progressive direct taxation and its equity attribute . . . when indirect taxation . . . [is] far more relevant administratively . . . and can be made progressive at low income levels by omitting basic foodstuffs, clothing, etc. . . .' (Please, 1985).

But pressing this view home required a more sophisticated descriptive methodology, given the fact that empirical allowance has to be made for the indirect taxation of inputs as well as the final outputs that households consume. At the end of the 1970s, this came with Ahmad and Stern's application of input–output methods to estimate effective indirect tax rates in India. This showed that, even with a fuller accounting for the shifting of input taxes, there was nothing about indirect taxation as such that prevented it being designed to be progressive.

The renewed focus on the potential of indirect taxation—even from an equity perspective—has in the 1980s been married up with the revival of applied welfare economics in the shape of optimal taxation theory (Newbery and Stern, 1987). This looks at the effects which the imposition of one indirect tax has on the demand for all other untaxed goods, as well as on demand for the taxed good itself, and aims at so ordering the indirect tax system in the light of these interdependences that the welfare cost of raising an additional unit of revenue is minimised. This 'modern' approach doubly distances itself from Kaldorian perspectives. It brings indirect taxation, which Kaldor relatively neglected, to centre stage, and it proposes the usefulness for policy prescription of general equilibrium analysis, which Kaldor would have vehemently denied on grounds already mentioned.

Nevertheless, some of the problems which obstructed Kaldor's efforts at tax reform may still affect the optimal taxation approach. Leaving aside the vexed question of the derivation of utility weights for different groups of taxpayers, the information requirements for designing an optimal tax system are quite substantial: consider the task of tracing out the general equilibrium consequences of a single tax rate change for prices and quantities. If the approach were to be extended from indirect taxation to income taxation, the information requirements would be even higher. If administrative costs were to be included, they would be higher still—and so on. There is obviously some danger of the optimal taxation theorists finding themselves in the same sort of quandary as Kaldor, in his early missions, found himself: creators of an ultra-elegant technical solution which assumes the availability of more information than can in fact be brought to bear.

It may be argued against this that adoption of an optimal taxation perspective does not imply any commitment in tax reform to move directly to the optimum design. In the absence of the required information, greater caution and smaller movements away from the status quo will be appropriate. Such caution is admirable, and indeed indispensable. Little is likely to be gained by a major effort to calculate the optimal tax regime for all the developing countries of the world.

One obvious reason, which constrains tax reformers with an optimal taxation approach no less than it constrained Kaldor, is the massive and continuing weakness of tax administration in developing countries. In the face of this constraint, the priority for tax reform must be the simplification of the tax system, combined wherever possible with the broadening of the tax base. Sophisticated arguments from general equilibrium theory to show that uniform tax rates are not necessarily optimal may serve as a distraction from the pressing task of simplification. With simple, uniform taxes, however, problems of equity will arise unless broad exemptions which favour the poor are made. Sophisticated arguments which show that (on stated assumptions) it is efficient to tax necessities (those items of consumption which are bought with little regard for their post-tax price) may make tax reformers hesitate to adopt a 'no taxes on the poor' policy.

The recalcitrant political forces of the developing world which plagued Kaldor are also—notwithstanding improved policy dialogue—still a major danger to tax reformers. Pakistan experienced riots when its 1987–88 Budget was presented. Newspaper reports claimed that disturbances in at least six Karachi districts were sparked by the budget's provisions, which included a defence tax and higher duties on oil and consumer goods. A 14-member committee of the Pakistan Muslim League party was then set up and given 24 hours to suggest budget revisions that would be 'acceptable to the masses' (*The Guardian*, 9th June, 1987). The defence tax (or general surcharge on imports) was probably to blame for the riots. Policy dialogue still may not dispose of the political and sociological problems that surround tax reform in developing countries. Today's tax reformers must be able to judge adequately the non-economic factors that influence the prospects of tax reform, in particular '. . . the psychological reaction to particular taxes and, in general, the tolerance or inertia of the general public towards a direct or indirect dip into their pockets and the ability of the national leadership to increase such tolerance' (Patel, 1986, p. 21). These are issues 'on which professional training in economics can throw only limited light: an economist is likely to speak of them in the light of his tastes and temperament rather than his training'.

In his classic survey of eleven development projects, Hirschman (1967) thought that he had discovered a consistent tendency of project planners to underestimate *ex ante* the problems and difficulties that arise in the execution of a project. He named this tendency 'the hiding hand'. It has had critics as various ideologically as Deepak Lal and Paul Streeten (Toye, 1987, pp. 21–2). But if tax reform in developing countries is interpreted as a special institutional type of development project, it would be hard to deny the evidence for the operation of the 'hiding hand' both in Kaldor's early contribution and in that of contemporary successors. It is not clear that any tax reform would ever occur in developing countries *unless* tax reformers consistently overestimated the political acceptability of their proposals. Tax reform (like development policy more generally) seems to contain irreducible elements of opportunism and optimism. Since the scientific validation of reform proposals is beyond anyone's reach, all that remains is a cheerful pragmatism grounded only on a mixture of professional commitment and ethical judgement. In his time, Nicholas Kaldor's taxation work represented the very highest quality of contribution to this inherently ambivalent endeavour.

Bibliography

Ahmad, E. and Stern, N. H. 1986. *The Analysis of Tax Reform for Developing Countries: Lessons from Research on Pakistan and India,* LSE Development Research Programme No. 2, September

Chelliah, R. J. 1969. *Fiscal Policy in Underdeveloped Countries* (second edition), London, George Allen & Unwin

Crossman, R. H. S. 1979. *The Crossman Diaries,* Condensed Version, introduced and edited by Anthony Howard, London, Magnum Books/Methuen Paperbacks

Friedrich, C. J. (ed.) 1949. *The Philosophy of Kant,* New York, Modern Library

Gellner, E. 1979. *Spectacles and Predicaments: Essays in Social Theory,* Cambridge, CUP

Gemmell, N. (ed.) 1987. *Surveys in Development Economics,* Oxford, Basil Blackwell

Harvey, C. 1986. On the art of giving economic advice: tactics, access, damage limitation, packaging, confessed ignorance and timing, *Public Administration and Development,* vol. 6

Hirschman, A. O. 1967. *Development Projects Observed,* Washington DC, Brookings

Hirschman, A. O. 1984. A dissenter's confession: 'The Strategy of Economic Development' revisited, in Meier, G. M. and Seers, D. (eds), *Pioneers in Development,* New York and Oxford, OUP for the World Bank

Kaldor N. 1955. *An Expenditure Tax,* London, Unwin University Books

Kaldor, N. 1980. *Collected Economic Essays,* 8 volumes, London, Duckworth

Kay, J. A. and King, M. A. 1986. *The British Tax System,* (4th edition), Oxford, OUP

Lim, D. 1983. Fiscal incentives and direct foreign investment in less developed countries, *Journal of Development Studies,* vol. 19, no. 2

Marshall, A. 1961. *Principles of Economics,* 9th Variorum Edition, London, Macmillan

Mathur, G. 1975. *Disparity Tax in a Composite Economy,* Delhi, Macmillan

Meier, G. M. 1984. The Formative Period, in Meier, G. M. and Seers, D. (eds), *Pioneers in Development,* New York and Oxford, OUP for the World Bank

Mosley, P. 1987. Conditionality as bargaining process: structural adjustment lending, 1980–86, in *Essays in International Finance,* no. 168, Princeton, N.J., Princeton University

Newbery, D. and Stern, N. 1987. *The Theory of Taxation for Developing Countries,* New York and Oxford, OUP for the World Bank

Patel, I. G. 1986. *Essays in Economic Policy and Economic Growth,* London, Macmillan

Please, S. 1985. Letter to Professor N. H. Stern and Dr E. Ahmed dated 29 November 1985

Pliatzky, L. 1984. *Getting and Spending. Public Expenditure, Employment and Inflation,* revised edition, Oxford, Basil Blackwell

Prest, A. R. 1985. *Public Finance in Developing Countries,* (3rd edition), London, Weidenfeld and Nicolson

Prowse, M. 1987. 'Thursday Book Review' of Thirlwall, 1987A, *The Financial Times,* 12 November 1987

Rawls, J. 1971. *A Theory of Justice,* Oxford, OUP

Reddaway, W. B. *et al.* 1973. *Effects of the Selective Employment Tax: Final Report,* DAE Occasional Paper No. 32, Cambridge, CUP

Rosen, G. 1985. *Western Economists and Eastern Societies,* Baltimore and London, Johns Hopkins University Press

Shah, S. M. S. and Toye, J. F. J. 1978. Fiscal incentives for firms in some developing countries: survey and critique, in J. F. J. Toye (ed.), 1978, *Taxation and Economic Development,* London, Frank Cass

Siegfried, A. (ed.) 1947. *L'Année Politique,* Paris, Editions du Grand Siecle

Tawney, R. H. 1971. *Equality,* London, Unwin Books

Thirlwall, A. P. 1987A, *Nicholas Kaldor,* Brighton, Wheatsheaf Books

Thirlwall, A. P. 1987B, 'Kaldor as a Policy Adviser', University of Kent Studies in Economics, No. 87/11

Toye, J. F. J. 1976. How Progressive are Indian Consumption Taxes? *Economic and Political Weekly* 26th March

Toye, J. F. J. 1987. Development theory and the experience of development: issues for the future, in L. E. Emmerij (ed.), 1987, *Development Policies and the Crisis of the 1980s,* Paris, OECD

Wood, A. 1987. Kaldor, Nicholas (1908–1986), in Eatwell, Milgate and Newman (eds), *The New Palgrave Dictionary of Economics*, London, Macmillan

World Bank 1985. *Ghana: Towards Structural Adjustment,* 2 volumes, Report No. 5854-GH, Washington, DC, October 7, 1985

World Bank 1988. *World Development Report 1988,* New York and Oxford, OUP

Appendix 1

The CGT tax reform plan of 1947 had the following component parts:

(a) a *wealth tax*, based on a regular assessment of wealth. The rate recommended was 0·5% per annum, which was supposed to represent the equivalent of a 16% income tax (assuming a 3% rate of capitalisation);

(b) a *capital gains tax* based on gains calculated to exempt saving and gains resulting from price inflation. However, gains from inheritance and gifts were chargeable to this tax;

(c) an *income tax* based on all categories of income, with an exemption threshhold and a regular upward progression of rates. The highest rate of 85% was recognised to be 'quasi-confiscatory', and operated at a taxable income of 170,000 Fr per month.

(d) a *business transaction tax* of 10% on value added, designed to replace assorted other indirect taxes with distorting 'cascade' effects and high rates which encouraged evasion. This tax would fall on agriculture as well as non-agricultural transactions;

(e) various *excises* on alcohol, luxury products and property transactions.

Kaldor endorsed the CGT Plan as 'the only satisfactory permanent remedy' for the problems of the French tax system, and in his comments on financial stabilisation in France worried only about whether transitional measures were necessary before the permanent remedy could come into effect (CEE 8, pp. 22–7).

In his tax recommendations for developing countries, the items (a), (b) and (c) are prominent in the reports on India, Sri Lanka, Mexico and Guyana. The only major difference is that Kaldor was hostile to the idea of a quasi-confiscatory marginal rate of income tax and argued strongly against it. Item (d), the value-added tax, by contrast, appeared only infrequently, the major example being the report on Turkey.

Thus the CGT plan was clearly the source of Kaldor's recurring recommendation for a cluster of mutually supporting direct taxes on wealth, capital gains, gifts, inherited wealth and income—to which the expenditure tax, once he had developed the idea, was added.

(The details of the CGT tax reform plan are given in Siegfried, 1947, pp. 126–7. I am grateful to Bruce Graham for supplying me with a copy of this publication.)

Kaldor on commodities

John Spraos*

The title could have been stretched to the even more alliterative 'Kaldor's continuous concern for commodities'. For the issue of primary commodities preoccupied Kaldor over almost half a century: from a theoretical discussion of the pricing of futures (though not just commodity futures) included in a paper of wider scope published at the beginning of World War II (Kaldor, 1939–40A) to a lecture near the end of his life (Kaldor, 1986A) where he reassessed his views on the supply of commodities as a factor limiting growth.

Yet in the autobiographical sketch of his professional life (Kaldor, 1986B) there is no reference to his thinking or writing on commodities. In part, this is probably due to the emphasis on Kaldor-the-theorist in this sketch. While there are several questions of theory related to primary commodities, Kaldor approached commodity issues as matters of urgent economic policy, abstracting and conceptualising to just the degree necessary to service his practical concerns. There are, thus, no milestones marked 'commodities' in his life's theoretical journey (except perhaps Kaldor, 1979). But a better indicator for gauging Kaldor's own assessment of the importance of commodity issues is the fact that, as recently as the mid 1970s, in a macroeconomically critical phase of the world economy, he chose to place primary commodity prices at the centre of the analysis of inflation and recession which he offered in his presidential address to the Royal Economic Society (Kaldor, 1976).

In keeping with Kaldor's policy-motivated approach, this paper, in reviewing his work on commodities, will revolve round the issue of the instability of prices and the policy proposals for countering it. Section 1 will deal with micro aspects and Section 2 with macro aspects.

Kaldor's preoccupation with the micro and macro aspects of commodity prices did not overlap. The former came first and, when his attention shifted to the macro aspects, he viewed a number of issues differently. Yet, while obsolete from the standpoint of his later thinking, there is much in Kaldor's micro phase which is of enduring interest and/or offers the opportunity for a more rounded treatment of commodity price issues. Nevertheless it is only proper that somewhat less space should be devoted to Section 1 than to Section 2.[1]

The paper ends with an epilogue, which may have some resemblance to a conclusion but is definitely not a summary. The wide-ranging nature of the paper does not lend itself to a

*University College London. The comments of anonymous referees and of David Vines are gratefully acknowledged, the latter's especially. The author's selective response to these comments adds to the reasons why he retains sole responsibility for the remaining errors.

[1] A policy issue related to commodity prices which Kaldor (1963) considered but which will not be reviewed here is that of price enhancement (but see Spraos, 1983, ch. VIII). The article therefore excludes consideration of policy proposals which involve concerted output restriction.

summary. Instead, there are itemised guides to the paper at the beginning of Sections 1 and 2 which describe the issues addressed and note such new insights as the perusal of Kaldor's writings and of some of the related literature have engendered.

1. Micro focus

Of Kaldor's writings, the most relevant to this section is his early paper on the International Wheat Agreement (IWA) (Kaldor, 1952). The specifics of this agreement raise interesting issues, but hovering above these is the question with which Kaldor actually began and which is taken up in sub-section 1.1—why intervene in the first place? Kaldor at that time was much concerned that the intervention scheme should preserve the market signals and devised a provision which would enable a multilateral price guarantee scheme, such as that incorporated in the IWA, to come very close to achieving this. Other important issues are distributional neutrality between producers and consumers and the income-stabilising potential of the scheme. These matters are covered in sub-section 1.2. Neutrality and income stability became important issues in the context of buffer stock schemes and sub-section 1.3 outlines the principal points which emerge from the literature in order to add a comparative touch. Sub-section 1.4 attempts to extend the rationale for intervention by identifying two market failures, and sub-section 1.5 draws attention to certain affinities between compensatory financing schemes and an IWA-type scheme.

1.1. The rationale for intervention

For Kaldor this hinged on the distinction between the resource allocation and the distributive effects of price movements.

Allocatively, market prices were efficient. Of this Kaldor had no doubt in his IWA paper. Since then much ink has flowed on Pareto efficiency in risk-laden situations and the conclusion is that its attainment requires not only perfect spot markets but the existence of futures markets for all maturities as well as rational expectations in the sense of Muth (1961) (i.e. agents acting on a theory which is always borne out *ex post*, subject only to a stochastic component) or, equivalently, in the sense of perfect foresight (perfect anticipation of the probability distributions of the relevant variables) (see Newbery and Stiglitz, 1981).

Since these are unfulfillable conditions, primary commodity markets are not Pareto efficient. As Ghosh *et al.* (1987, p. 137) observe, this is not sufficient to justify intervention, but in primary commodities the imperfections are so pronounced that they thrust intervention on the agenda. So the fall-back position of those who oppose intervention is that an intervening authority could not do better than the impersonal market forces can do despite the imperfections (for example, Henderson and Lal, 1976). At the time he was writing the IWA paper, it would appear that Kaldor shared this view as far as the allocative function of prices was concerned. For he wanted to preserve market signals intact.

Income distribution was, however, a different matter. Any price movement has distributional effects as between buyers and sellers. But when price elasticities are high, resource allocation effects dominate the distributional effects. However, it is the other way round when price elasticities are low. This they undoubtedly are in the case of primary commodities, and it is in dealing with the unwelcome distributional byproduct of price movements that commodity agreements found their microeconomic rationale in the view of Kaldor in his early phase.

There is a problem here, however. While for an interval of time smaller than that of a complete cycle distributional effects are obviously present, over the whole cycle the question is more complicated and the case for distributional effects would be strengthened if relevant asymmetries could be identified.

As an illustration of such an asymmetry consider a producer whose income falls below trend in one period by as much as it would exceed the trend in the next period if he stayed in business. But a coincidence of calamities (illness, underperformance of other sources of income) with low prices may force him to withdraw from the activity, so that he cannot take advantage of the next period.

The literature emphasises the less traumatic case, where the producer stays in the activity but, owing to diminishing marginal utility of income (implied by the utility function of risk-averse individuals), the utility gain in good times is less than the utility loss in bad times. (Newbery and Stiglitz, 1981, show that the welfare loss from this source is likely to be small.)

If producers had perfect access to borrowing, they could smooth out the income fluctuations associated with price movements and price instability would be no problem. But it must have amused Kaldor to see the problem blandly ascribed to capital market imperfection.

An asymmetry between groups of producers can serve as a second illustration. Suppose favourable weather in Brazil brings about a bumper coffee crop. The consequent fall in price is cushioned by the rise in volume for Brazilian producers. There is no such cushion for, say, West African producers. Suppose, next, that in the following period unfavourable conditions lower the West African output, which raises prices. Brazilian producers gain from the price rise in full. Not so the West Africans, who have a lower volume to sell. Over the entire cycle of low/high price the Brazilians gain and the West Africans lose. Over many cycles things could even out but that could take a long time and in the meantime the problems indicated in the first illustration, exacerbated by duration, are present.

What is true of producers is also true of governments when tax proceeds are positively associated and expenditure negatively associated with revenues accruing to major primary products. There is no perfect capital market even for governments.

These asymmetries are not strictly located in the producer/consumer interface, but they are directly associated with the income consequences of price movements and fall in the class of effects which Kaldor labelled an 'undesirable by-product of the price mechanism' (Kaldor, 1952). (A further distributional point is discussed in the latter part of sub-section 1.3.)

1.2. Efficiency-preserving intervention, distributional neutrality and income stability

The challenge, then, was to devise a scheme which retained the allocative effects of price movements but restricted the income effects. In Kaldor's view the IWA scheme could meet this challenge, subject to certain rules being adopted by participating countries for their internal arrangements.

The core of a multilateral guarantee scheme, such as the IWA of 1949, consisted of a commitment of m participating importing countries to buy no less than volume $\sum_{1}^{m} X_i$ at a price $= p^l$, if market price fell below p^l, and of n participating exporting countries to sell no less than volume $\sum_{1}^{n} Y_j$ at a price $= p^u$, if market price rose above p^u; $p^u > p^l$ (u for upper, l for lower).

For Kaldor, a critical condition that the scheme had to satisfy was that the volume to which the guaranteed prices applied was less than the current year's output, even in years of low production. If not, there would be no spare volume to be traded in the free market and the allocative role of prices would be lost. Moreover, this rule must operate at the level of the individual producer: each producer's quota at the guaranteed price must be less than his current output. Only by having to trade a margin of output at the market price will each producer respond to price incentives. This is the critical rule which countries participating in the IWA had to follow, in order to retain the efficiency benefits of markets alongside the income-stabilising properties of the agreement. Analogous arrangements had to apply on the buyer's side so that consumers retain the incentive to economise in response to price. (With billions of consumers, drastic shortcuts in the application of the rule would evidently be needed.)

If this rule were followed, Kaldor indicated that the market signals would come through undisturbed; the behaviour of price, it was implied, would be unaffected by the agreement. A couple of qualifications are called for here, but the broad message is clearly right: if you deduct the same constant from both sides of the demand-supply equation, the price is not affected.[1] The scheme espoused by Kaldor is tantamount to this: the volume which is subject to the scheme is the constant that is being deducted when market price falls below p^l or rises above p^u. The worries which have been expressed many times—particularly in the context of sugar, which has had large volumes preempted by bilateral or minilateral deals—that markets are rendered thin and volatile when only marginal quantities are traded, would be without foundation if the Kaldor rules were adhered to.

The core of the scheme, the guaranteed prices, will survive only if neither consumers nor producers as a group feel that they are net losers over the long term. For this reason Kaldor incorporates an error-correction mechanism: the mean between upper and lower guaranteed prices for the year $t+1$ will be adjusted by a fraction of the difference between the mean in year t and the average of market prices over the years $t-k$ to t. Naturally, the bigger k is, the more stabilising the influence of the scheme and over the long term it would keep both parties satisfied by keeping the mean prices under the scheme around the market trend, provided the path of market prices is predominantly cyclical. Thus market prices not only retain their allocative role, they also guide the guaranteed prices.

Two points deserve to be looked at more closely. First, the ability of the scheme to operate with zero net transfers between producers and consumers over the cycle. Second, its ability to stabilise producer income. Both are issues which have attracted much attention in the context of buffer-stock schemes (see next sub-section), and with respect to both an IWA-type scheme seems to be less problematical.

If zero net transfer is desired, it can be attained subject to a very simple condition, at least in the trendless case in which, under Kaldor's price-adjustment rule, the mean of p^u and p^l over the entire cycle would equal the mean market price. (Recall that the market price is unaffected by the scheme.) Zero transfer means that the producers' income/consumers' expenditure would be the same over the entire cycle both with and without the scheme. (Time discounting is neglected.) The necessary and sufficient condition for this is that $\Sigma X_i = \Sigma Y_j$, i.e. that the total buy and sell volumes subject to the multilateral guarantee should be equal. Sufficiency follows from the fact that the guaranteed volume would change hands at a mean price equal to the mean market price over the cycle, while the

[1] Kaldor (1952) establishes this point by arguing that, while volume is reduced, the elasticities are correspondingly increased: a given absolute change of volume in response to price constitutes a bigger percentage change when the base is reduced.

balance would sell at the (unaffected) market prices. Necessity can be inferred from the fact that if ΣY_j is, say, increased by one unit, while ΣX_i is held constant, the producers will gain the difference between p^u and market price, a gain that would not be offset in the down phase of the cycle since ΣX_i is not correspondingly increased.

Equally, of course, a desired transfer can be incorporated in the scheme by distancing ΣX_j from ΣY_j by the amount and in the direction required.

As regards income stabilisation, the scheme works in the right direction (except when demand is elastic, which is implausible for primary commodities, and the price cycle is generated by supply disturbances) since the volume(s) subject to the scheme is sheltered from the extremes of the market price. It might be thought that the higher the volume subject to the scheme (relatively to production) the greater the income-stabilising influence. But this is only correct when market price and quantity are positively correlated (cycle generated by demand shifts). When they are negatively correlated (cycle generated by supply shifts) and demand is inelastic, an optimum is reached at which income is completely stabilised. In a two-period cycle and in the limiting case where the spread between guaranteed prices is zero ($p^u = p^l$), this optimum is attained when the ratio of first period to second period residual volumes (those not in the scheme) equals the ratio of second period to first period market prices. Clearly, at this point, the proceeds from the volume outside the scheme are also equalised. Superhuman knowledge of the market outcomes is, of course, required but, as usual with exercises of this kind, one has to say that complete income stabilisation is *in principle* attainable.

A quick glance now at the two qualifications (noted above) to the proposition that market prices will not be affected by the scheme. The first relates to the 'lumpy' decision to enter or leave the sector. As the scheme will ease the adverse effects of bad times, some producers will stay in the sector when otherwise they would have been forced out. Also, to the extent that risk aversion keeps some potential producers out of the sector, the scheme will raise the number of producers.

The second qualification relates to tactical behaviour *vis-à-vis* the scheme. Suppose that each producer's quota subject to the scheme is some average of previous years' output. If, then, producers anticipate a lower market price than the price guaranteed by the scheme, they would, up to a point, benefit more from having an enlarged volume eligible for the guaranteed price in subsequent years than the profit they would forgo as a result of extending current production beyond the point where marginal cost equals current price. In the reverse case—expected market prices higher than those at which the scheme compels producers to surrender a certain volume—they would gain from a tactical curtailment of current output.

Note that the scheme's non-neutrality on account of the first reason is welfare-enhancing. As for the second reason, it can only be significant if the scheme's pricing is misperceived as biased *vis-à-vis* market prices over the coming years, otherwise the incentive to grab a higher quota would be roughly matched by an incentive to go for a smaller one. More serious may be an asymmetric compliance with the scheme. There is an incentive to cheat when market prices are high by feigning a production shortfall relatively to quota in order to divert more output to the free market. (Moral hazard problems are, of course, always present in any insurance scheme.)

1.3. Buffer stocks, income stability and income transfers

Kaldor was quite emphatic that a scheme along IWA lines was superior to a buffer stock scheme. He gave two reasons. The first was that a buffer stock does away with price signals, since the price range is constrained by the pre-specified intervention points. He did not deny that it was possible to incorporate an error-correction mechanism hinging on stock accumulation but, appealing to experience, doubted its efficacy. (This is one of the points about which he modified his position later.)

The second reason was that, in the event of supply shifts, price stabilisation would increase income instability by doing away with the offsetting price movements. This became one of the most celebrated arguments in the literature on commodity agreements. But it is only correct when demand is price-elastic. An IWA-type scheme is, however, also income-destabilising in that event. Moreover, price-elastic demand is of little interest in the context of primary commodities. Below unity elasticities—usually much below—predominate massively up to and usually including the very long run. This is one of the few empirical regularities which is not much doubted in a profession which has grown profoundly sceptical about econometric findings.

With inelastic demand, price stabilisation by buffer stock can in principle be so designed as to be always income-stabilising (i.e. variance-reducing) provided there is a spread between the buying and selling price of the buffer stock, the size of which can be varied to fit the circumstances. (If there is no spread, the elasticity condition is more stringent. See Nguyen, 1980 and Newbery and Stiglitz, 1981, pp. 26–27.) In the technical literature this emerged comparatively recently (Nguyen, 1980) but the idea, though largely neglected, has been hovering about for a long time (see Lipsey, 1963, pp. 110–12). In essence the buffer stock manager, by adding to market demand (by assumption inelastic) in periods of abundance and satisfying part of the market demand in periods of scarcity, raises the 'elasticity' of the combined demand (market plus buffer stock) nearer to unity and thus makes the incomes of producers more stable. The requirement that buffer stock net purchases (sales) over the cycle should be zero is always consistent with income stabilisation. And for demand elasticities that do not exceed a small fraction—typically the case for primary commodities—this extends to the case where private agents are governed by 'rational expectations' (Miranda and Helmberger, 1988).

But despite this, the income-stabilising properties of a scheme of the IWA type are more robust: as in the case of a buffer stock scheme, they come through, regardless of whether the cycle is generated by demand or supply shifts; if generated by supply shifts, complete stabilisation is in principle attainable when demand is inelastic and, unlike the buffer stock case, no particular spread is required between upper and lower intervention prices.

An IWA-type scheme also compares favourably under the income transfer heading. It is free of unwanted transfers, whereas a buffer stock scheme may result in transfers between producers and consumers. It has been shown, *inter alia* by Newbery and Stiglitz (1981, pp. 30–3, 95 and 295), that, when demand is inelastic *and* isoelastic, producers' income under a price completely stabilised by a buffer stock, the holdings of which do not expand over the cycle, would be less than the (arithmetic) mean income under a freely fluctuating price. (See also Kanbur, 1984.) The proposition does not extend to linear or concave demand curves or even to all convex ones[1] (but still inelastic in the sense that the arc-elasticity over the relevant price range is less than one). It is not therefore clear what significance should be attached to it. But it casts perhaps a small shadow. That it is a purely distributional matter between producers and consumers is no consolation. With many of the (losing) producers concentrated in the Third World, this is not something that would have left Kaldor indifferent.

[1] The lack of robustness of the result derived from the isoelastic case emerges when Newbery and Stiglitz (1981) turn to a more general treatment in ch. 18.

However, schemes of the IWA type have dropped out of view completely, while buffer stock schemes have remained continuously on the international agenda, though with varying degrees of urgency. One reason is that the quota provisions for each producer, as envisaged by Kaldor, required the centralisation of purchases through a marketing board or some other, administratively difficult, machinery. This was not a serious problem in the immediate post-war years because such machinery was in place in many countries and its creation elsewhere would have been in keeping with the climate of the period. But later the climate changed and the machinery was dismantled.

1.4. Market failures

However, even buffer stock schemes are now lower down on the policy agenda than at any time since World War II. This is partly because the record of those which were put into operation is patchy (Gilbert, 1987) and partly because of the growing belief that the private sector can step in to perform whatever useful functions buffer stock schemes are capable of performing.

The latter view neglects income distribution considerations on which, as we saw, Kaldor rested his case. It also neglects the macroeconomic aspects to be discussed in the next section. But it can, in any event, be met on its own ground, and not merely by vaguely invoking the impossibility of all the conditions for Pareto efficiency being satisfied.

The much-used argument that all participants gain from pure buffer stock commodity agreements, since less uncertainty is good for all parties to a transaction, does not help, on its own, to make the case for public provision. For it is precisely when there is a perceived potential gain and there are no significant losers to block the way that smart entrepreneurs will identify a profit-making niche and will hasten to provide the missing service—unless there are circumstances of market failure. To identify major sources of market failure is therefore important for the underpinning of price-stabilising commodity agreements.

Two such sources will be mentioned here, selected because they involve ideas which are not over-rehearsed in the literature.

The first is the non-existence or extreme thinness of future markets for long maturities, say longer than one year. This observation is of course commonplace. The matter becomes more interesting when we take one step back to enquire whether there are any fundamental reasons why this cannot be remedied.

In any futures market the gap between hedger-buyers and hedger-sellers is filled by speculators. But if the *ex ante* gap is very big, the market will not function unless the supply elasticity of speculation is very high. If, now, commodity producers are to gain substantial risk-reducing advantages from the futures market, they must enter it on a large scale as hedger-sellers. Suppose they are willing to do this despite the fact that the quantities to be hedged are subject to great uncertainty (weather, pests, plant diseases etc.). They obviously need long maturities for commodities with long gestation periods (coffee, cocoa, rubber). But they also need them for commodities with a growth cycle of a year or less (rice, wheat), because they must hedge a number of years ahead in order to even out the ups and downs of output in individual years. On the other side of the market are the hedger-buyers, mainly the manufacturers who use primary commodities as an input. They fix the prices of their product for a marketing season and, if risk-averse, they are prepared to incur some cost to cover themselves against fluctuations of input prices through the season. But beyond the marketing season (say, a year) they have no incentive to hedge because the new input prices, be they up or down, will be reflected in the price of the finished product.

This, then, is a source of asymmetry: for adequate protection against price instability, producers need to hedge a big fraction of total output for a long period ahead, but there are no hedging counterparts. To fill the gap, the speculators (if prepared to commit themselves at all to a view extending far into the future) will need to take on a huge volume in their books, not just the marginal volume that needs to be transferred intertemporally to iron out the price cycle. One would have to believe in a hugely elastic supply of speculation to avoid the conclusion that the gap could only be filled on terms that would drive out most hedge-sellers. Therefore, even if some life can be breathed into futures markets for long maturities, such markets will be wasteful compared to a buffer stock mechanism which needs to operate only on marginal volumes to achieve its purpose.

The asymmetry which is at the root of this point is associated with the distinction—a basic one in the subsequent thinking of Kaldor (1976)—between primary product prices determined through a market-clearing mechanism and the prices of manufactures set on a cost-plus-mark-up basis. It is because of the latter that (beyond the short run) there is a correlation between input and output prices of manufactures which obviates the need to hedge against input-price instability.[1]

The second source of market failure arises from a discrepancy between private and social costs. To reduce price instability, private markets must provide incentives for the carrying of stock across phases of the price cycle. Futures prices are supposed to do this by generating a relation between the futures price and the current spot price such as to make stock accumulation profitable/unprofitable. The interest cost of stock carrying is one of the factors influencing the profitability of the operation. But if the stock to be carried is a gift of God (good weather), the opportunity cost is zero and to incur the full interest cost of financing that stock can lead to a suboptimal outcome.

Suppose, for the sake of argument, that in the background first best conditions prevail; *inter alia* that market interest rate = opportunity cost of capital = marginal rate of time preference. Now, good weather brings in a big harvest. On account of time preference the rate of interest is still relevant to the choice between consuming in the present season and carrying stock into next season. Optimality will be attained when the stock to be carried is determined by the marginal condition: current spot price × (1 + interest rate) + non-interest marginal storage cost = next season's spot price (proxied by the current futures price).

The carriers of stock in excess of routine business requirements are those who arbitrage between the spot price (at which they can presently buy) and the current futures price (at which they simultaneously contract to deliver on maturity).[2] So, for the above condition to be satisfied through the actions of profit-maximising arbitrageurs, it is necessary that next season's spot price be accurately proxied by the current futures price. This will not occur if the speculators are inaccurate price forecasters or if a risk premium acts as a wedge between their forecast of next season's spot price (at which they will wind up their position) and the current futures price (at which they presently take up their position). But, sticking to the assumed first best background, neither of these things happens and so the attainment of the marginal condition is not thwarted on this account. On the other hand, the marginal condition cannot be satisfied unless arbitraging between spot and

[1] It should be added that Kaldor himself took the view, at one time, that for agricultural raw materials there would be an excess of hedger-buyers over hedger-sellers of futures (Kaldor, 1939–40B). But this is not inconsistent with what has been said in the text because it referred to actually traded maturities, i.e. not exceeding a year, with respect to which a significant presence of hedger-buyers is common ground.

[2] The carrying of unhedged stock, if not due to inertia, can be decomposed into pure arbitrage (which governs the stock carrying) and pure speculation. This convention is adopted here.

forward prices yields a positive total profit sufficient to keep arbitrageurs in business. Clearly, satisfying the marginal condition for profit maximisation does not necessarily imply positive total profits in the presence of overheads which in the present context include warehousing overheads in addition to general administration and forgone profits from alternative activities.

When this 'total' condition fails, the carrying of stock to the point that will satisfy the marginal condition does not take place.[1] If the stock to be carried had an opportunity cost correctly represented by the rate of interest, an intervention to recify the marginal discrepancy may or may not be Pareto-improving, depending on the resource cost of the 'excess overheads' that create the problem.

However, the interest charges do not represent resources diverted from elsewhere since the stock, as a gift of God, has zero opportunity cost. The failure of the total condition is attributable to private accounting which does not correspond to the social cost/benefit calculation. A lump-sum subsidy to a buffer stock scheme to cover losses $\leq$ interest charges on stock-carrying, combined with an obligation to borrow at market interest rates and to minimise losses (which implies satisfying the marginal condition for optimality if prices are forecast accurately) would restore the system to a first best position.

This is of course all very formal and oversimplified. But at least one putative difficulty can be placed in perspective. If rigid monetary targets were to impose a financial crowding-out when the buffer stock manager borrowed, then of course the social opportunity cost would not be zero. But that, like all divergences between monetary and real constraints, is a problem of monetary management. This point ties up closely with Kaldor's insistence, in the context of his macroeconomic arguments for commodity price stabilisation, on non-crowding-out financing of commodity stockpiles (see sub-section 2·4).

1.5 Compensatory financing

The compensatory financing schemes currently in operation do not fall in the microeconomic category, but a reference to them in this section is nevertheless appropriate because, in some ways, an IWA-type scheme has more in common with them, particularly with the EEC's STABEX, than with conventional commodity agreements.

In a version of the IWA scheme described by Kaldor (1952, section II) as 'perfectly conceivable' (though it was not his preferred version), producers and consumers would not be touched directly by the scheme. The difference between the market price and the scheme price multiplied by the agreed quantity would be transferred between governments. (The transfers referred to now are within a cycle-phase, not over the entire cycle as in sub-section 1.2.) So, like STABEX, prices and quantities would be determined by market forces, while money tranfers would compensate the economy in the aggregate. In both schemes the transfers are recyclable (though STABEX provides for outright grants for the least developed countries which, however, would be significant only if additive to the total aid budget) and there are no interest charges. Both schemes are commodity-related but action is triggered in the IWA by commodity prices while in STABEX it is triggered by commodity export earnings—a significant difference. There are, of course

[1] This way of putting it has an element of overkill: nobody engages in arbitage. It was easier to drive the point home in this way. If we introduce rising marginal cost for each arbitraging unit, the units with the lowest overheads would remain and would operate up to the point indicated by the marginal condition, but at a higher marginal cost of carrying stock than would have been the case had other arbitraging units (driven out by interest charges) remained in business. Thus the aggregate stock carried would be suboptimal.

differences in geographical and commodity coverage and the STABEX transfers are more marginal to the perceived needs than the IWA transfers were intended to be, but these are not differences of principle.[1]

2. Macro focus

As Kaldor's general professional interests came to be dominated by macroeconomic concerns, so his focus on commodities switched from their micro to their macro aspects. In the new perspective the signalling properties of prices are valued less and commodity stocks are accepted as alternative signallers; buffer stocks, previously criticised, are now endorsed. There is no reason to believe that this was a repudiation of the earlier analysis. There is just more at stake now; the macroeconomic objectives are dominant and that affects the ranking of the instruments. Some allocative efficiency is traded-off against greater macroeconomic stability or enhanced growth.

For his macroeconomic analysis of commodities Kaldor visualised a stylised world of two sectors: an industrial sector and a primary sector. The inter-sectoral asymmetries which provide the rationale for this dichotomy are discussed in sub-section 2.1. The terms-of-trade mechanism which keeps the two sectors in long-run harmony and which bears a distinctive Kaldorian mark is outlined in sub-section 2.2. But long-run harmony does not extend to the short and medium run where excessive price fluctuations are associated with deleterious effects. Kaldor had four, analytically founded, arguments for advocating the stabilisation of some average price of commodities. These are examined in turn here. The first and fourth have attracted most attention in the academic literature. But sub-section 2.3 raises doubts about the first argument: that an industrial depression is aggravated by falling commodity prices. In what is the longest sub-section of the paper it is pointed out that the outcome depends substantially on the Marshall-Lerner condition and satisfying this condition may not be consistent with either the econometric evidence or Kaldor's own perceptions.

However, waving these doubts aside, the first argument comes into its own and in sub-section 2.4 it is suggested that in certain circumstances stockpiling commodities is not inferior to fiscal policy as an instrument against a depression aggravated by falling commodity prices. But to be effective the financing of the stockpile must not lead to crowding out. The scheme for a commodity reserve currency, which was at one time espoused by Kaldor, satisfies this condition and is discussed (very selectively) in sub-section 2.5. Two other arguments for price stabilisation follow, one related to the niggardliness of nature (sub-section 2.6) and the other to the need for anchoring the absolute price level (sub-section 2.7). The next sub-section (2.8) is devoted to the most interesting and powerful of the arguments, one which focuses on the inflationary effects of sharp commodity price increases. The last sub-section (2.9) glances at recent policy concerns regarding commodity prices.

2.1 Intersectoral asymmetries

To articulate his macroeconomic concerns about commodities Kaldor conceptualised the world economy as consisting of two complementary sectors, one producing primary commodities and the other industrial products. But a meaningful disaggregation of the

[1] The IMF's Compensatory Financing Facility is not commodity-anchored; eligibility for it depends on a more general export earnings shortfall. It imposes interest charges and is subject to conditionality. For recent surveys of compensatory financing schemes see MacBean and Nguyen (1987, ch. 5) and Hewitt (1987).

macroeconomy depends not only on the questions one wishes to address but also on the presence of critical differences, major asymmetries, between the sectors into which the stylised world is being sliced up. In Kaldor (1976, 1979, 1983) two differences stand out conspicuously and make this particular disaggregation compelling: (1) the niggardliness of nature, which casts a shadow over the primary sector but not (directly) over industry, and (2) the contrast between market-clearing prices in the primary sector and cost-driven (or administered) prices in industry. Of these differences, the second was the more critical and the more enduring in his thinking.

The first is in the classical tradition: land (including mineral-bearing land) is the ultimate scarce factor which is liable to impose limits to growth. In contrast to the neo-classicals, labour is not viewed as scarce—pockets of persistent excess demand can be eliminated by migration from regions or sectors where the marginal product of billions of men and women is zero or negligible—and capital can be accumulated indefinitely, though the rate of accumulation is constrained.

Kaldor was of course fully conscious of the fact that the land constraint on growth had failed to bite for a very long time and conspicuously so in recent decades. This was due, in part, to a rapid rate of land-saving technical progress which could not be relied on to continue indefinitely. It also depended on the extreme poverty of two-thirds of the world's population which held down the demand for natural resources, and could also be attributed to the effects of farm support policies in the rich countries (see especially Kaldor, 1983) which, by reducing uncertainty, brought about a surge of investment, and hence of output in agriculture. The rocketing of all primary product prices in 1972–4 must have seemed an ominous warning of the growth-limiting potential of the niggardliness of nature and it is no doubt significant that Kaldor's stress on the sectoral asymmetry emanating from land scarcity was at its most emphatic at the time when this price episode was fresh in the memory (Kaldor, 1976).

Ten years later, however, his position shifted significantly (Kaldor, 1986A). By then, the primary price explosion of 1972–4 was seen as a unique episode; natural resources were not a constraint, primary products could, in the long term, grow in balance with industrial growth as required by the two sectors' complementarity. Land-saving technical progress could absorb all the strain, provided stock-carrying schemes were instituted to stabilise primary prices and to relieve the bottlenecks associated with slow output responses in the primary sector. It is not entirely clear whether this was meant to be a fundamental repudiation of his earlier position, or only a judgement limited to recent economic history. Much in Kaldor (1986A) is consistent with the latter interpretation. But the matter can be left open; the niggardliness of nature, as we shall see, strengthened Kaldor's policy recommendations; it was not the linchpin of his argumentation.

It is the second asymmetry—market-clearing prices in the primary sector: cost-driven prices in industry—which constitutes that linchpin. The price-setting practices in industry, based on prime costs plus mark-up, give rise to Keynesian variations of output in response to demand. But the enlargement of the Keynesian model with a primary sector, where market-clearing prices prevail, provided Kaldor with the insights which pointed to the macroeconomic case for the stabilisation of commodity prices (in some weighted average sense).

With large corporations now playing a big role in a number of primary commodity markets (copper, bauxite, bananas, cocoa etc., let alone petroleum), the distinction is a little blurred in practice and some authors have sought alternatives to market-clearing price in modelling commodities (Maizels, 1984). But the asymmetry in pricing behaviour which remains is still striking and seems more than enough to justify pride of place being given to it in a stylised treatment.

2.2 Intersectoral balance

The critical variable which in the long run keeps the output of the two sectors in balance is the terms of trade; but not through demand substitution effects, which were deemed to be weak or non-existent as between industrial goods and primary commodities. In a growth context, the channel of adjustment runs through investment. If industry is growing disproportionately fast, the terms of trade turn against it and investment becomes more profitable in the primary sector; and *vice versa*, if the primary sector is growing too fast. The consequent switch of investment closes the gap between the sectors. A well-defined relation between the level of the terms of trade and the rate of growth of this stylised world economy emerges as a neat theoretical vision for the long run (Kaldor, 1976 and, more formally, 1979; see also Thirlwall, 1986 and 1987, ch. 8 and Molana and Vines, 1987).

But in the short and medium run the adjustment of the system is painful, wasteful and even unstable. It was to obviate this that policy measures designed to stabilise commodity prices were called for.

2.3 Flexible commodity prices and demand deficiency

The first of Kaldor's macroeconomic arguments for price stabilisation was based on the view that falling commodity prices depress industrial demand. His analysis and conclusion on this topic can be seen in the following passage:

> The fall in the prices of primary products, by releasing purchasing power, ought, in principle, to generate additional demand within the industrial sector. But the fall in the purchasing power of the primary producing sector—reflected in reduced demand for manufactured goods—pulls the other way; and so does the fall in the scale of world investment in the primary sector which is normally also largely financed by the 'industrial' sector . . . allowing for these effects it seems quite likely that the *net* effect of a fall in the prices of primary products relative to manufactures is to depress, rather than to stimulate, the level of activity in the manufacturing sectors. (Hart, Kaldor and Tinbergen, 1964, p. 163).

Unbeknown to Kaldor, Keynes, too had reached the same conclusion in 1942 (published for the first time in Keynes, 1980, pp. 121 and 155.) But the conclusion is not at all heterodox and D. H. Robertson (1952) was among those who endorsed it. Something, however, is missing in Kaldor's analysis which would not be omitted in more orthodox versions. Nothing is said about substitution in demand between commodities and industrial goods in response to the relative price change. Yet, without some demand substitution it is difficult to sustain robustly the conclusion that flexible primary prices aggravate demand deficiency in the industrial sector. As demand substitution between primary and industrial goods is generally underplayed by Kaldor (see sub-section 2.2), it seems worth dwelling on this point.

Let us postulate a negative demand shock in the industrial sector and enquire whether the ensuing commodity price fall will exacerbate the depression by comparing the case of market-clearing commodity prices with the case where prices are held constant by a stabilising agency. Leave aside for the moment the point in the quoted passage concerning investment.

In the simplest specification, with constant prices in the industrial sector and constant output in the primary sector, the 'Keynesian' gross product equation in the industrial sector is

$$Y = E(Y) + B(Y, p) + \pi$$

where Y = output, E = expenditure, B = trade balance, p = price of commodities in terms of industrial goods, π = shift parameter. In equilibrium, when p is market determined, commodity output = commodity consumption and hence $B = 0$. A depressive shock ($d\pi < 0$) gives rise to incipient negative excess demand for commodities (via lower industrial sector imports as Y falls) but this is offset by a fall in p and, *provided* $\partial B/\partial p > 0$, the negative excess demand and hence the trade balance will end up at zero at the new equilibrium ($dB = 0$). In the alternative case, the same exogenous shock is not allowed to lower p because the stabilising agency buys up the excess supply of commodities and, at the new equilibrium, the industrial sector's trade balance improves ($dB > 0$, excluding from B the stabilising agency's activities) as a result of the lower imports associated with the sector's depression; the primary sector's deficit is financed by the debt of the stabilising agency which by assumption, has borrowed without crowding out any other demand.

Since the exogenous shock is the same in both cases, but in the second case is partly offset by $dB > 0$, while in the first case there is no such offset,

$$\frac{dY}{d\pi} \text{ (p market determined)} > \frac{dY}{d\pi} \text{ (p stabilised).}$$

As Kanbur and Vines (1986) say (in a somewhat different context) and as the literature on alternative foreign exchange regimes (which has close parallels) would lead us to expect, the multiplier is larger when commodity prices respond to market demand.

But the result is subject to the proviso—italicised above—that $\partial B/\partial p > 0$. If, instead, $\partial B/\partial p < 0$, the fall in p (in the case where p is market determined), far from bottling up the depression inside the industrial sector through keeping $B = 0$, would provide relief for the sector's depression, B turning more and more positive the more p fell. The Kaldor conclusion would not hold.

It is in relation to the sign of $\partial B/\partial p$ that demand substitution comes into the act. For $\partial B/\partial p > 0$ requires that the Marshall–Lerner (M-L) condition be satisfied, i.e. sum of import-demand elasticities of industrial and commodity-producing sectors $(e_i + e_c) < -1$. (Both are own-price elasticities; the own price of industrial goods is $1/p$.) If the substitution component of both elasticities is zero, the change of p is tantamount to a pure intersectoral transfer and (using the Slutsky equation) the M-L condition reduces to (an expression familiar from the transfer literature) $m_i + m_c > 1$, where m is the fraction of the transfer spent by one sector on the other sector's product. Since neither empirical evidence, nor intuition, nor theory can sustain a strong case for $m_i + m_c > 1$, it is evident that non-negligible substitution effects must be present if the contention that flexible commodity prices aggravate industrial depressions is to be at all robust.

Kaldor, it will be recalled, gave substitution no part to play in the mechanism by which the terms of trade keep the two sectors in balance. (Instead, he envisaged the terms of trade playing the balancing role by influencing the incentive to invest in this or that sector—see sub-section 2.2.) The empirical hunch which underlies this is that, if you partition the world economy along the industrial goods/commodities divide, you fence-in the substitution effects inside each sector and leave mostly income effects to operate across sectors. There is not much substitution between food and beverages as a group and other items in the consumer's basket, nor between raw materials as a whole and other industrial inputs.

The empirical evidence also suggests weak substitution effects. There are thousands of elasticity estimates for individual commodities, too many to be digestible,[1] but the impression they convey is that the empirical value of e_i is a very small fraction. As for the value of e_c, in a two-good context it is equal to that of e_i plus a term representing differential income effects. This does not add up to knowledge about the sum of the elasticities but plants some doubts about whether it numerically exceeds one by a significant amount.

A counter-argument would be that if the elasticities summed to less than one, the system would be set on an explosive path: the more the price fell, the bigger the excess supply of commodities. If this meant a world where prices shrink to zero or explode to infinity, it would be an implausible world and a sum of the elasticities in excess of unity would have to be embraced on this ground. But a slight extension of the model would get round this point. At some stage on the downward price path, commodity dealers will start accumulating stocks because they will perceive the upside potential of commodity prices as bigger than the downside. This would give time for an adjustment of capacity to take care of excess supply and the explosive movement would be contained. Kaldor would have been quite comfortable with this line of thought (see sub-section 2.2).

Note that in Kanbur and Vines (1986), where Kaldor is formalised, the sum of the elasticities does not emerge as a critical consideration. As it happens, the exogenous change which sets their model in motion is a rise in commodity output. But had it been a fall in industrial demand, their model would have yielded, seemingly unambiguously, the result that flexible commodity prices are depression-aggravating. The reason is that, through making the assumption of proportional expenditure functions (constant share of income for each commodity regardless of p), each price elasticity is implicitly constrained to unity, thus automatically and comfortably satisfying the M-L condition.[2]

Now turn, however, to another string which Kaldor had to his bow. The quoted passage also refers to the fall in the industrial sector-financed investment in the commodity sector. As commodity prices fall, fixed investment in the sector wanes. It is, presumably, no accident that when Kaldor restated his argument (Kaldor, 1976, p. 706) this point was explicitly repeated. He appreciated its importance in sustaining his position. It acts in an unambiguously depressive direction for industrial output. So, if the sum of the elasticities happened to be on the unity borderline, the investment effect of falling commodity prices would carry the outcome in the direction predicted by Kaldor's analysis.

This is perhaps a narrow foundation on which to rest the whole burden of the depression-aggravating role of commodity prices. However, additional support could be found in the Laursen–Metzler (1950) hypothesis. This amends the expenditure function from $E(Y)$ to $E(Y, p)$ and hypothesises that $\partial E/\partial p > 0$, either on (empirically weak) Keynesian grounds (savings ratio rises as real income increases) or on the basis of the permanent income hypothesis (change of p viewed as transitory). Now a fall in commodity prices depresses industrial demand by acting directly on the industrial sector's aggregate expenditure, not just through the trade balance. On the other side though, the redistribution of income in the primary sector associated with falling commodity prices would be

[1] Hundreds of commodity models are listed in Labys and Pollak (1984) and a synoptic view of elasticities can be found, *inter alia*, in Behrman (1977) and World Bank (1975). Conceptually, the estimates are not homogenous: there are own-price (Marshallian) elasticities, income-compensated elasticities, elasticities related to internationally traded volumes and others to total volumes—and most of them contain a component which reflects substitution among commodities (among coffee, tea and cocoa for example, or among copper, lead and aluminium) which should be netted out on aggregation.

[2] The assumption of proportional expenditure functions is also made in the Kaldor-inspired growth models of Thirlwall (1986 and 1987, ch. 8) and Molana and Vines (1987).

expected to lower the sector's savings ratio and thus exert an expansionary influence on the industrial sector. (As this will be exerted via a change in B, the primary sector must have borrowing capacity or assets to dispose in order to finance the deterioration of its trade balance.) Such an effect is the obverse of the contractionary influence exerted by the OPEC-engineered rise in petroleum prices in the 1970s, which was stressed by Kaldor (1976).

So, on balance, a question mark may be in order concerning Kaldor's position on this point. An early assessment by Kaldor himself was indeed extremely modest: 'At any rate, there is no presumption that the balance of forces would operate in one direction more that in another' (Hart, Kaldor and Tinbergen, 1964, p. 163). This assessment followed immediately his first exposition of the adverse link between flexible commodity prices and industrial activity. It is later that Kaldor's position hardened—the argument became part of a 'fundamental proposition' (Kaldor, 1976, p. 706).

Lastly, a wider comment. Although the macroeconomic literature of recent decades gives prominence to the role of financial assets, here they have hovered in the background and just entered by the back door once or twice. (The counterpart of dealers' stocking/destocking is financial asset decumulation/accumulation.) The most suitable assumption that would account for their non-prominence is that accommodating monetary conditions prevail in the industrial sector which keep the yields on financial assets constant. This is not arbitrary—and not just because it is implicit in Kaldor's own analysis of commodity issues and in the literature inspired by it, nor because the instinct of commerical banks is to accommodate prudentially acceptable demand for credit unless pressed otherwise. When there are no resource constraints in the economy, as under Keynesian unemployment, it is hardly appropriate to postulate under the *ceteris paribus* clause a constant money supply which, in an expansionary phase, would lead to finance-engendered crowding out, uncalled-for by resource scarcity. Deviations from accommodating conditions can be viewed as monetary policy initiatives, to be added to the discussion if desired, but to be left out if, as here, we must press on.

2.4 Steadying aggregate demand

Setting aside hereafter worries about the Marshall–Lerner condition and thus taking for granted the depression-aggravating role of falling prices, the counter-cyclical role of commodity price stabilisation is evident.

In a phase of underheating of the world economy, commodity prices would be subject to downward pressure. The stabilising authority would offset this pressure by purchasing commodities for its stockpile. Financed in ways that did not crowd out other expenditure, these purchases would constitute a net injection of demand accruing to the industrial sector as compared with the alternative of falling commodity prices, since with $\partial B/\partial p>0$, industrial demand does not stand to benefit from falling prices. If appropriate institutions were established, an automatic demand stabiliser would be in place. This would operate equally in a phase of overheating, when commodities would be sold from the stockpile (though Kaldor relied more on other arguments of an asymmetric nature, in support of price stabilisation in the phase of rising prices—see sub-section 2.8).

Johnson (1967, pp. 232–3), among others, has remarked that demand management by fiscal/monetary policy in the industrial countries would achieve the same macroeconomic result more efficiently. It is a plausible point but not necessarily correct. In a two-sector context, the purchase of commodities gives the same stimulus to demand for industrial goods, pound for pound, as direct budgetary spending on industrial goods. This follows from the fact that the entire amount spent on commodity purchases by the stabilising agency ends up as an improvement in the industrial sector's trade balance. Thus, the industrial sector's output ends up at the same level under either method of stimulating demand.[1] True; this would not be so if the primary sector diverted some of the proceeds into buying industrial sector assets, for then $\mathrm{d}B <$ spending to stabilise commodity prices. But nothing happens to induce such diversion when the price-stabilising action simply restores the *status quo ante* in the primary sector. In different circumstances and more complex models some superiority of direct fiscal action could come through. But, on the other side, counter-cyclical fiscal or monetary expansion cannot be undertaken by one country in isolation and, in the light of recent experience, it hardly needs saying that coordination does not come easily and has built-in inefficiencies.

2.5 Commodity reserve currency

Non-crowding out finance of the stockpile is obviously an essential ingredient of a price stabilisation policy as conceived by Kaldor. This was firmly secured in the Hart–Kaldor–Tinbergen (1964) proposal for an international commodity reserve currency (hereafter to be cited as HKT, 1964). At the time there was much concern about the shortage of international liquidity and the HKT proposal (of which Kaldor was the principal inspirer) was designed to tackle this problem while using the newly-created international currency to finance stockpiling. The initial deficiency of international liquidity would be met by a fiduciary issue and by taking over such stocks of commodities then held by national governments as these governments would be prepared to surrender in return for the new currency. At the margin the new currency would be on a 100% reserve basis (the fiduciary issue would be fixed, though subject to occasional revision), backed by a bundle of numerous commodities in fixed proportions. Full convertibility would ensure stability of the average price of the bundle but would not restrict the variability of prices of individual commodities. The volume of the new currency would wax and wane anticyclically as stocks of commodities accumulated/decumulated in response to downward/upward pressure on the level of commodity prices.

In the long run there would be no faster accumulation of commodity stocks than the rate of growth of world output, unless there was voluntary accumulation of the international

[1] Differentiating the equation for the industrial gross product set out in the previous sub-section and holding p constant.

$$\mathrm{d}Y = s\mathrm{d}Y - m\mathrm{d}Y + \mathrm{d}\pi,$$

where $s = \partial E/\partial Y =$ marginal propensity to spend and $m = -\partial B/\partial Y =$ marginal propensity to import.

Note that to keep p constant the stabilising agency spends $\mathrm{d}B = -m\mathrm{d}Y$. (Flows in or out of the agency's stockpile not included in B.)

Under the alternative of fiscal policy (to be designated by $\mathrm{d}G$) a flexible p clears the commodity market, hence, $\mathrm{d}B = 0$. Thus

$$\mathrm{d}Y = s\mathrm{d}Y + \mathrm{d}\pi + \mathrm{d}G.$$

When $\mathrm{d}G$ equals the amount spent on stabilising p under the previous policy (i.e. $-m\mathrm{d}Y$), the effect of $\mathrm{d}\pi$ on Y is clearly the same under both alternatives; $1/(1-s+m)$ is the multiplier of $\mathrm{d}\pi$ in both. However, with $\mathrm{d}\pi < 0$, p falls in the second case and the improved terms of trade make the industrial sector better off under the fiscal alternative. Kaldor could not argue on symmetry grounds that this is offset by deteriorating terms of trade when $\mathrm{d}\pi > 0$, because he denied symmetry. But, clearly, gains emanating from the terms of trade relate to distribution, not efficiency.

Note also that if a Laursen–Metzler effect is present ($\partial E/\partial p > 0$), industrial output will end up higher under price stabilisation than under an equal-spending fiscal stimulus.

currency. For suppose it was faster for a time. This would imply two things: first, growth in the primary sector faster than the industrial sector and second, a current account surplus of the industrial sector (paid for by the primary sector with that part of the international currency accruing to it which it did not wish to retain). The latter will induce either an expansion of industrial output, which would align the two sectors' growth rates and eliminate the initial excess supply of commodities, or an appreciation of the currency of the industrial sector which would do the same in due course by turning the terms of trade against the primary sector, thus diminishing the incentive to invest in that sector.

In practice things cannot be that smooth. For example, in industrial countries which comprise a primary sector (as most do) the prices of the primary sector's products must be lowered in the national currency when the latter appreciates, which may not be easy. Or, again, some of the intended benefits from price stabilisation (such as less uncertainty) are diluted when the nominal price is stable but the real price remains variable.

For HKT these difficulties would not have loomed very large, because their presumption was that the main source of adjustment would be the expansion of industrial output. Indeed, they considered it as the main advantage of their scheme that expansion in the primary sector would generate faster growth in the industrial sector instead of being dissipated (at least in part) in relative price changes (HKT, 1964, section IV).

Note, in any event, that it was not the intention of the scheme to accumulate indefinitely unwanted stocks of commodities. It was clearly, therefore, a price-stabilising, not a price-raising, scheme, even though some price enhancement could be an incidental by-product.

The idea of an international commodity reserve currency was first mooted by Graham (1944), while proposals for a broad commodity standard for national currencies go back to the nineteenth century. There is, therefore, a large literature on the subject. Some of the issues have been alluded to already. Superselectively, a couple more points will be taken up here.

The cost of holding and managing the stock of commodities is a substantial disadvantage, as the authors of the scheme acknowledged from the beginning. They were satisfied, however, that the gains outweighed the cost many times over. Here the estimate of costs is important and widely different estimates were put forward in the debate that ensued—see Grubel (1965) and Hart (1966). McKinnon (1979) considers a fractional commodity reserve as a way of reducing what would otherwise be, in his judgement, 'overwhelming social costs'. But whatever the economising merits of this, it would not do for Kaldor, for it would reduce the injections/withdrawals of demand associated with the scheme and hence blunt its anticyclical power.

For certain shocks to the system, a commodity-based currency would give a perverse response. Suppose that it was in operation during the OPEC-engineered second oil price increase of the 1970s and that oil was in the commodity bundle underlying the currency. To keep the commodity value of the currency constant, there would have had to be sales from stock, reducing international liquidity at a time when it should have been increased to offset the deflationary impact of the low absorption of oil-exporting countries (Stewart and Sengupta, 1982, ch. 7).[1]

In principle there is a correct response to such a shock within the HKT scheme: sell from the commodity stock as required by the convertibility rules and at the same time more than offset the resulting contraction of the international currency by expanding the fiduciary issue. When you have two targets (commodity price stability and international

[1] The commodity sales would have also lowered the price of commodities other than oil, thus pushing the burden of adjustment on poor non-oil primary producers.

liquidity) you obviously need at least two instruments, and the fiduciary issue is the second instrument. The only problem from the point of view of HKT is that they set much store by the automaticity of their scheme, and a discretionary manipulation of the fiduciary issue would destroy that.

More than a decade after the launching of the scheme, Kaldor (1976) was reiterating his belief in an international commodity reserve currency. But in Kaldor (1983), after an allusion in a footnote to unspecified 'inherent problems' of a currency convertible into a fixed bundle of commodities, he opted for a more flexible scheme of simultaneous buffer stocks of individual commodities operating subject to centralised control. In making this choice, he acknowledged the influence of Keynes's war-time proposals for commodity control which had recently been declassified (Keynes, 1980); a convergence towards the UNCTAD-sponsored multi-buffer stock Integrated Programme for Commodities linked to a Common Fund may also have been in his mind. Perhaps he also became conscious of the risk of perverse responses under fully automatic rules. He insisted, however, on the financing of the net buffer stock acquisitions through international money (SDRs) so as to preserve the non-crowding-out property of the buffer stock operations.

2.6 Alleviating the niggardliness of nature

A second ground for advocating a price stabilisation scheme related to its productivity-raising effect, especially significant in the context of the view that land/natural resources is the ultimate constraint on growth. As noted earlier, Kaldor (until close to the end of his life) viewed this constraint not as one that had played a binding role in recent decades but as a serious potential constraint, particularly in a vision of the world without grinding poverty for two-thirds of its population. Avoidable obstacles to bigger (renewable) output of land were wasteful in the most fundamental sense because they tightened the ultimate constraint. Wide fluctuations of commodity prices acted as such an obstacle by discouraging, through the uncertainty they engendered, land-saving investment in agriculture (Kaldor, 1976 and especially 1983). The experience since the 1930s of farm-support programmes, agricultural marketing boards and the Common Agricultural Policy of the EEC all confirmed (in the view of Kaldor, 1983) the pronounced productivity-raising effect of price stabilisation schemes.

In the neoclassical view this would only be a once-over effect, associated with an enlargement of the capital stock to a level in keeping with less uncertainty. But Kaldor was not a neoclassical and, in any case, once-over does not mean negligible and it can take many years to be completed.

Note, however, that while commodity-by-commodity buffer stocks would reduce the price variance for each commodity, a commodity-convertible currency would only stabilise on average, and this is consistent with increased price instability for a few commodities in the bundle.

The power of the present argument in support of price stabilisation is clearly enhanced by the fact that stabilisation is said to ease the scarcity of the ultimate scarce resource. When, therefore, in a change of view, Kaldor (1986A) came to discount the growth-constraining role of land/natural resources, some, but not all, of the strength of the argument was lost: the gain from productivity growth can still outweigh the cost of attaining it, though not if the increment of output is added to a perpetual mountain of unwanted stock. This, it should be noted, is the only argument the force of which is affected by how niggardly nature is perceived to be, which is why it was said earlier (subsection 2.1) that the niggardliness of nature was not crucial to Kaldor's general position.

2.7 Anchoring prices

The third ground for a stabilisation scheme is the excessive amplitude of price fluctuations. This is the problem now described as overshooting. The swing between boom price and depression price is big anyway because of low price elasticities; it is even bigger when there is overshooting in both directions. Raw experience in recent years has made many converts to the idea of price-overshooting and models incorporating the phenomenon in various contexts are proliferating. (Throw in a slow adjustment here and a sticky variable there and you can have overshooting even under the hypothesis of rational expectations.) Clearly, overshooting is wasteful; the ephemeral resource shifts associated with it involve not only transitional adjustment costs but also permanent write-offs of product-specific factors.

It will be recalled that in Kaldor's vision the terms of trade guide the system towards intersectoral equilibrium, not however through substitution in consumption but by affecting investment incentives and hence capacity adjustments (sub-section 2.2). This is a slow-acting mechanism and for this reason it exacerbates the risk and magnitude of overshooting. While the capacity adjustment is pending, only the stocking/destocking actions of commodity traders can stand as a barrier to huge and unnecessary price swings. If endowed with rational expectations, traders would perform this role adequately. But for Kaldor rational expectations was a naïve hypothesis, unworthy of a pivotal role even if capable of generating a few useful insights. Expectations were historically and institutionally conditioned and in the not too distant past the institutional setting was, in Kaldor's view, conducive to stabilising behaviour by commodity traders. They had a notion of 'normal' price and, while needing a perceptible deviation from that price before stepping in to act in a stabilising fashion, they kept price fluctuations within a tolerable range. This was at the time of the gold-linked monetary system—not just the classical gold standard but also the period of fixed dollar price of gold after World War II:

> . . . the formal though distant link embodied in the Bretton Woods system sufficed to maintain the illusion that dollars were as good as gold, and that commodities have a (long-run) *normal* dollar price around which their market prices fluctuate. The formal demonetisation of gold, as subsequent events have shown, has greatly weakened this stabilising force in the markets . . . (Kaldor, 1976, p. 714).

After the early 1970s, in the absence of any anchor, price fluctuations became wider because, in the more uncertain environment, traders needed a bigger movement of prices before commiting resources to the belief that it will be reversed. And not only wider but widening, as successive rounds of previous fluctuations entered into the calculation of how wide the next one was going to be. The monetisation of a large bundle of commodities proposed in the HKT scheme would restore the anchorage which had been provided by the gold standard and improve upon it. As Hart (1976) put it, such a scheme would provide 'a link between the monetary and the real spheres—the kind of link which conservatives have hoped could be forged in the form of the gold standard'. What was essential, however, was the anchorage—with or without monetisation. As we saw, Kaldor ended up by preferring the alternative of buffer stocks.

The anchor was not, presumably, to be fixed in perpetuity, come what may. Some concept of fundamental disequilibrium could be used to provide for (infrequent) shifting of the anchorage. But, in any event, prices would cease to be the main motivator in the adjustment mechanism of the primary sector. Like the industrial sector, capacity expansion would be undertaken when demand, current or expected, pressed against the limits of existing capacity and stocks ran down.

2.8 Severing the first link of an inflationary chain

Turn now to the fourth and last ground for price stabilisation, which is perhaps the most interesting and the most powerful.

With flexible primary prices, when the sector's growth is too slow relative to that of the industrial sector, prices will rise. But now, to the cost-driven industrial prices, add real-wage resistance by industrial workers, and the relative price mechanism breaks down. The incipient threat to living standards from a terms-of-trade deterioration faced by the industrial sector (when not sufficiently masked by productivity growth) triggers money-wage increases. Industrial prices rise to match the increasing cost of inputs and the terms of trade are pushed back to their initial level. The capacity bottleneck in the primary sector remains, so primary prices continue to rise but are continuously matched by industrial price increases. Thus, the relative price mechanism for intersectoral adjustment is thwarted and we have, instead, an inflation-generating mechanism.

Add, finally, contractionary measures by governments to combat inflation—not demand inflation, be it noted, but cost inflation—and we end up with an industrial recession (Kaldor, 1976). Note that, with the asymmetry of response to falling and rising commodity prices, we end up with a depressive influence in both directions. Kaldor attached much significance to this observation.

The analysis of the rising prices case was inspired by the inflationary explosion of the 1970s. At the time, monetarist explanations were being loudly propagated, but the subsequent breakdown of the monetarist paradigm has improved the receptivity to a Kaldor-type analysis. There are now at least a couple of empirical papers which identify the rate of change of primary product prices as a major influence on the rate of inflation.[1]

The welfare costs implied by the analysis are clearly high—both the costs of inflation incurred while it lasts, and the costs of recession, incurred for stopping it (see Kanbur and Vines, 1986 for an elegant formal demonstration). These costs are avoided under a scheme which stabilises commodity prices. Substantial stocks are, of course, needed to satisfy the excess demand for commodities (which caused the initial price upsurge) until such time as the (normally slow) expansion of capacity has had time to catch up and the cost of stock-holding must be deducted to arrive at the net gain. If anyone is so minded as to ask why, if there is gain to be had, are profit-seeking dealers not stepping in to fill the gap, the obvious answer is that the gains from avoiding inflation and recession are social gains that cannot be privately appropriated (see also sub-section 1.4).

It could be argued that an optimal solution to the problem outlined in the Kaldorian analysis would require that it be tackled at its source, by attacking the power which sustains real-wage resistance and not by stabilising commodity prices. But the social costs of such a strategy are high. Here, as elsewhere, when an alleged first best is made the enemy of a feasible second best, the argument needs watching.

2.9 Recent policy concerns in industrial countries

Commodity prices are a permanent concern of the developing countries, many of which are far too dependent on their primary exports. In the industrial countries policy concerns on this topic sometimes wane, but they keep bouncing back. Kaldor did not live to see the

[1] Beckerman and Jenkinson (1986) and Rowlatt (1987). Beckerman and Jenkinson focus on the fall in OECD inflation in the early eighties and its association with falling commodity prices. Commodity prices, therefore, appear in a benign role. Kaldor would not have expected symmetric inflation effects of rising and falling commodity prices. But even if symmetric, the influence is malign overall, having responsibility for generating or intensifying the inflation cycle in the first place.

recent resurfacing of the issue, in however attenuated a form, at a major policy forum. James Baker, then US Secretary of the Treasury, told the 1987 annual meetings of the IMF/World Bank that, as part of the multilateral surveillance process '... the United States is prepared to consider utilising, as an additional indicator ... the relationship among our currencies and a basket of commodities including gold. This could be helpful as an early warning signal of potential price trends' (*IMF Survey*, 19 October 1987).

At a less official level, the issue has surfaced also in the context of the 'target zones' proposal for exchange rate reform. If one country's currency is breaching the upper end of its target zone and another's the lower end simultaneously, which should act? One suggestion is that the strong currency country should initiate internal expansion if the price of a basket of commodities is falling and the weak currency country should engage in contraction if the price of the basket is rising (Williamson, 1987). This is bound to have a certain stabilising effect on commodity prices.

3. Epilogue

Kaldor's concern for commodities was life-long. The common thread has been the instability of their prices. He identified the microeconomic inefficiencies and (more persistently) the macroeconomic disorders associated with such instability. An activist by nature, he offered policy proposals for tackling the problem, placing them, as was typical of him, within a wider conceptual framework. He did not cast his proposals in iron. Not being dogmatic, he changed his mind more than once about the details. While preserving some role for relative prices at the microeconomic level, he aimed at reducing the amplitude of movement at the macro level and at providing some anchorage for the absolute price level.

At the policy-making level, interest in commodity prices has had its ups and downs but, at all times, Kaldor's thinking has been an essential part of the intellectual background, and one of the author's many pleasant memories of Nicky is serving with him on a committee of experts on the Indexation of Commodities convened by UNCTAD in 1975.

Bibliography

Beckerman, W. and Jenkinson, T. 1986. What stopped inflation: unemployment or commodity prices?, *Economic Journal*, vol. 96.

Behrman, J. R. 1977. *International Commodity Agreements: An evaluation of the UNCTAD Integrated Commodity Program*, Washington DC, Overseas Development Council

Ghosh, S., Gilbert, C. L. and Hughes Hallet, A. J. 1987. *Stabilizing Speculative Commodity Markets*, Oxford, Clarendon Press

Gilbert, C. L. 1987. International commodity agreements: design and performance, *World Development*, vol. 15

Graham, B. 1944. *World Commodities and World Currency*, New York, McGraw-Hill

Grubel, H. G. 1965. The case against an international commodity reserve currency, *Oxford Economic Papers*, vol. 17

Hart, A. G. 1966. The case for and against international commodity reserve currency, *Oxford Economic Papers*, vol. 18

Hart, A. G. 1976. The case as of 1976 for international commodity-reserve currency, *Weltwirtschaftliches Archiv*, vol. 112

Hart, A. G., Kaldor, N. and Tinbergen, J. 1964. The case for an international commodity reserve currency, in Kaldor, N. (1964)

Henderson, P. D. and Lal, D. 1976. UNCTAD IV, the commodities problem and international economic reform, *ODI Review*, no. 2

Hewitt, A. P. 1987. Stabex and commodity export compensation schemes: prospects for globalisation, *World Development*, vol. 15

Johnson, H. G. 1967. *Economic Policies Toward Less Developed Countries*, Washington DC, The Brookings Institution
Kaldor, N. 1939–40A. Speculation and economic stability, *Review of Econimc Studies*, vol. 7
Kaldor, N. 1939–40B. A note on the theory of the forward market, *Review of Economic Studies*, vol. 7
Kaldor, N. 1952. *A Reconsideration of the Economics of the International Wheat Agreement*, Rome: FAO, Commodity Studies No. I, reprinted in Kaldor (1964)
Kaldor, N. 1983. Stabilising the Terms of Trade of Underdeveloped Countries, *Economic Bulletin for Latin America*, vol. 8, reprinted in Kaldor (1964)
Kaldor, N. 1964. *Essays on Economic Policy II*, London, Duckworth
Kaldor, N. 1976. Inflation and recession in the world economy, *Economic Journal*, vol. 86
Kaldor, N. 1979. Equilibrium theory and growth theory, in Boskin, M. J. (ed.), *Economics and Human Welfare. Essays in Honor of Tibor Scitovsky*, New York, Academic Press
Kaldor, N. 1983. The role of commodity prices in economic recovery, *Lloyds Bank Review*, no. 149
Kaldor, N. 1986A. Limits on Growth, *Oxford Economic Papers*, vol. 38
Kaldor, N. 1986B. Recollections of an economist, *Banca Nazionale del Lavoro Quarterly Review*, no. 156
Kanbur, S. M. R. 1984. How to analyse commodity price stabilisation? A review article, *Oxford Economic Papers*, vol. 36
Kanbur, S. M. R. and Vines, D. 1986. North-South interaction and commod control, *Journal of Development Economics*, vol. 23
Keynes, J. M. 1980. *The Collected Writings of John Maynard Keynes*, vol. 27, Macmillan and CUP
Labys, W. C. and Pollak, P. K. 1984. *Commodity Models for Forecasting and Policy Analysis*, London, Croom Helm
Laursen, S. and Metzler, L. A. 1950. Flexible exchange rates and the theory of employment, *Review of Economics and Statistics*, vol. 32
Lipsey, R. G. 1963. *An Introduction to Positive Economics* (first edition), London, Weidenfield and Nicolson
MacBean, A. I. and Nguyen, D. T. 1987. *Commodity Policies: Problems and Prospects*, London, Croom Helm
McKinnon, R. I. 1979. Commodity reserve money, special drawing rights, and the link to less developed countries, in Boskin, M. J. (ed.), *Economics and Human Welfare. Essays in Honor of Tibor Scitovsky*, New York, Academic Press
Maizels, A. 1984. A conceptual framework for analysis of primary commodity markets, *World Development*, vol. 12
Miranda, M. J. and Helmberger, P. J. 1988. The effects of price stabilisation programs, *American Economic Review*, vol. 78
Molana, H. and Vines, D. 1987. 'North-South Growth and Terms of Trade: A Model on Kaldorian Lines', University of Glasgow Discussion Papers in Economics, no. 8710
Muth, J. F. 1961. Rational expectations and the theory of price movements, *Econometrica*, vol. 29
Newbery, D. M. G. and Stiglitz, J. E. 1981. *The Theory of Commodity Price Stabilisation*, Oxford, OUP
Nguyen, D. T. 1980. The effects of partial price stabilisation on export earnings instability and level: implications for the North-South negotiations, in Sengupta, A. (ed.), *Commodities, Finance and Trade*, London, Frances Pinter
Robertson, D. H. 1952. The terms of trade, in Robertson, D. H., *Utility and All That and Other Essays*, London, George Allen & Unwin
Rowlatt, P. A. 1987, 'Analysis of the Inflation Process', Government Economic Service Working Paper No. 99
Spraos, J. 1983. *Inequalising Trade?*, Oxford, OUP
Stewart, F. and Sengupta, A. 1982. *International Financial Cooperation*, London, Frances Pinter
Thirlwall, A. P. 1986. A general model of growth and development on Kaldorian Lines, *Oxford Economic Papers*, vol. 38
Thirlwall, A. P. 1987. *Nicholas Kaldor*, Brighton, Wheatsheaf Books
Williamson, J. 1987. Exchange rate flexibility, target zones and policy coordination, *World Development*, vol. 15
World Bank 1975. *Price Forecasts for Major Primary Commodities*, Report No. 814, Washington DC

Nicholas Kaldor's contribution to the analysis of international monetary reform

Stephany Griffith-Jones*

1. Introduction

Nicholas Kaldor was both actively involved with practical problems of economic policy and reform, as well as contributing to the theoretical understanding of how economies function. In the field of international monetary reform, his work provides a clear example of a lucid application of theoretical insights on the malfunctioning of the international monetary and economic system to proposals on reform of the system, that could help overcome such problems.

Kaldor wrote on international monetary affairs very much in the tradition and the spirit of Keynes's thinking; this refers not only to the importance which he attached to the sustainment of world aggregate demand as a major objective of an efficient international monetary system, but also to the specific characteristics of Kaldor's proposal for international commodity control.[1] But on international monetary reform, Kaldor was far more than a neo-Keynesian, as he also drew—and contributed to—the tradition of development economics, pioneered by Raul Prebisch, Hans Singer and Arthur Lewis. One of Kaldor's most valuable contributions to the field of international monetary reform is precisely that he is one of the first economists to approach this issue clearly from a development perspective. Indeed, as we shall see below, amongst the main objectives of Kaldor's proposals for international monetary reform were to 'permit a balanced distribution of economic progress in the world ... between developed and developing countries' and to 'provide an effective instrument for stabilising the terms of trade between primary products and manufactured goods, and for accelerating the rate of growth of world industrial production'.

It could thus be argued that the significance of Kaldor's proposals for international monetary reform—first made in the early sixties—lie not so much in the detailed schemes themselves, but in the agenda of objectives which he puts forward, an agenda which seems particularly relevant in the eighties. In the next section (2), I shall elaborate further on the sources on which Kaldor based his analysis of the international monetary system. In Section 3, I shall describe and analyse Kaldor's proposal for an international commodity

*Institute of Development Studies, Sussex. I should like to thank Ricardo A. Lagos for his valuable research assistance, and Adrian Wood for his extremely valuable comments. I am also grateful to the referees of the article for stimulating comments.

[1] As Kaldor (1983) points out, Keynes's plan in this field has become known only in 1980, with the release of war-time British Government papers under the 30 years' rule, and their subsequent publication in Keynes' *Collected Writings* (Moggridge, 1980).

reserve currency, as well as mentioning his contribution to the setting up of compensatory financing schemes. Section 4 will evaluate Kaldor's contribution in the field.

2. The background to Kaldor's analysis

2.1 The concern with the fragility of the international monetary system

Kaldor shared with other economists, of which the most distinguished was Robert Triffin, a concern about the fragility of the Bretton Woods international monetary system, and its unsustainability. Triffin had pointed out the inherent financial contradiction of the system, that existed till 1971, based on the dollar being the 'key currency', and having a fixed price in terms of gold. In order for the key currency to be acceptable, it should not be too abundant, nor should the country issuing it be seen to have excessive balance of payments deficits. This contradiction, which has been called the 'Triffin dilemma', was a source of major concern to Kaldor. Throughout the 1950s and 1960s, mainly in correspondence, but also in some of his articles, Kaldor warned of the fragility of the system, and of the increase in dollar liabilities (see Thirlwall, 1987). This concern with the fragility of the existing system was one of the two pillars on which Kaldor based his plans to replace the gold exchange standard with a commodity-backed international money, independent of any national currency.

It is worth noting here that Kaldor also added an important insight into the analysis of the final breakdown of the Bretton Woods system, with the suspension of the gold convertibility of the dollar on August 15, 1971. This explained the contradictions of the Bretton Woods system not merely in financial terms, but also in terms of the evolution of the world economy. Kaldor (1973) explained the progressive over-valuation of the dollar that had occurred in the fifties and sixties, mainly 'as a result of the cumulative trading advantages of countries which have been gaining an increasing share of world trade in manufactures, and the cumulative handicap of those whose market shares were curtailed in consequence'. Kaldor thus attributes the weakening of the dollar to the fact that the US pursued 'consumer led' economic growth, in which exports grow at a rate similar to that of industrial capacity and output; on the other hand, countries which like West Germany pursued an 'export-led' model, allowed their fast-growing industries to sustain far higher rates of growth than they could if they were mainly dependent on the growth of domestic demand. The faster rate of resulting productivity growth—caused by the more rapid growth of exports—led to a further improvement of their share of world trade. It was these mechanisms of self-reinforcing divergences in the trends of industrial productivity and competitiveness which in the last instance explained, according to Kaldor, the unsustainability of a world financial system based on firmly fixed exchange rates. Thus, Kaldor used his analysis of virtuous and vicious cumulative causation in long-term growth to explain what was initially seen by so many economists purely as a breakdown of a financial mechanism.

2.2 The concern with world growth and development

The other pillar on which Kaldor based his proposals for international monetary reform was his concern with the deterioration of the terms of trade of developing countries and its negative effect on their (and the world's) economic growth. As early as 1964, Kaldor in his joint piece with Hart and Tinbergen (Hart *et al.*, 1964)—clearly stated that

'The present world concern with monetary reform seems to us to present a rare opportunity to adapt the world monetary structure so as to foster the growth of world production and trade, and in particular, for us to contribute to the stabilisation and expansion of trade in primary products (Kaldor, *Essays in Economic Policy II*, pp. 131–2).[1]

Kaldor starts with the concern that increased availability of primary products in the world economy—due to technical progress and/or increased investment—will not necessarily lead to an expansion of manufacturing production, basically because of *insufficient world demand, as the prices of primary commodities may decline*. Such a decline in commodity prices, leads, firstly, to a fall in the purchasing power of the primary producing countries—reflected in their reduced demand for manufactured goods, produced in the industrial countries; secondly, it leads to a decline in world investment in the primary sector, mainly (in Kaldor's model) within the developing countries; and, thirdly, it leads to a decline in the purchasing power of the primary producers in the developed countries. These three effects will probably, according to Kaldor, more than compensate the expansionary effect of aggregate demand in the industrial countries, owing to the increased purchasing power caused by cheaper primary products. Kaldor here takes Keynes's concern with lack of world aggregate demand,[2] but disaggregates it into primary and industrial sectors—and countries. This integration of macroeconomic and broad sectoral concerns (particularly the relation between industrial and primary producing sectors and countries) is a major contribution by Kaldor to the field of development economics, which seems insufficiently recognised in the relevant literature.

Kaldor was fundamentally concerned with the wasted opportunity for growth and development which this situation presents since, at a time when supplies of primary products are rising relatively fast, there is scope for acceleration in the rate of growth of world manufacturing production.[3] According to Kaldor's vision for the world as a whole (and for each under-developed country with prospects of industrialisation), the flow of the primary products represents the materials necessary to operate industry, and the food necessary to expand urban employment. Even if a given rate of expansion of primary production may be more than required to support the industrial expansion of already industrialised countries, it clearly cannot be viewed as excessive if accelerated industrialisation of relatively under-developed areas is considered. Hart *et al.* (1964) clearly summarise this point: 'If an acceleration of agricultural production fails to induce an acceleration of industrial production, it is primarily because it fails to generate the increase in effective (world) demand' (p. 164).

[1] This paper was submitted to the United Nations Conference on Trade and Development (UNCTAD) in 1964. As Kaldor writes in the introduction to the second volume of his *Essays on Economic Policy*, he had prepared a first draft by himself in April 1963, which found support from A.G. Hart and Jan Tinbergen. They then decided to prepare a joint submission to the forthcoming UNCTAD conference, on which Kaldor and Hart worked jointly at the end of 1963. Though Tinbergen was not able to participate in the actual drafting, he added his signature, subject to a few minor changes which were acceptable to Kaldor and Hart. Though Kaldor was too modest and loyal a colleague to say it, Thirwall's (1987) interpretation that 'the plan was Kaldor's brainchild' seems an accurate summary of the authorship of the piece, though Hart's and particularly Tinbergen's backing clearly added prestige and weight to the piece.

[2] See Moggridge (ed.) (1980); for a discussion, see, for example, Griffith-Jones and Sunkel (1986), ch 2.

[3] Kaldor believed that technical progress is more exogenous in the primary sector than in industry, thus representing a relatively inflexible upper limit on the long-term rate of growth of primary production. This technically determined upper limit was seen by Kaldor to be the main long-term constraint on industrial production growth, as well as an overall economic growth. For a clear and brief analysis of Kaldor's thinking in this and other areas, see Wood (1987); see also, Kaldor (1983), for his own statement and Thirlwall (1987), for a formalisation of the analysis.

In their view, here lies the *central* advantage of a scheme of commodity price stabilisation via an international commodity reserve currency. (For details of the scheme, see Section 3 below.) Under such an arrangement, an increase in primary production would (according to the authors) generate a *proportionate increase in the effective demand for industrial products.* Such an element of income generation would have a powerful multiplier effect, not only in increased consumption, but also on 'induced investment'; manufacturing producers, whose markets lie in the primary producing sector, would find a market that is *not only larger, but more reliable*, which will allow them to expand their own capacity with greater confidence. The commodity reserve system's virtue is thus to provide a mechanism through which the expansion of primary production induces *a corresponding expansion* in manufacturing production: 'the balance between the two sectors will be restored through an accelerated rate of industrialisation, rather than through cuts in investment and in the growth of output in the primary sectors—the latter being the adjustment mechanism that operates through prolonged periods of depressed prices' (p. 165). This type of analysis is of course particularly relevant in the late eighties, a decade which has been characterised precisely by the negative type of adjustment which Hart, Kaldor and Tinbergen wished to avoid.

Those authors went beyond the pure aim of sustaining short-term world aggregate demand, into perceiving the stability of primary product prices as an engine of industrialisation and development, particularly in the poorer countries. They thus argued that the process of expansion set off by the commodity reserve system would *diffuse* demand from the central to the outlying areas of industrialisation; if demand for additional industrial goods could not be met by increased supply from industrial countries (owing to full capacity utilisation) the expansive pressure would be diverted to the industrial sectors of less developed enconomies.

With this line of argument, Kaldor provided a clear rationale not just for the commodity reserve currency which he proposed with Hart and Tinbergen, but to other schemes where the main aim was to stabilise the prices of commodities; this is a subject to which Kaldor (1983) returned much later, when he argued in favour of schemes such as the Common Fund, proposed by developing countries, or the International Commodity Control, originally proposed by Keynes in 1938, to stabilise commodity prices. Kaldor points out that such schemes were coldly received by the 'establishment' in industrial countries, because they were seen mainly to benefit developing countries. Kaldor stressed however that stability of commodity prices was also in 'the vital interests' of the industrialised countries, as it is a pre-condition for securing long-term investment necessary for sustained growth.

Particularly in his later work (1976, 1983), Kaldor was concerned not only with the negative effect of deteriorating terms of trade on the development of poorer countries and on the world economy, but also with the negative effect of *any* major instability of commodity prices (whether upwards or downwards). We have already described Kaldor's concern with the deflationary effect of falling commodity prices. However, as Kaldor pointed out, sharp increases in commodity prices can also have negative (stagflationary) effects on the world economy.

Kaldor's analysis of the latter (see Kaldor, 1976) is based on the perception that while commodity prices are demand-determined, industrial prices are cost-determined; as a result, rises in commodity prices have a very powerful inflationary effect operating on the cost side, which is multiplied by its passage through the various stages of production.

Thus, according to Kaldor's analysis, the industrial sector—owing to its 'superior market power—will resist any compression of real income by countering commmodity price rises through a cost-induced inflation of industrial prices. The rise in the price of raw materials and fuels is, according to Kaldor's analysis, passed through the various stages of production into the final price with an exaggerated effect—'blown up' by a succession of percentage additions to prime costs. This initially causes a rise in the profit share (in the value added of manufacturing), which—in countries with strong trade unions—is a strong factor in causing pressure for wage increases. Added to this is the price-induced rise in wages caused by the reluctance of workers to accept a cut in standards of living. Through these different mechanisms, the industrial sector resists any compression of its real income by countering the rise in commodity prices through a cost-induced inflation of industrial prices. Furthermore, this inflation will have a *deflationary* effect on real demand for industrial goods, for two reasons. One of them is that the rise in producers' profits is not matched by a rise in their spending; the other is that the governments of industrial countries will tend to react to increased domestic inflation by deflationary fiscal and monetary measures, that reduce consumer and investment demand. In Kaldor's analysis, excess demand of primary products thus results in an acceleration in the world rate of inflation, but no relative price change between primary and manufactured products. Equilibrium is achieved by income changes, which reduce the demand for primary products, that may ultimately lead to a relative decline of commodity prices!

Kaldor thus initially stressed the negative effects—on growth, particularly, but not only, of developing countries—of deteriorating commodity prices; he became equally concerned with the negative effects of rapidly rising commodity prices, such as occurred with the major rise in the price of oil in the seventies. Thus, the key problem was instability of commodity prices, determined by the inappropriate operation of commodity markets, without government regulation.

3. Kaldor's proposals for international monetary reform

A solution which attempted to tackle simultaneously the fragility of the international monetary system and the instability of commodity prices, with its negative implications for the world economy, was presented jointly by Kaldor, Hart and Tinbergen, in their 1963 article quoted above.

Though proposals for an international commodity reserve currency had been developed since the nineteenth century, the Kaldor, Hart, Tinbergen proposal (Hart *et al.*, in short) is clearly one of the most elaborate and influential schemes in this tradition, as reflected in the fact that it tends always to be quoted in any discussion on the issue. Perhaps one of the reasons for this is that they provided a very detailed justification and a blueprint for the operation of such a scheme, even though accepting that there would have to be subsequent modifications to the blueprint.

The scheme had the following characteristics:

(a) The IMF would have its own currency, convertible into both gold and a bundle of commodities, consisting of thirty or so principal commodities in world trade, which combine a high degree of standardisation with reasonable durability in storage. In the tradition, and presumably in honour of Keynes, this currency would be called 'bancor'.

(b) Bancor should be fully covered by gold and commodities, except for a fixed fiduciary issue.

(c) Only central banks of member countries should be entitled to hold bancor balances with the IMF, and countries should accept bancor in settlement of claims.

(d) A suggestion was made for an initial issue of bancor equivalent to $30 billion (at the time), made up of $5 billion in exchange for gold, $20 billion in exchange for commodities, and $5 billion as the fiduciary issue.

Once the scheme could enter into full operation (when the IMF would have built up its reserve of commodities), the convertibility of bancor into both gold and commodities could ensure that the price of primary commodities in the bundle would be stable in terms of gold, irrespective of variations in the exchange rate of individual currencies. Tendencies to price declines would be met by an absorption of stocks by the IMF, an increase in the basic income of primary producers and an increase in world liquidity; if prices fell, the reverse mechanism would operate.

The plan presented by Kaldor, Hart and Tinbergen to the UNCTAD Conference was not seriously discussed there, being referred instead to a study group. Kaldor himself wrote already in 1964: 'In submitting this scheme, none of us were under any illusion that the central bankers of the main industrial countries would be prepared to give serious consideration to a plan of this kind', however, they were anxious—at a time of widespread discussion on international monetary reform—to present 'the case for alternative schemes which would produce a *more powerful and more widely diffused benefit to the world economy*' (Introduction to Hart, Kaldor, and Tinbergen, 1964).

The IMF did agree to issue a new international monetary unit, the Special Drawing Right (SDR), in 1960. The SDR is valued in terms of a basket of currencies and not, as Kaldor *et al.* had proposed, by commodities; there are no automatic rules for its issue, a decision which depends on a majority in the Executive Board of the IMF. The SDR is a fairly insignificant part of international monetary reserves; between 1981 and 1988, as a result of the opposition of certain industrial governments—and particularly the US—there has been no new issue of SDRs. Though the world economy since 1981 had many of the characteristics outlined by Kaldor—low and falling commodity prices, slow growth or declining GDP in many developing countries, with negative effects on industrial economies' exports and production—counter-cyclical mechanisms have not been used internationally to reverse these trends. A commodity reserve currency would have operated automatically in such a direction; however, the existing SDR currency could have also been used in a counter-cyclical manner, as many economists and governments have argued. This logic was not accepted by the US and other governments, which blocked new issues of SDRs between 1981 and 1988.

Thus, not only has Kaldor's scheme been rejected, but in the eighties even the spirit of counter-cyclical international financial measures to combat recession in developing countries, so eloquently defended by Kaldor, was also rejected, even though such measures could have been implemented with existing mechanisms. The cost of such a rejection has been dramatic, particularly in the developing world (see, for example, Cornia, Jolly and Stewart, 1987).

Just as there has been no new issue for SDRs in the eighties, and any attempt to link SDR issues to the needs of developing countries was even less 'feasible' politically, so commodity price stabilisation schemes have received very little and even decreasing support internationally, and particularly from industrial governments. As the ideological preferences of the governments of leading industrial countries have shifted towards 'free' markets and towards tight control of government issued currency (nationally *and* internationally), the climate for accepting Kaldor's scheme has, if anything, deteriorated since the mid sixties. However, if and when these trends are reversed, the climate may again improve.

As described above, there has been strong ideological rejection, particularly in the eighties, not only of Kaldor's scheme, but also of the use of other counter-cyclical international financial mechanisms which Kaldor advocated and to whose creation he had contributed (see below). This opposition has come with particular strength from those who are ideologically committed to the pure operation of market forces, both nationally and internationally. As these latter views became more dominant in major industrial countries (particularly during the Reagan years of the US administration), opposition both to the letter and the spirit of Kaldor's proposal was strengthened.

A more long-term reason for resistance to Kaldor's scheme by industrial governments may arise from the view that industrial and developing countries have conflicting interests in the matter of commodity prices; if it is perceived that industrial economies actually benefit from lower commodity prices (e.g. by lower costs of imports, lower inflation), then there is no reason for industrial governments to support and even less to fund commodity prices stabilisation mechanisms or a commodity backed currency, with a similar effect. Again the ideological perspective is important here. If emphasis is placed on controlling inflation as a key (and possibly major) objective for industrial governments, as the monetarist school does, then lower commodity prices provide a welcome contribution to the fight against inflation. Clearly, lower commodity prices in the eighties have contributed to a reduction in inflation in the industrial world. However, if a Kaldorian or a Keynesian view is adopted, both as regards the operation of the world economy *and* the objectives of economic policy, then there is a 'positive sum' gain to be obtained from higher and—above all—more stable commodity prices; these would be a pre-condition for long-term and sustained investment in the primary sector as well as providing an additional source of aggregate world demand (see Section 2 above). Furthermore, a Kaldorian perspective would give far higher priority to sustaining economic growth, particularly but not only in the developing world, than would a monetarist one.

The extent to which higher commodity prices should be viewed in a zero–sum perspective (as harmful to industrial economies) or in a positive-sum perspective (as beneficial to both industrial *and* particularly developing economies) may be largely related to the perception of supply elasticities (and idle resources) in the industrial economies. To the extent that there is idle capacity in industrial economies, and no structural bottlenecks, then the increased demand from the developing world, generated by higher commodity prices, could be accommodated by higher production in the industrial world. Negative effects on inflation via increased costs of imported commodities would be reduced or eliminated by the reduction in unit fixed costs caused by an expansion of production volumes. Should there be no (or scarce) space capacity in industrial countries, or if there are structural bottlenecks, then the effect both of the rise in commodity prices (via higher costs) and of increased aggregate demand would be basically an inflationary one, and therefore an undesirable one, from the perspective of industrial countries' consumers. However, the positive long-term effect—pointed out by Kaldor—of higher investment in the primary producing sector, particularly in developing countries, would still occur even in this case; indeed, such investment could tend to reduce future inflationary pressures.

Table 1. *Selected data for world merchandise trade, 1985 (billions of dollars)*

Origin/Destination	Developed	Developing	World
Developed countries			
Total primary products		51	310
Primary products excluding fuel		43	210
Total manufacture		195	940
Total exports		253	1275
Developing countries			
Total primary products	196		294
Primary products excluding fuel	58		96
Total manufacture	96		145
Total exports	295		440

Source: GATT, *International Trade, 1986–87*, Geneva, 1988.

It should also be stressed in this context that it is increasingly incorrect to view the developing countries only as primary commodities exporters and the richer countries only as industrial goods exporters. Increasingly, the 'North' has become a major commodity producer and exporter, while several 'Southern' countries have become major exporters of manufactures. As a result, schemes like Kaldor's which would favour sustained and stable commodity prices would not merely favour in the first instance developing economies, but primary producers anywhere in the world. Indeed, as can be seen in Table 1, total exports (in US $) of primary products by developed countries (at $310 bn) *was higher* than total exports by developing countries (at $294 bn). If fuels are excluded (given that its prices have had a far more favourable evolution since the seventies than those of other commodities), total non-fuel primary exports from developed countries (at $210 bn) are far higher than from developing countries (at $96 bn). Furthermore, if trade between the 'North' and 'South' is examined, non-fuel primary exports from South to North (at $58 bn) are of a not very different order of magnitude to non-fuel primary exports from North to South (at $43 bn).[1] Thus, a scheme that would stabilise commodity prices—and possibly maintain them at a slightly higher level than the average in the eighties—would not only be of great benefit to developing economies (given the high share of primary exports in their total exports), but would also benefit producers and exporters of those commodities in the industrial world.

Looked at from this perspective, Kaldor's scheme has today far fewer potential negative distributional implications for industrial countries than it could have had in the mid sixties, as the structure of trade has been quite significantly modified.

Even though a commodity backed currency faces strong—and perhaps insuperable—opposition from industrial governments either owing to their ideology or to their

[1] It should be stressed that the definition of primary commodities used in the GATT data is broad, and therefore that of manufactures narrow; thus, many processed primary products (e.g. canned goods, refined oil), which would be regarded as manufactures in domestic production statistics, are excluded from the manufactured category in the trade statistics given in Table 1. This further strengthens the point that raw primary product exports from developing countries are not as major an item in world trade as is generally perceived.

perception of their economies' self-interest, such a proposal still either receives support or at least serious consideration from those concerned with the prospect of international monetary reform, from the point of view of the interests of the developing countries. Thus, the Arusha *South North* Conference in 1980 had, as its central recommendation, 'the establishment of an international currency unit as the international means of exchange and primary reserve asset' (see *Development Dialogue*, 1980). Authors, like Stewart and Sengupta (1984), Williamson (1987) and Bird (1987) who analyse international monetary issues, either partly or mainly from a developing country perspective, tend to give consideration to a commodity-backed currency, though they are not necessarily convinced of its technical advantages.

This leads us to an examination of the more technical criticisms of Kaldor's scheme of a commodity-backed currency, mainly voiced by critics sympathetic to his scheme. Even if the ideological and political climate changed very significantly (which seems at present fairly unlikely, thought not impossible) and there was greater support for the governments' deliberately regulating the world economy as well as for a greater acceptance of developing countries' interests in the structuring of the international monetary system, it is unclear whether a commodity-backed currency would be technically an optimal solution. It is to these more technical objections to Kaldor's scheme to which we now briefly turn.

The clearest disadvantage of a commodity-backed international currency is the high cost of commodity storage; this problem was in fact recognised by Hart *et al.* themselves, who estimated the *gross* cost to amount to as much as 3–3½% *a year* of the value of the stock; an opponent of the scheme, Grubel (1965) estimated a higher cost, of around 6%. Stewart and Sengupta (1984) estimated that at 1980 prices this would imply an amount in the range of US $20 billion to US $80 billion, clearly a very significant figure! The above estimates reflect the gross private running costs of such a scheme. However, it could be argued, as Bird (1987) does, that, firstly, the net private cost could be lowered, if the buffer stock made a profit in its commodity transactions. More importantly, the net social cost would differ from the net private cost for several reasons. The existence of the 'Kaldorian' buffer stocks could reduce the need for other stocks; also, confidence in the long-term viability of the stock could encourage private speculators to operate in a price stabilising way; most importantly, the world economy would benefit from the scheme owing to more stable growth, higher levels of employment and a lower rate of inflation. However, in any attempt to implement the Kaldor scheme, it would be the gross private running costs which would initially have to be financed, and for which financial support, mainly from the industrial governments, would have to be found. This seems a major barrier, not only in present circumstances but also in future ones.

More specific technical objections have also been raised. For example, Bird (1987) has argued that stabilising prices may in some cases not stabilise export earnings, but in fact de-stabilise them. Stewart and Sengupta (1984) have also argued that a commodity reserve currency provides stability of commodity prices in terms of the bancor units, but not in terms of manufactured goods prices. Such technical problems could probably be overcome, but at the cost of introducing further complexity in an already much complicated scheme.

The advantages of a commodity reserve currency are basically those so lucidly outlined in the writings of Kaldor, as well as in Hart *et al.* (1964) (see Section 2.2 above). These relate to more rapid and stable world economic growth, to more stable commodity prices, and—particularly—to more sustained growth amongst primary commodity exporting economies. Some of the functions of such a commodity reserve currency could however be achieved by unbacked international currency, if it were properly developed.

Given that, unlike in 1964, there already exists an unbacked international currency, the SDR, the discussion today needs to relate to the extent to which replacement by a commodity reserve currency would be superior to an improvement of the SDR itself. For governments concerned with improving the international monetary system in ways which make it both more stable *and* more functional to stable and widespread economic growth, a strong pitch for a commodity reserve currency would be justified only if the technical advantages were very obvious and a sufficient number of influential governments could easily be persuaded of this. So long as this is not the case, pressure for commodity backed currency would be a waste of both technical expertise and bargaining time.

A commodity currency could potentially have important advantages over the existing SDR system, some of them clearly demonstrated by recent experience. In particular, the counter-cyclical element of issue would operate far more automatically under a commodity currency than under the existing SDR system, which has no trigger criterion for issuing SDRs automatically or semi-automatically, when the world economy—or sections of it—have a scarcity of international liquidity. This problem could be overcome by providing an element of automaticity into SDR issue, but such automaticity would emerge more naturally from a commodity-backed currency. A commodity-backed currency would also have other advantages, if viewed from the point of view of the developing countries, in that it would be particularly counter-cyclical in the first instance, as regards their own economies, as the variable to be stabilised would be commodity prices. For those who view world economic growth as a positive-sum game, this could be an advantage. However, for those who (incorrectly according to Kaldor) view world economic growth as more of a zero-sum game, the fact that in the *first* round the counter-cyclical benefits go to developing countries could be viewed as a disadvantage for industrial economies, and could be therefore opposed.

On tactical terms, Stewart and Sengupta's (1984) conclusion seems correct, that it is better to focus bargaining energy in the short term on improving the SDR, and attempting to incorporate some of the advantages of a commodity currency in those improvements, than to attempt the replacement of the SDR by a commodity-backed currency. This relates to the fact that commodity price stabilisation has even less support amongst industrial governments than improving the SDR. Kaldor's scheme tries to address simultaneously two major problems in the world economy: instability of commodity prices, as well as the possible relative deterioration of commodity prices *and* the resulting deflationary tendencies in the world economy, particularly in developing nations. Tactically, the problem is that opposition to any scheme which would try to stabilise commodity prices is stronger in industrial government circles than opposition to measures which could lead to increases in world demand (e.g. new issues of SDRs, or even expansion of compensatory financing for cases of commodity price decline). Thus, if developing country governments were to push all out for a Kaldor type scheme, they would risk destroying potential progress on more expansionary world demand, owing to opposition to a scheme that would also help stabilise commodity prices.

However, it should be stressed that progress in expanding world economic demand (e.g. via SDR issues or other measures) may not be enough to deal with commodity price problems. Indeed, during several years in the mid eighties, even when industrial countries' aggregate demand grew at a fairly rapid pace, commodity prices—in nominal terms and, even more, relative to manufacturing prices—either continued at their very low levels or—even worse—declined further. Although, since 1987, this negative trend in commodity prices has been somewhat reversed, the de-linking of growth in industrial countries and improved commodity prices that occurred in the mid eighties is a source of concern. It is possible that this combination in the mid eighties can be explained by factors specific to that period such as widespread debt crises; as many developing countries simultaneously faced the need to expand export volumes so as to increase export earnings, to fund their higher net financial transfers abroad, the aggregate sum of their actions implied an expansion of total commodity supply that had a deflationary effect on commodity prices. Thus, declining commodity prices were both an initial important cause of widespread debt crises, as well as an important consequence; this link occurred not only in the eighties, but also in previous periods, e.g. the thirties. A scheme such as Kaldor's would have broken such 'perverse' inter-linkages. If it is politically infeasible, ideologically unacceptable, or technically problematic (see above) to adopt price stabilisation schemes, alternative measures need to be designed internationally to face the problem of fluctuating—and, in certain periods—declining commodity prices. Amongst such measures are the improvement and broadening of international compensatory financing facilities as well as the financing of, and international support for, export diversification and import substitution for the countries whose exports are too heavily concentrated on one or a few commodities. These measures, differently from Kaldors's scheme, accept as inevitable market fluctuations of commodity prices, and seek to protect countries from these fluctuations, in the short term, by compensatory financing; and/or in the long term, by supporting and funding economic restructuring and diversification, in sectors which generate or save foreign exchange. Particularly to break the 'perverse' interaction between widespread debt crises and declining commodity prices described above, it would be useful to design lending instruments which link repayment of debt to commodity price evolution of countries' main exports, for example via commodity bonds; for handling the current debt crises of the eighties, measures of debt or interest relief could be related (amongst other factors) to the evolution of the commodity prices of countries' main exports.

Finally, in this context it should be stressed that, particularly in the 1981–88 period, there has been *no* significant movement *either* towards improving the SDR, enhancing its role or indeed issuing it, in a context when an important part of the world was starved of foreign exchange reserves. Political realism, at least in the Reagan years, did not take us far on any road of international monetary reform, or even of use of existing, potentially counter-cyclical, instruments for international monetary management!

Returning to Kaldor's own work, it should be perhaps mentioned again that in one of his final works (1983), Kaldor recognised that his 1964 scheme was very complex and had some inherent problems. He therefore not only simplified his scheme, but also related it to the existing SDR. As mentioned above, drawing far more directly on Keynes's recently disclosed work, Kaldor (1983) proposed a simpler scheme, in which separate buffer stocks operated for various commodities. Kaldor proposed that the net expenditure on these buffer stocks—run by an international agency for stabilising commodity prices—would be funded by SDRs. Though simpler and less detailed his later scheme ends up with a fairly similar product to that of his 1964 scheme, 'a basic money unit which can be guaranteed to be stable in terms of basic commodities'.

Finally, reviews of Kaldor's work in this field tend to focus exclusively on his brilliant schemes which are not—and perhaps never will be—implemented. However, it seems appropriate to stress a far more neglected aspect: that Kaldor made an important contribution to providing the theoretical background for the establishment of the compensatory financing facility (CFF) of the IMF. This is particularly important because the CFF was for a long time the only significant modification of the international monetary system, achieved mainly as a result of the pressure of developing country governments; it is also one of the few counter-cyclical mechanisms existing in the international monetary system (see, e.g., Griffith-Jones, 1986).

As early as 1952, Kaldor had prepared a paper that analysed the problem of how to offset, or minimise, the international propagation of cyclical fluctuations, a paper which contributed to the theoretical analysis beginning then within the United Nations and elsewhere on this subject. This debate contributed clearly to the establishment in 1962, by the IMF, of the above mentioned Compensatory Financing Facility. Hart *et al.* (1964) correctly welcomed this innovation, 'as the most encouraging development in the international monetary system since 1953'. The same principle behind the CFF was later applied to the EEC's compensatory facility, STABEX.

It is unfortunate, however, that in the mid 1980s, compensatory (and counter-cyclical) mechanisms were weakened by a reduction in the size of the CFF, and of its semi-automatic nature (Dell, 1985), precisely at a time of low and falling commodity prices as well as widespread debt crises when they were particularly important.

4. Kaldor's contribution

Nicholas Kaldor was perhaps the first major economist, after Keynes, to address the issues of international monetary reform from the perspective of growth in the world economy. In one sense, Kaldor went beyond Keynes in that he related the structure of an ideal international monetary system not just to the sustainment of aggregate demand and short-term growth but also to sustained investment and long-term development, particularly in the poorer parts of the world. It is especially in this context—of linking long-term development concerns with the operation of the international monetary system—that Kaldor's contribution to the latter field is the greatest. Though his work in this case is fairly widely quoted, it perhaps has not got the full attention it deserves, particularly as a basis for providing a powerful rationale for international monetary reform.

Thus, Kaldor's work on the commodity reserve currency is lasting not so much in the actual details of the scheme he proposed, as in the broad agenda of policy objectives and methodology of analysis which it sets.

Kaldor contributed in an important way to the creation of a school of economists, who analyse the operations of the international financial system in depth, but who do so from a perspective which gives priority to the achievement of goals in the real economy, with particular, though not exclusive, concern for the development needs of poorer countries. This tradition of analysis, embedded in Keynes's thinking, is represented by economists such as John Williamson, Sidney Dell and Gerald Helleiner; it seems appropriate to note that one of the distinguished followers of that tradition is Frances Stewart, Kaldor's daughter.

Like Kaldor—and Keynes before him—this school of economists have perceptively analysed the working and limitations of the international monetary system, and made innovative proposals for its improvement and reform. The proposals of this school of analysis have to an important extent—though *not* entirely—been unheeded, with rather serious costs to world economic growth and indeed with growing risk to the stability of important parts of the international monetary system. It is to be hoped that their influence will increase as time passes, and as the cost of ignoring their policy advice is more clearly perceived.

Bibliography

Bird, G. 1987. *International Financial Policy and Economic Development*, London, Macmillan

Cornia, A., Jolly, R. and Stewart, F. 1987. *Adjustment with a Human Face*, Oxford, OUP

Dell, S. 1985. The fifth credit tranche, *World Development*, vol. 13, no. 2

Development Dialogue 1980. no. 2

Griffith-Jones, S. 1986. Ways forward from the debt crisis, *Oxford Review of Economic Policy*, Spring

Griffith-Jones, S. and Sunkel, O. 1986. *The Crises of Debt and Development in Latin America*, Oxford, OUP

Grubel, H. 1965. The case against an International Reserve Currency, *Oxford Economic Papers*, vol. 17, no. 1

Hart, A. G., Kaldor, N. and Tinbergen, J. 1964. The case for an International Commodity Reserve Currency, in Kaldor, N., *Essays on Economic Policy, Vol. II*, Duckworth (originally 1963 as a memorandum submitted to UNCTAD)

Kaldor, N. 1964. Introduction, in Kaldor, N. *Essays on Economic Policy, Vol. II*, London, Duckworth

Kaldor, N. 1964. Foreign Trade and the Balance of Payments, in Kaldor, N., *Essays on Economic Policy, Vol. II*, Duckworth (originally 1952)

Kaldor, N. 1973. Problems and Prospects of International Monetary Reform, *The Banker*, September

Kaldor, N. 1976. Inflation and Recession in the World Economy, *The Economic Journal*, December, pp. 703–714

Kaldor, N. 1983. The Role of Commodity Prices in Economic Recovery, *Lloyds Bank Review*, July 1983; also reproduced in *World Development*, vol. 15, no. 5, 1987

Moggridge, D. (ed.) 1980. *The Collected Writings of J.M. Keynes Vol. XXVII, Activities 1940–46. Shaping the Post-War World: Employment and Commodities*, London, Macmillan

Stewart, F. and Sengupta A. 1984. *Framework for International Cooperation*, Oxford, Frances Pinter

Thirlwall, A. 1987. *Nicholas Kaldor*, Brighton, Wheatsheaf Books

Williamson, J. 1987. Valuation of the SDR: the case for a standard five currency basket, in S. Dell (ed.), *The International Monetary system and its Reform*, Part II, North Holland

Wood, A. 1987. Kaldor, N. (1908–1986), in Eatwell, J. *et al.* (eds) *The New Palgrave*, London, Macmillan innovative proposals for its improvement and reform. The proposals of this school of analysis have to an important extent—though not entirely—been unheeded, with rather serious costs to world economic growth and indeed with growing risk to the stability of important parts of the international monetary system. It is to be hoped that their influence will increase as time passes, and as the cost of ignoring their policy advice is more clearly perceived.

Bibliography

Bird, G. 1987. *International Financial Policy and Economic Development*, London, Macmillan

Cornia, G., Jolly, R. and Stewart, F. 1987. *Adjustment with a Human Face*, Oxford, OUP

Dell, S. 1985. 'The Fifth Credit Tranche', *World Development*, vol. 13, no. 2.

Development Dialogue 1980, no. 2.

Griffith-Jones, S. 1986. 'Ways forward from the debt crisis', *Oxford Review of Economic Policy*, Spring

Griffith-Jones, S. and Sunkel, O. 1986. *The Crisis of Debt and Development in Latin America*, Oxford, OUP

Grubel, H. 1963. 'The case against an International Reserve Currency', *Oxford Economic Papers*, vol. 15, no. 1

Hart, A. G., Kaldor, N. and Tinbergen, J. 1964. 'The case for an International Commodity Reserve Currency', in Kaldor, N., *Essays on Economic Policy*, Vol. II, Duckworth (originally 1963 as a memorandum submitted to UNCTAD)

Kaldor, N. 1964. 'Introduction', in Kaldor, N., *Essays on Economic Policy*, Vol. II, London Duckworth

Kaldor, N. 1964. 'Foreign Trade and the Balance of Payments', in Kaldor, N., *Essays on Economic Policy*, Vol. II, Duckworth (originally 1962)

Kaldor, N. 1973. 'Problems and Prospects of International Monetary Reform', *The Banker*, September

Kaldor, N. 1976. 'Inflation and Recession in the World Economy', *The Economic Journal*, December, pp. 703–714

Kaldor, N. 1983. 'The Role of Commodity Prices in Economic Recovery', *Lloyds Bank Review*, July; also reproduced in *World Development*, vol. 15, no. 5, 1987

Stewart, M. 1983. *Controlling the Economic Future*, [illegible]

Stewart, F. and Sengupta, A. 1982. *International Financial Cooperation*, London, Frances Pinter

Thirlwall, A. P. 1987. *Nicholas Kaldor*, Brighton, Wheatsheaf Books

Williamson, J. 1987. [illegible]

Worswick, [illegible] Macmillan

Nicholas Kaldor on Indian economic problems

Sukhamoy Chakravarty*

Nicholas Kaldor was a very well known name in Indian economic circles long before he visited India to teach at the 'Summer School' which was organised by the International Economic Association at Poona in 1955. He made a profound impact on the minds of his audience, especially on the younger generation of economists most of whom had started their careers as University teachers. I remember quite well how some of our own teachers at Calcutta University who had been to Poona came back with a fresh perspective on issues relating to growth and development. Amongst the lecturers at Poona the two who seemed to have left the greatest imprint on the perceptions of their students were Nicholas Kaldor and Joan Robinson. Joan Robinson had by that time completed her major piece of work *The Accumulation of Capital*, which shook the complacency of many who had earlier led themselves to be persuaded that there was little scope for major new thinking in the theory of production generally presented in the Hicksian fashion. I am here referring to the Hicks of the *Theory of Wages* and also of *Value and Capital*. Kaldor was at that time engaged in the complementary job of working out a non-neoclassical theory of distribution. In fact, his deservedly famous paper, 'Alternative theories of distribution' was published in the *Review of Economic Studies* in 1955–56, and has continued to remain influential.

After the Summer School was over, Kaldor was invited by Professor P. C. Mahalanobis, then the presiding spirit at the Indian Statistical Institute, to deliver some lectures. Mahalanobis was at that time busy working out the 'plan frame' for the Indian Second Five Year Plan at the special request of Prime Minister Nehru. Kaldor was initially requested by Mahalanobis, and subsequently by the Government of India, to look into the resource mobilisation dimension of the newly proposed Five Year Plan, which envisaged a quantum jump in size over the previous Plan.

This was an important request as the Second Plan reflected a new economic strategy, not merely in terms of size, but also in terms of its priorities. A Taxation Enquiry Committee had already submitted a report on the structural aspects of the problem of taxation, but, in view of changed economic perceptions, it was judged somewhat inadequate. Kaldor had just finished his work on *An Expenditure Tax* (1955) and was willing to have a look at the Indian tax system, which he believed would provide him with an occasion to assess the relevance of his ideas on taxation. He took up his assignment to write a comprehensive report on the Indian tax system in the middle of January, 1956 and worked continuously on it till the end of March. In his letter of transmittal to the then

*Delhi School of Economics.

Finance Minister, C. D. Deshmukh, who was also Chairman of the Indian Statistical Institute, he clearly stated that his approach constituted a radical departure from the practice prevailing at that time and that, therefore, a national debate was urgently called for, if the government was to implement the suggestions it contained.

Kaldor's report entitled 'Indian Tax Reform', issued by the Department of Economic Affairs, Ministry of Finance, indeed provoked a great deal of discussion amongst economists, policy makers and revenue administrators.[1]

It is sometimes thought that the 'Report' was merely an attempt to render plausible for India the proposal for an expenditure tax, an idea that Kaldor had already developed in the context of the earlier work in UK.[2] This is, however, an oversimplification. First, the Report was a fairly comprehensive document, although it concentrated on issues of personal and business taxation, because of limitations of time. Second, Kaldor put forward a philosophy of taxation which was geared towards the need for greater resource mobilisation which would permit the required acceleration in growth to take place in the Indian situation without putting undue upward pressure on prices. Third, it was a very healthy complement to Mahalanobis' 'physical' view of planning when applied in real time to conditions of an economically backward mixed economy. Mahalanobis, it may be recalled, was inclined to think that what was physically possible must be financially feasible. This had led him to leave a large 'uncovered gap' on the resources side in his 'Plan frame', a feature which had generated a great deal of anxiety about inflation. It was part of Kaldor's job to show that, with a suitable re-definition of taxable capacity as well as a thorough reform of tax administration, the additional revenue projected for the Second Plan could indeed be realised to a very substantial extent.

Kaldor was quite enthusiastic about his assignment, as he believed himself to be in fundamental agreement with Mahalanobis on the need to accelerate the growth rate as well as on the enhanced role of the state in promoting economic development.

Throughout his life Kaldor remained of the opinion that developing countries which had opted for a mixture of institutional motive forces, private, public and cooperative, must adopt a sound programme of taxation, which would promote growth while leaving the degree of inequality in the distribution of income and wealth at a low level. India seemed to provide him with an interesting opportunity to try out these ideas. His basic convictions on this point are expressed not only in his 'India Report', but also in several articles which are printed in Vol. II of his *Essays on Economic Policy* (1964B). To illustrate this point, we may quote one typical passage from the opening paragraph of the article that he published in *Economic Weekly*, Annual Number, January 1958. Kaldor writes there,

> An effective system of progressive direct taxation is vital to the survival of democratic institutions in India. The need for this arises not merely on financial grounds—to raise adequate resources for purposes of accelerated economic development—but in order to bring about the degree of social cohesion and cooperation that is essential for the successful functioning of the democratic system (1958A).

This shows that Kaldor was not merely looking at the tax reform problems as narrowly defined revenue generating exercises, but as part of a wider process of bringing about broader structural changes within a democratic economic environment.

[1] This report has now been reprinted without the letter of transmittal in Kaldor, 1980B.

[2] For example, a well-known expert on public finance, Professor Raja J. Chelliah, wrote in his book, *Fiscal Policy in Underdeveloped Countries*, 'Kaldor's ideas on direct taxation have been expounded at length in his book *An Expenditure Tax*. For the most part, his "Report" to the Indian context seeks to apply these ideas to the Indian case' (Chelliah, 1969, p. 129).

This viewpoint is reinforced if we recall the fact that Kaldor was an economist of the highest standing, who had recently shifted his attention from his earlier preoccupation with economic theory and problems of stabilising employment levels in mature economies to problems of development and underdevelopment. He may have been influenced in this regard by the example of G. Myrdal, with whom he had worked in Geneva at the Secretariat of the Economic Commission for Europe.

Even before Kaldor first visited India, he was therefore becoming concerned about the unduly divergent growth rates that the world economy had experienced since 1750 and the likely outcomes for global stability, a concern that only increased over the following years and which is also reflected in his last published book, *Economics without Equilibrium*(1985). His early essay on this subject, delivered at Milan in 1954, had already emphasised two points which are relevant in the present context (see Kaldor, 1960). The very first point he highlighted was the emergence of an 'agricultural surplus' in presently developing countries and its deployment in productive pursuits. The second point was connected with '*technical dynamism*', which was reflected in the growing share of profit incomes in national production characteristic of fast-growing capitalist market economies. Kaldor was not clear what caused certain societies to be more dynamic technologically than others. He was of the opinion that an adequate answer must go beyond the narrow limits imposed by formal economic theory. He was highly appreciative of the work of Marx and Schumpeter on these issues, but felt that a great deal more analysis was called for, especially in regard to contemporary capitalism. Amongst the factors influencing technical dynamism he felt that attitudes towards risk taking were particularly important.

For an economically backward country like India, with 80% of the population engaged in agriculture in the mid fifties, an agricultural transition was first order business. He felt that this transition could be facilitated by an appropriate system of land taxation. While the report he prepared for India was not directly concerned with this problem, in work contemporaneous with or subsequent to his 'India Report', he strongly emphasised the vital necessity for an effective land tax both for increasing the efficiency of land use, as well as for mopping up the agricultural surplus for productive investment outside agriculture (see Kaldor, 1964A, pp. 225–54, especially pp. 232–7). Kaldor did not believe in a 'squeeze agriculture' thesis; what he was emphasising was the necessity for siphoning off a considerable part of the agricultural surplus which went into satisfying merely 'rentier' consumption, in order to sustain additional wage payments in industry. He believed that a two-way relationship between industry and agriculture could be mutually self-propelling in an upward direction. The argument is stated most succinctly in his Cornell Lectures on 'Strategic factors in economic development' (Kaldor, 1967), although it appears in several other places as well. Kaldor's basic perception on this point would appear to me to be fundamentally valid for Indian economy even today, although in many other ways the economy has changed since he wrote these essays (see Chakravarty, 1987).

As is well-known, Kaldor's argument for an expenditure tax was based on a neo-Keynesian approach to 'public finance'. The heart of this approach was the use of taxation as an instrument to regulate the level of private spending in relation to the capacity for generating output. Private spending may have to be restrained in order to release real resources for sustaining real public investment in infrastructure, health or directly productive sectors. Kaldor believed that, in devising a tax policy, primary emphasis has to be on the 'release of real resources', while care should be taken not to blunt the incentives for economic agents to a undue extent. He did not subscribe to the view that savings acted as a direct constraint on growth. In Kaldor's view, causality ran from investment to savings, a common feature of post-Keynesian thought. But he did not believe that a high level of public investment was sustainable without adverse distributional shifts unless private spending power was curbed to release resources which would allow long-run growth potential to be built up. This was particularly true of a developing country like India, which needed investment in health, education, infrastructure, etc. which the market would either not undertake at all, or at best undertake on an inadequate scale. That is why he believed that two changes were especially important. One was to restrict the growth of luxury consumption and the other was to check tax evasion. He favoured expenditure as an important measure of 'taxable capacity', in India, to be used alongside taxation of income, and net wealth. The logic of this 'multi-criterion approach' is argued in his 'India Report' and not in his original book 'An Expenditure Tax'.[1] He also felt the need to devise a self-checking system of reporting for tax purposes. He suggested an integrated approach to income, expenditure and wealth taxation in order to create such a system of taxation, which would provide economic incentives while reducing the degree of inequality in the long-run distribution of wealth. This was no doubt a very complex task and it is doubtful whether Kaldor, despite all his ingenuity, was able to fathom all the institutional complexities pertaining to the Indian situation. While he was not lacking in boldness, he was careful (to the extent time permitted) to go into the details of revenue administration with the support provided by the Ministry of Finance.

Very briefly, the proposals for tax reform which he put forward and were much discussed at the time his Report was released consisted of the following items:

(a) limiting the maximum marginal rate of taxation to 45% of taxable income plus the existing surcharge. Taxable income was inclusive of capital gains;

(b) a property tax ranging from one-third of 1% to $1\frac{1}{2}$%, with a minimum exemption limit at Rs. 100,000;

(c) levying of an expenditure tax on personal outlay in excess of Rs. 10,000 per adult (a child counted as one-half adult);

(d) the imposition of an inheritance tax and gift tax;

(e) drastic reform of company taxation, which struck him as 'a perfect maze of unnecessary complications, the fruits of years of futile endeavour to reconcile fundamentally irreconcilable objectives'; and

(f) a reform of business profit tax by disallowing various types of so-called business expenses. In particular, entertainment expenses were not to be allowed at all, or allowed only to a limited extent.

Kaldor's proposals were tried out by Mr T. T. Krischnamachari, the then Finance Minister of India, in one of the rare attempts at innovative budget-making in India. However, the reforms based on Kaldor's recommendations which emerged from the parliamentary debates were limited and half-hearted, because of the opposition from various quarters. Besides, there was always the argument based on administrative feasibility. Kaldor himself expressed great unhappiness over the way in which the attempt was actually made to implement his proposals, especially because what he believed to be the essential props of his system were found to be missing, i.e. the main reporting system he prepared and the large reduction in existing rate schedules, especially on income tax.[2]

[1] This partial change in point of view was subsequently endorsed by him in a paper that he wrote for a Brooking Conference in 1978. It was reprinted in Kaldor, 1980B, pp. 230–249.

[2] On Kaldor's reaction to T. T. Krishnamachari's budget efforts, see Kaldor, 1958A. In the Brookings paper (1978), Kaldor reviewed the Indian experience. While dismissing the 'outcome as a joke', he said that the main provision that crippled the tax was that 'liability to the tax was tied to an income limit and not a minimum expenditure limit' (see Kaldor, 1980A, p. 238).

In 1983, Kaldor visited India to deliver the newly initiated C. D. Deshmukh Memorial Lecture at the Reserve Bank of India. The lecture was devoted to a critique of 'monetarism' and was largely a reiteration of Kaldor's views on this topic. He decided to refrain from discussing the question of an appropriate monetary policy for India, probably because he had very little time to study the problem during his short visit. At the request of the then Prime Minister, Mrs Indira Gandhi, he wrote a brief paper on 'An Exchange Rate Policy for India', which was published in the *Economic and Political Weekly* a few months later (see Kaldor, 1984). This brief paper is more interesting for providing Kaldor's assessment of Indian development strategy as it had evolved over the years since the Second Plan than for suggesting any policy initiative that Kaldor had not broached earlier in his writings. The main policy proposal concerned the institution of a dual exchange rate system along with a phased reduction of tariffs over time. Kaldor expressed the view that the process of import substituting industrialisation had almost run its full course in India, while admitting that the so-called 'Mahalanobis strategy' had greatly broadened India's economic base. He feared that sustained growth in home demand through increased agricultural production as well as through public investment might be inadequate for achieving a high enough growth rate for industry. It was necessary therefore to devote serious attention to export promotion. Kaldor rejected, however, the usual IMF proposal for devaluation with respect to India, more or less for the same reasons that he had expressed for several other semi-industrialised countries.

Basically, Kaldor thought that the proposal for a dual exchange rate, mooted for the first time in the sixties in an ECLA paper, would apply in the case of India in the 1980s. However, he was realistic enough to suggest that 'given the weight of existing import controls, it might cause too much disruption if all forms of controls were abolished at the same time as the dual exchange rate is introduced' (1978, pp. 202–13).

Kaldor's proposals for reforms of the exchange rate system were not worked out in any degree of detail and were largely based on the impressions that he had gathered from discussions with concerned officials. Furthermore, since the rupee was not consistently floating down with the dollar, and the government were soon to embark on a policy of import liberalisation, Kaldor's proposals did not give rise to any significant debate on this occasion.

The interesting point to note is that Kaldor did not display any great concern in his 1984 article with the general problems facing the world economy, possibly because he thought that India's trade share was too insignificant to matter. Furthermore, he had, I believe, too easily dismissed his own earlier argument for treating the growth of marketable surplus from agriculture as leading to an expansion of the home market for Indian industry. It is not quite clear whether he was properly briefed on this point about the state of India's agriculture, or whether he had changed his basic argument on this point. The latter explanation seems less plausible, as his subsequently published volume 'Further Essays on Economic Theory' shows (Kaldor, 1978).

How do we assess the significance of Kaldor's writings on India? There are basically two approaches that one can adopt. The first, and the obvious one, would be to take up for re-examination the specifics of various proposals that he made in the area of taxation as well as in the area of reform of exchange rates. During the fifties, as noted, Kaldor's work on India largely centred around the reform of the tax system. As regards his ideas on dual exchange rates, they were first published in the ECLA *Bulletin* in the early sixties. It was only in the context of his last visit to India in 1983 that he was persuaded to produce a memorandum for consideration by the Government of India which dealt with the problem of how best to increase India's exports in the context of newly emerging pressure on the balance of payments. While Kaldor's tax proposals were never really given a chance to show their effectiveness, they were at least discussed widely and left some impression on the intellectual climate of opinion.[1] In contrast, his proposals on the reform of the exchange rate regime were hardly discussed, perhaps because they were already well-known from his early writings and partly because they were not backed up by the kind of detailed analysis that went into his early work on taxation.

It would appear to me that not much of substance can be gleaned from the study of the detailed set of recommendations that Kaldor devised to show the administrative feasibility of his integrated system of income, expenditure and wealth taxation. Kaldor's analysis on the details of feasibility of his proposed tax reform have (understandably) dated a great deal. The same cannot be said to be true of his general approach towards taxation. Much of what he had to say on the role of taxation in creating a progressive and equitable society remains valid for India even today. If anything, the importance of restraining the growth of non-essential consumption through a carefully balanced set of taxes has increased. This is often contested on the grounds that Kaldor-type tax proposals will take away incentives and thus dampen the growth of productive forces. It is further contended that the state should reduce its draft on private incomes, because the efficiency of public investment is low relative to that of private investment. These arguments cannot be accepted as analytically sound, even if one were to concede that methods of tax collection leave considerable scope for evasion and lead to large, effectively unequal, burdens on different segments of the population.

One of Kaldor's major points was to emphasise that, in the context of overall economic management, it is necessary not merely to raise the ratio of tax to GDP, but also to make sure that the increase in the tax revenue is achieved in a desirable way. In other words, it is not merely the magnitude of the additional tax effort that matters, but also its *composition*. I believe that there are three principal reasons why Kaldor's general approach remains valid today. First of all, even if India's ratio of taxation to gross domestic product has come up from around 7%, which was Kaldor's estimate at the time he submitted his report, to around 20% in 1985–86, an increase which cannot be regarded as insignificant, it is also a fact that the composition of revenue has shifted very sharply away from direct taxation towards indirect taxation. The following table shows the picture at a glance:

Table 1. *Tax ratios in the Indian economy as % of GDP*

Period	Direct tax	Indirect tax	Total tax revenue
1970/71 to 1974/75	3·15	11·40	14·55
1975/76 to 1979/80	3·67	14·16	17·83
1980/81 to 1984/85	3·19	15·52	18·71
1985/86	3·03	16·99	20·02

Source: National Accounts Statistics, CSO.

Kaldor would definitely have deplored the composition shift shown in the table as he always considered indirect taxes as very blunt instruments from the point of view of ensuring equitable growth, even if they were selectively designed to fall upon upper class

[1] For a careful contemporaneous assessment of Kaldor's tax proposals, see Lakdawala, 1956.

consumption, which is not the case in India. The reasons for his view are, of course, not difficult to discern. They are stated very clearly in his book on *An Expenditure Tax* (1955) and could hardly be seriously questioned. Yet the fact remains that the Indian tax administration has found it increasingly convenient to rely on this undesirable mode of revenue raising. The explanation lies to a certain extent in the area of administrative convenience, but more importantly in the domain of fiscal sociology.

The second argument highlighting the need for appropriate tax reform is that the pattern of public current expenditure has shifted in the direction of interest payments, subsidies and defence, and cannot therefore be said adequately to offset the regressiveness of the tax system.

Third, the positive role of the state in the economic arena still lies mainly in the area of public investment, especially in the sectors dealing with irrigation, health, education, transport, the environment, etc. This growing need has to be met not through a policy of tapping private savings through borrowing at fairly high rates of interest with the aim of avoiding what some people describe as an 'internal debt trap', but through a system of progressive direct taxation, if the desired goals of growth with equity are to be met.

In order of importance, what is most urgently needed is a progressive land tax (a tax whose importance Kaldor strongly emhasised), a system of taxation of income fully inclusive of capital gains, and an effective system of taxation of net wealth. Given the difficulties of administration, a general expenditure tax would probably be less effective than a properly chosen system of partial outlay taxation.

Furthermore, what Kaldor had to say in his memorandum for the Planning Commission in 1958 on the size of the Third Plan is still applicable for determining the size of the Eighth Plan. 'The problem as a whole', he wrote, 'should be considered far more as one of increasing the production of various kinds of goods, rather than as one of attaining certain investment targets either in terms of crores or as a percentage of the national income' (Kaldor, 1958B).

Our analysis has shown that Nicholas Kaldor's interest in Indian development problems led him to formulate suggestions concerning taxation and plan financing which involved both an application of ideas developed in a more general setting to the Indian situation, as well as a number of relevant extensions. It is well-known that Kaldor's interest in taxation was derived from a much more fundamental concern with problems of steering economic change and progress in a mixed economy. While much of his applied writing had as its principal focus problems facing the UK economy, he found time to study the problems of Latin America and India. In addition, as a theorist he was profoundly influenced by the work of Allyn Young who presented a highly perceptive, and as yet incompletely worked-out analysis of economic growth. The paradigm of growth that emerges from Kaldor's later writings can be best described as the Smith–Young–Kaldor paradigm. While Kaldor himself did not attempt any application of such an ambitious scheme of reasoning to the development problems of India, in his last book *Economics without Equilibrium*, economists, both in India and abroad, have been offered an analytical perspective which deserves to be explored in depth.

Bibliography

Chakravarty, S. 1987. *Development Planning—The Indian Experience*, Oxford, OUP

Chelliah, R. J. 1969. *Fiscal Policy in Underdeveloped Countries* (2nd edition), London, George Allen & Unwin

Kaldor, N. 1955. *An Expenditure Tax*, London, George Allen & Unwin

Kaldor, N. 1956. 'Indian Tax Reform', New Delhi, Government of India, Ministry of Finance, Department of Economic Affairs

Kaldor, N. 1958A. 'Tax Reform in India', *Economic Weekly*, Annual Number, January, reprinted in Kaldor, 1964B (vol. I)

Kaldor, N. 1958B. 'Problems of the Indian Third Five Year Plan', reprinted in Kaldor, 1964B (vol. II)

Kaldor, N. 1960. 'Characteristics of Economic Development', reprinted in *Economic Stability and Growth*, London, Duckworth

Kaldor, N. 1964A. 'The Role of Taxation in Economic Development', reprinted in Kaldor, 1964B

Kaldor, N. 1964B. *Essays in Economic Policy*, vols I and II, London, Duckworth

Kaldor, N. 1964C. 'Dual Exchange Rate and Economic Development', reprinted in 'Essays in Economic Development', pp. 178–200, London, Duckworth

Kaldor, N. 1967. *Strategic Factors in Economic Development*, Ithaca, Cornell University Press

Kaldor, N. 1978. 'What is wrong with Economic Theory', reprinted in *Further Essays in Economic Theory*, London, Duckworth

Kaldor, N. 1980A. *Essays on Taxation—I,* London, Duckworth

Kaldor, N. 1980B. *Reports on Taxation—II,* London, Duckworth

Kaldor, N. 1984. 'An Exchange Rate Policy for India', *Economic and Political Weekly*, July 14, pp. 1093–95

Kaldor, N. 1985. *Economics without Equilibrium*, Cardiff, University College, Cardiff Press

Lakdawala, D. T. 1956. *Taxes and the Plan*, Bombay, Popular Book Depot

Kaldor on the 'discreet charm' of the Chilean bourgeoisie

J. Gabriel Palma and Mario Marcel*

1. Introduction

Nicholas Kaldor belonged to a rapidly disappearing breed of economists who take the problems of the 'real world' seriously, and who in so doing recognise that mathematics is not a useful substitute for economic analysis. Kaldor's contribution to political economy covers an amazing range of topics, to which his eight volumes of *Collected Economic Essays* testify. Thus, it comes as no surprise to find in one of them an article on the economic problems of Chile, which he wrote during a visit to that country in 1956, as a consultant to the United Nations' Economic Commission for Latin America (ECLA).[1] In this article, Kaldor attempts to answer the difficult but fundamental question of why a country with such enormous potential for economic development (human and natural) could only manage a disappointing rate of economic growth:

> Chile, like many other countries in Latin America, is apt to strike the European observer as a country of vast economic potentialities which remain unexploited ... There can be little doubt that the combination of natural and human resources of the country—its climate and geology, its mineral resources as well as the potential fertility of its soil, the natural vitality and intelligence of its population derived from a combination of strains of European stock which in the similar climatic but different social environment of North America produced spectacular results—are as favourable, if not more favourable, than that of the economically most developed nations of the globe ... If it remains essentially an under-developed country—as by the test of the standard of living of the bulk of its population, it must undoubtedly bo so classified—this must perforce be due to predominantly social factors which hamper the free development of productive forces ... *Indeed, one's general impression is that the obstacles in the path of an accelerated improvement are neither natural, technical nor economic, but essentially political* ... 1956B, pp. 234–5; the emphasis is ours).

The essence of his analysis can be summarised in two propositions. First, Chile's low rate of accumulation was not the result of insufficient capacity to generate investable resources, but of the peculiar consumption, savings and investment behaviour of the local property-

*University of Cambridge and CIEPLAN, Santiago respectively. We should like to thank Lord Kaldor's family and Professor Thirlwall for having allowed us access to Kaldor's private files. We should also like to thank those of ECLA's 'old guard' of the 1950s, particularly Celso Furtado, Anibal Pinto, Alfonso Santa Cruz and Osvaldo Sunkel for providing us with very helpful information. Finally, we should also like to thank Geoff Harcourt, Tony Lawson, Ana Maria Olivares, Ann Newton, Luis Ortega, Ajit Singh, John Sender, Ignês Sodré, Daniel Sodré Hahn, Elizabeth Spillius, Frances Stewart, Lance Taylor and Tony Thirlwall for their stimulating co-operation. Lastly, we are very grateful to two anonymous referees for their many contributions.

[1] Kaldor (1956B). Quotations in the text are from the 1964B version. Kaldor also published the part on inflation of his paper in *Panorama Economico* (1957B).

owning class. Second, Chile's persistent inflation had not provided the economic environment conducive to fast and sustained economic growth.

Kaldor's analysis of Chile's accumulation and inflation problems have to be understood within the context of wider debates in the North at that time. The first relates to the controversies surrounding the post-Keynesian analysis of growth and distribution, initiated by Harrod's seminal work, and to which Kaldor had already made important contributions. His analysis of this persistent inflation, in turn, should be understood within the context of a growing school of thought—including Harrod, Kalecki and the emerging Latin American 'Structuralist School'—which attempted to analyse inflation as the result of both 'capacity constraints' in some sectors of the economy (which produce 'primary', or 'initial' upward pressure on prices) and 'propagation mechanisms' (by which price increases feed back into themselves).

Finally, it is important to point out that Kaldor's analysis, although connected with the 'Structuralist School', did not follow the mainstream of ECLA thought at the time. While the latter located the essence of the LDC's economic problems *outside* the LDCs (in the international division of labour and the unequal distribution of gains from trade), Kaldor emphasised that the key problem for Chile's economy did not lie outside the country but *inside* it—basically, in the absence of a really *progressive entrepreneurial class*. The 'external factors' did add to the country's economic problem, but by themselves could not account for Chile's unsatisfactory economic record.

2. Kaldor in Chile

Kaldor visited Chile for three months in 1956, having been invited by Raul Prebisch to work for ECLA at its headquarters in Santiago. His main task was to advise this Institution in their first studies on fiscal policies for developing countries. Prebisch had written to him:

> . . . I had hoped that you would be able to come here for an extended period in order to familiarise yourself thoroughly with the material we have gathered on fiscal policy in relation to economic development. With time to study this material properly, you would be in a position to make a contribution to the practical and theoretical aspects of the influence of fiscal policy on investments in countries at various stages of development (Prebisch to Kaldor, 25 May, 1955).

As it happened, Kaldor worked for ECLA between June and September 1956, but he partially modified the original purpose of the visit by also writing his paper on the Chilean economy.

The 1956 sabbatical year was one of the most influential periods for Kaldor's thinking on development economics. Before coming to Chile, Kaldor visited India to advise the government on the tax issues concerning the Indian Second Five Year Plan. This gave rise to his well-known *Report on Indian Tax Reform* which laid down the basis for his subsequent advice to several developing countries on taxation. While in India, Kaldor was unexpectedly invited to China; he considered this a unique opportunity to visit the country, then practically closed to Westerners. In China, he met Mao Tse Tung and delivered his well-known critique of the Marxist theory of capitalist development (1956A). Later, he toured several Japanese universities, lecturing on some of his favourite topics, leaving for the US early in June, where he stayed with Tibor Scitovsky at Stanford. Finally, after brief stops in Mexico and Lima, he arrived in Santiago at the end of June. Later in the year, Kaldor travelled to Brazil, where he attended a meeting of the International Economic Association and gave several lectures that contained his first systematic formulation of the link between agriculture and industrialisation in developing countries (1957A).

During his first month in Santiago, Kaldor gave about twenty lectures to a special training programme for Latin American economists organised by ECLA.[1] As Thirlwall has noted, these lectures (which were never published) put forward for the first time several topics—for example, the principle of cumulative causation—which would become major features in Kaldor's later thinking (see Thirlwall, 1987, p. 202).

In the remaining two months at ECLA, Kaldor was asked to assist its staff in the preparation of a study on 'monetary and fiscal policies' in relation to the requirements of economic development in Latin America', to be presented at the following general session of ECLA, in May 1957.[2]

During these last two months Kaldor wrote his paper on the economic problems of Chile. The latter puzzled a large number of economists and justified several UN missions to the country—one of them led by Lindahl—and several books by well-known economists in the US (e.g. Fetter, 1931 and Ellsworth, 1945). Kaldor had the major advantage of being able to use the (then still unpublished) first Chilean National Accounts.[3]

The study of the Chilean economy raised some new hypotheses that became central in Kaldor's work on developing countries. The first one concerned the violation in the LDCs of the traditional post-Keynesian assumptions of the saving behaviour of the capitalist class. In particular he stressed that contrast between the disproportionately high share of profits in Chile's national income and the strikingly low level of private saving. This made it economically (although not necessarily politically) possible to raise domestic saving substantially through taxation, without the need to reduce workers' income, and without requiring large capital inflows from abroad.[4]

The second hypothesis postulated by Kaldor concerned the peculiar macroeconomic role of the agricultural sector in developing countries. He identified agriculture as the main bottleneck that constrained growth and boosted inflation in the Chilean economy.

Kaldor's ideas certainly had a 'structuralist' flavour, but they were quite innovative in a period when most Latin American economists within this tradition were emphasising the 'external factors' affecting LDCs.[5] Although Kaldor's stress on the 'internal factors' was received with some scepticism by some leading ECLA economists, he was told that the paper would be published in their *Bulletin* by the end of that year.

Almost immediately after Kaldor left the country the paper came under open criticism in ECLA and its publication was delayed several times. Initially, the criticism concentrated on the statistical basis of Kaldor's study (the new National Accounts) and his interpretation of some of the concepts of these National Accounts;[6] and then, on the

[1] This was the ECLA/TAA Training Programme for Economic Development, an intensive programme organised by the Chilean economist Jorge Ahumada and attended by a dozen economists from all over Latin America, mostly holders of senior government posts in their countries.

[2] Unfortunately, there is no trace of this document nor evidence that it was ever presented at the ECLA meeting.

[3] CORFO (1957). These were the first Chilean National Accounts. The work had been carried out by CORFO, the public corporation in charge of the government's industrial policy which had actually been the leading institution in the development of the strategy of industrialisation through import substitution. CORFO had the most able group of technicians in the country and had carried out a wide range of studies on the Chilean economy. These National Accounts were later updated in CORFO (1963).

[4] For Kaldor, in a country like Chile when capital inflows become necessary, it would be for balance of payments purposes and not because of savings constraints.

[5] The exceptions to this rule were the studies on inflation. See section 3.2 below.

[6] This criticism can be found in a memorandum written by Juan Noyola and Osvaldo Sunkel, which was sent to Kaldor in August 1957. They emphasised the possibility that inappropriate exchange rates had been used in converting flows into foreign currency.

political feasibility of his main policy recommendation—to increase domestic saving by taxing capitalists' consumption.[1]

It was difficult for Kaldor to revise his figures and answer his critics from Cambridge and he became increasingly worried about the destiny of the paper, of whose main conclusions he remained convinced. His concern was increased by the leaking of some of its content (particularly his policy recommendations on taxation) during the presidential election campaign in Chile in 1958.

During the 1957/8 academic year Celso Furtado, who had previously worked for ECLA, was in Cambridge and shared Kaldor's concern over the mounting difficulties surrounding the paper's publication (see Furtado, 1985). Finally, in September 1958—two years after Kaldor had finished the article—ECLA's Executive Secretary told him that the paper was not going to be published in ECLA's *Bulletin*. He wrote to Kaldor:

> . . . to put the matter bluntly we have decided not to publish your article on Chile. The principal reason is that it has strong political overtones which make it inadvisable to publish it in a UN document . . . in the changed circumstances here in Chile where a new administration is taking over the Government (Swenson to Kaldor, 25 September 1958).

In fact, the right-wing parties supporting the newly-elected President had strongly criticised Kaldor's leaked article during the election campaign on account of its 'leftist' propositions, even though he was only proposing

> a more effective system of taxation (including special tax measures designed to increase the proportion of profits retained by enterprises) in order to reduce the proportion of property income allocated to personal consumption to a figure nearer to that of Britain (1956B, p. 261).

In search of a way out of the problem, ECLA's Executive Secretary wrote to the Mexican journal *El Trimestre Economico* to support its publication there. That journal was only too happy to accept it, and the article appeared immediately in April 1959.

During the next decade, Kaldor travelled with some regularity to Latin America, and he further elaborated some of the hypotheses and policy recommendations of his paper on Chile. He also advised the governments of Mexico, in 1960, and Venezuela, in 1976 (see Kaldor, 1960B and 1976, respectively).

In the 1960s Latin American economists became increasingly interested in Kaldor's thought. When in 1961 the Latin America Centre for Monetary Studies (CEMLA) published his lectures given in Mexico (see Kaldor, 1961), the book had an enthusiastic reception, and Kaldor was asked for permission to include his article on Chile in its second edition.

During the 1960s, Kaldor's analysis focused on the 'external factors' of Latin America's development, studying the foreign trade and terms of trade of the sub-continent. Kaldor wrote two articles on these subjects for ECLA and (this time) they were published in ECLA's *Bulletin* (see Kaldor, 1963 and 1964B).

From this point on, Kaldor reduced his visits abroad as he had become economic adviser to the Labour governments in the UK. However, he continued writing on Latin America, particularly on exchange rate policies and industrialisation (see, for example, Kaldor, 1974), remaining particularly well-informed about Chile. After the military coup of 1973 he used the new economic policies in Chile as an example of the ineffectiveness of monetarism in developing countries (Kaldor, 1985). He was amused when he learned

[1] It was obvious that ECLA's objections to Kaldor's paper were only related to his analysis of accumulation and his radical tax proposals. In fact, ECLA raised no objection to Kaldor immediately publishing the second part of his paper, the one relating to inflation and the role of agriculture (Kaldor 1957B).

from his old Chilean friend Alfonso Santa Cruz that the military dictatorship (quoting his name) was attempting to introduce an expenditure tax in the early 1980s.

> It is ironical [Kaldor wrote to Santa Cruz] that a government such as yours should take up my ideas from 25 years ago. When I elaborated them I certainly thought it would be a very left wing reform which could only be carried out by a left wing government; but I dare say there are ways of giving effect to this idea which could have quite different applications (Kaldor to Santa Cruz, 29 May 1982).

The new expenditure tax in Chile was certainly different from Kaldor's original idea and in fact resulted in a reduction of the tax burden of the upper income groups and an incentive to acquire financial assets (see below, Section 4).

3. Kaldor's view of Chile's economic problems

At the time when Kaldor wrote his study of the Chilean economy, the country was in the middle of an economic and political crisis. As a result of economic mismanagement and external instability, in 1955 inflation increased abruptly from its 'normal' level of around 25% per annum to 75%, real wages dropped significantly and the economy was stagnant from 1953 onwards (see CORFO, 1957).

Widespread economic disarray had provoked two general strikes in 1954 and 1955, and the government had lost most of its popular support. Then, in a drastic U-turn, the Ibañez Government decided to combat the crisis through an orthodox stabilisation programme designed by a foreign firm, the Klein-Saks Mission, which began its work at the end of 1955. It was within this context of frustration and disappointment in the country and of the re-emergence of conventional economic policy that Kaldor decided to make his unorthodox contribution to the understanding of Chile's economic problems. His most important and innovative contribution was to explain the country's economic problems on the basis of its underlying economic and political structures and the peculiar behaviour of some of its key economic agents.

3.1 A low rate of accumulation and unequal income distrubution

Examining Chile's National Accounts figures Kaldor noticed that gross fixed capital formation had only occasionally exceeded 10% of GNP since 1940 (1956B, p. 251), just above the annual depreciation of the capital stock, and lying substantially below the investment rate of countries with a much more egalitarian income distribution.[1] Moreover, more than half of domestic investment was carried out by the public sector, which was developing the country's infrastructure and building large public enterprises in energy and basic industry.

At the same time, Chile's national income was not only unequally distributed, but was so to an increasing degree. National Accounts figures showed that this process had led to a share of wages in national income of about half that of developed countries like Britain, and that the gap with respect to profit earnings had broadened since the early 1940s.[2]

[1] According to the National Accounts *net* investments in fixed capital (deducting depreciation measured in terms of current replacement costs) for 1952, 1953 and 1954 were *0·2, 2·3 and 1·5%* of the net national product, respectively. Whilst, for the year 1953 the corresponding figures [for other countries] were: Norway 21%, West Germany 14%, Italy 12%, Turkey 9%, France 7%, Belgium and the UK 6%, [and] USA 7·6% (Kaldor, 1956B, pp. 251–2).

[2] The National Accounts showed that during the period studied by Kaldor (1940–54) there had been an 84% increase in real national income. This improvement, however, was very unevenly distributed: whilst the aggregate wage bill had only risen by 36% (or 9% per capita, an increase of 0·6% per year), profits and dividends had gone up by 120%. Thus, the share of wages in national income had fallen from 28 to 21%, whilst profits and dividends had gone up from 23 to 27%. (In 1954, the remainder of the national income was made up by: salaries, 20%; profits of the self-employed, 23%; and rent, 10%; see CORFO, 1957 and Kaldor, 1956B, p. 244.)

Yet, for Kaldor, the most striking feature of the Chilean economy (and many other LDCs) was that the disproportionately large share of profits in national income was not accompanied by high levels of saving. For him, it was clear that the low propensity to save of the private sector in Chile was not the result of any 'crowding-out' process but simply and directly of the profit-receivers' and rentiers' high propensity to consume—in fact, personal saving remained *negative* in most of the period examined by Kaldor (see Appendix 2):

> ... [The] high propensity to consume of the capitalist class [can be found in the fact that they] appear to have spent on personal consumption more than two-thirds of their gross income, or three-quarters of their net income after tax. In comparison to other countries, the luxury consumption of the property-owning classes appears to take up an altogether disproportionate share of national resources, part of which would be automatically released for investment purposes if a more efficient system of progressive taxation were introduced and/or if effective measures were taken to encourage the retention of profits by enterprises (1956B, p. 266).

According to Kaldor, therefore, the Chilean capitalist class was the weakest link in the country's economic structure and the productive mobilisation of the resources wasted by this sector deserved to be a first priority in the formulation of economic policy. This phenomemon of a low propensity to save on the part of the Chilean capitalist class in a context of an increasingly unequal income distribution clearly contradicted the popular view that (through its supposedly positive effect on saving) worsening income distribution was a necessary condition for growth in LDCs.

To put Chile's income distribution into the perspective of the experience of developed countries, Kaldor compared it with the corresponding figures for the US and the UK. After adjusting the figures to make them comparable, he found that in 1953 the proportion of wages and salaries (including insurance contributions) in the US was 59% of national income, while in Chile it was 45%. At the same time, profits of enterprises after tax were 5% of national income in the US and 17% in Chile. When the comparison was made with the UK, the proportion of wages (without taking into account salaries) in gross national product at factor cost was 41% in the UK and only 19% in Chile. On the other hand, that of gross profits, interest and rent were 24% in the UK and 36% in Chile (Kaldor, 1956B, pp. 248–50). Yet,

> The most important difference is that in Chile the personal consumption of property owners appears to take up *21·2%* of national resources, [but] in Great Britain it appears to take up only *7·4%*. Since in Britain the category of property owners includes a relatively large number of small rentiers (which does not appear to be the case in Chile) the implication is that the proportion of national resources engaged in producing goods and services for the luxury consumption of the well-to-do is at least three to four times as high in Chile as in Britain ... The proportion of gross property income allocated to personal consumption is only 30% in Britain whilst it is over 60% in Chile. British property owners, in addition to paying 42% of their gross incomes in taxation, save (on balance) a further 27·4%, whereas Chilean property owners who pay only 16·5% in taxation, save only 22%. Or, starting from the gross disposable income after taxation, British property owners appear to have saved *48% of their post-tax income and spent 52% whereas the Chileans saved 26% and spent 74%* (Kaldor, 1956B, p. 261; the emphasis is ours).

This finding convinced Kaldor that for a developing country with the characteristics of Chile he had to use a different theoretical framework than the one he had hitherto used in his work on growth and income distribution in industrial economies.

Some remarks on Kaldor's theoretical background in the 1950s: the post-Keynesian debates on growth, accumulation and income distribution. In the 1930s Harrod began an attempt to introduce a 'moving equilibrium growth path' for the economy, i.e., to introduce the concept of steady-state growth within Keynesian macroeconomics. Keynes had already shown how an economy can reach full-employment, but he had not studied sufficiently how this full-employment could be maintained in the long run. Harrod, and later (more comprehensively) Domar, showed that there were two fundamental conditions for this to happen. First, the rate of growth should be sufficient to induce investment equal to full employment saving; second, the rate of growth of output must equal the growth of the physical labour force, plus the rate of increase in labour productivity (see Harrod, 1939, 1948; Domar, 1946). Since the market did not have any in-built mechanism to achieve both conditions, it was not likely that an economy would be able to achieve long-lasting full-employment: a Keynesian result which follows naturally from Harrod's Keynesian assumption (Eltis, 1987, p. 602).

Kaldor entered this debate with his models of growth and income distribution (the first of which was published in the year of his stay in Chile; see, 1956C and 1957B). Following the post-Keynesian tradition, he started from the classical principle according to which profits are the main source of finance for investment, and he investigated the macro-economic implications of this assumption for the analysis of effective demand. One of the main implications of this type of analysis is (as in Ricardo) the unification of the theory of accumulation and of income distribution. He tried to show that shifts between the share of wages and profits in national income could adjust the saving ratio to the required level to achieve long-term full-employment. His steady-state models had a theory of distribution in which the share of profits in national income is determined by the share of investment, and it in turn depended on the aggregate capital-output ratio and the growth rate.

The post-Keynesian macroeconomic relation between profits and investment can be seen in a simple way through the macroeconomic identities of a closed economy without a government, with two social classes, the capitalist and the workers.

From the point of view of the income recipients, national income can be disaggregated into profits and wages, $Y = P + W$. From the point of view of expenditure, it can also be disaggregated into consumption and investment, $Y = C + I$. Workers spend all their income on consumption; i.e. $S(w) = 0$. From the first three equations, profits are equal to capitalists' expenditure on consumption and investment, $P = Y - W = C(c) + I$. If capitalists save a fixed proportion of their profits, then $P = [1 - s(c)]P + I$, and $I = s(c)P$. That is to say, there is a basic macroeconomic relationship between profits and investment which depends on the capitalists' saving propensity (see Kaldor, 1956C; Kalecki, 1968; Ocampo, 1980).

At the same time, both Kaldor and Harrod attempted to adapt their post-Keynesian approach on growth and distribution to LDC economies. It is within this context that Kaldor wrote his article on Chile (see also Kaldor, 1958A, B; Harrod, 1959). These distribution models were essentially closed economy/full employment models that could not be mechanically applied to LDCs with large export activities and with only a proportion of the workforce in the 'modern' (capitalist) sector. At the same time, some of the basic assumptions—particularly the most popular extreme form of the Kaldorian hypothesis 'workers save nothing and capitalists consume nothing'—had to be drastically changed. Indeed, the basic 'stylised fact' of the Chilean economy was precisely that capitalists consumed a totally disproportionate share of their income.

Kaldor's main proposition from this point of view was that a developing country like Chile *does* generate a surplus large enough to sustain the level of investment needed for a fast rate of growth and high levels of employment. Nevertheless, too large a proportion of that surplus was wasted in luxury consumption by the high income groups. For this reason his original prescription for developed economies—adjusting long-term saving to the required levels of investment via shifts in the relative shares of wages and profits in national income—was not applicable to LDCs: an increase in the share of profits in national income would have very little effect on saving. Government intervention, particularly through taxation *and an effective investment policy by the public sector*, was the most appropriate way to achieve a dynamic equilibrium. In other words, what Kaldor proposed were institutional changes that would make the Chilean public sector both a high-saving (through better taxation) *and* a high-investing affair.

Returning to the simple equations shown above, if only capitalists save, then $S=s(c)P$. Dividing by national income, to express the relationship in proportion to income, we obtain $s=s(c)p$. Then, Harrod's 'warranted' rate of growth ($g=s/k$, where $s=S/Y$ and 'k' is the incremental capital-output ratio) becomes $g=p[s(c)/k]$. For Kaldor, it was possible to obtain the required 'g', given '$s(c)$' (basically determined by the propensity to consume of capitalists) and 'k', through shifts in 'p' (the share of profits in national income); i.e. there was a level of 'p' that would achieve the long-run dynamic equilibrium between saving and investment and between aggregate demand and productive capacity. (For a critique of this approach see James Tobin's article in this volume.)

However, if the rate of investment was too low and the propensity to consume of capitalists too high, as in Chile (according to his calculations in that country the proportion of after-tax profits ploughed back into investment was only about 15% whilst in the UK it was around 60%; 1956B, p. 231), 'p' will adjust in such a way that the country would end up with both unequal income distribution and a low rate of investment. Given the high propensity to consume out of profits, an attempt to increase private investment 'through market mechanisms' would require further worsening of the income distribution, i.e. the share of profits in national income required for long-term dynamic equilibrium with growth and high levels of employment would be absurdly high. Therefore, instead of increasing 'p' (the share of profits in national income), a more efficient way of finding a long-term dynamic equilibrium would be to increase the taxation of profits *and* to implement an effective investment policy in the public sector:

> There can be little doubt that with a more efficient system of taxation (including, if necessary, special tax measures or other restraints designed to raise the proportion of profits that are retained by enterprises) it would be perfectly possible in Chile to reduce the proportion of property income allocated to personal consumption to a figure nearer to that of Britain ... If the proportion of consumption in gross property income were reduced to the UK percentage of 30%, the personal consumption of property owners would fall from 21·2% to 10·3% of national resources; and the resources thereby released would be more than adequate *to double* the rate of gross investment in fixed capital and in stocks—which means, in accordance with the official estimates, *an increase in the rate of net investment from some 2% to 14% of the net national income* ... These estimates contradict the frequent contention that Chile, owing to its very poverty, is incapable of generating the savings necessary for an accelerated rate of capital formation. For the figures tend to show that if luxury consumption could be reduced to a more modest proportion of the income of property owners, the

proportion of savings in the national income could be considerably raised without lowering the standard of living of the mass of the population.[1]

3.2 Persistent inflation

One of the most remarkable features of the Chilean economy in the 1950s was its inflationary record. As Kaldor noted, Chile had experienced continuing inflation for a longer period than almost any country in the world (see Kaldor, 1956B, p. 267).

Inflation in Chile, when seen from the perspective of the mid 1950s, was characterised not only by its endurance but also by its cyclical pattern and year-to-year fluctuations. For Kaldor (as for the 'structuralist' school), it was essential to distinguish between the 'initial' upward pressure on prices (mainly attributed by Kaldor to the inelastic nature of agricultural supply) and the 'propagation mechanism' through which price increases feed back into themselves. This type of approach to inflation had been pioneered by Keynes (1940) and Kalecki (1941A and B) for wartime Britain.

Inflation and unbalanced growth. Kalecki saw the problem of inflation arising in wartime 'because the level of employment is maintained or even increased, whereas the output of consumption goods falls considerably' (1941A, p. 115). The increase in employment raises the wage bill and thereby the demand for consumption goods, which in these circumstances cannot be fulfilled. Later on (particularly in his 1954 article), Kalecki described a similar mechanism in the LDCs where the agricultural sector is often unable to increase food production at a rate similar to the increase in the demand for its products.

He developed a model of the way in which the rate of increase of the supply of necessities, as fixed by institutional barriers to the development of agriculture, determines the growth of national income. The characteristic of inflation would be an increase in the price of agricultural goods in relation to wages, reducing real wages. As a result 'this type of growth involving inflationary price increases of necessities . . . is definitely to the advantage of the upper classes' (1970, p. 106); and 'it is not only an evil in itself but it tends also to reduce productivity of labour' (1941B, quoted in Sawyer, 1985, p. 120).[2]

[1] Kaldor was well aware that a more effective system of taxation of the property owning class '[was] a political, and not only a narrowly economic question; but the present analysis is entirely confined to an examination of the economic and technical, rather than of the political possibilities [of that new system of taxation]' (1956B, p. 263). Nevertheless, maybe it was political considerations which led Kaldor not to discuss at all the low propensity to save *of the middle classes.* One of the most striking aspects of the information contained in his paper is the relatively large share of income paid as salaries. Thus, while white-collar workers represented some 10% of the working population, they received nearly 20% of gross income—a figure similar to that of the UK (20·8% in 1953). Moreover, real salaries seemed to have been rising as fast as income from capital since 1940, with wages progressively losing ground. In addition, the Chilean middle class, closely related to the state bureaucracy and more influential than many blue-collar groups, had won substantial benefits from the welfare state, including considerably subsidised loans from the social security institutions. (Pinto relates this special status occupied by the middle classes to their strategic position in the balance of power existing in Chile; see 1959, p. 290). One could, therefore, argue that Kaldor should have also asked why the middle-class had such negligible savings, and not direct that question only at the property-owning class.

[2] In his analysis of the negative effects of low real wages on productivity, Kalecki was following the pioneer work of Marshall in 1890: 'it was only in the last generation that a careful study begun to be made of the effects that high wages have in increasing the efficiency not only of those who receive them, but also of their children and grandchildren . . . the application of the comparative method of study to the industrial problems of different countries of the old and new worlds is forcing constantly more and more attention to the fact that *highly paid labour is generally efficient and therefore not dear labour*; a fact which, though it is more full of hope for the future of the human race than any other that is known to us, will be found to exercise a very complicating influence on the theory of distribution (1890, p. 510; quoted in Dasgupta and Ray, 1986, p. 1011. The emphasis is ours).

In 1956, two years after the first publication (in Mexico) of Kalecki's 1954 article (which was a summary of a series of lectures he gave in that country), and in the year when Kaldor was writing on Chile, the Mexican economist Juan Noyola sketched the first 'structuralist' theory of inflation along similar lines to those of Kalecki and Kaldor (see Noyola, 1956, 1957). Then, Ahumada (1958), Sunkel (1958), Pinto (1959) and Prebisch (1961) made important further contributions to this insightful approach to inflation in LDCs (see also Grunwald, 1961; Seers, 1962; Thorp, 1971; and Pinto, 1968, 1973). Probably, the most significant ones were to add distributional problems, constraints in the foreign sector and rigidities in public finances to the inelastic supply of agricultural goods, as further possible 'initial' (or primary) upward pressures on inflation.

Kaldor on Chile's inflation. For Kaldor it was evident that in Chile, after twenty years of two-digit inflation, different sectors had developed effective mechanisms to protect their incomes and assets from the erosion of inflation. As a consequence, a system of *de facto* 'indexation' had been developed which introduced a substantial inertial component into price dynamics. In this context, advancing what would become an essential argument of his attack on monetarism twenty years later, Kaldor argued that it was a mistake to blame just monetary policy and credit expansion for inflation and to derive a one-way causal relationship from the correlation between prices and money supply:

> If the demand for credit is not speculative in origin, but is merely a consequence of the appreciation in the value of working capital caused by a rise in costs, it is idle to expect the banking system to be able to withstand the pressure for more credit (1956B, p. 271).

Therefore, Kaldor ruled out the possibility that Chilean inflation resulted simply from excess aggregate demand (although for him there were important *sectoral* imbalances) generated by excessive monetary expansion. Similarly, the fiscal deficit also seemed to be a consequence of inflation or disequilibria generated elsewhere rather than a systematic source of demand-pull inflation. This view was particularly relevant in the 1950s when the Chilean government was implementing a deflationary stabilisation programme based on the contraction of demand and restriction of bank credit. As in the case of similar programmes, the consequence was recession, with workers bearing the costs of the adjustment, and with only partial (and temporary) success in bringing down inflation.[1]

These factors, he argued, supported the hypothesis that inflation in Chile was essentially caused by the inability of the wage-goods sector, and particularly of agriculture, to keep up with the growth in demand resulting from the rapid process of urbanisation, the expansion of manufacturing employment and workers' attempts to raise real wages proportionally to productivity increases in manufacturing. If agriculture was unable to generate a surplus that could constitute the real basis for an increase in industrial labour incomes, the result would be a lower 'inflationary barrier' to upward pressure on wages and salaries.

[1] The Klein-Saks mission delivered a programme of macroeconomic adjustment and reforms aimed at stabilising the economy and 'rationalising' the foreign sector, the financial sector, and the public sector. In relation to stabilisation, the weight of the programme was put in compressing wages, rationing bank credit, and balancing the budget through a prospective increase in revenue from a reform of the tax and social security system. The latter two, however, were never implemented owing to strong oppositions from the upper-income groups and the employers' organisations. (It is important to note that Kaldor and Klein-Sacks were not on the same taxation wavelength—the former wanted to increase taxation to make the Chilean public sector both a high-saving and a high-investing economic agent, whilst the latter wanted a reform of the tax system simply to reduce the public sector borrowing requirement.) As a result of opposition to the tax reform, the whole burden of the programme had to be borne by workers, without any sustained success in bringing inflation down. Finally, the government abandoned this programme altogether.

In this way, if workers attempted to realise their higher earnings by catching up with wage-goods prices, the result would be a self-reinforcing inflation process, i.e. price increases feeding back into themselves. In Kaldor's words:

It was the rise in food prices which caused the increase in the demand for higher wages and salaries—in order to restore real wages to the levels they had already, if only temporarily, attained—thereby raising the general level of industrial costs and prices. The inflation therefore was *'demand induced' as far as agricultural products were concerned; and it was 'cost induced' as far as the non-agricultural sectors were concerned* . . . If this analysis is correct, no lasting cure of the inflationary tendencies in Chile can be found either in stricter monetary and credit policies or even in administrative reform which secured more effective taxation of the upper classes. No doubt both monetary and fiscal policy could make important contributions towards the attainment of monetary stability . . . But the lasting cure for inflation can only be found through a more rapid increase in food availabilities—either through a more rapid increase in the productivity of agriculture (which in turn hinges upon the reform of land tenure) or a more liberal policy for importing foodstuffs from abroad (1956B, pp. 274 and 277).[1]

This analysis of inflation in Chile led Kaldor to the first formulation of a two-sector model which he was later to apply to the analysis of LDCs. Later on, Lance Taylor, David Vines and Tony Thirlwall, among others, further developed the important contributions of this approach to development economics.

Kaldor's model highlighted the crucial two-way dynamic relationship between agriculture and non-agriculture (basically manufacturing) in the development process. In a sense, in the same way that as a post-Keynesian he was emphasising the need for a dynamic equilibrium between *ex ante* saving and investment in industrialised economies, his model for developing countries focused on the need for a 'horizontal' balance between the growth of agriculture and industry (Kaldor was always a strong advocate of balanced growth in LDCs). This arose from the fact that leakages from the manufacturing sector in the form of purchases of food from agriculture must be offset by autonomous expenditure on manufactured goods in the form of the demand for manufactured goods by agriculture. As Thirlwall has shown, the determination of the equilibrium level of output in manufacturing then turns out to be the Harrod trade multiplier result (see Thirlwall, 1987, p. 213; see also Thirlwall, 1986).

Following this approach, Kaldor based his analysis of inflation in developing economies on the structural differences between agriculture and industry. For him, such differences arose from the absence of a proper 'capitalist' class in agriculture and particularly from the prevalence of what he called 'semi-feudal' institutions:

If agriculture is in the hands of traditional peasants or of feudal landlords and, in consequence, production is stagnant and unresponsive to increased demand, the mere fact that aggressive-minded entrepreneurs existed in the community who could make large profits in agriculture, would not ensure that the dynamic elements would displace the traditional elements—for the simple reason that these agressive-minded entrepreneurs cannot challenge the position of the existing producers unless they first get hold of their land, and they cannot get hold of their land unless they drive them from it through competition which in turn presupposes that they *have* the land necessary for increased production (1961, p. 40, emphasis in the original).

The pre-capitalist character of agrarian property thus rendered the market mechanism quite incapable of finding a dynamic equilibrium between both sectors. The only way in which price movements could act as an equilibrating force in the economy was by redistributing real income between both sectors. However, for the same reason that the low

[1] On the concentration of land tenure (and the need for land reform) Kaldor notes that 'according to the 1936 census, over 94 per cent of the farms in Chile were under 200 hectares and only 5·7 per cent above 200 hectares, but the latter accounted for nearly 88 per cent of the total farming area' (1956B, p. 239).

propensity to save of the property-owning class in LDCs rendered shifts between wages and profits ineffectual as a policy prescription for growth and high levels of employment in these countries, the lack of output response of the agrarian sector to price increases rendered a distribution of real income between agriculture and industry ineffectual as a dynamic equilibrating force in these countries. The latter would simply produce a system of rewards *for the very inefficiency of agriculture* and a continuous source of inflationary pressures, which (as our earlier quotation from Kalecki emphasises) is only to the (short-term) advantage of the property owning class.

A structuralist critique of Kaldor's theory of inflation. Kaldor's two-sector model has been subject to criticism as a general model of economic development, and especially as a theory of inflation. For example, Noyola, Prebisch, Ahumada, Sunkel, Pinto and other 'structuralist' thinkers have criticised Kaldor's emphasis on agriculture as the main (and almost only) 'initial' (or primary) source of inflationary pressure. They argue that he did not pay enough attention to other sources of inflation such as foreign trade (particularly the terms of trade/fiscal cycle), the structural characteristics of the public sector, and some distributional conflicts.

Firstly, the usual combination of export price instability, low diversification of exports and a generally overvalued exchange rate policy have turned the foreign sector into an additional source of inflationary shocks. As many analysts stressed in the late 1950s, there was a recurrent terms of trade/fiscal cycle in LDCs. Normally, it was put into motion by an increase in export prices which raised tax revenues and improved the current account. Invariably, governments used these resources to expand much needed public expenditure and to sustain the usually over-valued local currency. As a result, there was an internal expansion which lasted until the terms of trade deteriorated.[1] This phenomenon generated a trade deficit which forced devaluations and 'cost-push' inflationary pressures. At the same time, owing to the high share of export (and import) taxes in total revenues, a fall in the terms of trade also seriously affected public revenues. In this way, the terms of trade/fiscal cycle were transformed into a mechanism of reproduction of the basic inflationary impulses (owing to the rigidities of current public expenditure) which acted together with the wage-price–exchange-rate leap-frog. Once such forces were unleashed it became very difficult to keep inflation, public expenditure and the balance of payments under control.

Secondly, the fiscal system presented several additional deficiencies (on top of being vulnerable to the terms of trade/fiscal cycle) that made it both a source of autonomous pressure on prices and a mechanism for the propagation of inflation.Together with the procyclical character of fiscal revenues, public finances at that time (and up to the mid 1970s) were characterised by an extreme downward rigidity in current expenditure, and by a steady narrowing of the social security suplus. The downward rigidity of current public expenditure was essentially the result of the large share taken by rigid wages, salaries and pensions. Under these circumstances, public investment was the only relatively flexible component of expenditure and suffered accordingly (with an important contractionary effect on output).

[1] As it is well known, the terms of trade of primary producing LDCs are characterised by extreme instability. A UN study has shown that between 1901 and 1950 the prices of 18 'essential' primary commodities, which were exported by 47 LDCs, oscillated, on average, *27%* per year during this period (quoted in Ffrench-Davis, 1979, p. 86). If a LDC exports, say, 25% of its GDP, and assuming no change in real output and import prices, this export price instability alone would produce, on average, fluctuations equivalent to some 7% per year in national income. The same level of fluctuations in total public revenues would occur (7% per year), if export taxes have a similar share (25%) in total revenues (assuming other public revenues constant).

On the other hand, despite the long-standing inflationary tradition of the country, direct taxes were not satisfactorily indexed against inflation. This was mainly due to the existence of significant lags in tax collection (particularly from business and the self-employed) and to the inadequate method of adjusting the value of property for tax purposes. Tax reforms were extremely difficult to pass in Congress, to the extent that most of them had to be included in other bills, like those for the indexation of wages and salaries. Even then, the tax proposals were subject to substantial amendments.

Moreover, the public sector was also a source of autonomous inflationary pressures because of the key role played by the State in the struggle for income distribution. On the whole, the State was highly responsive to pressures for favourable incomes policies and social security benefits from some privileged groups. These expenditures involved substantial transfers of resources from the State to those who benefited from it and created further disequilibrium when fiscal revenues declined.

As there was no significant market for public debt, fiscal deficits were almost automatically transformed into monetary expansion, thus giving additional impetus to inflationary pressures.

Finally, we ought to mention the peculiar social structure of the country—particularly the large size and power of the urban middle class (the so-called *capas medias*)—as a relevant factor in explaining inflation. Given their increasingly strong position in Chilean society, this group was able not only to push its earnings beyond productivity increases, but it also set the pace for wage increases in the economy. This 'demonstration effect' involved a built-in inflationary mechanism because wages in general (and in the modern sector in particular) not only tried to keep up with rising food prices, but also with the levels of salaries in the public and private sectors.

This 'structuralist' critique of Kaldor's analysis, however, does not deny his analysis of agriculture as a significant 'primary' source of inflationary pressures, nor support the view that fiscal and monetary policy have no relevance in propagating inflation. What it attempts to do is both to complement Kaldor's analysis of the 'structural' causes of inflation and to emphasise the fact that, to the extent that inflation mostly responded to 'structural' causes and that economic agents had learnt how to accomodate to it, a strict monetary and fiscal control could have been effective only at an enormous (and unnecessary) economic, social and political cost. The experience of the last fifteen years of monetarism in Chile corroborates this point.

3.3 An inadequate tax systmem

Kaldor's favoured solution to the problems of accumulation, distribution and inflation in LDCs was a radical tax reform. For him, an appropriate tax system could stimulate efficiency in production and provide the public sector with sufficient funds for investment. The tax system in Chile at the time of Kaldor's visit was very different from the one favoured by him. It was extremely inefficient, complex and unfair, and was mainly the result of successive measures implemented throughout many years of political bargaining. According to his calculations, in relative terms, taxes on profit were less than half those of the UK, and only marginally higher than those on wages and salaries (see Appendix 2). Moreover, agriculture was hardly taxed at all. This system was unable to provide sufficient funds for public expenditure and was very vulnerable to inflation. As a result, there was a chronic deficit and continuous monetary expansion.

A thorough tax reform was necessary to raise domestic saving, since it was predicted that an increase in the tax burden of the property-owning class would reduce private saving much less than the larger revenue could increase public saving. Moreover, a rationalisation of the fiscal system would have the additional effect of establishing a more appropriate system of incentives for the private sector (particularly in agriculture).

These ideas became familiar in Kaldor's policy recommendations for developing countries. For example, in his advice to the Indian Government in 1956 (the same year as his visit to Chile), Kaldor designed a programme of reforms with emphasis on the rationalisation of the tax administration. He also advocated an expenditure tax, largely on the equity grounds that expenditure provides a better measure of ability to pay than income, particularly in the absence of a wealth tax. In Latin America, Kaldor put the emphasis on taxation as a means of increasing domestic savings and as a way of transforming the agricultural sector. Later, when he developed the concept of the 'taxation potential' of a country—the excess of its actual consumption over the minimum essential consumption of the population, plus private saving—Kaldor stated that, in view of the high share of profits devoted to personal consumption (expressed as a proportion of gross national product),

> the taxation potential of the semideveloped countries of Latin America . . . must be [proportionally] fully as large as that of the highly developed countries, although their actual tax revenue is typically only one-third or one-half as large (1965, p. 73).

However, fiscal reform in Chile was very difficult to implement. The elaborate compromise of vested interests made it politically dangerous to attempt any major change, and the complexity of the institutional arrangements on taxation played against wide-ranging reforms. Moreover, there was hardly any public consciousness of the need for these changes since taxes on exports (mainly on foreign multinationals) provided a much easier potential source of additional government revenues.

On the other hand, increasing the effective tax burden of the industrial bourgeoisie clashed with one basic orientation of public policy: the alliance between large manufacturing firms and the state in the development of the import-substituting industrialisation. During this period CORFO, the government's development agency, had built a 'core' of large public enterprises and supported the modernisation of the private sector in selected activities, generating a nucleus of industrial entrepreneurs which developed in association with the state. Such an alliance between the public sector and the 'modern' segments of manufacturing formed a strategic balancing factor against the political power of the land-owning oligarchy and other backward groups, and was an essential requirement for overcoming the 'absorptive capacity' constraint of an investment push. The basic idea was that, eventually, the process of industrialisation would stimulate structural change and modernisation in other sectors of the economy. This view was held specially strongly by economists like Prebisch, who came from a country, Argentina, where the land-owning class was far more powerful, and the prospect of industrial development more attractive, than in Chile.

In the case of agriculture, Kaldor also suggested that a drastic reform to the tax system of agriculture could be an effective alternative to land reform and a possible solution for the price inelasticity of supply of this economic activity. He believed that a purpose-built increase of the tax burden of the owners of large and scarcely exploited estates could stimulate their productivity; the new tax system should be so designed as to leave increases in production as the only way to offset reductions in disposable income. Since many large and inefficient landowners would not be able to manage sustained increases in productivity they would be left with no option but to sell part (or all) of their property in order to reduce their tax burden. This would produce a higher fluidity in the market for land and would act as an indirect form of land redistribution towards a more efficient structure of the agrarian sector; therefore, it would help to transfer land from the traditional land-owning oligarchy, with its roots in colonial times, to a more modern entrepreneurial class which could release the latent forces of growth in agriculture (see Kaldor, 1961, pp. 74–7).

As it happened, a tax along Kaldor's line proved to be politically unworkable in countries with powerful land-owning classes—who had consistently succeeded in avoiding almost any form of taxation since colonial times. Yet, this same resistance of landowners to any kind of reform was, in some cases, counterproductive when, in frustration and with enormous political pressure from the peasantry, some progressive governments opted for the more straightforward alternative of compulsory land reform. This was the case in Chile, where the process mostly took place during the Frei and Allende Governments in the late 1960s and early 1970s.

4. Thirty years later

Although it is beyond the scope of this paper to make a thorough evaluation of whether Chile's development since 1956 has confirmed Kaldor's views on the main economic problems of the country, it is important to attempt to analyse, at least briefly, whether the Chilean economy is still characterised by Kaldor's 'stylised facts', and whether his policy recommendations are still relevant today. We shall concentrate on three main issues (i) his hypothesis that the low rate of accumulation of the Chilean economy is due to the perverse combination of a large share of property earnings in national income and the high propensity to consume of the capitalist class; (ii) his identification of agriculture as the major bottleneck to economic growth and the main structural source of inflation; and (iii) the effectiveness of fiscal reform as a way of solving these problems.

4.1 A low rate of accumulation and unequal income distribution

Despite the fact that income distribution and the level of saving by different economic agents are two of the most important economic issues in a country like Chile, their estimates today are still as unreliable as they were thirty years ago.

As we mentioned earlier, after Kaldor left the country the official figures of income distribution showed such a deterioration in the share of labour and became, therefore, so controversial, that the Government decided to stop their publication. Since then, there have been two major attempts to rebuild them.[1]

Unfortunately, the three series were constructed with such different methodologies and coverages that any comparison between them has to be done with extreme caution. However, very few people will doubt that income is more unequally distributed today than in the mid 1950s, when Kaldor analysed it.

The main exceptions to this trend were the first years of the Frei Administration and the Popular Unity years: between 1969 and 1972 the share of wages, salaries and social security contributions increased from 49% to 62% of national income; nevertheless, this improvement was as dramatic and short-lived as the Allende Government.

[1] Therefore, in all, there are three main studies of income distribution in Chile during this period. The CORFO series (covering the period 1940 to 1954, the figures used by Kaldor), the first ODEPLAN series, and the 'revised' figures produced by the military regime, ODEPLAN's New National Accounts, 1977. The latter figures have been strongly criticised by CIEPLAN (see for example Cortazar and Marshall, 1980; Marcel and Meller, 1986).

The other side of Kaldor's analysis of Chile's accumulation problems was to investigate how much of the (high share of) income appropriated by the property owning class was actually saved and invested by them. As we mentioned earlier, the results obtained by Kaldor were very disappointing; the figures for the period after he left Chile are of a similar nature. During the 1960s, for example, the saving of both public and private corporations amounted to only 3·2% of GNP, less than a third of the resources required for depreciation alone. The saving of households and private non-profit institutions were again negative, −4·2% of GNP, an amount larger than the level of 'external saving' of the period (equivalent to 3·2% of GNP). Household dis-saving approached 9% of household disposable income. (For these figures and an analysis of these negative household savings in Chile, see King, 1971, and our statistical Appendices.)

The latest available figures for recent years show a similar picture. Between 1979 and 1985 (when financial markets were radically de-regulated) total gross saving of the country (internal and external) amounted to approximately 14% of national income; of this total only *a quarter* was provided by 'corporate and personal' saving, despite the fact that these sectors of the Chilean economy appropriated more than three-quarters of total disposable income. At the same time, again, the non-financial private sector had negative saving (see Arellano and Marfan, 1986 and 1987). Financial 'deepening' was not accompanied by higher private savings.

Yet, of all the many figures we could quote to illustrate this peculiar aspect of the Chilean economy, probably the most striking one refers to what happened to private saving between 1976 and 1982, the years of easy external borrowing. During this period, Chile, like most middle-income LDCs, could borrow almost unlimited amounts of funds in the international financial markets; as a result, in these six years the country's external debt grew from US$ 4·7 billion to US$ 17·6 billion—an annual rate of growth of *25% per year* (see Marcel and Palma, 1988). This large inflow of foreign capital had a negative effect on (already low) domestic saving. For example, in 1981, the year of the height of the credit boom and the so-called 'Chilean economic miracle' (widely praised in the financial press of the North)—and despite a real rate of interest of 28·7% paid to deposit accounts of 30 to 90 days —the level of both 'corporate and personal' saving only reached *1·8% of national income* (see Arellano and Marfan, 1986).

At the same time, according to Meller's calculations, between 1977 and 1982 the level of 'excess' imports of non-food consumption goods amounted to US$ 6.5 billion (Meller, 1988A, p. 19).[1] As a result,

> If there had not been for this import binge, in 1985 Chile's foreign debt would have been 31 per cent lower, and today the country would have been able to import 70 per cent more non-food consumption goods (Meller, 1988A, p. 19).

Thus, despite the unprecedented increase in foreign debt, productive investment in the country was on average only 15% of GDP (see CIEPLAN, 1988, p. 1). In fact, even according to much criticised official estimates, the share of investment in GDP in the 15 years of the military regime has been 25% lower than during the 1960s (Central Bank statistics, quoted in CIEPLAN, 1988, p. 1).

As Taylor has emphasised:

> [financial and trade] liberalization and regressive income distribution were not a wise policy mix (1987, p. 19; see also Palma, 1989).

[1] 'Excess' imports of non-food consumption goods are understood by Meller as those imports that exceeded the level that would have been achieved if these imports had 'only' increased at a rate of 10% (real) per annum. Ffrench-Davis and de Gregorio (1986) reached a similar figure using different assumptions and methodology.

This phenomenon confirms—if any confirmation were needed—Kaldor's hypothesis that economic backwardness in Chile is not the result of lack of investible resources (both domestic and foreign), but simply and directly the result of the tendency of the upper income groups to squander, in luxury and wasteful consumption, a large proportion of the investible resources available in the country.

Therefore, as regards Kaldor's first—and probably most important—observation of the Chilean economy, the last thirty years have clearly tended to confirm his hypothesis: in fact, it seems more obvious today than what it was during Kaldor's visit.[1]

4.2 The effect of agricultural development on growth and inflation

Inflation, and the role of agriculture as its main 'structural' source, is probably the main difference between the Chile of today and that of the time of Kaldor's visit. First, inflation has not just continued to oscillate within a certain 'normal' range, but has presented wide fluctuations, including a period of hyper-inflation between 1972 and 1974. Second, agriculture does not seem to be today as important a source of inflationary pressure as it was in the 1950s.

As noted above, during the Allende period a strong initial upward pressure on prices arose from distributional conflict and excess demand, particularly of agricultural products; in turn, indexation played an important role as a propagating mechanism, with price increases quickly feeding back into themselves. Together with political turmoil, these phenomena drove price increases to nearly 500% in 1973. After the *coup d'état*, the Pinochet regime pursued strict, orthodox stabilisation policies, by the drastic contraction of aggregate demand. As a result, inflation came down to 35%, having been halved every year for four years.[2] Nevertheless, after the initial 'success', inflation stubbornly refused to come down any further. Despite ten more years of continuous orthodox efforts to reduce it, it is still fluctuating around 20%.

In the meantime, agriculture has gone through a radical process of transformation (see, e.g., De Janvry, 1981; Muñoz and Ortega, 1987; Ortega, 1987).[3] As a result, a significant penetration of capitalist relations of production has taken place in the countryside.

Even though aggregate growth rates of this sector have not been very impressive (1·2% per year between 1970 to 1985, or 1·5% between 1974 and 1985; see Marcel and Meller, 1986, p. 126)—and are only marginally higher than the 1·1% of Kaldor's period (see Kaldor, 1956B, p. 243)—at least agriculture has performed better than manufacturing industry, which has had an output decline of 8% during these years (see Cortazar and Meller, 1987, p. 7). Furthermore, agriculture has recently been transformed into an important source of foreign exchange earnings for the country (see, e.g., Cruz and Leiva, 1982; Cruz, 1987).

[1] It is striking that these issues were not taken up by the progressive parties for quite a long time. In fact, the Left, which developed in the Dependency School tradition, put most (if not all) the responsibility for stagnation and inequality onto foreign exploitation. And when the unsatisfactory performance of the local capitalist class was analysed, it was simply associated to the vicious circle of dependency and underdevelopment; (see Palma, 1978). As a result, the solution favoured by the Left was to change the whole system, without really being interested in 'mere' radical tax reforms.

[2] However, as Taylor has noted, *en route*, the growth rate was minus 13% in 1975, real wages were cut 30% by 1977, and (counting people on the dole) unemployment reached one-quarter of the labour force. Chile was a partial success for old-fashioned monetarist stabilization, at the cost of creating a stagnant economy (1987, p. 17).

[3] Owing to the Frei and Allende governments, agrarian reforms, in 1979 farms with more than 64 'basic irrigated' hectares accounted for 21% of the agricultural land, as opposed to 55% for those with more than 80 in 1965. See p. 255, n. 1 for the much larger share of big farms noted by Kaldor for an earlier period.

In addition, average real wages for the whole economy declined by 18% between 1970 and 1985 (Cortazar and Meller, 1987, p. 7), with the real value of the minimum wage in 1987 being only 56% of its 1981 level, and family allowances being equivalent to 40% of their level in that year (Ffrench-Davis, 1988, p. 39; Chile now has one of the lowest minimum wages in Latin America! see CIEPLAN, 1988, p. 4). At the same time, the level of employment remained stagnant until 1985 (Cortazar and Meller, 1987, p. 7). Therefore, it should come as no surprise that, even according to official statistics, *consumption per capita dropped 8% between 1970 and 1987* (Central Bank figures, in CIEPLAN, 1988, p. 3).

Taking all these facts—and the policy of trade liberalisation—into account, it is easy to understand why agriculture cannot have the same inflationary role today that it had when Kaldor visisted the country. On the one hand, the aggregate demand for agricultural products has been significantly reduced; on the other, complete import liberalisation[1] and a more price-responsive domestic agriculture have lessened the output constraint with which this sector used to saddle economic growth. All these factors have so far significantly changed the role of agriculture on inflation.[2]

Therefore, if one is searching today for 'initial' or 'primary' sources of inflation in order to explain why monetarist policies have failed to eradicate inflation after 15 years of relentless application, one should look to other sectors of the economy. The obvious target would be the foreign sector, particularly the policy of continuous devaluations, which are necessary to create the large (and increasing) surplus in the balance of trade required to service the foreign debt.

4.3 The evolution of the tax system

One of Kaldor's main policy recommendations for LDCs was fiscal reform. As we mentioned earlier, he conceived it primarily as a tool for the transformation of the public sector into a dynamic agent for development and for establishing an adequate system of incentives and regulations. In addition, Kaldor thought that adequate tax reform could make a substantial contribution towards increasing aggregate saving and serve as a tool for structural changes in the backward sectors of the economy which acted as a bottleneck to economic development (as in the case of land tenure).

Unfortunately, in the case of Chile, Kaldor did not make fiscal policy recommendations as concrete as those he made for other LDCs that asked his advice specifically on this topic. Nevertheless, from his analysis of the Chilean economy, his work on the role of taxation in economic development (1965) and the tax reforms he suggested for other developing countries (see Kaldor, 1980 and John Toye's contribution to this volume), we can safely assume that the main elements of a tax reform for Chile on 'Kaldorian' lines would have included: (i) a reform of direct taxation to transform it into a comprehensive and uniform system for incomes from all sources, with a progressive scale but a relatively low maximum marginal rate so as to reduce the incentive for evasion; (ii) the creation of a system of indirect taxation more efficient and less distorting than the turnover tax in operation in

[1] Kaldor and Kalecki mainly used closed economy models, and when they discussed open economies, they tended to assume (implicitly or explicitly) either relatively stagnant export earnings or significant quantity restrictions for the import of necessities. None of these situations characterises the Chilean economy of the last 15 years: there are no restrictions to the import of necessities (other than a flat 10% import duty), and exports grew at an average rate of 8% per year between 1974 and 1987 (see CIEPLAN, 1988, p. 2).

[2] Nevertheless, it is difficult to predict what could happen to the relationship between agriculture, inflation and growth if Chile returned to a more civilised economy (and society), in which real wages and employment recovered the lost ground of the last 15 years.

Chile at the time of his visit;[1] (iii) the introduction of inflation-adjustment mechanisms in all direct taxes in order to avoid the erosion of revenues; and (iv) a radical transformation of the tax regime of agriculture, so as to increase the burden on rents and to discriminate against large and inefficiently run farms.

Although it is obvious that the Chilean tax system differed substantially from Kaldor's model at the time of his visit, it was probably more developed than that of the other LDCs which he had advised. Its main shortcoming was its inefficiency, as revenues from copper exports had facilitated the multiplication of exemptions and postponed their required modernisation (see Ffrench-Davis, 1973, pp. 153–8; Arellano and Marfan, 1986, pp. 139–44; and 1987).

No major tax reforms took place between Kaldor's visit in 1956 and the late 1970s. Some partial modifications were attempted by the Alessandri Government (1958–64) to provide incentives to private investment through the reduction of the tax burden on business, and by the Christian Democratic and the Popular Unity Governments (1964–70 and 1970–3, respectively) to help the implementation of structural changes leading towards broader democratisation of both society and the economy. As the most ambitious proposals on tax reform encountered fierce opposition in Congress, only administrative changes and partial modifications could be implemented.

The Frei administration (1964–70) devised a thorough programme of fiscal reforms, which even included constitutional changes in order to broaden the Executive's command over economic policy.[2] Nevertheless, the Government clashed with the Conservative establishment as well as with the Left, and failed to pass many of its original proposals through Congress. The Popular Unity, in turn, did not have specific plans on the subject when it reached power in 1970, as it assumed that its vast programme of nationalisations would make the surplus of the most profitable private businesses available to the public sector. As it happens, only the nationalisation of copper mines owned by US multinationals achieved this aim, as it made the whole surplus from copper exports available to the public sector.[3]

Among the most important changes in the tax system that took place between 1956 and 1973 was the gradual simplification of direct taxation and the introduction of new indirect taxes. In the first case, several distortions were eliminated, the 'cedular' system was simplified in the 1964 reform and revenue protection against inflation was facilitated with the introduction of the PAYE system in 1972. In relation to indirect taxation, a new tax on domestic transactions was introduced shortly before Kaldor's visit in the form of a 'turnover' tax (*impuesto a la compra-venta*). Despite the increasing criticism made of this

[1] The turnover tax was introduced in 1954. Before that date, domestic transactions were hardly taxed at all.

[2] With regard to fiscal matters, these constitutional reforms (when they were finally passed in 1970) gave the Executive more power to increase public expenditure. The Congress could ony specify 'indications' to the Government's annual Budget, and make sure that increased expenditures had an appropriate financing. This reform was particularly important in Chile, since Members of Parliament had frequently used fiscal financing as a political weapon against the Executive.

[3] See Meller, 1988B. Nevertheless, despite this substantial increase in revenues from copper exports the deficit of the Central Government rose from 3% of the GDP in 1970 to 10% in 1971, 12% in 1972 and 21% in 1973. Public enterprises—including the recently nationalised ones, but excluding copper—also faced an increasing financial disequilibrium and in 1972 their overall deficit exceeded even that of the Central Government. However, it is important to consider this problem within the context of the economic turmoil of the three years of the Allende Government, and the political and economic warfare unleashed by the Chilean oligarchy, the industrial bourgeoisie and the US Government of Richard Nixon against a Socialist Government that they saw as a major threat to their vested interests. For an analysis of the Popular Unity Government's economic policies see Palma (1973); for one of the political and economic developments of the period, see de Vylder (1979).

tax because of its distorting economic effects,[1] it became the most important source of revenue—it provided more than two-thirds of all non-export public revenues—and all modifications up to 1970 were towards increasing its rate. During the Allende Government, however, this tax was transformed into a wholesale tax applied to a relatively reduced number of large producers. This had the advantage of limiting tax evasion and eliminating the damaging 'cascading' effect of the turnover tax, so that the taxable base actually shifted towards value added. The Government clearly preferred the wholesale tax to a direct value added tax,[2] since the former was more consistent with the Government's distributive policy.

In real terms, non-copper fiscal revenues rose steadily during this period at an average of 5% per year, increasing their proportion of GDP from 13% to 18·6% between the early 1960s and the beginning of the 1970s. Most of this increase was due to the growth in revenue from indirect taxes.

The most significant attempt to change the structure of the tax system during these three decades (other than the nationalisation of copper) was the Christian Democratic Government's introduction of a wealth tax in 1965. This Government had to overcome fierce opposition from the Conservative sectors in Congress, but had the support of the Left. After hard bargaining, the tax was approved with so many modifications that its effectiveness was largely undermined and its actual revenue irrelevant—during the years it was applied it only contributed 0·5% of total revenues.

The orthodox economic team of the military régime which took power after the *coup d'état* of 1973 attempted to integrate the many reforms which had been introduced piecemeal in the previous twenty years, and introduced some new ones. As a result, a general reform of taxation took place in 1975. The wealth tax and most of the existing exemptions to the income tax were eliminated, and the wholesale tax was replaced by a VAT of wide coverage (see Marcel, 1986; Arellano and Marfan, 1986).

Subsequently, the public sector and public enterprises were incorporated as taxpayers into the system and, in 1981, the Government began to reduce direct taxes. Nevertheless, these cuts had to be reversed in 1983 owing to the severity of the economic crisis which started the year before, the worst since the 1930s. At the same time, the social security system was privatised, adding an enormous weight to the budget during the long transition period.

As the crisis that started in 1982 deepened, the military régime had to postpone its more radical reform proposals until 1984, when a new tax reform was carried out. This was an attempt—quoting (of all people) Kaldor's authority—to transform the current income tax into an expenditure tax.[3] The changes involved, however, pointed in a different direction to that of Kaldor's favoured reform, and actually amounted to a stimulus for the purchase of existing financial assets. Not surprisingly for such a régime, the reform also brought about a reduction in the effective burden of direct taxes on the higher income

[1] These distortions came from the application of the tax to *every* stage of production and distribution—the so-called 'cascade effect'. This generated an irrational distribution of the effective burden on different commodities, which stimulated vertical integration and made almost impossible the application of drawback policies for exports. Moreover, this type of tax is very difficult to check, providing an important incentive for evasion. For an evaluation of this tax, as well as the other indirect tax systems in LDCs, see Goode (1980).

[2] VAT had been enthusiastically supported by Kaldor—against the opinion of many Latin American experts—in the 1962 ECLA/IDB/OAS Conference on Taxation in Latin America, held in Santiago. The introduction of this tax was included in the Christian Democrat Manifesto of the 1970 presidential election.

[3] See Kaldor's letter to Alfonso Santa Cruz, quoted above, on his amazement that his name could be mentioned by such a régime to justify a tax reform.

groups.[1] Overall, the reform involved a US$ 400 million reduction in public revenues. Since 1985, this reform and futher tax cuts have been financed by revenues from the privatisation of public enterprises—and the military régime has made every effort to emphasise the similarities of these policies to those of the Thatcher Government! Between 1986 and 1988, the proceeds of the sale of public companies amounted to nearly US$ 900 million (see Marcel, 1989).

The Chilean tax system at the end of the 1980s looks, therefore, substantially different from the one that prevailed at the time of Kaldor's visit. The most effective changes took place in indirect taxation, where VAT became a highly efficient tax and a regular source of public revenue. Moreover, public finances have become fully indexed to inflation. Direct taxation has been simplified, but as a result of the orthodox character of economic policy during the military government, its burden has been reduced to the almost exclusive benefit of the richest sectors of the population.

The only sector which has been impervious to any tax changes is agriculture. Its tax régime remains today as inadequate as ever, even though the land reform of 1965–72 did produce important structural transformations of this sector, with a substantial redistribution of land which not even the military régime could ignore. In the last decade this sector has substantially increased its profitability and become a major source of foreign exchange earnings for the country. There is, therefore, absolutely no reason now—if there ever was one—to keep such a backward tax regime for this sector.

In 1956 Kaldor outlined a tax reform for Chile which, in essence, proposed that the surplus the property-owning class was wasting in luxury consumption should be taxed, so that the country could increase, through public investment, its extremely low rate of accumulation. At the same time, he proposed that a new tax system should be devised to encourage structural changes in the agricultural sector. Thirty years later, despite the many changes in the tax system, the first task remains as relevant and necessary as it was in 1956. As for the second, despite important productivity increases in the agricultural sector, the (almost non-existent) tax system of this sector remains as backward as it was in the 1950s—or, indeed, as deficient as it has been since colonial times (for an analysis of the tax system of agriculture in the nineteenth century see Palma, 1979, and during the 1920s and 1930s, Palma, 1984).

Some concluding remarks

It requires a particular quality of genius for a person to be able to visit briefly a country, which has never previously been a subject of his/her investigation, and write in a few weeks one of the most insightful papers about its economic problems that has ever been written. Those of us who were lucky enough to know Kaldor are not really surprised he was able to do just that.

At the same time, the realisation that after thirty years most of his policy proposals are still on the agenda is rather depressing. Nevertheless, those who are familiar with the developing world know well enough that there seems to be nothing more resistant to change than a social formation in the South. Classical economists from Adam Smith to Karl Marx firmly believed that capitalism—which drastically changed the *ancien régime* in Europe in a relatively short period of time—was going to transform the newly emerging

[1] As a result of this reform the taxpayers in the highest income bracket increased their disposable income by 40%. For those earning less than US$ 250 per month, the benefit was negligible. For an analysis of the 1984 reform, see Marfan (1987).

societies in the developing world with ease. This mode of production has certainly been able to develop the productive forces of these societies, but this development has had enormous difficulties in inducing some of the other transformations which were expected of it; those in the composition of productive forces, in resource allocation, in class relations and in the character of the state, that is, those transformations in the different structures of these societies which, in many cases, were necessary for its own continuous economic development.

However, even if Kaldor's article (1956B) has not yet influenced Chilean economic policies in the way that it obviously should, it has at least had a significant influence on development literature, particularly by thoroughly destroying the case for worsening income distribution as a necessary condition for growth in developing countries.

The property-owning classes of most developing countries—and certainly of Chile—are clearly not satisfied with having for their own consumption the same *relative* amount of resources as their counterparts in the industrial countries: they persist in trying to have the same *absolute* amount. Indeed, they may not be very sophisticated in their forms of production—or in their politics—but they certainly are in their consumption. It will probably take more than reason or logic, even if it is of Kaldor's calibre, to change the 'discreet charm' of this type of bourgeoisie.

Bibliography

[**Note:** the letters referred in the text are from Kaldor's private files.]

Ahumada, J. 1958. *En Vez de la Miseria*, Santiago, Editorial del Pacífico

Arellano, J. P. and Marfán, M. 1986. Ahorro-inversión y relaciones financieras en la actual crisis económica chilena, *Colección Estudios CIEPLAN*, no. 20

Arellano, J. P. 1987. *25 years of fiscal policy in Chile*, Tokyo, United Nations University, Project on the Political Economy of Fiscal Policy

Banco Central de Chile 1984. *Cuentas Nacionales de Chile, 1960–1983*, Santiago, Banco Central

CIEPLAN 1988. *Documentos*, Santiago, April

CORFO 1957. *Cuentas Nacionales de Chile, 1940–1954*, Santiago, Editorial del Pacífico

CORFO 1963. *Cuentas Nacionales de Chile, 1940–1963*, Santiago, Dirección de Planificación, Departamento de Investigaciones

Cortazar, P. and Marshall, J. 1980. Indice de precios al consumidor en Chile, 1970–1978, *Colección Estudios CIEPLAN*, no. 4

Cortazar, P. and Meller, P. 1987. Los dos Chiles y las estadísticas oficiales: una versión didáctica, Santiago, CIEPLAN, *Apuntes* no. 67

Cruz, J. M. and Leiva, C. 1982. *La fruticultura en Chile despues de 1973: un area privilegiada de expansión del capital*, Santiago, GIA

Cruz, J. M. 1987. 'Los nuevos empresarios en la agricultura chilena: el caso del sector fruticola', Santiago, CIEPLAN, mimeo

De Janvry, A. 1981. *The Agrarian Question and Reformism in Latin America*, Washington, Johns Hopkins University Press

Dasgupta, P. and Ray, D, 1986. Inequality as a determinant of malnutrition: theory, *Economic Journal*, December

Domar, E. 1946. Capital expansion, rate of growth, and employment, *Econometrica*, April

Eatwell, J., Milgate, M. and Newman, P. 1987. *The New Palgrave, a Dictionary of Economics*, London, Macmillan

Ellsworth, P. T. 1945. *Chile: an economy in transition*, New York, Macmillan

Eltis, W. 1987. Harrod- Domar growth model, in J. Eatwell *et al.* 1987

Fetter, W. W. 1931. *Monetary Inflation in Chile*, Princeton, PUP

Ffrench-Davis, R. 1973. *Políticas Económicas en Chile, 1940–1954*, Santiago, Ediciones Nueva Universidad

Ffrench-Davis, R. 1979. *Economía Internacional, Teorías y Politicas para el Desarrollo*, México, Fondo de Cultura Económico

Ffrench-Davis, R. 1988. Despues de 15 años, *Revista de CIEPLAN*, no. 12

Ffrench-Davis, R. and De Gregorio, J. 1986. Orígenes y efectos del endeudamiento externo en Chile, CIEPLAN, mimeo; forthcoming in *El Trimestre Económico*

Furtado, C. 1985. *La Fantasia Organizada*, Buenos Aires, Editorial Universitaria

Geithman, D. T. (ed.) 1974. *Fiscal Policy for Industrialization and Development in Latin America*, Florida, University of Florida Press

Goode, R. 1980. *Government Finance in Developing Countries*, Washington, The Brookings Institution

Griffin, K. 1971. *Financing Economic Development in Latin America*, London, Macmillan

Grunwald, J. 1961. The 'Structuralist' School on price stability and development: the Chilean case, in A. Hirschman (ed.), 1961

Harrod, R. F. 1939. An essay in dynamic theory, *Economic Journal*, March

Harrod, R. F. 1948. *Towards a Dynamic Economics*, London, Macmillan

Harrod, R. F. 1959. Inflation and investment in developing countries, in Ohlin (ed.), (1959)

Hirschman, A. (ed.) 1961. *Controversia Sobré América Latina*, Buenos Aires, Editorial del Instituto

Instituto de Economía, 1956. *Desarrollo Económico de Chile, 1940–1956*, Santiago, Universidad de Chile

Instituto de Economía, 1963. *La Economía Chilena en el Período 1950–1963*, Santiago, Universidad de Chile

Joint Tax Programme 1965. *Fiscal Policy for Economic Growth in Latin America*, Baltimore, Johns Hopkins Press

Kaldor, N. 1956A. Capitalist evolution in the light of Keynesian economics, lecture delivered at the University of Peking on May 11th, 1956. In (1960A), and *El Trimestre Económico*, July–September, 1956

Kaldor, N. 1956B. Economic problems of Chile, ECLA, mimeo; also in *El Trimestre Económico*, April–June 1959; and in Kaldor (1964B)

Kaldor, N. 1956C. Alternative theories of distribution, *Review of Economic Studies*, no. 2

Kaldor, N. 1957A. Caracteristicas do desenvolvimento economico, *Revista Brasileira de Economia*, March. Also in *Ensayos Sobre Desarrollo Económico*, CEMLA, 1962

Kaldor, N. 1957B. La inflación chilena y la estructura de la producción, *Panorama Económico*, November

Kaldor, N. 1957C. A model of economic growth, *Economic Journal*, December

Kaldor, N. 1958A. Observations on the Problems of Economic Development in Ceylon, in (1964B)

Kaldor, N. 1958B. Problems of the Indian Third Five-year Plan, in (1964B)

Kaldor, N. 1960A. *Essays on Economic Stability and Growth*, London, Duckworth

Kaldor, N. 1960B. Report on Mexican tax reform in (1980)

Kaldor, N. 1961. *Ensayos Sobre Desarrollo Económico*, Mèxico, CEMLA

Kaldor, N. 1963. Stabilising the terms of trade of underdeveloped countries, *Economic Bulletin for Latin America*, March. Also in Kaldor, N. (1964B)

Kaldor, N. 1964A. Dual exchange rates and economic Development, *Economic Bulletin for Latin America*, September. Also in Kaldor, N. (1964B)

Kaldor, N. 1964B. *Essays on Economic Policy II*, London, Duckworth

Kaldor, N. 1965. The role of taxation in economic development, in Joint Tax Programme, 1965

Kaldor, N. 1974. The role of industrialization in Latin American inflation, in Geithman (ed.), 1974

Kaldor, N. 1977. Observations on the fiscal reform in Venezuela, in (1980)

Kaldor, N. 1980. *Reports on Taxation II*, London, Duckworth

Kaldor, N. 1985. How monetarism failed, interview in *Challenge*, May–June

Kalecki, M. 1941A. What is inflation?, *Bulletin of the Oxford University Institute of Statistics*, May

Kalecki, M. 1941B. Inflation, wages and rationing, *The Banker*, October

Kalecki, M. 1954. The problem of financing economic development, *El Trimestre Económico*, Oct–Dec

Kalecki, M. 1968. *Theory of Economic Dynamic*, New York, Monthly Review Press

Kalecki, M. 1970. Theories of growth in different social systems, *Scienta*, nos 5–6

Kalecki, M. 1976. *Essays on Developing Economies*, Brighton, Harvester

Keynes, J. M. 1940. How to pay for the War, in Moggridge, D. (ed.) (1972) *The Collected Writings of J. M. Keynes* vol. 9, London, Macmillan for the Royal Economic Society

King, T. 1971. Private savings, in Griffin, K. 1971

Lundhal, M. (n.d.) 'Savings and Property income in Chile, 1940–54: the Kaldor estimates revisited', Lund University, Department of Economics, mimeo
Mamalakis, M. 1967. 'Negative personal savings in the Chilean National Accounts: an artifact or reality?', New Haven, Centre Discussion Paper no. 36, Economic Growth Centre, Yale University
Mamalakis, M. 1976. *The Growth and Structure of the Chilean Economy*, New haven, Yale University Press
Mamalakis, M. 1977, *Historical Statistics of Chile, 1840–1965*, New York, Greenwood Press
Marcel, M. 1986. Diez años de IVA en Chile, *Colección Estudios CIEPLAN*, no. 19
Marcel, M. 1987. 'Social security, the consumption function and macroeconomic analysis', Cambridge, mimeo
Marcel, M. 1989. La privatización de empresas públicas en Chile, 1985–1988. *Notas Técnicas* No. 125, CIEPLAN
Marcel, P. and Meller, P. 1986. Empalme de las cuentas nacionales de Chile, 1960–1985. Métodos alternativos y resultados, *Colección Estudios CIEPLAN*, December
Marcel, M. and Palma, J. G. 1988. Third world debt and its effects on the British economy: a southern view on economic mismanagement in the North, *Cambridge Journal of Economic*, September
Marfán, M. 1986. 'Two Essays on Fiscal Policy for the Chilean Economy, unpublished PhD. Dissertation, Yale University
Marfán, M. 1987. Reactivación y restricción externa: el rol de la política fiscal, *Colección Estudios CIEPLAN*, no. 22
Marshall, A. 1890. *Principles of Economics, Vol. 1*, London, Macmillan
Meller, P. 1988A. Un enfoque analítico-empírico de las causas del actual endeudamiento externo Chileno, *Colección Estudios CIEPLAN*, no. 20
Meller, P. 1988B. El cobre y la generación de recursos externos durante el régimen militar, *Colección Estudios CIEPLAN*, no. 24
Ministerio de Hacienda, 1986. *Exposición Sobre el Estado de la Hacienda Pùblica*, Santiago, Ministerio de Hacienda
Mũnoz, O. and Oretega, H. 1987. La agricultura Chilena y la política económica, Santiago, CIEPLAN, *Notas Técnicas*, no. 98
Noyola, J. 1956. El desarrollo económico y la inflación en México y otros paises La inoamericanos, *Investigación Económica*, 4th quarter
Noyola, J. 1957. Inflación y desarrollo económico en Chile y México, *Panorama Económico*, July
Ocampo, J. A. 1980. 'De Keynes al análisis post-Keynesiano', Bogotá, mimeo
Ohlin, T. B. 1959. *Economi, Politik, Samhalle*, Stockholm, John Bergvall
Ortega, E. 1987. *Transformaciones agrarias y campesinado*, Santiago, CIEPLAN
Odeplan, 1977. *Cuentas Nacionales de Chile, 1960—1975*, Santiago, ODEPLAN
Palma, J. G. (ed.) 1973. *La Vía Chilena al Socialismo*, México, Madrid and Buenos Aires, 1973
Palma, J. G. 1978. Dependency: a formal theory of underdevelopment, or a methodology for the analysis of concrete situations of underdevelopment? *World Development*, July
Palma, J. G. 1979. *Industrialization in a Primary-Commodity Export Economy: Chile, 1830–1929*, D. Phil. Dissertation, Oxford University, forthcoming, Oxford, OUP
Palma, J. G. 1984. From an export-led to an import-substituting economy, Chile 1918—1935, in R. Thorp, 1984
Palma, J. G. 1989. Chile 1976–82. 'Negative interactions between trade liberalization and financial liberalization' mimeo
Pinto, A. 1959. *Chile, un caso de desarrollo frustrado*, Santiago, Editorial Universitaria
Pinto, A. 1960. Ni estabilidad ni desarrollo—la politica del FMI, Santiago, Editorial Universitaria
Pinto, A. 1964. *Chile: Una Economía Difícil*, México, Fondo de Cultural Económico
Pinto, A. 1968. Raices estructurales de la inflación en América Latina, *El Trimestre Económico*, January–March
Pinto, A. 1973. *Inflación: raices estructurales*, México, Fondo de Cultura Económico
Prebisch, R. 1961. Economic development or monetary stability. The false dilemma, ECLA, *Economic Bulletin*, no. 1
Sawyer, M. 1985. *The Economics of Michal Kalecki*, London, Macmillan

Seers, D. 1962. A theory of inflation and growth in underdeveloped economies based on the experience of Latin America, *Oxford Economic Papers*, June
Sunkel, O. 1958. Inflation in Chile: an unorthodox approach, reprinted in 1960 in *International Economic Papers*, no. 10
Sunkel, O. and Paz, P. 1970. *El Subdesarrollo Latinoamericano y la Teoría del Desarrollo*, México, Siglo XXI Editores
Taylor, L. 1987. 'Varieties of stabilization experience', Marshall Lectures presented at the University of Cambridge, 6–7 May, mimeo
Thirlwall, A. P. 1986. A general model of growth and development on Kaldorian lines, *Oxford Economic Papers*, July
Thirlwall, A. P. 1987. *Nicholas Kaldor*, Brighton, Wheatsheaf Books
Thorp, R. 1971. Inflation and the financing of economic development, in Griffin, K. (1971)
Thorp, R. 1984. *Latin America in the 1930s*, London, Macmillan
Thorp, R. and Whitehead, L. (eds) 1986. *La Crisis de la Deuda en América Latina*, México, Siglo XXI Editores
Vylder, S. de. 1975. *Allende's Chile: The Political Economy of the Rise and Falls of the Unidad Popular*, Cambridge, CUP
Woods, A. 1987. Nicholas Kaldor, in Eatwell, J. *et al.*, 1987

Appendix 1. Statistical sources

Ever since Kaldor wrote his paper, there have been fierce controversies about the quality of the statistical sources he used for his analysis of the Chilean economy. As we pointed out before, he was one of the first economists to be able to use the (still unpublished) first National Accounts (CORFO, 1957).

His most controversial conclusion rested on the saving and income distribution figures of the National Accounts, which contained some of the least reliable estimates.[1] According to the CORFO methodology, personal saving was obtained as the residual between gross investment and the sum of corporate and government saving, and the balance on current account of the balance of payments.[2] As a result of this procedure, mistakes in estimating any of these terms would be reflected in the personal saving figure,[3] which was particularly distrusted owing to its persistent negative value over the period covered by the accounts.[4] Nevertheless, getting personal saving as a residual is a common practice in calculating national accounts. What still has not been proved is why it might be especially misleading in Chile.

An experimental correction of Kaldor's figures on the basis of some of Mamalakis' criticisms and assumptions, our own assumptions and new information now available for the public sector, shows the sensitivity of private saving figures. According to our calculations, the average propensity to save out of after-tax property income in 1952–54 would increase from the 26% estimated by Kaldor[5] to

[1] These figures and the National Accounts in general came under strong criticism as a result of the controversial nature of Kaldor's paper and the debate that followed the failure of the aforementioned Klein-Saks stabilisation programme. As an outcome of this debate, the Government stopped producing income distribution estimates, following the well-known policy that it is always easier to 'shoot the messenger who brings the bad news', than to do something about it.

[2] See, e.g., Mamalakis, 1976, pp. 323–39. According to this author, this estimate was further adjusted in the CORFO methodology to balance the personal income and outlays account.

[3] For example, several criticisms were made to the CORFO figures. Firstly, it was believed that the gross investment figure was underestimated owing to the exclusion of some items like non-monetary investment (especially in the agricultural sector) and repair and adaption of machinery (which was included only if it extended its useful life), and Chile's undervalued exchange rate underestimated the value of capital goods' imports in local currency. Secondly, the measure of public saving lacked some adjustment for the implicit taxation of foreign mining companies through the application of differentiated exchange rates, and the distribution of tax revenue through the year, since the lag in actual tax payments involved a substantial loss of real income for the public sector. Finally, and probably most importantly, the depreciation estimates were thought to be clearly overestimated. On these issues, see specially Mamalakis, 1976, ch. 13, and Lundhal, n.d.).

[4] According to CORFO's National Accounts, personal saving was positive during only four years between 1940 and 1954.

[5] We have re-calculated Kaldor's figure for the property-owning classes average propensity to save out of after-tax property income for 1952–54, using his own methodology, and obtained a slightly different figure from the one he did. The figure we arrived at was 27·3%—as opposed to Kaldor's 26%. The small difference is probably simply the result of some assumption in the calculations and it does not in any way alter the nature of Kaldor's argument.

31·7%, if gross investment, depreciation allowances, tax revenues and exchange rates are adjusted as suggested earlier. This new figure of 31·7%, however, is still *less than two-thirds* of the UK's level of 48%, which Kaldor used as a point of reference.

Another important attempt at correcting Kaldor's (and CORFO's) figures was made by Lundhal (n.d.). He also based his calculations on some of Mamalakis' assumptions (particularly those of 1976), and re-estimated the figures for the entire period covered by the CORFO series, 1940–54. He arrived at a *median* propensity to save out of after-tax property income of 39·4% for the 14-year period. But his median value for the 1952–4 period—the years used by Kaldor for his calculations—is only *24·4%*. This figure is actually lower than the 26% (average) found by Kaldor and the 28·6% median, and 31·7% average found in our adjusted figures for these years. Nevertheless, Lundhal's figures (as well as our own) present absurdly wide yearly fluctuations. For this reason, as he correctly acknowledges, they should not be taken 'too seriously [if looked at individually]' Lundhal, p. 13).

Therefore, it is obvious that a correction of the statistics along Mamalakis', Lundhal's, or our lines (or on some other assumptions) is very tentative and purely speculative, and no real substitute for research leading to some better *direct* information on the subject. In the meantime, the weight of the available information for this period, *and even more so for recent years*, still remains firmly on Kaldor's side.

Furthermore, private savings—despite all the criticism and the continuous correction of the National Accounts by governments of very different political orientations—have remained negative for long periods of time. This phenomenon does not lack some behavioural support. For example, at least up to the mid 1960s, and again during the Allende Government in 1970–3, the presence of negative real interest rates did stimulate large amounts of borrowing by the private sector and reduced the real value of loan repayments. Moreover, the inflationary process, as well as the uncertainties of economic policy in Chile, probably drove a substantial share of potential savings into the acquisition of durable consumer goods (which are included as 'consumption' in the National Accounts), or into speculation and hoarding of foreign currencies. In turn, real estate could be another important potential saving sink.

Appendix 2

Table A2.1. *Incomes and saving, 1952–54 (US$ 1985 million)**

	1952	1953	1954
Personal income			
Salaries and wages	3071	3093	2964
Self-employed	1532	1444	1366
Property income	2418	2402	2287
Tax burden (%)			
Salaries and wages	15·6	15·6	16·9
Income and self-employed	11·5	11·9	13·3
Property income	18·2	15·6	17·6
After tax personal income			
Salaries and wages	2592	2610	2464
Self-employed	1356	1273	1185
Property income	1978	2028	1885
Private saving			
Personal savings	−518	212	−942
Corporate savings	1083	1449	910
Total private saving	565	1661	−32
Saving by income source			
Salaries and wages**	0	0	0
Self-employed**	68	64	59
Property income	497	1597	−91
Propensity to save			
(i) out of after-tax income			
Wages and salaries**	0·0	0·0	0·0
Self-employed**	5·0	5·0	5·0
Property income	25·1	78·7	−4·8
(ii) out of gross income			
Wages and salaries	0·0	0·0	0·0
Self-employed	4·4	4·4	4·4
Property income	20·6	66·5	−4·0
Corrections			
overestimate depreciation[a]	191	174	165
non-registered taxation of mining companies[b]	65	42	24
underest. gross savings[c]	61	56	53
Adjusted gross income			
Wages and salaries	3071	3093	2964
Self-employed	1532	1444	1366
Property income	2227	2228	2121
Adjusted taxation			
Wages and salaries	478	483	500
Income of self-employed	176	172	181
Property income	506	417	425
Adjusted after-tax personal income			
Wages and salaries	2592	2610	2464
Self-employed	1356	1273	1185
Property income	1722	1812	1696
Adjusted private saving			
Personal savings	−331	400	−747
Corporate savings	892	1274	744
Total private savings	561	1674	−3

Table A2.1. *(Continued).*

	1952	1953	1954
Corrected savings by income groups			
Wages and salaries**	0	0	0
Self-employed**	68	64	59
Property income	493	1610	−62
Propensity to save			
(i) out of after-tax income: corrected			
Wages and salaries**	0·0	0·0	0·0
Self-employed**	5·0	5·0	5·0
Property income	28·6	88·8	−3·6
(ii) out of gross income: corrected			
Wages and salaries	0·0	0·0	0·0
Self-employed	4·4	4·4	4·4
Property income	22·1	72·3	−2·9

Sources: Adapted from Kaldor (1956B), CORFO (1957) and Mamalakis (1976).
*pesos converted into US$ and corrected by US Wholesale Price Index.
**These propensities to save were those assumed by Kaldor.
[a]Assumes a 25% overestimate of depreciation.
[b]Corresponds to the non-budgetary revenues from mining companies due to the application of differentiated exchange rates. This implicit tax, however, is partially accounted for in the National Accounts through an application of a single exchange rate, obtained as a weighted average of the actual ones, to all values in foreign currencies. According to Kaldor's correspondence, about 22% of the difference with the values obtained through a parity exchange rate methodology would have been left out of this adjustment. Therefore, we have applied this rate to the original estimates of implicit taxation.
[c]8% of gross savings. This figure arises from the comparison of CORFO and ODEPLAN-Central Bank accounts at current prices.

Table A2.2. *Incomes and saving: average 1952–54 (millions of pesos at current prices)*

	Kaldor series	Adjusted series
After-tax personal income		
Wages and salaries	134,895	134,895
Self-employed	66,365	66,365
Property income	103,597	92,358
Private saving		
Personal saving	−27,200	−17,037
Corporate saving	58,833	49,608
Total private saving	31,633	32,571
Average propensity to save out of after-tax income[a]		
Wages and salaries	0·0	0·0
Self-employed	5·0	5·0
Property income	27·3	31·7
Average propensity to save out of gross income		
Wages and salaries	0·0	0·0
Self-employed	4·4	4·4
Property income	22·7	25·3

Sources: as for Table A2.1.
[a]The averages of the figures at current prices are obviously different from the averages at US$ 1985 values.

Index of names

Index of subjects